# The Victorian City

## Images and Realities

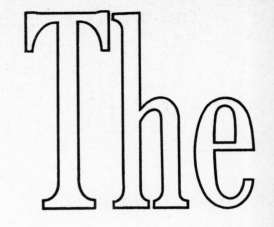

Edited by

# H. J. Dyos and Michael Wolff

Routledge & Kegan Paul
London, Henley and Boston

# Victorian City

## Images and Realities

Volume I    **Past and Present**
and
**Numbers of People**

To H. L. BEALES in his eighty-fifth year

Pioneer and Exponent of the Victorian World

*The Victorian City: Images and Realities*
first published in two volumes in 1973
Past and Present *and* Numbers of People
first published as a paperback in 1976
by Routledge & Kegan Paul Ltd
39 Store Street,
London WC1E 7DD,
Broadway House, Newtown Road,
Henley-on-Thames,
Oxon RG9 1EN and
9 Park Street,
Boston, Mass. 02108, USA
Set in Monotype Modern Extended Series No. 7
with Gloucester Extra Condensed
Designed by Joseph J. Hart
Printed in Great Britain by
William Clowes & Sons Limited
London, Beccles and Colchester

ISBN 0 7100 8458 7

# Contents

Preface to the First Edition     ix

Preface to the Paperback Edition     xiv

Acknowledgments     xvi

## I   Past and Present

1   The Urbanizing World     Eric E. Lampard     3

2   Voices from Within     Paul Thompson     59

## II   Numbers of People

3   The Human Aggregate     Asa Briggs     83

4   The Contagion of Numbers     J. A. Banks     105

5   Comers and Goers     Raphael Samuel     123

6   Pubs     Brian Harrison     161

7   The Literature of the Streets     Victor E. Neuburg     191

8   The Metropolis on Stage     Michael R. Booth     211

Index

# Illustrations

## Plates

|    |                                          |                              |
|----|------------------------------------------|------------------------------|
| 1  | Sailors' Home in the East End            | *Between pages 150 and 151*  |
| 2  | The Strangers' Home, Limehouse           |                              |
| 3  | The Bull's-Eye in Whitechapel            |                              |
| 4  | Gypsy encampment in Notting Dale         |                              |
| 5  | Gypsies on Epsom Downs                   |                              |
| 6  | 'Out of the parish'                      |                              |
| 7  | 'All the way from Manchester . . .'      |                              |
| 8  | Spring herrings at Yarmouth              |                              |
| 9  | Casual ward at Marylebone workhouse      |                              |
| 10 | Labour-yard at Bethnal Green             |                              |
| 11 | Frost fair in St James's Park            |                              |
| 12 | Thaw in Cheapside                        |                              |
| 13 | London gypsies                           |                              |
| 14 | Moved on by the police                   |                              |
| 15 | On the tramp                             |                              |
| 16 | Van-dwellers at the Agricultural Hall    |                              |
| 17 | Sandwich-board man                       |                              |
| 18 | Italian street musicians                 |                              |
| 19 | Mobile circus                            |                              |
| 20 | Suffolk maltsters                        |                              |

21 Navvies at the Crystal Palace

22 Hop-pickers

23 Whitby fishermen

24 Dundee whaler

25 The King's Head, Southwark    *Between pages 182 and 183*

26 The White Horse, Fetter Lane

27 The Bull and Mouth, St Martin's-le-Grand

28 London street-corner on Sunday

29 Ginshop interior

30 The Old Oak, Hampstead

31 Tom Spring's Parlour

32 The Cyder Cellars, Covent Garden

33 Cream ginshop

34 'Father, don't go'

35 The Rosemary Branch, Islington

36 The Surrey Music-Hall

37 Dinner at the London Tavern

38 Discussion at the Belvedere

39 Signing the pledge

40 The Band of Hope

41 Catnach's shop    *Between pages 198 and 199*

42 A ballad-seller

43 'Marriage of the Queen'

44 'John Bull & his Party'

45 'Mister Billy Roupell'

46 'Strike of the London Cabmen'

47 'Shocking Murder'

48 *Cross Roads of Life!*    *Between pages 214 and 215*

49 *After Dark*

50 *The Great City*

51 *Lost in London*

52 The Surrey Theatre

53–4 The Adelphi Theatre: Old and New

55 The London Pavilion

56 The Alhambra Theatre of Varieties

57 Theatre Royal, Haymarket

58 The Garrick Theatre, Whitechapel

59 The Gaiety Theatre

60 The Grecian Theatre

61 The Britannia Theatre

62  *The Streets of London*, Princess's Theatre
63  *The Great City*, Drury Lane Theatre
64  *Lost in London*, Adelphi Theatre
65  *The Long Strike*, Lyceum Theatre

# Maps

|  |  |  |
|---|---|---|
| I | Licensed premises, Bethnal Green, 1899 | 164 |
| II | Licensed premises, Strand, 1899 | 165 |
| III | Licensed premises, dockland, 1899 | 166 |
| IV | Licensed premises, Bloomsbury, 1899 | 167 |
| V | Drink map of Oxford, 1883 | 177 |
| VI | London theaters and music-halls, 1875–1901 | 214 |

# Preface to the First Edition

The idea for this book was planted, though we did not realize it at the time, in a conversation we had in London in the summer of 1965. We were looking for a theme for a symposium which the editors of *Victorian Studies* planned to hold at Indiana University (the home of the journal since its inception in 1957), under the auspices of the University and the American Council of Learned Societies.

The occasion demanded a theme which was capable of being handled in different ways by scholars from as wide a range of disciplines as possible. The choice eventually and, as it now seems, naturally fell on the Victorian City. Urban history, of course, was already beginning to make its mark, and the growth of cities in the nineteenth century was understandably one of its chief preoccupations. The ways in which the circumstances of urban life had influenced, or were influenced by, the ideas, the values, and the creative expressions of men and women living through that experience were being studied perhaps less explicitly but with increasing curiosity. It struck us that it might be particularly interesting to hear what some of the academic disciplines engaged on this common ground had to say to each other. Here, it seemed, was the most promising topic we could find to provide a focus for the immense range and variety of Victorian experience. Not only so, however, for the global process of urbanization we could see going on around us first gathered momentum in Victorian Britain. To study the inhabitants of Victorian Britain as city-dwellers was therefore to come upon them in their most telling role, the prototype of modern urban man. We could not conceivably have found a theme to touch the sinew of our respective subjects more directly. This book is an outcome of the dialogue that ensued.

The thirty or so scholars who faced each other in Bloomington in March 1967 mined no golden interdisciplinary nuggets and probably no one expected that they would. Indeed, it had become clear before they dispersed that a great synthesis of disciplines was as undesirable as it was unattainable. Yet we could not shrug off the fact that any man's experience of life—or any community's either—transgresses all conventional academic boundaries: that the various professional approaches to the study of man in his time are all more or less artificial as compared with the totality of his experience. However difficult it may be, it is vital to the ultimate purpose of the social sciences or the humanities that people should be recognized as having *lived* in the round. What was undeniably valuable, therefore, in our discussions was the pooling of specialized knowledge, the demonstration of unfamiliar ways into familiar problems, the atmosphere of freedom from arbitrary academic constraints. These things helped to put old thoughts into new contexts, brought new thoughts out of old settings, generated unexpected insights. It is our hope that we have not lost the momentum of those exciting exchanges in the even more ambitious programme of papers we have gathered into this book. For the underlying purpose remains—not only to encircle our subject more completely than any one of us might do alone but also to blaze trails of new ideas for each other. As far as we know, the combined pursuit of such a theme as ours by a team of scholars so large and multifarious is something new in itself.

Of the papers included in this book, not one is an untouched relic of the Bloomington conference, though four—those by Banks, Best, Briggs, and Stange—are more or less developed versions of papers first presented there and subsequently printed in two special numbers of *Victorian Studies*; four more—those by Dyos and Reeder, Keating, Himmelfarb, and Marcus—contain some material that has already appeared elsewhere. The remaining twenty-nine papers have not been published in any form before and have been written specially for this book. Sixteen of the present contributors, in fact, took part in the Bloomington symposium though the majority of them did so as discussants or chairmen of the discussions. Every contributor to this book, without exception, was invited to write on a specific topic and to keep in view the scope of the other papers and of the book as a whole. This entailed a very substantial amount of redrafting as the book took shape. In these respects it represents in its finished form a co-operative effort of an unusual order and, in a very real sense, a continuing discussion of its theme.

Exacting though some of this has been, we cannot pretend to have beaten all the bounds of our subject, nor should we like to believe that we have said the last word on any of its aspects. The study of the past cannot divest itself of the present, and the questions forced from us now about the past are unlikely to serve for an indefinite future. Despite the size of this book, we think of what we have tried to do, not (as the Victorians themselves might have done) as an encyclopedia to be consulted for verified fact, but as a connected series of essays, some weightily empirical but others deliberately speculative, all of them brief incursions into territory which they could not hope to subdue at a swoop. Every chapter has had to be pruned, some of them severely, and many topics which we would have liked to include have had to be left out. A full bibliography of the subject as treated would require a volume to itself, and we hope that we may later be able to attend to that, but the notes to each chapter are generally extensive and are a guide to the larger literature.

It may not be amiss to add that the book has been designed to be read straight through. There is hardly any cross-reference between chapters and no editorial superscriptions to them. We hope that the logic of its own structure will make the book's connections clear. One small but important point of presentation will be noticed in the spelling and other literary conventions. We have deliberately retained both United Kingdom and North American usages in the belief, formed by our own experience, that to force either into the mould—or mold—of the other does damage to what is being said. This having been such a transatlantic experience in the writing and editing, it seems to us entirely apt that the reader also might be alerted to its extent.

We should explain here that the main title to this book is purely descriptive and not generic. We are concerned with the city in the Victorian period but are not concerned to isolate it as a type in a whole declension of urban forms and, more particularly, to differentiate it from what might be inferred from it, namely the Georgian city or the Edwardian city. One reason for this is that much of the physical fabric and many of the underlying attitudes governing the way in which urban life was shaped in the first half or more of the period were an unexpended legacy, not only from the most recent, but from the remoter past. Nor was the vast investment of capital and creative energies in the Victorian city suddenly liquidated when Victoria died. Indeed, there are some respects in which a great many cities of the present day, wherever they may be, can fairly be described as Victorian without decrying them—a point to which we shall return at the end of the book. It would, therefore, seem unduly pedantic to be too precise about terminal dates, and this we have tried to avoid. It would be equally fatuous for us to contend for the distinctiveness of the Victorian experience without extending the comparison in a number of other directions, though we are inclined to think that some of the most lasting impressions of the cities dealt with in this book will be formed when the next logical step is taken of making more intercultural comparisons. For the time being we have had to be content for the most part with inter-city comparisons within the United Kingdom.

It makes sense to us, too, not to define 'city' with episcopal nicety. The English legal authorities of the seventeenth century maintained that a city was not such unless it was an incorporated town or borough which was or had been the see of a bishop. Whenever a borough was elevated to an episcopal see before that time, it generally became known as a city, though there were boroughs, like Sherborne and Dorchester, which had once had bishops but never became cities; there was also at least one place, Ely, which could boast a bishop but no borough charter; no doubt there were others, like Leicester, where the terms 'city' and 'borough' were mixed up promiscuously in their charters. It was, and remains, confusing. Though lexicographers went on repeating each other over these things, the first edition of the *Encyclopaedia Britannica* declared soothingly in 1771 that 'city' was used in England as little more than a synonym for 'town', 'while at the same time there is a kind of traditional feeling of dignity connected with it.' That understanding seems to have remained undisturbed for over a hundred years. When any 'mere village'—as Manchester was to Defoe—grew sufficiently in economic strength it aspired, especially after 1835, to be chartered as a borough, as Manchester itself was in 1838. By comparison London, encumbered in this respect by an ancient corporation presiding over the affairs of a mere particle of London proper, though popularly known as a whole as the largest city in the world, could never usurp the style of the City of London, and it eventually became a county instead. In the same year in which this came about, 1889, a rather smaller industrial town, Birmingham, though not an episcopal see either, acquired the style of 'city' by royal charter—the first to have done so in these circumstances. The concept of city we prefer to use in this book, therefore, is what might be called the common-sense one. We mean by it simply any large centre of population which was generally regarded as such at the time. We use it in preference to 'town' just because it is the larger places that occupy us. No one yet knows for certain what the necessary and sufficient distinguishing marks of an urban as distinct from an agrarian society are in the modern world. It is not even clear that these things are a matter of scale. However, we suspect that, to some extent at least, they are, and in choosing to concentrate on the largest places we hope to illuminate some of their inherent characteristics.

There is little we need say here about the basic theme of the book itself. In discussing just now what a city meant at law and to its citizens we were palpably enough dealing at once with certain images and realities of the city in fact. We were referring to actual places and verifiable occurrences as well as to attitudes towards them both. We could reasonably speak of a local image of these municipal realities, and if we wished to know better what forces were actually controlling them in a particular place we would pay as much attention, not merely to what was said to have happened, nor even to what people thought about what was happening, as to what they thought about themselves or others as it did so. We can—mercifully perhaps—seldom listen to such things so closely. Almost all the evidence that can be admitted is indirect and woefully incomplete and fragile. We cannot make any ropes from such sand. But the tissue we have is generally more serviceable than is commonly supposed. The vocabulary people use, the conventions they obey or disregard, the actions they perform, the things they find funny, the beliefs they find acceptable, the circumstances they tolerate, the fantasies they project—all these leave some kind of observable residue. There are, we think, more valid documents to be read than historians sometimes like to believe.

In trying to show how to read some of them in this book we should perhaps add one word more about its arrangement. Just as we have avoided any territorial or thematic division of our editorial labour, so we have deliberately avoided polarizing the images and realities to be treated. None of the contributors deals exclusively with one category or the other. We are not in fact making any arbitrary or sustained distinction between opposing forces, so to speak. We do not see in one camp the historians of fact all brimming with realities and in another the historians of values all burnishing their images. The realities cannot sometimes be communicated without the appropriate images; they cannot sometimes be perceived because of them. Both the realities and the images are of many different orders and it becomes a matter of discovering just how much each is revealed by the other, and which is really which. That is what this book is all about.

We must here record our most heartfelt thanks to every contributor to this book. We thank them particularly for accepting our editorial criticisms, suggestions, and incessant demands, and we can but hope that in reading the book as a whole they will think their efforts worthwhile and ours justified. We are also grateful in due measure to all those friends and colleagues whose names appear among the more formal acknowledgments set out below. We thank them for their invaluable encouragement and for the opportunities, advice, and practical aid they gave us, sometimes perhaps without realizing it. Whatever weaknesses there may be in the finished work we accept unreservedly as our own; whatever strengths there are we are happy to share to the full with all who have been concerned.

Finally, we take pleasure in the opportunity this book affords of offering our salute to the man who, in his long years as Reader in Economic History at the London School of Economics, gave so freely and unselfishly of his unrivalled store of knowledge about the Victorians.

H. J. Dyos
Michael Wolff

# Preface to the Paperback Edition

It is now almost ten years since the original contributors to this symposium first engaged in a conference on its theme, and over three years since the greatly augmented transcription of that many-sided discussion was published in these volumes. The aim was and remains to find a set of issues touching as closely as possible the most widely-shared experience of modern man and the most widely-gathered interpretation that might be provided for a significant aspect of it. We are delighted to find that the focus we chose should have justified so soon a larger and cheaper printing of the work in its entirety and just as it first appeared. The basis of the subdivision into four volumes instead of the original two is set out elsewhere.

We were well aware from the beginning that a work as ambitiously multi-disciplinary as this could never become definitive. We knew from wrestling with each other and ourselves, let alone our contributors, that there were many alternative structures for the book and many topics that we might have continued to seek to bring into it. We would, had the condition of the book trade under such inflationary conditions as we now endure allowed it, have been happy to have taken this opportunity to add new material: But we see more immediately how much more use might yet be made of the book as it stands. Our original purpose of finding a means of promoting the most subtle and far-reaching study of our subject might have been served, quite simply, by publishing now another volume containing the scores of highly-informed and searching reviews that have been addressed to the book. In the hope of carrying the discussion of our central theme as far as we can in present circumstances we take the unusual step of listing below every critical review of substance, both favourable and unfavourable, to which the book has been submitted. We aim to include at the end of the fourth of these paperback volumes our own reflections on the scope and direction of further research in this field and, in doing so, to take account of these and other writings that have appeared since we first went to press.

H.J.D. and M.W.

1 *The Times,* 30 August 1973: Michael Ratcliffe.

2 *Financial Times,* 30 August 1973: C. P. Snow.

3 *Guardian,* 30 August 1973: E. J. Hobsbawm.

4 *The Economist,* 1 September 1973: Unsigned.

5 *Sunday Times,* 2 September 1973: Cyril Connolly.

6 *Observer,* 2 September 1973: Angus Wilson.

7 *Sunday Telegraph,* 2 September 1973: Peter Conrad.

8 *Yorkshire Post,* 3 September 1973: Derek Linstrum.

9 *Daily Telegraph,* 6 September 1973: Margaret Lane.

10 *Times Literary Supplement,* 7 September 1973: Unsigned.

11 *Times Higher Education Supplement,* 7 September 1973: Sidney Pollard.

12 *Spectator,* 8 September 1973: Mark Girouard.

13 *Listener,* 20 September 1973: Rosalind Mitchison.

14 *New Society,* 4 October 1973: E. P. Thompson.

15 *New Statesman,* 5 October 1973: John Clive.

16 *Times Educational Supplement,* 12 October 1973: E. M. Sigsworth.

17 *Books and Bookmen,* October 1973: Francis Sheppard.

18 *History Today,* November 1973: Michael Greenhalgh.

19 *New York Times Book Section,* 4 November 1973: Raymond Williams.

20 *Municipal Review,* December 1973: G. W. Jones.

21 *RIBA Journal,* December 1973: Patrick Nuttgens.

22 *Connoisseur,* January 1974: Benedict Read.

23 *Architectural Review,* January 1974: Godfrey Golzen.

24 *Encounter,* May 1974: E. P. Hennock.

25 *Dickensian,* May 1974: Anthony Burton.

26 *Country Life,* 23 May 1974: James Stevens Curl.

27 *New York Review of Books,* 30 May 1974: Frank Kermode.

28 *British Journal of Sociology,* June 1974: Gareth Stedman Jones.

29 *Victorian Studies,* June 1974: Alexander Welsh.

30 *Essays in Criticism,* July 1974: Valentine Cunningham.

31 *Urban History Yearbook, 1974:* François Bédarida.

32 *Technology and Culture,* July 1974: Carl W. Condit.

33 *Economy and Society,* August 1974: Nigel Harris.

34 *Journal of the Royal Society of Arts,* August 1974: John Hayes.

35 *Labour History,* Autumn 1974: F. B. Smith.

36 *Urban Studies,* October 1974: Asa Briggs.

37 *History,* October 1974: Anthony Sutcliffe.

38 *Journal of Modern History,* December 1974: Neil Harris.

39 *Archiv für Kommunalwissenschaften,* No. 2, 1974: Wolfgang Hofmann.

40 *Journal of Historical Geography,* January 1975: Richard Lawton.

41 *Journal of Urban History,* February 1975: David M. Fahey.

42 *London Journal,* May 1975: D. E. C. Eversley.

43 *Criticism,* Summer 1975: Robert L. Patten.

44 *Economic History Review,* November 1975: Dudley Baines.

45 *Isis,* March 1975: Robert H. Kargon.

# Acknowledgments

To the Editor of *Victorian Studies* for permission to reprint, in amended or developed form, material first published in its pages and now forming part of chapters 3 and 4.

To each of the following for their courteous permission to reproduce paintings, drawings, or photographs in their possession, as indicated: Aberdeen University Library (56); the Curators of the Bodleian Library (26, 40); the Trustees of the British Museum (35); Brown, Son & Ferguson Ltd (24); Faber & Faber Ltd (20); Mr David Francis (19, 23); Greater London Council Photograph Library (25); the Keeper of Prints and Pictures, Guildhall Library (13, 17, 18, 27, 31, 32, 37, 53, 55); Miss Caroline Herschel (40).

# I    Past and Present

# 1    The Urbanizing World

## Eric E. Lampard

Each day newspaper readers, radio listeners, and television viewers around the world are confronted with the torrent of events. If the headlines of 1973 were merely updating yesterday's unresolved problems, the public might well relax. Their parents also lived with these problems and the world is still there. Besides, the mass media provide many distractions, and the commercialization of anxiety is a notorious vice of our time. Only the increasing reference to population explosions, urban implosions, and an alleged crisis in human ecology, perhaps, need give rise to the uneasy feeling that, beneath the familiar epiphenomena of tumult and wars, the old frameworks of interpretation and understanding are no longer sufficient.

Certainly many parts of the Victorian framework are no longer there. Britain's queen is not an empress and some two dozen sovereignties have risen in place of her empire. The specter of communism that haunted the old Europe of Victoria's innumerable kin has, in the present century, conjured up a global counter-spook more potent and resourceful than the holy alliance against which Marx and Engels inveighed. The concert of great powers which, in Victoria's twilight years, still held a world in fee has given way before a nuclear deadlock of super-powers around which the proliferating nations of the earth must form as satellites or supplicants.

We have entered upon a new era of world history which, however obscure and shapeless it may be at present, will nevertheless come to be as conventional in the future as modern, medieval, and ancient history became to historians of Europe in Victorian times. That is the major premise of 'contemporary history,' which has been defined as beginning when the problems which are actual in the world today

3

first took visible shape. The promise of contemporary history is to construct a framework within which the world can be interpreted and understood as a *unit*. One of the major tasks confronting contemporary historians is, therefore, 'to clarify the basic structural changes' which have been shaping the world scene and which, notwithstanding a certain overlap with the more recent past, will eventually give our era a definitive character and identity of its own.[1]

This essay is such an exploration in contemporary history. Its theme is the Victorian city in an urbanizing world. Its object is to review the urban climax of late-Victorian times from the global vantage point of the 1970s and delineate, however tentatively, those of its societal processes which have been pressing the world forward into the mold of the twentieth Christian century.

## The First Urban Transformation

We look first at the urban transformation of the nineteenth century. During the first half of that century Victorian Britain became the world's first urbanized society. In 1801 one-fifth of the population lived in cities and towns with 10,000 or more inhabitants; one in every twelve persons was a Londoner. By the year of the Great Exhibition, the proportion of the greatly enlarged population resident in such places was 38 percent, and London's 2,362,000 inhabitants now represented a slightly smaller share of the national population. For the first time, the census in 1851 reported an aggregate 'urban' population which exceeded the 'rural' population in size, albeit by less than one percentage point. At the beginning of the century only the Dutch Netherlands had surpassed Britain in the proportion of her population resident in towns with 10,000 or more inhabitants, and the Dutch *gemeenten* of that size included a considerable segment of rural population. Elsewhere, with the exception of the nine provinces that would shortly unite as Belgium, fewer than one person in ten could be found residing in concentrations of even this modest size.[2]

By mid-century the Belgian level of concentration had risen to one person in every five, approximating the level of Great Britain in 1801. But in the Netherlands, meanwhile, the rural segment had grown faster than the town segment and, if anything, the Dutch population was slightly less 'urban' in 1849 than it had been at the end of the eighteenth century. Elsewhere, only France, Saxony, Prussia, and the United States could yet claim more than one person in ten residing in concentrations of 10,000 and over. Thus the early-Victorians who, following Robert Vaughan, had designated their era 'an age of great cities' had somewhat missed the point. Great cities there were, larger perhaps and more numerous than ever before, but in Great Britain this phenomenon was only an outward symptom of a more profound tendency: the urbanization of society. In the rapidity and extent of the urbanization of her growing population, Great Britain was without peer (see Table 1.1). If the distinctive achievement of Britain in the latter part of the eighteenth century was to inaugurate the Industrial Revolution, her no less remarkable feat in the first half of the nineteenth century was to accomplish the first urban transformation.[3]

Table 1.1  *Annual rates of urban concentration, cities 10,000 and over, selected countries, 1800–50 and 1850–90*

| Country | 1800–50 | 1850–90 |
|---|---|---|
| England and Wales | 0·36 | 0·56 (1)* |
| Scotland | 0·30 | 0·44 (6) |
| Belgium | 0·18 | 0·32 (8) |
| U.S.A. | 0·16 | 0·39 (7) |
| Saxony | 0·14 | 0·52 (2) |
| Canada | 0·11$^c$ | 0·22 (13) |
| Switzerland | 0·11 | 0·24 (11) |
| Prussia | 0·10 | 0·47 (4) |
| France | 0·10 | 0·29 (9) |
| Hungary | 0·07 | 0·21 (14) |
| Bavaria$^a$ | 0·06 | 0·24 (12) |
| Ireland | 0·05 | 0·20 (16) |
| Norway | 0·05 | 0·20 (16) |
| Russian Empire (Europe) | 0·04 | 0·14 (18) |
| Austria | 0·03 | 0·21 (14) |
| Portugal | 0·00 | −0·01 (19) |
| Australasia | — | 0·46 (5) |
| Argentina$^b$ | — | 0·48 (3) |
| Chile | — | 0·26 (10) |

N.B.: Annual rate of concentration is percentage point shift in level of urbanization over intercensal years nearest terminal dates, $\delta(u/p)$.

* Figures in parentheses, rank order, 1850–90.

$^a$Cities $\geq$ 20,000.    $^b$Cities $\geq$ 2,000.    $^c$1820–50.

For dates of census or estimates: A. F. Weber, *The Growth of Cities in the Nineteenth Century* (New York, 1899), Table cxii.

It is significant that, despite the antiquity of its Latin root, the word *urbanize* was scarcely used in English before the late nineteenth century. People commonly spoke of ' the growth of towns,' the life of townsmen was 'urban life,' but when the verb 'to urbanize' was employed it generally had the connotation 'to render urbane': courteous, refined in manner, elegant or suave. To urbanize was almost synonymous with civilize: to bring out of barbarism, to enlighten, and it is not surprising that as the word took on the more literal meaning, 'to render urban,' the lexicographers spoke simply of 'removing the rural character' of a place or population.

The reluctance of lexicographers to commit themselves to a more positive definition is understandable. No less an enthusiast for the factory system than William Cooke Taylor had suggested in 1840 that the northern industrial towns revealed 'a system of social life constructed on a wholly new principle, a principle yet vague and indefinite but developing itself by its own spontaneous force and daily producing effects which no human foresight had anticipated.' Two years later he conceded that a stranger passing through the towns 'cannot contemplate these crowded hives without feelings of anxiety and apprehension . . . The population is hourly increasing in breadth and strength. It is an aggregate of masses.' In 1850 most of the manufacturing and mining aggregates were still small 'walking towns' made up of mills, chimneys, pitheads, and tips, narrow cobbled or dirt streets with grimy row (terraced) houses running out over hill and dale into the countryside. In the larger places the social landscape was already more varied, with wholesale and retail areas, warehouses, parks, church steeples, and public buildings, with cuttings and viaducts carrying canals or railways into the congested factory districts. The horse-drawn omnibus had appeared on improved roads, and, in order to escape the soot, odors, and noise, the proprietary classes were moving to the edge of town. For the masses the countryside lay further away.[4]

During the third quarter of the century, when the census classified more than half the population as urban, the loss of rural character could no longer even imply a passage to urbanity. Work, work places, and the working day were increasingly differentiated from the inherited routines of domestic life and livelihood. Provincial accents and manners still combined with local materials to give an outwardly variegated texture to a deepening uniformity of the industrial urban fabric. A growing segment of the town population was thought to be dangerously uncivilized and the prospect of 'rural depopulation' a social disaster. 'Civilized man,' de Tocqueville said, 'is turned back almost into a savage.' The social philosopher J. S. Mackenzie was uttering a commonplace by the 1890s in stigmatizing the growth of large cities as 'perhaps the greatest of all the problems of modern civilization.' Amidst a continuing celebration of material progress and the enlargement of individual opportunity and experience, some Victorian critics remembered the 'marks of weakness, marks of woe' which Blake had seen on the faces of eighteenth-century Londoners, or echoed Rilke's contemporary judgment on 'the cities' guilt.'[5]

There is no need to rehearse what Asa Briggs has termed 'the international debate' about cities. 'If it has to be a choice between Beverley and Jarrow,' declared J. B. Priestley in 1933, 'write me down a medievalist.' But neither pessimists nor optimists could win the debate, for the issue was never put to the question in either the nineteenth or the twentieth centuries. The population, meanwhile, was voting with its feet. It was rendering itself urban. By the year of Victoria's death, three-quarters of the population of Great Britain was classified by the census as urban. Whether the people were really better off in the grim industrial towns of the Midlands and the North, Priestley still could not decide in 1933 but 'they [had] all rushed into the towns and mills as soon as they could . . . which suggests that the dear old quaint England they were escaping from could not have been very satisfying.' What was it about Merrie England, he queried, 'that kept the numbers down?'

The style of urban life in Britain was changing rapidly by 1933. Two years earlier the census of England and Wales had reported 79·9 percent of the population living in urban areas with 2,000 or more inhabitants. Of the twenty-five places with 20,000 or more residents which had increased their populations by more than 30 percent between 1921 and 1931, nineteen were situated in the Home Counties. With one exception, the others were city suburbs or seaside resorts. This fringe development had, in fact, become marked since the census of 1881, especially around London, and had only been temporarily arrested by the First World War. This was a Britain not of Garden Cities but of arterial roads and petrol pumps, of wireless sets and Woolworths, of suburban council estates and semi-detached bungalows, of new factories and cinemas that looked more like exhibition buildings. It was a style, Priestley thought, belonging more to the age itself than to 'this particular island . . . America, I supposed, was its real birthplace.' In the course of his *English Journey*, Priestley had found three townscapes: the Old, the Nineteenth-Century, and the New, all co-existing, 'variously and most fascinatingly mingled in every part of the country.'[6] The urban transformation of Britain had gathered momentum in the latter part of the nineteenth century. By means of restrictive legislation, the reform of public administration, and prodigious feats of engineering, the late-Victorians had striven, however tardily and ineffectually, to make urban life livable. For better and for worse the economic system had done the rest. In the early 1930s Priestley had found his more numerous townspeople better off materially, even when living on the dole, but lacking a little of the spontaneity he could remember from his Bradford childhood at the turn of the century.

Only in the last quarter of the nineteenth century could people anywhere begin to get the urban transformation in perspective. Amidst the welter of blue books, white papers, census volumes, social surveys, tracts, and dissertations that poured from the printing-offices on one aspect or another of the Social Question, a new kind of 'scientific monograph' appeared, dealing with the subject of urban and rural populations and the relationships between them. The focus of the new studies was not so much the growth of great cities and their problems as population growth and redistribution and the related processes of concentration and agglomeration. By 1899 Adna F. Weber concluded that 'the concentration of population in cities' was now commonly recognized as 'the most remarkable social phenomenon of the present century.' For him also it was not of one particular country but of the age. Whereas in 1790 the United States, a virgin country with undeveloped resources, had little more than 3 percent of its 3·9 million inhabitants living in cities, Australia in 1891, still an undeveloped country, had more than 33 percent of its 3·8 million inhabitants doing so. 'But Australia is of the nineteenth century; and that is the vital fact which explains the difference in the distribution of population . . . What is true of Australia,' Weber affirmed, 'is, in a greater or lesser degree, true of the other countries in the civilized world. The tendency towards concentration . . . is all but universal in the Western world.'[7]

At no point in his monumental study of the growth of cities did Weber use the term 'urbanization.' He wrote instead of 'the tendency towards concentration,' a measure of urbanization in international and historical comparison which has not been improved upon to this day. He expressed the tendency simply as the share of a country's population resident in cities of a given size, usually 10,000 or more inhabitants. In some cases he was able to push his urban threshold down to 5,000 and even 2,000, but most demographers would nowadays agree that a minimum size of 20,000 for the 'agglomerated population' is the only one that can be used with any prudence in international studies. It is impossible, of course, to compare the variety of classifications of 'urban' population employed in national censuses, owing to the diversity of conditions of settlement and administration that prevail throughout the world at any time. By most national criteria, the size threshold of 20,000 is somewhat high and probably represents divergent combinations and degrees of urban character-istics in different countries.[8] Equally, not all population in places with less than 20,000 inhabitants can be sensibly classified as 'rural.' For many comparative pur-poses the size limit of 100,000 is quite satisfactory, but in most nineteenth-century situations, as well as in developing countries today, that threshold is unduly high.

If we adopt the measure of 20,000 and more for the agglomerated population *c.* 1890 and compare the level of concentration prevailing in the fifty-nine countries for which Weber furnishes data with that achieved in England and Wales in 1801— 16·9 percent—then the universal tendency remarked by Weber at the end of the century does not appear to have gone very far—even in 'the Western world.' Hardly more than a dozen countries had yet surpassed the level attained by England and Wales at the beginning of the century. Of fifteen countries, outside England and Wales, with more than 16·9 percent of their population urbanized, all, with the exceptions of the Netherlands and Scotland, had achieved that level since mid-century. By 1891, Scotland with 42·4 and Australia (six colonies) with 40·9 percent of their populations urbanized were the only countries to have surpassed the level of England and Wales in 1851—35·0 percent. Of the sixteen countries which exceeded the 16·9 percent level *c.* 1890, ten were located in Europe, three in Latin America, two in Australasia, and one in North America. Only six of them could yet be char-acterized as 'industrializing societies' in which a rapidly expanding share of their labor forces had been committed to full-time employment in manufacturing, mining, and construction industries. Among the other ten countries, six had comparatively small populations resident within a confined national territory, while two had com-paratively small populations in very extensive national territories. In several cases the aggregate level of concentration reflected the numerical predominance of one large 'primate' city rather than a pyramid of different-sized centers extending throughout the entire size-distribution. Thus, apart from Great Britain itself, what was true of Australia in 1891 was true of other 'civilized' countries, only to a much lesser degree.

At the close of the Victorian era it was still possible for Weber to carry out a revealing analysis of urban growth within the successive size-classes: 2,000–10,000; 10,000–20,000; 20,000–100,000; and 100,000 plus. Almost everywhere the largest cities were growing more rapidly than the smaller but, for all the talk about 'great cities', only Britain and the United States yet appeared to have been developing a class of cities over 500,000. There were about twenty such agglomerations in the early nineties—four in Great Britain; two in European Russia; five in the rest of

Europe (including Constantinople); three in the United States; two in East Asia, one in South Asia; and two in Latin America (see Table 1.2). Peking was almost certainly in this class, and, by 1900, Budapest, Warsaw, Madrid, Birmingham, Greater Brussels, Melbourne, Sydney, Madras, and possibly Shanghai were as well.[9]

Table 1.2  *World's largest agglomerations, 1890, 1920, 1960*

(000s)

| | 1890 | | 1920 | | 1960 | |
|---|---|---|---|---|---|---|
| 1 | London | 4,212 | New York-N.J. | 8,047 | New York-N.J. | 14,163 |
| 2 | New York-N.J. | 2,741 | London | 7,236 | Tokyo-Yokohama | 13,534 |
| 3 | Paris | 2,448 | Paris | 4,965 | London | 8,190 |
| 4 | Berlin | 1,579 | Tokyo-Yokohama | 4,168 | Shanghai | 7,500 |
| 5 | Tokyo-Yokohama | 1,390 | Berlin | 4,025 | Paris | 7,140 |
| 6 | Vienna | 1,342 | Ruhrgebiet | 3,730 | Buenos Aires | 6,775 |
| 7 | Chicago | 1,100 | Chicago | 3,315 | Los Angeles | 6,568 |
| 8 | Philadelphia | 1,047 | Manchester | 2,306 | Moscow | 6,150 |
| 9 | St Petersburg | 1,003 | Philadelphia | 2,302 | Chicago | 5,998 |
| 10 | Constantinople | 874 | Buenos Aires | 2,275 | Calcutta | 5,810 |
| 11 | Moscow | 822 | Boston | 2,210 | Osaka | 5,158 |
| 12 | Bombay | 822 | Osaka | 1,889 | Ruhrgebiet | 4,960 |
| 13 | Rio de Janeiro | 800 | Vienna | 1,845 | Mexico City | 4,825 |
| 14 | Osaka | 800 | Calcutta | 1,820 | Rio de Janeiro | 4,700 |
| 15 | Calcutta | 741 | Shanghai | 1,700 | São Paulo | 4,375 |
| 16 | Hamburg-Altona | 712 | Birmingham | 1,694 | Bombay | 4,040 |
| 17 | Manchester | 703 | Glasgow | 1,630 | Philadelphia | 3,655 |
| 18 | Buenos Aires | 677 | Hamburg-Altona | 1,545 | Detroit | 3,560 |
| 19 | Glasgow | 658 | Leeds | 1,445 | Peking | 3,500 |
| 20 | Liverpool | 518 | Rio de Janeiro | 1,325 | Leningrad | 3,400 |
| 21 | Budapest | 492 | Bombay | 1,275 | Cairo | 3,320 |
| 22 | Melbourne | 491 | Pittsburgh | 1,261 | Berlin | 3,274 |
| 23 | Warsaw | 485 | Budapest | 1,225 | Djakarta | 2,850 |
| 24 | Birmingham | 478 | Liverpool | 1,201 | Tientsin | 2,750 |
| 25 | Madrid | 470 | Detroit | 1,119 | Boston | 2,700 |
| 26 | Brussels | 465 | Brussels | 1,070 | Hongkong | 2,614 |
| 27 | Naples | 463 | Istanbul | 1,000 | S. Francisco Bay | 2,442 |
| 28 | Madras | 452 | St Louis | 978 | Manchester | 2,427 |
| 29 | Boston | 448 | Moscow | 950 | Seoul | 2,400 |
| 30 | Baltimore | 434 | Cleveland | 924 | Birmingham | 2,300 |

Source: Tokyo-Yokohama and Osaka populations based on populations resident 1890s reported in *Encyclopaedia Britannica*, 11th edn rather than on place of *legal* residence, *honseki*: see I. B. Taeuber, 'Urbanization and Population Change in the Development of Modern Japan,' *Economic Development and Cultural Change*, ix (1960), Part 1, 1–28. Other 1890 figures: A. F. Weber, *The Growth of Cities*, Table clxiii. 1920 and 1960: U.N. Dept of Economic and Social Affairs, 'Growth of the World's Urban and Rural Population, 1920–2000,' unpublished, corrected to 9 Dec. 1968.

These international comparisons suggest the singularity of the Victorian urban achievement. While Saxony, Prussia, Australasia (seven colonies), and perhaps Argentina and the United States, now approached Britain's rate of concentration around 1890, their degree of concentration still lagged. Apart from Australia, in so many respects a *rara avis*, no country yet had more than 30 percent of its population urbanized. Great Britain, with four or five of the world's largest conurbations, with more than half her population resident in cities of 20,000 or more, and with almost three-quarters of the population classified as urban, presented a situation at the end of Victoria's reign as 'unique' as that perceived by Cooke Taylor and others at its beginning. Britain had made its painful adjustment to the first urban transformation. This alteration profoundly affected the quantity and quality not only of town life and livelihood but also of rural life and livelihood. It is understandable that, amidst the pomp and circumstance of the Jubilees, the predominant mood was self-congratulatory and that, at the time of the Queen's death, the nation's genuine mourning was tinged with self-satisfaction.


## The Demographic Transition in the Cities

The second peculiar achievement of Victorian Britain was to be the first to make what may be called the urban demographic transition from high to low birth- and death-rates at a comparatively late stage in the urban transformation we have been considering. This transition was completed between about 1890 and 1910. From this time the growth of the total population became largely dependent on the natural increase of the urbanized population itself.

During Victoria's reign the population of Great Britain had doubled. In 1901 the censuses reported almost 77 percent of thirty-six million inhabitants resident in urban areas. Notwithstanding the phenomenal growth of the towns, Britain's crude death-rate, which peaked around 24–25 per 1,000 in 1849, had fallen from 22–23 per 1,000 in the later sixties to about 17–18 per 1,000 at the close of the century. Unfortunately this change had not yet affected the very young. The numbers of deaths under one year per 1,000 live births was as high again in the late 1890s, 155–160 per 1,000, as it had been in the late sixties. Meanwhile the crude birth-rate, which had risen from about 30 per 1,000 in the late 1830s to 36 per 1,000 in the late sixties, had fallen steadily thereafter to less than 29 at the time of the Queen's death. In so far as these improvements had persisted over the two decades of highest incremental urbanization, 1870–90 (see Table 1.3), they reflected not only the advances in social medicine and vast expenditures on water systems and sanitation, but also very real gains in the material level of living brought by industrialization.[10] Average real wages in England and Wales, adjusted for unemployment, had fluctuated upwards over the second half of the century and by 1901 the index stood at more than eighty points above the level for 1850. By no means all of the increase can be attributed to price changes. Average retail prices had followed much the same pattern as crude

Table 1.3  *Population concentration and industrialization of labor force and product, England & Wales and the United States, by decades, 1800–1900*

| Date | Urban shift | England & Wales Labor force shift | | National income shift | | Urban shift | United States Labor force shift | | Commodity value-added shift |
|---|---|---|---|---|---|---|---|---|---|
| | | N-A | MMC | N-A | MMC | | N-A | MMC | N-A |
| | | | | (percentage point shifts) | | | | | |
| | (1) | (2) | (3) | (4) | (5) | (6) | (7) | (8) | (9) |
| 1800–10 | 1·2 | 2·9 | 0·5 | −3·2 | −2·6 | 0·9 | −1·2 | — | — |
| 1810–20 | 1·6 | 4·6 | 8·2 | 9·6 | 11·1 | 0·0 | 5·0 | — | — |
| 1820–30 | 2·6 | 3·8 | 2·4 | 2·7 | 2·5 | 1·8 | 8·2 | — | — |
| 1830–40 | 2·5 | 2·4 | −0·3 | 1·3 | 0·0 | 1·8 | 7·5 | — | — |
| 1840–50 | 3·3 | 0·5 | 2·4 | 1·8 | −0·1 | 4·0 | 8·3 | 6·3 | 12·2 |
| 1850–60 | 2·8 | 3·0 | 0·7 | 2·5 | 2·2 | 3·6 | 1·9 | −0·8 | 4·2 |
| 1860–70 | 2·1 | 3·6 | −0·5 | 3·6 | 1·6 | 4·8 | 0·4 | 6·5 | 2·9 |
| 1870–80 | 5·9 | 2·5 | 0·4 | 3·8 | −0·5 | 1·8 | 1·2 | −0·8 | 3·6 |
| 1880–90 | 8·7 | 2·1 | 0·4 | 1·8 | 0·8 | 6·3 | 8·6 | 1·5 | 11·6 |
| 1890–1900 | 1·7 | 1·8 | 2·4 | 2·2 | 1·8 | 3·9 | 2·5 | 1·0 | 4·1 |

N.B.: Urban shift is intercensal δ(u/p) in percentage point terms. E & W concentrations ≥ 20,000; U.S. concentrations ≥ 8,000.

N-A labor force is non-agricultural; MMC is the manufacturing, mining, and construction segment of the N-A labor force. The same notation applies to national income in the case of England & Wales and to commodity value-added in the U.S.A. N-A labor force shift is intercensal δ(N-AL/LF) in percentage point terms and similarly for national income and commodity value-added.

Source: E. E. Lampard, 'Historical Contours of Contemporary Urban Society,' *Journal of Contemporary History*, iv (1969), Table II.

birth-rates, rising until about 1873 and then falling steadily to 1901 when the index stood fully ten points below the mid-century level. Over the entire length of Victoria's reign, gross national product had roughly quadrupled in size. Net national income *per capita*, adjusted for price changes, had more than doubled, rising from £18 in 1855 to £42 in 1901. These figures reveal little about changes in the distribution of income among different classes in the population. The numbers of 'the poor' may well have increased in this period, but that they ever formed a growing share of the labor force, except in periods of severe economic depression, seems unlikely.

What underlay these long-run achievements was, of course, the unfolding of the Industrial Revolution. While population multiplied in the countryside, it was in the manufacturing towns that industrial reorganization created the jobs. Industrialism soon put its stamp upon emerging urban society in every country and was itself stimulated and shaped by the related concentration of population. The coincidence of high rates of population growth with still higher rates of concentration identifies the demographic processes underlying the early industrial-urban transformation, while the later transition to low vital rates among the more highly-urbanized populations marks the completion of the transformation from the economic and demographic regimes of preindustrial society.

National populations may grow from an excess of births over deaths and/or from net migration. But population increases that are not accompanied by even greater *relative* increases in concentration cannot achieve higher levels of urbanization. Since there is no evidence before the late-nineteenth century that urban rates of natural increase were higher than rural rates, in Great Britain or elsewhere, the rapid and sustained rates of concentration experienced throughout much of that century could have resulted only from (1) a rural-to-urban shift brought about by net migration.[11] Unless concentration is arrested, the transformation enters another critical phase (2) when the magnitude of the migration comes to exceed that of the rural natural increase. At this juncture the *absolute* size of the rural population begins to fall and, barring immigration from abroad, the pool of potential migrants to the cities also declines. Thereafter the rate of concentration appears to increase and the rate of national population growth tends to slacken unless and until (3) the urban segment begins to reproduce itself at more than replacement levels. There is thus an interval, of longer or shorter duration in different countries, when the process of concentration portends 'race suicide.' Only when urban mortality falls, and more especially the mortality of infants, do the industrial cities cease to be 'devourers of population' and does their own excess of births assure the growth of total population.

The growth and redistribution of population between town and country will meanwhile have involved great changes in the relative numbers of children, adults, and old people in each place, as well as alterations in the demographic contributions of the different socio-economic classes. The lower, largely newer, strata in the urban population now provide the greater part of the increment, since the middle strata tend to have smaller families as their level of living improves. Thus, while the urban demographic transition allows the survival of 'the race,' it threatens a new regime in which the city proletariat outbreeds the higher and more economically productive strata. As the socio-economic and spatial structures of the urbanized population are further differentiated during (4) the metropolitan phase of the transformation, the fertility of the entire population subsides as people from the lower orders 'rise' to occupy either the new niches created by economic change or older ones vacated by the less fecund middling strata. This final turn to low fertility among *all* classes generally offsets the incremental effect of low mortality and removes the 'menace' to society from proletarian fecundity. The industrial-urban order thus achieves the low vital rates and structural stability that characterizes the high *per capita* income countries of the mid-twentieth century.

## The Changing Balance of Migration and Natural Increase

Migration was the major component of the urban increase in Victorian Britain even after some of the towns had begun to show a slight excess of births over deaths. Assuming that all births and deaths occurring in the London area are attributable to London population, it would seem that the deficits of the eighteenth century were turned into a positive increase quite early in the nineteenth century. One set of figures based on pre-registration data suggests that the ratio of net migration to total London increase during the first decade was less than one quarter. Migration continued to grow in absolute terms and probably reached its maximum in 1841–51, when it formed 40·2 percent of the increment, but it fell off again during the sixties and, in 1881–91, finally turned negative with the 'export' of population to suburbs outside the registration district. Except for this suburban trend of the eighties, the other large towns in England and Wales followed London's demographic tendencies, although their ratio of net migration to total increase was higher. Between 1821 and 1871 that ratio was always above a third and it peaked during the forties at almost half.[12]

The diversity of experience among the larger towns is well illustrated, however, by the following examples which show the proportion that in-migration contributed to total increase per thousand in each instance over the decade 1881–91: Manchester 717, Belfast 654, Leeds 300, Birmingham 257, and Edinburgh 94. At this point in the century, too, some of the large towns were beginning to export population beyond their boundaries, while increasing in size. The following examples show the proportion which out-migration bore to total increase per thousand during the eighties: Sheffield 4, Dublin 120, Bristol 785, and London 1,289. Liverpool, with 2,481, actually experienced an absolute decline over the decade 1881–91, although, if the areas which were annexed before 1901 are included in the totals for these census years, the population of Liverpool had grown—by less than one percentage point.[13]

Thus, by the closing decades of the century, Victorian society was remarkable not only in the degree of concentration but also in the fecundity of its urban population. In no other European country for which data are available does the urban population come so near to reproducing itself. Of course, large cities were growing rapidly in most European countries at the time, but in few instances does the contribution of natural increase seem to have *outweighed* that of migration. Émile Levasseur cited a study reported in 1877 which showed that migration had furnished more than half the growth of twenty-three of Europe's thirty largest cities. Without this influx seven of the cities would have rapidly decreased in size, since even their natural increase was heavily dependent on the city-born children of migrant parents. Six of the twelve large cities of France were also found subject to an excess of deaths. In a survey of eighty-eight European cities, 200,000 and over, for the years 1880–1890, Richard Boeckh concluded that at least half of their population increase was attributable to net migration and the balance to a combination of natural increase and annexation. A. F. Weber summarized his evidence with the conclusion that migration had played 'the largest role in the growth of French and Italian cities, then in the German and Scandinavian, and finally in the English cities.' He might have added the Russian cities (St Petersburg, Odessa, and probably Moscow) to the French and Italian centers among the class of 'devourers of population' in Europe and, in the light of Irene Taeuber's researches, we may include the large cities of Japan before and after the Meiji restoration. The fact that Victoria's great capital had grown so conspicuously from natural increase was due, Weber thought, to 'London's precedence in the making of sanitary improvements.'[14]

There is no reason to suppose that the United States' experience differed very greatly from that of continental Europe. The phenomenal growth of such Middle and Far Western cities as Chicago, Minneapolis, Cleveland, and San Francisco, or Detroit, Los Angeles, and Seattle by the turn of the century, could only have stemmed from an influx of foreign as well as native-born migrants. Between 1865 and 1890 the population of Boston, for example, had risen by 133 percent, of which roughly half was attributable to net migration, about 20 percent to excess of births, and the residual 30 percent to political annexation. If Boston's natural increase had furnished 'a subordinate part' of its growth, as one observer reckoned, it is noteworthy that its crude birth-rate none the less was already higher than its death-rate. Taking the six-state New England region as a whole, in which the urban population ('towns' of 10,000 and over) almost equaled the population of the rural 'towns' (under 10,000) by 1890, the crude urban birth- and death-rates were 29·7 and 21·0 respectively, compared with 20·0 and 18·7 for the rural districts. The rate of urban increase was thus 8·7 per 1,000 and the rural rate only 1·3. As a consequence of both rural-to-urban and net interregional migration, this slight excess of births did not suffice to maintain the region's rural population; it had been in *absolute* decline since the decade of the Civil War. Hence the greater part of the region's urban growth was probably contributed by foreign-born migrants and their foreign- or native-born children.[15]

There is no evidence that the urban rate of natural increase nationwide equaled the rural rate; there are no grounds for believing that the urban population could yet reproduce its numbers, let alone grow, without sizeable in-flows of migrants. This was still true for Europe, although the natural increases of town and country in England and Wales were virtually equal by the late eighties. One estimate by Charles Booth gives the two segments natural increase-rates of 14·03 per 1,000 and 14·13 per 1,000 respectively. Only in Sweden, still a comparatively rural country, did the crude rates approach this degree of parity, 12·3 per 1,000 for rural population and 11·3 per 1,000 for urban over the decade 1881–90. Urban death-rates in Europe were already somewhat lower than in the United States but urban birth-rates in Europe were, in general, much lower than in the United States.[16]

The United States also differed from Europe in the relative contribution of international migration to its urban increment. No country, with the possible exception of Australia before 1890, had accepted such a large proportion of foreign-born into its population as the United States. By 1890, with the flood tide of immigration still more than a decade away, some 31·8 percent of the residents of the twenty-eight largest cities, 100,000 and over, were foreign-born. These cities contained 15·5 percent of all US population but only 12·4 percent of the native-born and 33·4 percent of the foreign-born. Canada and some of the Latin American countries also had higher proportions of foreigners living in their cities than any European country, but in both volume and proportion their levels of immigration fell far short of the United States. In Europe, Scotland and Saxony had the highest proportions of non-natives living in their cities, about 13 and 10 percent respectively, but their foreign shares include the natives of other parts of the British Isles or other German states whose presence, apart from sectarian differences, scarcely betokened cultural pluralism. Among the great European cities of 1890, Vienna, with 11 percent foreign-born, was the most cosmopolitan and almost three-quarters of her alien element were natives of the confederated state, Hungary.[17]

By the close of the Victorian era, therefore, internal migration was generally contributing less to the urban increment than it had during the third quarter of the century. Among larger, more developed European countries, only France and Italy, perhaps, lagged in this respect. In Great Britain, on the other hand, the towns came closest to reproducing themselves. In England and Wales the *absolute* decline in rural population, marked since 1871, was arrested by 1901 with the spread of population to suburbs which lay outside town boundaries. With rural population rising again, except for the war years 1914–18, and the population of cities of 20,000 and more continuing to grow, it is not surprising that, in the decades on either side of the First World War, the population of smaller towns and urban districts, 2,000–19,999, declined. In other words, population concentration was no longer a predominantly rural-to-urban movement but, over and beyond the suburban spread, a movement within the city-size distribution itself.[18]

If the growth of cities in the more urbanized countries was becoming less dependent on rural-to-urban migration by the 1890s, this does not mean that the volume of internal migration was subsiding. The most highly urbanized populations were generally still the ones with the most mobile populations. In 1890–1 England and Wales had less than 72 percent of total population residing in the county of birth (a smaller share if Scotland is included), Saxony, with only 69 percent, and Prussia, with 70 percent, dwelling in the *Ort/Kreis* of birth, were the most internally-mobile countries on the Continent and were, if anything, becoming more mobile. In ten other European countries, from 79 to 90 percent were enumerated in their native county or equivalent district and half to three-quarters of these people were actually living in their locality of birth. The United States, with 21·5 percent of its natives living outside their state of birth in 1890, probably contained the most internally mobile population in the world. Most internal movement seems to have been over relatively short distances. This was especially true for females. Only the very largest European cities exercised much international allure although, in general, the larger the city the more likely it was to attract migrants from remoter provinces. Younger males appear more frequently in the long-distance movement than females, and this difference may have reflected the influence of large industrial labor markets and, in some instances, the location of garrison towns.[19]

## Sex and Age Structure of Urban Populations

By 1891 there were 1,064 women in the population of England and Wales for every 1,000 males. For London the figure was 1,116, for the urban sanitary districts 1,090, and for rural districts only 1,010. In Scotland the imbalance of females was slightly larger. In the German *Reichsgebiet* the *Frauenüberschuss* in 1890 was 1,040, but in small towns, 5,000–20,000, there were only 994 females; in cities 20,000–100,000, there were 1,004 females, and in the largest cities, over 100,000, the preponderance was 1,057. Evidence from a dozen other European countries broadly confirms the fact of the imbalance, the notable exceptions being Russia and Serbia, where the preponderance of men seems to have been greater in the cities than in the country-side. One explanation may be that many of the men in the larger Russian towns were there temporarily, returning later to their families in the country. In 1891 the colony of New South Wales had a female deficit of more than 8 percent in the rural areas, but in Sydney the sex ratio virtually balanced. Parts of the American West also resembled New South Wales, but in the United States as a whole a female deficit of 1·2 percent turned to a slight surplus in the urban population ($\geq 2,500$). Nevertheless, in the twenty-eight large cities of 1890 ($\geq 100,000$) there were 999 females for every 1,000 males. It is noteworthy that in countries which benefited so much from international migration, such as Australia and the United States, the female surplus did not occur nationwide.[20]

Registration data from a number of countries indicate that the surplus of women was largely the outcome of heavier mortality among infant males 'which within the first year usually effaces the superiority of male births.' Since infant mortality was usually higher in the cities, the excess of females had become characteristic of the urban population in many countries. The heavier mortality of men in working ages—owing to physical hazards of certain male occupations and, as many Victorians believed, to effects of 'vice and crime'—tended to confirm the male deficit in the towns.[21] The in-migration differential augmented an existing female surplus, while the greater out-migration of men from a number of large cities further distorted the sex ratio in that part of the city-size distribution.

At the close of the nineteenth century the age structure of most urban populations differed from that of most national populations. The latter resembled a pyramid; the more rapidly a population was growing from its own natural increase, the greater the proportion in the younger age groups, the broader the base of the pyramid, and the more gradual the slope of the structure to its apex formed by the oldest age groups. The age structure of the urban population departed from the national pyramid, however, largely as a consequence of the greater proportion of city folk in the productive adult years and the correspondingly smaller shares of dependent children and retired people.[22]

That migration contributed to this bulging of city age structures in the productive adult years is clear enough. However, most of the nineteenth-century evidence reveals little about age *at the time* of migration. Charles Booth reported that among

295 male and female migrants to London from English villages, 235 or 85 percent had been between the ages of fifteen and twenty-five; only 16 were under fifteen years and only 17 above the age of thirty. Over half the migrants resident in Frankfurt-am-Main in 1890 were of the age groups twenty to forty years, while in Berlin the number of migrants per thousand population in 1885 clustered in five-year groups between thirty and sixty years. Some 80 percent of the male labor force, aged thirty to sixty years, had been born *outside* the capital. Native Berliners constituted 42·3 percent of the population but the natives, of course, included the children of the new-comers. About half the entire adult population, twenty-five years and over, in this city of 1,315,287 had in 1885 lived there for less than fifteen years.[23]

As populations experienced later phases of the urban transformation, differences in the age composition and sex ratios of urban and national populations would be reduced. This would tend to erode the rural bulges in age groups under fifteen years, and thereby dry up the historic reservoir for migrants to the city. If the rate of natural increase also declined, the population would, barring foreign immigration, tend to 'age'; a smaller share would be younger persons and a growing proportion would be older people. Such changes could be expected to have important reper-cussions on both the production and consumption sides of the economy as the shares of households in different phases of the life cycle expanded or contracted.

## Urban Fertility and the Socio-Economic Environment

The exceptional size and fecundity of the British urban population have already been noted in reference to the relative contribution of natural increase to city growth. A number of conditions incident to this first urban transformation—especially the growth of economic opportunities—should be noted. While the proportion of married adults of all ages and both sexes had risen in England and Wales since mid-century (less in Scotland, especially for adult males), the census of 1891 revealed a marked difference in the levels of nuptiality for urban and rural adults of each sex in the ages fifteen to forty years. In the highly urbanized county of Lancashire, for example, 469 males and 475 females in every thousand adults of each sex in these ages were married; in London the figures were 464 males and 456 females. The predominantly rural population of Herefordshire had 402 males and 422 females married and little Rutland only 388 males and 427 females.

Dr W. Ogle had already noted, however, that the marriage-rate among single men, twenty to forty-five years, was highest for the rural population of Bedfordshire where employment opportunities for women were exceptionally good owing to the localization of the lace and straw-plaiting industries in that county. His unromantic hypothesis, that men would propose more readily to girls who were themselves earn-ing money, seemed to be confirmed by the proportion of girls, fifteen to twenty-five years, gainfully occupied in industry. This condition held generally for the larger towns in England and was especially notable where opportunities for employment were greatest, as in the textile factories of Lancashire.[24]

The effect of economic environment was also noteworthy on the high refined marriage-rate prevailing in the textile towns of Massachusetts. Nevertheless, the married state of the adult population in the twenty-eight largest cities of the United States in 1890 was, unlike that for England and Wales, well below the national average for both men and women. Contrary to public opinion, moreover, it was not the large foreign-born element which lowered their aggregate level of nuptiality; rather was it the native-born white population of native parentage. The Negro was also a depressing factor in the nuptiality of large cities (not for the U.S. population as a whole), but the black proportion of their population was only 4·3 percent nationwide and insignificant outside of the four large cities of the South. A marked tendency on the part of the native white population in large cities to postpone marriage, a function of their improved socio-economic status perhaps, reduced the nuptiality of the city populations below that of the rest of the country. In so far as the age and socio-economic selectivity of the suburban trend may already have carried a greater share of the married native adults out beyond the boundaries of the older and larger cities, it could have contributed to the same result.[25]

In England and Wales both the high marriage-rate and the level of nuptiality for all adult ages in the urban population exceeded those for the rural population. In the United States, where younger unmarried people were quitting the rural areas in large numbers, the same was only true for the marriage-rate. The refined marriage-rate in some European countries may also have been higher for the city populations, but this was not generally the case. Denmark provides a well-documented exception where the large city of Copenhagen encouraged marriage at an earlier age than was possible in the Danish countryside. But in Sweden, Austria, and such German states as provide data, marriage-rates and nuptiality were generally lower among the urban populations than among their rural counterparts, except in the heavy industrial centers of the Ruhr. In the higher age groups which included older migrants and natives, the difference in nuptiality was less marked.[26]

By the early 1890s, nevertheless, crude birth-rates were generally higher among urban populations than they were among rural. With the exceptions of Sweden and Prussia, J. E. Wappäus had found the same to be true for seven European countries around mid-century. To the extent that cities were the destinations of young adult migrants and had a *Frauenüberschuss* in the child-bearing age, the explanation of their fertility seemed obvious. In Sweden the higher rural fertility, as measured by crude rates, had disappeared during the decade 1861–70 but in Prussia it had persisted and by 1890–1 stood at 40 per 1,000 compared with 36·3 for the urban population. Refined birth-rates based on the same census failed to change the picture and showed, moreover, that female fertility in ages sixteen to fifty *decreased* with size of city, especially above the 100,000 level. Even the incidence of illegitimacy was slightly higher in the Prussian rural districts, except for the very largest cities. On the other hand, refined birth-rates for Saxony for 1879–83 indicated that in all but

18

one of the five *Regierungsbezirke* legitimate births were higher in the urban districts than in rural districts, although this did not hold for the large cities of Dresden, Leipzig, and Chemnitz. Only in the Leipzig *Bezirk* did the rate of urban illegitimacy surpass the rural rate, but this did not hold for the great commercial city itself. The refined urban birth-rate in Denmark, outside of Copenhagen, was also higher than the rural rate, but illegitimacy in the capital was reported twice as frequently as in other urban and rural communities.

In regard to family size Wappäus had shown that, around mid-century, the numbers of children per marriage in six of seven European countries was greater in their rural districts than in the cities. By the 1890s, however, it was no longer true that the large city was the peculiar resort of relatively sterile families.[27] Marital fertility appeared to be falling in a number of countries which were more and less urbanized. In the United States, a country with falling fertility but with a comparatively high birth-rate, the number of persons per census family nationwide— 4·93 in 1890—was slightly smaller than in the twenty-eight large cities—4·99. The average for the nation was raised considerably by the size of family units in the South which contained the overwhelming majority of large Negro families but only four of the large cities. Among the ten largest centers, ranging in size from New York to Cleveland, seven showed a greater number of persons per family than did the states in which they were situated; two had a smaller number; and one virtually the same number as its particular state. While the proportion of foreign-born residents may have been a variable affecting family size in some of the larger cities, data for the registration state of Massachusetts and its Boston metropolis showed that married women of native parentage in the cities also had more children than their counterparts in rural areas. Three of the four largest cities in Germany, on the other hand, Berlin, Leipzig, and Munich, had a refined birth-rate that was below the average for the Reich's twenty-six largest cities, whereas in Hamburg and the six smallest of this class the birth-rate was above the average.[28]

In a number of countries, therefore, there was no direct relation between size of agglomeration and fertility. The mere concentration of population did not account for either the tendency to marry or the fecundity of married life. Since cities of more or less equal size in the same country or province commonly exhibited wide variations in their birth-rates, A. F. Weber was right to conclude that the 'conditions affecting the fruitfulness of marriage are so numerous and complicated that statisticians and social philosophers are still in dispute.'[29]

## Urban Mortality and the Physical Environment

The issue of mortality in cities posed no such complexities to understanding. At the end of the century it was almost universally true that rates of mortality were lowest in country districts and increased steadily with size and density of agglomerated population. Death expectancy was still highest in great cities. In 1893 the Registrar-

General, whose office coextended with Victoria's reign, apportioned the population of England and Wales into fifteen groups, increasing in density from 138 to 19,584 persons per square mile and in crude mortality from 14·75 to 30·70 per 1,000. He also grouped together certain 'selected healthy districts' with low mortality, 14–15 deaths per 1,000, embracing about one-sixth of the population, mostly rural, and contrasted their life expectancy at birth, 51·48 years, with that of the Manchester district, 27·78 years, and with that of the entire country, 43·66 years. Thus a Manchester-born man in Manchester might expect to live just over half as long as his country cousin.

In the United States the crude death-rate among the rural population of the census registration states in 1890 was 15·34—not much greater than that of the 'healthy districts' of England and Wales. The rate for their urban segments was 22·15 for all ages, but in the special 'metropolitan district' of New York it was 24·61. Almost without exception city mortality increased in severity for every period of life with the agglomerative size of a population and was at all ages heavier than rural mortality. The crude death-rate for the twenty-eight large cities of 1890 was 23·28 and, for similar cities of 100,000 and more residents in the registration states, 21·62 for all ages. Weber vividly summarized the cheapness of human life in cities at the time:[30]

> whereas the average person born in Massachusetts may expect to live 41·49 years, the average person born in Boston may expect to live only 34·89 years . . . while 426 out of 1000 men born in Prussia survive to the age of 50 years, only 318 native Berliners reach the same age . . . while the mean age at death is 42 years and 2 months in France, it is but 28 years and 19 days in Paris . . . while the average duration of life in the rural population of the Netherlands is 38·12 years, in the urban population it is only 30·31 years.

The decades on either side of 1890 mark a turn from the old mortality to the new. In 1891 the crude death-rate in Manchester was 26·0 per 1,000 but, over the years 1895–1904, the average rate was only 22·6. Among the large cities of England and Wales, Manchester was exceeded only by Liverpool, whose average was 23·2. London's average mortality was 18·2 per 1,000 and was surpassed by Newcastle, 20·9, Birmingham, 20·2, Sheffield, 19·6, Leeds, 18·7 (as well as Liverpool and Manchester). The average mortality in Bradford was 17·7, while Bristol, 16·9, and Leicester, 16·7, fell well below the rate for the capital. By the year of the Queen's death crude mortality in Glasgow had fallen to 21·0 per 1,000. Within little more than a quarter of a century after the Prince Consort's death, the life expectancy of the average Londoner had risen from twenty-five to thirty-seven years; over the middle years of the reign the crude death-rate for the capital had averaged 23·4 (1861–80), but by 1905 it had fallen to 15·6 when the rate for England and Wales stood at 15·3 per 1,000. In the latter year the crude rates for Bristol and Leicester were already below those of the lowest-density population groups reported by the Registrar-General as recently as 1893.[31]

In view of the death-rates obtaining in the industrial cities during the middle period of Victoria's reign the achievements of the closing years were remarkable. It is clear from Table 1.4 that by the early 1900s the mortality of England's great

Table 1.4   *Crude mortality in twelve selected cities, c. 1900*

| | City | Average death-rate per 1,000, 1895–1904 | Death-rate per 1,000 1905 | Net change (permillage point) |
|---|---|---|---|---|
| 1 | Manchester | 22·6 | 18·0 | −4·6 |
| 2 | Newcastle | 20·9 | 16·8 | −4·1 |
| 3 | Birmingham | 20·2 | 16·2 | −4·0 |
| 4 | Liverpool | 23·2 | 19·6 | −3·6 |
| 5 | London | 18·2 | 15·6 | −2·6 |
| 6 | Brussels | 16·7 | 14·5 | −2·2 |
| 7 | New York | 20·2 | 18·3 | −1·9 |
| 8 | Paris | 19·2 | 17·4 | −1·8 |
| 9 | Vienna | 20·0 | 19·0 | −1·0 |
| 10 | Berlin | 17·8 | 17·2 | −0·6 |
| 11 | St Petersburg | 25·9 | 25·3 | −0·6 |
| 12 | Rome | 19·1 | 20·6 | +1·5 |

Source: Data from 11th edn *Encyclopaedia Britannica*, XVI, p. 946.

manufacturing centers was on a par with that of the capitals of Europe and the two largest cities in the world. Nor was this improvement merely a consequence of the very high death-rates ruling in the older manufacturing towns as recently as 1890. The ancient woollen-city of Leicester, which in the nineteenth century had become a center for the boot and shoe industry and whose population had reached 212,000 by 1901, also achieved a net decline of 3·4 permillage points from its comparatively low average rate of 16·7 for the years 1895–1904. Newcastle's experience was particularly significant, since Tyneside had some of the most 'overcrowded' housing in Britain and, as late as 1933, struck Priestley as the grimmest part of England outside the dock districts of Liverpool.

The relationships between mortality and the socio-physical environment had been generally understood throughout Victoria's reign. Poor housing, impure water, lack of fresh air and sunlight, the prevalence of dirt and disease were the common lot of those living in the compact 'walking towns' of mid-century and especially of the poorer working classes. The *sine qua non* of the city, as in one way or another of every human habitation, was the water supply. Whether for sustenance, sanitation, fire-fighting, or industrial use, water was the original public utility and, historically, the first urban 'problem.' Londoners had been obliged to seek 'sweete waters abroad' in Hertfordshire even before the upsurge of the city's population in the early seventeenth century. By Victoria's time, when nine water companies competed to supply the capital, conditions had probably deteriorated and, regardless of whether it was obtained from fountains, dug wells, or the companies, 'a drop of London water' was not likely to be any purer than that depicted in the notorious *Punch* cartoon in 1850. Urban water systems were a natural breeding ground for typhoid and cholera and any real improvement had to await advances in hydraulic engineering and the development of bacteriological science, almost all of which belong to the last quarter of the nineteenth century.[32]

It was impossible for the nineteenth-century market-economy to house the growing, urbanizing, population in any but the most rudimentary way. Public and philanthropic efforts could do little more than advertise the 'problem.' In his *Housing Problem in England* Ernest R. Dewsnup cited twenty-eight major public Housing and Health Acts between 1851 and 1903. Their terms were largely permissive and depended for their implementation and enforcement mostly upon the initiatives and resources of local authorities. The authorities were generally more responsive to health regulation than to housing legislation, except when their influences were combined, as in the standards imposed upon builders for *new* construction. Although the Nuisances Removal Act of 1855, for example, had given statutory recognition to 'overcrowding' and had indicated its dire consequences to health, the abatement provisions were nugatory. An early report of the London County Council's Medical Officer of Health, nearly four decades later, showed that the death-rate increased in the same ratio as the proportion of the population residing more than two in a room in tenements with less than five rooms. Newsholme's *Vital Statistics* revealed that the death-rate in Glasgow was 27·7 for families living in one or two rooms, 19·4 for those in three and four rooms, and only 11·2 for those in five or more rooms. In one English town the death-rate was reported as 37·3 in districts containing 50 percent of 'back-to-back' houses compared with 26·1 in districts without them. Between 1885 and 1905 Manchester closed down nearly 10,000 'back-to-back' houses and allowed only about half to be reoccupied after thorough reconstruction.[33]

The English statutory definition of overcrowding, more than two persons per room, proves to be a far better measure of urban living conditions than the crude demographic criterion of density. In 1901 the census reported 8·2 percent of the population overcrowded, 8·9 percent in urban districts as against 5·8 for the rural. London with 16·0 percent overcrowding (Finsbury had 35·2 percent and a death-rate exceeding 19 per 1,000) was poorly housed by the national standard, but the situation ranged from Gateshead (35·5 percent) and Newcastle (30·5 percent) to places like Leicester (1·0 percent) and Bournemouth—'the Garden City of the South'—with only 0·6 percent overcrowded. Making no allowance for population changes, Huddersfield led the country over the decade 1891–1901 in reducing its overcrowding by seven percentage points and Nottingham appears to be unique among eighty-four towns of more than 50,000 population in showing no improvement.

North of the border the housing situation was far more grave. Compared with

8·2 percent overcrowding in England and Wales, the corresponding figure for Scotland was 50·6 percent. Dundee reported 63·0 percent of its residents in tenements of one or two rooms, Kilmarnock 62·2 percent, Glasgow 55·1, Edinburgh 41·3, and Aberdeen 39·3 percent. Even Ireland was better off in respect of overcrowding: 40·6 percent in Dublin (24·7 percent in one room), 31·7 percent in Limerick, but only 16·7 in Derry and 8·2 percent in Belfast. In England and Wales, at least, E. R. Dewsnup was convinced that 'gross overcrowding' probably affected no more than 2·8 percent of the population by 1901 and he implied that the 'housing shortage' was only gravely acute in a few highly publicized localities.[34]

Given the variety of local circumstances, the almost universal reduction in overcrowding during Victoria's last decade was extraordinary. One contemporary, Arthur Shadwell, insisted, however, that 'the most important' element in the recent improvement of English housing conditions was the electric tramcar, which from 1896 had made the outskirts of towns accessible to more people and presented private builders with more opportunities for profit. The declining birth-rate, he thought, had also reduced pressure on housing; many imprudent parents, such as those residing in the small antiquated miners' houses in Durham or the tenements of Finsbury, Shoreditch, and Bethnal Green, had been obliged to relocate their homes at great cost and inconvenience. Much overcrowding, he declared, was in any case 'voluntary' as evidenced by the many large families taking in lodgers, or the tendency of foreigners to 'herd together' in London, the ports, and a few of the manufacturing centers. Finally, and most gradual in its effect on housing, there was the improvement in public-health administration revealed, for example, in the accounts of building renovations given by the medical officers of London's metropolitan boroughs. In varying degrees, Shadwell concluded, these three tendencies indicated that 'the process of urbanization has been modified by one of suburbanization.'[35]

## Infant Mortality: Key to the Urban Demographic Transition

However much the experts might still dispute the relative significance of housing and health regulations in reducing urban mortality, they were agreed that the stubborn predominance of city deaths over those of the countryside was a consequence of the heavier mortality of the city's children. The gradual approximation of urban and rural death-rates in England and Wales since the late 1860s was largely a result of the decline in deaths among people aged fifteen to forty-five and, to a lesser extent, five to fourteen. The widest divergence between the age-specific death-rates of town and country populations was still under five. As late as 1890 the towns had achieved a lower rate only for females between the ages of fifteen and thirty-five. Nationwide the infant mortality-rate (deaths under one year per 1,000 live births) was edging upwards again as more people concentrated in the towns.

Among nine functionally-grouped categories of socio-economic environment, only seaside resorts and pleasure places yet enjoyed age-specific death-rates approaching those of the rural districts. For females aged five to forty-five, their rates were already below the corresponding rural rates. The highest death-rates for children of both sexes under five years were reported from the Staffordshire potteries and the Lancashire manufacturing districts, while Manchester itself and the northern colliery districts were unique among the nine categories in having somewhat higher death-rates for children five to fifteen years than for those under five. Even so, mortality among the under-fives in Manchester was well above the national average for that age group during 1881–90 and far above the average for the Registrar-General's 'selected healthy districts.' Yet chances for survival beyond the age of fifteen in Manchester tended to approximate those for the corresponding age groups in the healthy districts, at least until the age of thirty-five.[36]

In his consideration of causes and remedies for infant mortality, the Registrar-General revealed in 1893 that the town rate exceeded the rural rate in the first week of life by 23 percent and that the differential increased to 97 percent by the fourth week, reaching its maximum of 273 percent in the sixth month; throughout the balance of the first year of life the two rates converged rapidly. By the late nineties death-rates in England and Wales were declining for both sexes at every age, except from sixty-five to seventy-four, and the parents of city-born infants who survived the first six months could reasonably expect all their children to live longer, fuller lives than if they had been born only five years earlier. The national infant mortality-rate reached its peak of 160–3 per 1,000 in 1898–9 and then declined rapidly. By 1905 it was down to 128; in 1910, when the population was more than 78 percent urbanized, the rate was 105. The average rate for 1899–1901 was 146, but for 1909–11 was 114—the greatest decline in any decade since registration began in 1837. After 1915 infant mortality never again exceeded 100 and after 1933 fell below 60 per 1,000. Thus, by 1910, the last great barrier to the cities of England and Wales reproducing themselves had been overcome and the urban demographic transition had been accomplished.[37]

Elsewhere in Europe infant death-rates mostly lagged far behind those of England and Wales. While the crude death-rate in London had fallen below 20 in the late 1880s and infant deaths had hovered around 164 per 1,000, Vienna's crude rate fell to 23 and the infant rate to 203. From 1881 to 1890 the infant death-rate in the sixteen largest cities of Prussia fell by more than twenty-five permillage points, standing at 241·7 in 1891 (250·5 in Berlin). Slums were less prevalent in Prussia than in England owing to the comparatively recent development of most German industrial cities; but during the 1890s living conditions in the working-class districts of German cities deteriorated with the influx of newcomers; there were no uniform standards and overcrowding tended to increase. In 1900 Königshütte, for example, one of the chief coal and iron centers of Silesia, had 70·4 percent of its rapidly growing population 'overcrowded' by the English standard of two or fewer rooms per dwelling unit; Breslau had 49·9 percent overcrowded; Chemnitz, with the highest infant mortality in Saxony, had 36·5 percent overcrowded. By the end of the century, however, crude death-rates in German cities generally were beginning to fall and children were among the principal beneficiaries. In Bavaria, for example, notably in the ancient city of Munich which had 28·7 percent of its population overcrowded in 1900, the infant death-rate in the towns had already fallen below the level prevailing in the countryside.[38] In the Netherlands an infant death-rate of 195 per 1,000 for the twelve largest cities in 1891–2 was already below the countrywide average of 203. In Switzerland, where infant mortality was almost fifty permillage points above the English rate in 1890–2, the rate for the fifteen largest cities, 157·5, had actually fallen below that for the thirty or so largest centers of England and Wales.[39]

There was less cause for congratulation in the United States. The crude death-rate in New York City, to be sure, had fallen from around 32·2 per 1,000 at mid-century to 21·5 in 1896 and to 16·8 in 1908. But the infant death-rate for the twenty-eight largest cities of 1890 was 236·8 per 1,000, exceeding that for the German *Grossstädte* outside Prussia, while the rate for the metropolitan district of New York, 264·4, surpassed even that for Berlin. The rate for the entire urban population of the registration states of 1890 was 243·3 compared with only 121·2 for their rural populations. The state of Massachusetts could take pride, perhaps, in the fact that by 1885 infant mortality in Boston and three densely populated suburbs was already down to 185·8 per 1,000.[40]

Making due allowance for shortcomings of American statistics outside of the census registration states, the situation is still hard to understand. Average population densities, outside lower Manhattan and a few blocks in other major centers, were much lower than in Continental cities, owing to the preference for home ownership and to the fact that, on the whole, boundaries were more flexible and not circumscribed by lines of ancient walls and fortifications. While the proportions of home ownership in English cities were generally lower than in the United States, the preference for individual houses was marked in both countries, but the average number of persons per census dwelling in the United States (7·64 in the twenty-eight largest cities of 1890) was considerably higher than in England and Wales. Yet public standards for sanitation and sewage disposal were much lower. The U.S. Commissioner of Labor in 1894, reported that in New York some 360,000 people lived in 'slum' conditions—162,000 in Chicago, 35,000 in Philadelphia, and 25,000 in Baltimore, where 530 families were living in single rooms—the highest proportion in the country. In New York 44·6 percent of families lived in two rooms—27·9 percent in Baltimore, 19·4 percent in Philadelphia, and 19·1 percent in the huge 'spread city' of Chicago, the older parts of which had been substantially rebuilt since the great fire of 1871. Although average earnings per family in all of these cities were high by European standards, the high proportions of families living in overcrowded housing showed, according to one observer, that the worst kind of Continental conditions 'reproduce themselves in American cities.'

If bad housing in the United States was nevertheless not so widespread as in Europe, conditions in lower Manhattan had been publicized into a 'world-wide scandal.' Density in New York City in 1890 at fifty-nine persons per acre was no greater than it was in London but whereas London's density was decreasing, that of

New York appeared to be increasing. The *Report* of the New York Tenement House Committee in 1894 revealed that density was increasing in ten of the city's twenty-four wards. Two of these, it is true, were residential suburbs north of 42nd Street, but three which lay on the lower East Side below 14th Street were the most densely populated in North America. A. F. Weber claimed that the 10th Ward, with a density of 523·6 persons per acre, was 'the densest district in the Western World, Josefstadt in Prague having 485·4, the *quartier* Bonne-Nouvelle in *arrondissement* Bourse in Paris 434·19, and Bethnal Green North in London 365·3.' By 1900 density in Manhattan was 149, on the lower East Side 382, and in the 10th Ward, 735 persons per acre. Between 1900 and 1905 density was generally increasing all over Manhattan and in 1905 there were reported to be twelve city blocks with from 1,000 to 1,400 persons to the acre. In 1901 London's most densely populated borough had 182 persons per acre, but its most densely settled district, much smaller in area than the lower East Side, was 396. Nevertheless, the crude death-rate in New York did not increase. The figure for the predominantly 'Russian Jewish' 10th Ward in 1894 was no more than 17·1 per 1,000, a rate which was bettered in only two wards of the city, one a business district and the other an up-town suburban ward. The mortality of children under five years in the 10th Ward was 58·3 per thousand compared with rates ranging up to 183 in some other wards, and 76·6 for the city as a whole.[41] The corresponding rate for London children in 1891 was 66·4 per thousand. Clearly the experience of the 10th Ward demonstrated that domestic and personal hygiene could do much to save the lives of children among a population that had many of the outward characteristics of a 'culture of poverty.' The Peabody and Octavia Hill ventures in London had likewise shown that in 'properly managed' buildings, selected poor at any rate could be trained to save themselves.

Child mortality in New York declined rapidly around the turn of the century even as housing conditions deteriorated in many working-class districts. Medical inspection of school children, isolation of contagious diseases, and more stringent inspection of milk, all helped. By 1906 the city had reduced its death-rate for all children under five years to 55 per 1,000. Infant mortality itself was more intractable. In Massachusetts the last third of the nineteenth century had witnessed death-rates for infants ranging from the 150s to the 220s. The rate for 1890–4 averaged 163·2 per 1,000 when more than 80 percent of its population was classified as urban. By 1910, nevertheless, the decline in infant deaths was unmistakable; the average for 1905–9 was 134·3, the lowest for any quinquennium in Massachusetts since the late 1850s. During the years 1915–19, which included the postwar influenza epidemic, the infant rate was averaging 100·2, only slightly above the level for England and Wales.[42]

The situation in the United States as a whole is less clear. The population of the country's death registration area, established in 1900, was heavily weighted by the inclusion of large urban populations from outside the regular registration states of the North East. Infant mortality in this population, which covered about 40 percent of the whole, remained somewhat above the rate for Massachusetts during the early 1900s. The impact of the secular fall in infant deaths was nevertheless strong enough to effect a marked improvement in crude mortality for most of the nation's larger cities. By 1905 the death-rate for New York (five boroughs) was already down to 18·3 per 1,000 and to 16·8 in 1908 when, by this measure, the city ranked ninth among the fifteen largest centers whose individual rates ranged from a high of 22·7 in the case of New Orleans and 19·3 in Washington, D.C., to lows of 14·1 in Chicago and 13·6 in Milwaukee. If it was true, as one English critic affirmed, that 'American cities have nothing to learn from other countries in regard to bad housing' and 'nothing to teach in the way of reform,' their crude mortality at least could compare with any but the most advanced industrial states such as Great Britain and Belgium and was already much better than in backward states such as Italy or European Russia.[43]

The mortality aspect of the demographic transition in the cities posed fewer difficulties of interpretation than the fertility side. The cumulative effects of improved diet, more sanitary dwellings, public health, and medical services were generally reflected in lower death-rates for all ages and classes, but only the most involved social and economic analysis could begin to 'explain' the peculiar turn in fertility. What emerged as a demonstrably negative correlation between family fertility and socio-economic status confirmed the observations of men such as A. F. Weber that 'the birth rate in large cities diminishes as one goes from the poor to the rich quarters, and that the age at marriage increases, and the size of the family diminishes as one passes from classes low in the social scale to the responsible mercantile and professional classes.'[44] Only with the steep decline in infant mortality after 1890, however, could the lower orders begin to develop a more prudential control over their own fertility. The demographic transition within the urbanized population was thus a behavioral correlate of the social and spatial structural-differentiation which marks the transformation of the Victorian industrial city into the twentieth-century metropolis.

## Alternative Urban Futures: The Vision of 1900

The demographic transition produced a mood of *fin de siècle* among late nineteenth-century social thinkers no less pessimistic and confused than that which pervaded the literary world. Since the costs of raising children in the city tended to be higher than in the country (for both private households and public authorities), and inasmuch as city children were less of an economic asset than farm children (especially among the poorly-paid lower-middle classes), a growing number of urbanites was evidently substituting a higher level of consumption for the larger families of earlier generations. But, in so far as the absolute size as well as the fertility of the ageing rural population was also beginning to fall in more 'civilized' countries, while the lower urban strata tended to breed more prolifically than the middle strata, the decline in urban mortality could no longer be regarded as an unmixed blessing. However much pundits like Herbert Spencer, Francis Galton, Georg Hansen, or Alfred Marshall had differed on the principles and details of the change, they seemed to imply that life in the industrial cities was becoming at once essential and inimical to the further progress of civilization. The selective processes of the urban transformation had brought out the noblest and the worst in mankind. Such experts left little doubt that they identified themselves with the former tendency and the ignorant and imprudent masses with the latter.

At the very dawn of the industrial era Adam Smith had predicted some such outcome for the populations of manufacturing towns. The division of labor which was the source of enhanced productivity and material betterment in both town and country would reduce the ordinary tasks of manual workers 'to a very few simple operations.' Lacking any power of judgment concerning 'the ordinary duties of private life,' and incapable of judging 'the great and extensive interests of his country,' the town worker would eventually become 'as stupid and ignorant as it is possible for a human creature to become.' His industrial skill would be acquired at the cost of his 'intellectual, social, and martial virtues.' Smith insisted that 'in every improved and civilized society this is the state into which . . . the great body of the people must necessarily fall, unless government takes some pains to prevent it.' The Scot's judgment on the social character and outlook of the urban merchant or manufacturer was only less uncomplimentary than his view of the worker.[45]

More than a century after Smith, J. A. Hobson preserved many of the same doubts. Town life, as opposed to town work, was doubtless 'educative of certain intelligence and moral qualities.' The competitive stimulus of town life, Hobson thought, more than offset the deadening effect of town work, but the 'character of town education and intelligence' was none the less limited. Smartness, glibness, 'half-baked information' and prejudice among workers and businessmen alike had produced a shallow, self-seeking outlook which paid off on the job, perhaps, but remained essentially unscientific and anti-social. While he conceded Alfred Marshall's point that the progressive mechanization of work tended to substitute 'higher or more intellectual forms of skill' for the older manual skills, Hobson insisted that this description was 'not yet applicable to most factory trades.' More significant, there had been 'a progressive weakening of the bonds of moral cohesion between individuals' and he concluded that, the growth of production notwithstanding, 'the forces driving an increased proportion of our population into towns are bringing about a decadence of *morale*, which is the necessary counterpart of the deterioration of national physique.'[46]

The demographic transition in the cities had now added a note of urgency to the century-long debate concerning the effects of specialization of roles on citizens and their social environments. From across the Atlantic, W. Z. Ripley declared, in a somewhat overdrawn contrast between urban and rural populations, that marriage and family life, unless deferred, had become 'an expensive luxury' for the more enterprising people and 'every child . . . a handicap for further advancement.' Arthur T. Hadley, shortly to be elevated to the presidency of Yale, expressed the fear of many observers that the poorer classes, now relieved of both their hunger and their high mortality, would soon out-multiply the more ambitious and prudent members of society, the builders of industrial civilization. While still adhering to the tenets of Christian Darwinism, Hadley was no longer sure that those 'fittest for civilization' could necessarily survive: 'It is not that social ambition *in itself* constitutes a greater preventive check to population than the need of subsistence; but that the need of subsistence is felt by all men alike, emotional as well as intellectual, while social ambition stamps the man or race that possess it as having reached the level of intellectual morality.' The emotional masses, he opined, were incapable of 'ethical selection.'[47]

Against these confusions, other observers looked back to proposals such as Charles Kingsley's fusion of city and country modes of life or Andrew Jackson Downing's 'country cottage residences' as the best hope for the industrial city and its threatened civilization. For such people, the countryside had to be brought into the city, and a part of the city, at least, returned to the land. Charles H. Cooley, like Hadley a student of modern transportation, posed the late-Victorian dilemma most succinctly as 'a permanent conflict between the needs of industry and the needs of humanity. Industry says men must aggregate. Humanity says they must not, or if they must, let it be only during working hours and let the necessity not extend to their wives and children.' It was 'the office of the city railways,' Cooley declared, 'to reconcile these conflicting requirements.' Cooley's vision of the industrial city was of a new order of space and time: rapid transit and the residential suburb were conceived as the most practical and benign remedies for the physical and moral 'problems' afflicting the impacted populations of great cities.[48]

There was a certain myopic quality to the late-Victorian belief in the suburbs. Suburbs were as old as the cities themselves; the clustering of populations on the edges of towns was, if anything, an older form of city growth than their concentration at the core. The peripheral areas of early industrial towns had sometimes grown faster than their centers, even before the coming of steam railways in the 1830s. London, Manchester, Brussels, Philadelphia, Boston, Chicago, Berlin, and Sydney were essentially agglomerations of 'suburbs' and 'satellites,' some of which were later consolidated or annexed. The suburbs of one generation were often indistinguishable from the town of the next; sometimes yesterday's suburbs became today's slums. In *Sesame and Lilies* Ruskin had bitterly condemned the 'festering and wretched suburb.'

If the Victorians had studied the social morphology of city growth more closely, they might have been more guarded in their belief in the redemptive powers of suburban life. The fact that developments in technology and organization now permitted spatial differentiation on an unprecedented scale was surely as much cause for concern as for congratulation. While reducing the difference that had grown up between town and country environments, a much more intensive differentiation of land uses and social space would now be achieved over a greatly extended urbanized area. The city population might well become even more divided from itself.[49] The subjective gravity of 'the problem' was such that many otherwise informed observers grasped this particular panacea uncritically.

Here was the remedy for a deteriorating social environment that went beyond restrictive housing legislation or countrified neighborhoods. By increasing the speed of public transportation to ten miles per hour, the electrified street-car could more than double the journey-to-work distance attained by horse-drawn cars. Its promoters claimed that the electric tramway would be more flexible than cumbersome rackrailways or cable cars, and much cheaper to install than either tube or open-cut subway systems. New modes of electric power generation and transmission, moreover, could lead to a rapid dispersion of manufacturing jobs to the outskirts of towns, if not back to the countryside. Alfred Marshall had, in fact, been urging the decentralization of London's clothing industry and its poorly-housed working people on economic as well as civic grounds since the early 1880s. A. F. Weber agreed that, in so far as concentrated poverty and overcrowding had once been concomitants of agglomeration, the planned movement of people to new 'colonies' in the country, such as Marshall proposed, would certainly mitigate 'the evils of city life.'

Marshall had made many other suggestions for improvement which Weber could endorse: piped water, steam heat, compressed and 'ozonized' air in compact multi-tubular tunnels beneath city streets. Weber upheld Marshall's technical recommendations for reducing air pollution from household and industrial smoke and he applauded the economist's vision that 'every house might be in electric communication with the rest of town.' But the optimism of Weber, the most informed student of the city at the turn of the century, was grounded on something more substantial than a trendy confidence in quick technological solutions to intractable social and moral problems. He added Marshall's insights to his own hard evidence to show that, for all the real danger of the city, the general forces of economic and social progress were already in the ascendant.

Even before Weber, Marshall had maintained that advances in medical science, improvements in public health services, and the growth of material wealth 'all tend to lessen mortality and to increase health and strength and to lengthen life.' The very rapid growth of town populations, on the other hand, lowered vitality and tended to raise death-rates while 'the higher strain of the population' inclined 'to marry later and have fewer children than the lower' strain. The former impulses, unchecked by the latter, could, if overpopulation were avoided, bring man 'to a physical and mental excellence superior to any that the world had yet known; while if the latter act unchecked he would speedily degenerate.' Recent experience with the Victorian cities had convinced Marshall that the former set of impulses was 'slightly preponderating.' The population of England and Wales was still growing; 'those who are out of health in body and mind are certainly not an increasing part of the whole' while the rest were better fed and clothed and, with few exceptions, stronger than ever before.[50]

The qualified affirmation of the economist was carried over into the luminous vision and confident practice of the stenographer-turned-inventor, Ebenezer Howard. Published in 1898, Howard's seminal tract *Tomorrow: A Peaceful Path to Real Reform* had more citations to Marshall's writings than to any other single source. Howard's 'plan' for Garden Cities was an explicit critique of the sprawling peripheral development so familiar to late-Victorians and their descendants. For Howard the suburbs were a 'railway chaos' and should be replaced by towns linked with each other and with a central city by a 'railway system' including rapid public transit; the intervening spaces should be preserved for uses other than commerce or residence. Howard's 'town-country magnet' was, in Lewis Mumford's words, *'not a suburb but the antithesis of a suburb: not a more rural retreat, but a more integrated foundation for an effective urban life.'* He hoped that the Garden City experiment would not only relieve congestion and economize in the use of land but also serve as 'the stepping stone to a higher and better form of industrial life generally throughout the country.' Long before the private automobile, Howard foresaw the kind of 'alien' settlement and encompassing smog through which Priestley would pass on his English journey in 1933. The subsequent failure of the British town-planning movement to grasp more firmly Howard's design for 'social cities' is no reflexion on the practicality of his idea.[51]

No planner ever penetrated more deeply into the changing character of the late Victorian city than the indefatigable Scottish biologist and human ecologist, Patrick Geddes. Like Howard, Geddes recognized that the city of the future would differ as much from the mid-Victorian city of his childhood as that city, Perth, has done from the burghs and villages of preindustrial Scotland. If the existing city was to be reconciled with the needs of both industry and humanity, then its future development must be 'one capable of increasingly conscious evolution,' in course of which *quantitative* growth in wealth and population must be transformed into *qualitative* progress. Under a commission from Andrew Carnegie to his native Dunfermline in 1903, Geddes had opportunity to demonstrate his remarkable gift for mediating between a 'community's' past and future. Although Carnegie's initial interest had not gone far beyond introducing 'more sweetness and light into the lives of working people,' and despite the fact that Geddes' plan failed to induce the canny Dunfermline burghers to spend much more of Carnegie's money, *City Development. A Study of Parks, Gardens, and Culture Institutes*, published in 1904 at the author's expense, established Geddes as a master whose works and influence would be spread halfway round an urbanizing world.

Geddes predicted that 'the world is now rapidly entering upon a new era of civic development.' In the more urbanized countries 'the last generation has had to carry out great works of prime necessity, as of water supply, sanitation and the like; elementary education, too, has been begun; so that to some, even pioneers in their day, our city development may seem wellnigh complete.' In fact, city development had entered on an urgent new phase 'that of ensuring healthier conditions, of providing happier and nobler ones.' Coming generations would have to study the social history and needs of their particular communities and regions in order to relate their 'culture' to opportunities and limitations shown by a study of their physical environments. Meanwhile, technical education and technology, unless infused by an intimate knowledge of science and art and consciously directed to social and civic ends, would only tend to exacerbate the condition of man in cities. Thus, beginning with 'the fundamental problem of purifying our stream and cultivating our garden,' men would have to progress 'naturally and necessarily . . . towards the idea, first of bettered dwellings of the body, and then to that of higher palaces of the spirit.' Without a fusion of the 'material and intellectual, domestic and civic, scientific and artistic' into the 'fundamental basis of natural and industrial reality much of our present-day idealism but flutters in the void; while our would-be practical world . . . is continually sinking into material failure or stagnation, moral discouragement, or decay.' Though the would-be practical world would often decry Geddes' pronouncements as 'utopian' or 'anti-urban', he was consistently seeking to pose an alternative to the present, to awaken an urbanizing world to the necessity for *eu-technics* and to the promise of *Eu-topia*, the best of each place in its fitness and beauty.[52]

## The Urbanizing World and the Social Question

The urbanizing world at the close of Victoria's reign was still a western world. High rates and levels of urban concentration had been achieved only in countries of predominantly European population and culture. By 1890 the very rapid concentration in Australia and the northeastern United States had already indicated that the transformation was no longer peculiar to Europe itself. The case of Australia was particularly significant since it had achieved both high levels of urbanization—with more than a third of the population living in four colonial capitals in 1891—and comparatively high levels of material living without benefit of industrialization on the pattern of either Britain or the United States.

By 1900 two-thirds of the world's rapidly growing urban population was located in Europe (excluding the Russian Empire), North America, and Australasia (see Table 1.5). The proportion in Asia continued to fall and the fraction in Africa barely held its own. In contrast to the first half of the nineteenth century when the fastest growing share of world urban population had been situated in Europe, it was the Americas, notably North America, which were registering the greatest share of the increment during the last quarter of the century. Over the first half of the twentieth century, the Americas' share of world urban population continued to grow steadily, but Europe's declined almost as rapidly as that of Asia in the latter part of the nineteenth century. Between 1900 and 1950 the absolute numbers of city dwellers in Asia grew by nearly 450 percent, and in the Soviet Union by 495 percent, compared with only 160 percent for the combined urban populations of Europe and both Americas.

Since 1950 many of these tendencies have persisted. As of 1970 the Soviet Union and Latin America appear to be undergoing the most rapid structural change from rural to urban, followed by Australasia, North America, and East Asia in that order (see Table 1.6). The decadal rate of urban concentration in South Asia and Africa does not appear to be accelerating, although it is somewhat above the rates experienced in those regions during the years between the two World Wars. Meanwhile, the rate of concentration in Europe is currently the slowest among the eight major world regions. By the mid-twentieth century the urbanizing world had long ceased to be an exclusively 'western' world.

Table 1.5   *Growth of world population and world urban population, 1800–1970*

|  | Population (millions) | Percent urban (≥ 20,000) | Percent urban (national definitions) | Share of world urban population (≥ 20,000) in Europe, N. America and Australasia* |
|---|---|---|---|---|
| 1800 | 906 | 2·4 | — | 30·8 |
| 1850 | 1,171 | 4·3 | — | 48·3 |
| 1900 | 1,608 | 9·2 | — | 65·4 |
| 1920 | 1,860 | 14·3 | 19·3 | 61·6 |
| 1930 | 2,069 | 16·3 | 22·0 | 58·6 |
| 1940 | 2,295 | 18·9 | 24·8 | 51·1 |
| 1950 | 2,515 | 21·2 | 28·0 | 47·0* |
| 1960 | 2,991 | 25·4 | 33·1 | 41·0 |
| 1970 | 3,584 | 28·1 | 37·1 | 36·3 |

*1900 and earlier, in cities ≥ 100,000; 1950, 43·5 percent in cities ≥ 100,000.
Source: 1800, 1850, 1900: K. Davis and H. H. Golden, cited by P. M. Hauser, ed.,
    *Urbanization in Asia and the Far East* (UNESCO: Calcutta, 1957), pp. 55–60. Since
    1920: U.N. Dept of Economic and Social Affairs, provisional data, 9 Dec. 1968.

Table 1.6   *Levels and rates of world urbanization, by regions, 1920–70*

| Region | Percent of population agglomerated (≥ 20,000) | | | | | | Rate of urban concentration (percentage point shift) | |
|---|---|---|---|---|---|---|---|---|
|  | 1920 | 1930 | 1940 | 1950 | 1960 | 1970 | 1920–50 | 1950–70 |
| N. America | 41 | *46* | 46 | *51* | 58 | 62 | *+10* | *+11* |
| Australasia | 37 | 38 | 41 | *46* | 53 | 58 | *+9* | *+12* |
| Europe | 35 | 37 | 40 | 41 | 44 | 45 | *+18* | *+4* |
| U.S.S.R. | 10 | *13* | *24* | 28 | 36 | 43 | *+18* | *+15* |
| L. America | 14 | *17* | 20 | 25 | 33 | 38 | *+11* | *+13* |
| World | 14 | 16 | 19 | 21 | 25 | 28 | +7 | +7 |
| E. Asia | 7 | 9 | 12 | 14 | *19* | 22 | +7 | *+8* |
| S. Asia | 6 | 7 | 8 | *11* | 14 | 16 | +5 | +5 |
| Africa | 5 | 6 | 7 | 10 | 13 | 16 | +5 | +6 |

N.B.: Italicized figures indicate a rate of regional concentration, δ(u/p), above world rate in
    preceding decade. The last two columns present summary rates for three and two
    decades respectively.
Source: U.N. Dept of Economic and Social Affairs, provisional data, 9 Dec. 1968.

The world-wide process of urbanization since the 1920s is the outcome of much the same economic, technological, and demographic forces as were felt in parts of Europe and North America during the Victorian era. There, however, the metropolitan form of organization after 1890 had tended to mitigate some of the older central city problems, although it aggravated others by dispersing political and fiscal resources as well as population over a wider and more socially-fragmented urban area. By the 1920s the metropolitan ring populations of North America and some European countries were growing faster *nationwide* than the populations of their central cities and by 1970 the aggregate population residing in suburban and satellite rings of United States metropolitan areas actually outnumbered the aggregate population of the central cities themselves. Only in the interwar years did the pace and form of population concentration in a few of the less urbanized countries begin to assume a metropolitan pattern. The phase began early in Japan, and in certain Latin American countries such as Argentina, but the fuller impact of urbanism and metropolitanism has only been registered in most parts of the 'Third World' since the 1940s.[53]

For a period after the Second World War the average rate of population growth was rising in most parts of the world. During 1950–60, the less developed areas were growing at a faster annual rate, 1·9 percent, than the more advanced areas, 1·3 percent, with the single exception of Australasia, 2·3 percent, a major beneficiary of international migration. Latin America led the world in the 1950s with an annual rate of 2·8 percent, while its average rate of urban population growth (as distinct from its rate of urban concentration), 5·5 percent, far exceeded that of any other major continental region except Africa, 5·4 percent. United Nations' projections of population growth for the period 1960–80 likewise give Latin America the fastest rate, 2·9 percent per annum, for the immediate future. The projected rate of urban population growth for Latin America, 4·4 percent, however, will lag behind that for Africa, 4·6 percent, during the 1970s, but will far exceed that for any other region except South Asia, 4·1 percent.[54] Latin America is now therefore the most critical region for both population and urban growth.

Some of the recent effects of these changes are exhibited in Table 1.7 which also presents comparable data for high-income countries. Perhaps the most startling fact to emerge from it is that, by 1960, crude death-rates in India and many Latin American countries *already approximated those* of the more economically advanced countries. This accomplishment indicates the effectiveness of cheap health technologies, such as D.D.T., in the control of some forms of pandemic disease which had hitherto taken a heavy toll of life.[55] It also reveals, in light of high infant mortality-rates, the comparative youthfulness of the Indian and Latin American populations. The wide discrepancy between infant mortality-rates of high- and low-income countries, on the other hand, underlines the inadequacy of medical facilities, and relatively unhealthy conditions in the under-developed areas. Countries with comparatively high infant mortality-rates are, with the exception of Argentina, also countries with comparatively high birth-rates and, with the exceptions of Argentina and Chile, countries with comparatively low levels of urbanization. As of the early 1960s, Japan appears to be the only country outside of Europe, North America, and Australasia to have yet passed through anything resembling the urban demographic transition to low fertility and low mortality for infants as well as older age groups.

Table 1.7   *Level of urbanization, crude vital rates, infant mortality, numbers of persons per room, daily calorie intake per person, for selected countries, 1960–5*

| Per capita output range ($)[a] | Country | Level of urbanization, percent ($\geq 20,000$) | Birthrate | Deathrate | Infant mortality | Persons per room | Average daily calorie consumption |
|---|---|---|---|---|---|---|---|
| | | | | Per 1,000 | | | |
| Over 1,200 | U.S.A. | 59 | 18·5 | 9·5 | 23·4 | 0·7 | 3,140 |
| | Canada | 53 | 19·6 | 7·6 | 23·6 | 0·7 | 3,090 |
| | Australia | 66 | 19·6 | 8·8 | 18·5 | 0·7 | 3,160 |
| | N. Zealand | 59 | 22·5 | 8·9 | 17·7 | 0·7 | 3,410 |
| | Sweden | 40 | 15·8 | 10·0 | 13·3 | 0·8 | 2,950 |
| 601–1,200 | U.K. | 69 | 18·3 | 11·5 | 19·6 | 0·7 | 2,360 |
| | German F.R. | 52 | 17·9 | 11·2 | 23·8 | 0·9 | 2,900 |
| | Belgium | 52 | 16·4 | 12·1 | 24·1 | 0·6 | 3,150 |
| | Netherlands | 60 | 19·2 | 8·1 | 14·4 | 0·8 | 2,890 |
| | France | 48 | 17·7 | 11·1 | 22·0 | 1·0 | 3,050 |
| 301–600 | Italy | 47 | 18·9 | 9·5 | 35·6 | 1·1 | 2,810 |
| | German D.R. | 40 | 15·8 | 11·2 | 23·2 | 1·0 | — |
| | U.S.S.R. | 36 | 18·4 | 7·3 | 27·0 | 1·5 | — |
| | Japan | 46 | 18·6 | 7·1 | 18·5 | 1·2 | 2,320 |
| | Argentina | 55 | 22·5 | 8·2 | 60·7 | 1·4 | 3,040 |
| | Chile | 53 | 32·1 | 10·7 | 107·1 | 1·7 | 2,370 |
| 101–300 | Mexico | 35 | 44·2 | 9·5 | 60·7 | 2·9 | 2,660 |
| | Peru | 26 | 43–45 | 14–15 | 66·5 | 2·2 | 2,160 |
| | Ecuador | 25 | 46–50 | 15–18 | 93·0 | 2·5 | 1,970 |
| Under 100 | India | 14 | 38·4 | 12·9 | 139·0 | 2·6 | 1,980 |
| | Pakistan | 10 | 43·4 | 15·4 | 145·6 | 3·1 | 2,260 |

[a]Conversion to U.S. dollars by means of current exchange rates: E. E. Hagen, 'Some Facts about Income Levels and Economic Growth,' *Review of Economics & Statistics*, xlii (Feb. 1960), 63.
Source: Statistical Office, United Nations, *Statistical Yearbook, Demographic Yearbook*, and *Population and Vital Statistics Report*.

It is clear from Table 1.7 that levels of *per capita* output and degree of urbanization among high-income countries do not in themselves explain differences in vital rates or quality of the socio-physical environment. It must be remembered that some of the more obvious differences in socio-economic and demographic characteristics among low-income countries may well reflect divergences in the relative size and condition of their respective urban and rural components. Data from Japan, for example, suggest that as recently as 1926–30, when the population was about 28 percent urbanized, mortality in cities was still very much higher than in the country-side. In the immediate postwar years this was narrowing rapidly and by 1950, when the country was nearly 40 percent urbanized, registered infant deaths in Tokyo, 42 per 1,000, and Osaka, 50 per 1,000, for example, were already below the national rate of 60 per 1,000. Some fairly reliable data from four countries in South Asia indicated that, as of 1950, the national rate of infant deaths had been declining since the 1930s but some less complete data for large cities, such as Calcutta and Bombay, showed that an increasing rate had prevailed up until the late 1940s and had only recently been reversed. In 1950, however, the rate of infant mortality among the national populations of Ceylon, 82 per 1,000, and India, 127 per 1,000, was still considerably below the rate for such large cities as Colombo, 112, and Bombay, 152. Even if the rate in the large cities was no longer rising, Table 1.7 shows that, for the Indian population as a whole, average infant mortality over the decade 1951–61 *was* higher than at the mid-century, with no more than a two percentage point shift in the interim level of urban concentration.[56]

A more reliable measure of effective fertility in a population is given by the child–woman (c–w) ratio, or the number of live births less childhood deaths under age five per 1,000 women of child-bearing ages. In most East and South Asian countries the c–w ratios around 1950 were still very high compared with the more industrial-urban countries of 'the West.' Nevertheless, the c–w ratios for large Asian cities were almost always lower than for their respective national populations. In Tokyo, 454 per 1,000, and Colombo, 467 per 1,000, at least, the ratio was no greater than in Canada, 498, Chile, 480, or Finland, 476, whose populations then showed the highest c–w ratios among the more developed non-Asian countries. Making due allowance for the quality of Asian data it is clear, nevertheless, that the registered rates of infant deaths in East and South Asian cities during the early 1950s were already well *below* the rates prevailing in the larger cities of Continental Europe and North America at the turn of the century. Thus, while infant mortality may possibly increase and c–w ratios decline somewhat, especially in South Asian countries, the further urbanization of their populations is not likely to have quite the same 'braking effect' on total population growth as it did in the more urbanized parts of Europe and North America in the late-Victorian era.

In regard to the urban demographic transition the Japanese model may be more relevant to Asia than was the earlier experience of Europe or the United States. The drastic steps taken by the Japanese after 1950 to curb their own population, however, occurred at a comparatively advanced stage in their process of industrialization. Table 1.7 shows that in the early 1960s Japan already compared quite favorably with the high-income countries by most measures other than *per capita* product. By 1970 *per capita* product was rising steadily and Japan appears to have accomplished its urban transformation—more than 51 percent of population resident in cities of 20,000 and over—very successfully.[57]

Meanwhile, fertility remains highest in Latin America. In tropical American countries crude birth-estimates ranged up to 44–50 per 1,000 in the early 1960s, comparable to the rates achieved in parts of North America early in the nineteenth century. The more reliable child–woman ratio allows us to make a more careful analysis of the urban-rural differentials in Latin America. It was highest in the Dominican Republic, 749 per 1,000 in 1950, and lowest in highly urbanized Argentina, 423 per 1,000 in 1947. All other countries, except Chile and Haiti, however, had c–w ratios above 500, but Chile was one of the most urbanized countries in the region and Haiti the very least; hence the relation between level of urbanization and the effective fertility of Latin populations does not seem to be a very systematic one. Nevertheless, a comparison of the c–w ratios for total and for non-single women between the principal city and national populations in six countries led U.N. observers to assert 'an inverse association of the level of fertility with the size of the locality.' In general, they concluded, 'the fertility of the urban population is uniformly below that of the total population.'[58]

Data for nine Latin American countries, based on national intercensal periods prior to mid-century, reveal that the greater part of incremental urban growth in Mexico (58 percent), Chile (53 percent), and Brazil (51 percent) already stemmed from urban natural increase. Venezuela (29 percent) and Colombia (32 percent) were the countries whose urban increments had benefited least from natural increase and most from the migration of native and foreign-born elements. The annual average percentage growth in major urban areas in the ensuing years was, not surprisingly, highest in Venezuela, 7·6 percent in 1950–5, and Colombia, 6·6 percent, 1951–5, compared with rates of less than 4·0 percent for Brazil, Mexico, and Chile. Buenos Aires appeared to be the only major urban area with a rate of population growth lower than its country's national rate. U.N. observers of Latin America in the late 1950s endorsed the view of their counterparts in East and South Asia at the time that 'while the volume of rural-urban migration is largely dependent on the economic situation, the demographic characteristics of the migrants are conditioned by long-established social patterns.'

The situation in many developing countries today is perhaps more complex than this conclusion suggests. Some low-income countries are said to be 'over-urbanized in relation to [their] degree of economic development.' The massive urban housing deficits reflected in the growth and size of Indian *bustees*, Brazilian *favelhas*, or Peruvian *barriadas* are cited as evidence of the recent concentration of rural poverty, the spread of underemployment, and of the general explosiveness of the resulting social situation. Such conditions are thought to preclude the achievement of 'political stability and economic growth' which is said to have characterized the development of most 'Western nations' in the past.[59]

Victims of modern warfare such as Korea or Vietnam, and countries such as Egypt, Iraq, Peru, or Colombia in the late 1950s did indeed appear to have reached quite high levels of urbanization and non-agricultural employment in relation to their national levels of *per capita* income. Middle East countries, with about 23 percent of population living in cities of 20,000 and over by 1960, had an average level of gross domestic product *per capita* of only $75 in 1958. Was India at the time, with but 14 percent of her population urbanized and a *per capita* G.D.P. only $5 below the level of the Middle East, achieving a more balanced development? Was the U.S.S.R. with 36 percent of its population urbanized, and a *per capita* G.D.P. above $700 more balanced than Japan with 46 percent of population urbanized and a G.D.P. of only $650 *per capita*? Was New Zealand, at the same level of urbanization as the United States in 1960, but with a *per capita* G.D.P. of only $1,454 compared with $2,324 for the U.S., overurbanized and underdeveloped?

Clearly, the formulation implies some criterion of *balanced* urban and economic growth. Data from 150 countries around mid-century showed a high correlation between the level of urbanization and the degree to which the labor force was employed outside of agriculture. There was, likewise, an inverse relation between dependence of the labor force on agriculture and the level of *per capita* product. At any time it is possible to derive a regression line that summarizes the strong statistical association between (a) the proportion of population found, say, in cities of 20,000 and over, and (b) the proportion of total labor force or product contributed by the non-agricultural sector. Such an operation would reveal some conspicuously deviant countries in which a higher than 'expected' portion of the population is found in cities on the basis of the country's industrial composition and, by the same measure, cases of 'underurbanization' as well. But it does not follow that the only 'justifiable' balance is one that approximates the figment of the regression line. One might well inquire whether in such a deviant case as the Middle East, for example, any substantial numbers in urban places could be justified in the context of extremely low rural *and* urban productivity? But we do not know whether conditions in the urban places are in fact worse than in the alternative rural places and, as was the case in early nineteenth-century Britain, 'those best in a position to judge are continuing their migration.' What we do know is that the situation in the low-income countries today is, to say the least, uncomfortable and often desperate. As Britton Harris has suggested with reference to Indian urbanization, 'if . . . the cities are overlarge in relation to opportunity, so too are the rural areas.' Overurbanization combined with 'overruralization' probably means no more and no less than overpopulation.[60]

Another feature of contemporary urbanization in low-income countries gives rise to a more reasonable concern. In some parts of the world, population concentration is increasing the predominance of one national center within the size-distribution of city populations or the national population as a whole. Buenos Aires, Santiago, and Caracas are prominent examples in Latin America, although the phenomenon is not peculiar to that part of the world either today or in the past. Metropolitan Sydney had developed its primacy in New South Wales by 1861, almost a decade before Buenos Aires had assumed a similar position in Argentina. By 1891 Glasgow contained nearly 20 percent of the population of Scotland and Glaswegians outnumbered the aggregate of its seven next largest cities. London had also been steadily enlarging its share of the population of England and Wales during Victoria's reign and by the 1890s contained just over 20 percent of the whole. Nevertheless, the aggregate for the next sixteen largest cities (of 1871) had grown more rapidly than London over every census decade. By 1901 some thirty cities in England and Wales outside of London contained more than 100,000 population and, in the aggregate, more than a quarter of the nation's population. On the Continent, however, Stockholm, Oslo, Paris, Brussels, Berlin (Prussia), Budapest (Hungary), and Athens (Greece) were at one time or another primate cities in the manner of Glasgow in Scotland in 1891.[61]

It appears from this that there is no close empirical connection between the fact of primacy and economic underdevelopment. There is evidence, nevertheless, that a progression from primacy to a log-normal type distribution of city sizes often does occur as a society develops toward greater complexity and as the patterning effect of any single socio-economic variable is obscured. The examples of London and New York in their respective city-size distributions appear to illustrate this progression at least since the early nineteenth century. But the several patterns of city-size distribution obtaining in the contemporary world do not appear closely related to either the level of economic development or the degree of urbanization of national populations.[62] Very large centers are often unable to provide either adequate public services or full-time employment for a sizeable portion of their residents; alternatively, they are thought to exercise a constraining or 'parasitical' influence over the development of their national or provincial populations. The long history of controversies concerning the optimum size of cities and the effects of 'overcentralization' suggests, however, that such problems, real or imagined, are not entirely novel.[63] Nor does the existence of the primacy phenomenon anywhere in the world necessarily constitute evidence of either 'internal' or 'external' colonialism.

In the contemporary world the term 'colonialism' is a politically-charged expression to denote, in Richard Morse's phrase, 'a relationship between two systems showing discontinuities of structure and inherent purpose.' But the dominance which large cities exert over smaller centers and intervening countryside is as much a cause of their preponderance as it is the consequence. They grow larger, if not always faster, than provincial and local centers because, historically, they have served to integrate the social systems of which they form a part. Their integral role with respect to transport and communications, information flows, credit resources, and so on induces the gravitation of many other functions which benefit from 'cost' or other friction-reducing access to the node. Inequalities and inequities inhere in such a structure, to be sure, but they arise as much from the reciprocal relationships involved as from any others. The subordination of provinces to a metropolis is not indisputable evidence of rival systems with contradictory purposes, though provincial feelings of being victimized can certainly subvert their essentially symbiotic relations with the metropolis.

Morse affirms that, in Latin America at least, the term 'colonialism' may be analytically useful when applied to certain 'inter-ethnic situations' and even to 'certain forms of international influence and manipulation,' but that 'applied to the workings of a total society the expression becomes tendentious, while applied to relations between "city" and "country" it merely obfuscates.' He concludes that in the larger realm of 'collective attitude and social action,' now even more than in the past perhaps, 'the city becomes a theater, not a player—a node of forces, not a quantum of energy.' The conception of cities as theaters of forces or, less elegantly, as foci of generalized nodality, is central to an understanding of recent alterations in the organization of human ecosystems and many related phenomena of social change.[64]

Cities have become the focus for the twin forces of specialization and differentiation which have contributed so greatly to the making of the contemporary world. During the Victorian era exceptional numbers of people were concentrated in impacted areas of different size, density, and function. Land-extensive activities, such as staple agriculture, were excluded from the vicinity of cities, whose internal spaces were meanwhile reorganized and reshaped into specialized districts of work and residence and whose populations were required to allocate particular time for labor and domesticity, switching from production to consumption roles at specific times. By the early twentieth century a metropolitan city-dweller in many parts of Europe and North America was already obliged to play increasingly differentiated roles at work, at home, on the lengthening journey between, and in his increasingly fragmented 'community.' During the span of an individual's career, the sequence and specificity of his roles were modulated, not by ageing alone, but by changes in socio-economic status as well. Over the generations the daily routine and unfolding life-histories of individuals departed quite radically from those of their ancestors, urban or rural. The growing specializations of cities and countrysides and the integral linking of small towns, cities, and metropolitan centers were also manifestations of the same specialization-differentiation-reintegration tendency which, as in the case of vertically-integrated factory systems and large business enterprises, yielded increasing returns to scale. Notwithstanding distinctive sets of institutional-legal constraints on individual production units and corporate bureaucracies there is, by analogy, a similarly centralized mode of organization and control over 'systems of cities'—metropolitan hierarchy—which inheres in technological progress.[65]

Perhaps the most striking behavioral manifestations of the industrial-urban transformation were: (1) the generally inverse relation between family fertility and socio-economic status, and (2) the age and status selectivity of population movements to different suburban amphitheaters. Thus the climax of the Victorian city inaugurated and institutionalized a new order of space and time that ultimately penetrated the most intimate realms of personal consciousness and private judgment.[66] By and large, a majority of urbanites adjusted to the demands and disciplines of the emergent order, reconciled to it because for them at least the benefits in real income and acquired status outweighed the heavy costs that mostly fell on other segments of society. In its most recent metropolitan phase, the process of transformation has involved—in aspiration, if not actuality—the *embourgeoisement* of virtually the entire population.

Until the 1940s the spread of urbanization to the world was a gradual and highly selective process. Temporal as well as cultural and contextual differences from late

Victorian Europe and North America almost certainly assured that the outcome would diverge from any nineteenth-century model of change and adjustment. Before the mid-twentieth century, the very phenomena of urbanization and economic growth had ceased, so to speak, to be historical happenings and had become the subjects of highly self-conscious sets of competing ideologies. During the inter-war years, however, no country outside of A. F. Weber's 'western world,' except Japan and the Soviet Union, appeared to be undergoing anything resembling a rapid industrial-urban transformation (see Table 1.8). But in the two decades after 1940,

Table 1.8   *Rates of urban concentration, leading countries, 1920–60*

*(percentage point shifts)*

| 1920–40 | | | | 1940–60 | | | |
|---|---|---|---|---|---|---|---|
| Japan | 16 | S. Africa | 8 | Venezuela | 26 | Finland | 14 |
| U.S.S.R. | 14 | Morocco | 8 | Uruguay | 18 | Brazil | 13 |
| Spain | 10 | Uruguay | 8 | Mexico | 17 | Peru | 13 |
| Denmark | 9 | Venezuela | 8 | Colombia | 17 | U.S.S.R. | 12 |
| Chile | 9 | France | 8 | Chile | 16 | Bulgaria | 12 |
| Korea | 9 | Greece | 8 | Korea | 16 | Egypt | 12 |
| New Zealand | 8 | Sweden | 8 | New Zealand | 15 | Canada | 12 |
| Iran | 8 | Finland | 8 | Argentina | 14 | Australia | 12 |

Rate of urban concentration: $\delta(u/p)$, cities $\geq 20,000$.
Source: U.N. Dept of Economic and Social Affairs, provisional data, 9 Dec. 1968.

there were few countries which did not experience a marked surge in their rates of concentration. Only in Great Britain, the most urbanized country in the world, did the situation appear to have stabilized with about 70 percent of population concentrated in urban areas of 20,000 and over. The most awesome change occurred in Latin America, while in Korea and a few North African and Middle Eastern countries, levels of concentration rose by more than 10 percentage points. The absolute numbers of people moving to cities in India, Pakistan, or Indonesia could likewise no longer be ignored.[67] Even the United States, which had been conspicuously unsuccessful among developed nations in implementing any kind of 'urban' policy at home, became publicly concerned with the urban problems of low-income countries.

In view of population growth, the *per capita* domestic resources available in most low-income countries were judged to be inadequate if economic growth was to be achieved under conditions of 'political stability.' Resources that could be earned from the normal course of international trade, moreover, seemed uncertain and, depending on the terms of trade, comparatively expensive. Under Cold War conditions, moreover, neither the United States nor Soviet blocs could rely upon the United Nations to serve as the agency for devising and implementing assistance policy; they each preferred to make bilateral arrangements. Given the necessity for 'development,' as the problem is defined and measured by developers from high-income countries, the need for international assistance in the contemporary world is great, almost without regard to political-ideological strings attached by its donors.

The experience of Australia and New Zealand indicates, nevertheless, that on the product side at least, developing countries need not follow the form of Great Britain, Germany, the United States or Japan in their respective transformations. Certain tendencies in the structure of consumption in the economically-developed countries are more alike, however, although the proportion of actual goods and services comprising private and public expenditures differ greatly over time according to technologies and tastes. The proportions of disposable incomes spent on such basic consumption needs as food, clothing, furniture, or shelter do not necessarily increase over time.[68] Thus coefficients derived from cross-sectional structural associations between levels of urbanization, shares of manufacturing in total labor force or product, and additions to total real income and product in the advanced countries, even when they agree in broad direction, may differ greatly in *magnitudes* owing to the numerous variables involved: the size of populations, grades of raw materials, quality of the labor force relative to changing technologies, involvements in international trade, and, ultimately, to differences in social and cultural tradition.

All this implies a high degree of contingency in the social transformation required to accomplish economic growth. It also helps to account for the selective character of urbanization in different parts of the world. More important, it suggests that low-income countries are not doomed to recapitulate the 'modernizing' experiences of the more developed worlds, western or eastern. There is a margin for hope that, *if* certain acceptable minimum levels of material existence were reached, no social catastrophe need follow, nor even 'development.' Indeed, forced development, western or eastern style, might bring catastrophe. The outcome might depend very often on the extent to which the average number of persons 'per private household' can be lowered. High death-rates notwithstanding, the average size of 'private households' in countries with *per capita* G.D.P. under $200 in 1958, five members, was almost one-and-a-half times as large as in moderate and high-income countries with *per capita* G.D.P. of $575 and over. The proportion of total household population in the 'under $200' countries contributed by households of seven or more members was close to half at the time, compared with little more than 15 percent in the higher-income countries. One barely credible means of raising *per capita* incomes to some locally defined and tolerable minimum might be an effort to substitute such an acceptable level for the seventh, sixth, and fifth births per household by successive target dates before the *annus mirabilis vatum*, A.D. 2000. Only when one has contemplated the full complexity of factors, social and normative, affecting fertility in different cultures, perhaps, can one turn back to consider alternative, if scarcely less complex, strategies for stimulating economic growth![69]

## The Human Eco-System in an Urbanizing World

While the reduction in fertility might lessen some of the more obvious pressures making for social catastrophe in newly-developing countries, a comparable achievement in many high-income countries might prove to be a greater boon to the entire planet. In a world of finite resources there are boundary conditions, albeit uncertain, which set limits to all human procreation. The *effective* population in the human ecosystem is not mere numbers, but rather the impact of numbers on physical and social environments. With less than 6 percent of world population in 1970, for example, the United States consumes 40 percent of the annual world production of raw materials. If, on a very rough calculation, one additional North American birth has an effect on natural resource consumption of approximately twenty-five births in India or Pakistan, the recent decline in U.S. fertility might be regarded as providing some ecological relief for the rest of mankind. During the 1950s the refined fertility of American women averaged 3·35 children but by 1970 the figure had dropped to 2·45; the U.S. population is currently growing by little more than one percent per annum (and in some high-income countries of Europe the rate is already less than one percent). A fertility-rate in the United States of 2·11 children would, barring immigration, eventually produce zero population growth. If the trend continues, the Director of the U.S. Bureau of the Census confidently predicts a near doubling of average family income to $15,000 (constant) by the year after 1984 when, he affirms, the nation will be transformed into 'a society of an affluent majority.' But the effect of near-zero population growth, without some radical change in consumption patterns, might actually involve even greater demands upon physical resources than are currently being made.[70]

Unfortunately the United States, like other industrial-urban countries, is also an effluent society. Even at the very low rate of population increase obtaining today, consumption of electric energy is growing at an annual rate of 8 percent and, according to René Dubos, the quantity of accumulated thermal pollutants is doubling each decade. Eventually the production of electric energy by any technological means, Dubos insists, will have to be halted because the heat pollution of the earth has no *technical* solution. At some point conversion to solar energy sources will become literally vital.[71]

There are two features of the ecological problem which have become critical. With increasing control over mortality, the industrial-urban environment has been unable to generate sufficiently powerful resistances to moderate the mounting abuse of the human ecosystem. Information has been signaled too slowly and resulting feedbacks have been too weak to bring about corrective action. As a consequence, we have no very dependable knowledge of the time remaining in which such actions can be instituted—whether, for example, the horizon is five, fifty, or five hundred years.

Climatic changes are already apparent. For example, between 1957 and 1963 the observed dust-content of the air over the United States, outside the cities, doubled. This had the effect of making the earth brighter and reducing the penetration of sunlight to its surface. From 1950 to the early 1960s a 5 to 10 percent rise in turbidity is estimated to have produced a fall of from 0·6 to 0·7 of a degree centigrade in average temperature—an amount equivalent to the warming achieved over the previous century. The effects of these climatic changes are felt differently, but in the more industrially urbanized areas certain tendencies are common. The built-up areas of cities form surfaces which are from 50 to 60 percent waterproof and as a consequence city surfaces become much drier and dustier than those of open country which has organic cover. Since industrial and household chimneys are also emitting vast quantities of solid pollutants every day, the combined effects of waterproof surfaces and air turbidity are unmistakable. By the mid-1960s there were from ten to fifteen times as many dust particles on average in the air over open country as in 1950, and 10,000 times as many particles over the more polluted parts of cities. Over the urbanized region that sprawls along the Atlantic seaboard from north of Boston to south of Washington, D.C., the dust load of the air increased in less than fifteen years by a factor of twenty. The possibility of adapting solar energy was thus to some extent impaired. There was said to be 30 percent less penetration of sunlight and 90 percent less ultra-violet light and a concurrent increase in the nuclei available for fog condensation (in addition to the rising level of chemical pollution reflected in measures of lead or mercury in human blood samples).[72]

The time horizon is part of the ecological dilemma. We do not know how long the industrial-urban populations have before their opportunities for exercising rational options will be foreclosed by, say, river and ocean pollution, air poisoning, or heat accumulation. We are no less ignorant of the time-telescoping effects, in newly urbanizing countries, of the introduction of new forms of transport, new sources and forms of heat energy, or of electronic modes of communication in advance of general literacy. Even if more residents of high-income countries become less mesmerized by G.N.P. as it grows grosser in its content and ecological aftermath, the population of developing countries will, short of some Gandhian conversion, still have to raise their own levels of output and income somewhat if they are to attain hypothetically acceptable standards in regard to nutrition, medical services, or housing. Moreover, in default of profound changes in the outlook and behavior of populations in high-income countries, it will not be easy to convince either governments or masses in the Third World that they must now forgo the greater part of the 'progress' which has belatedly been offered them in the form of economic growth. Yet the decisions made by people in low-income countries in regard to growth will also determine the range of options remaining open to their own children in the not too distant future. There is a real danger that, if they adopt the environmentally-destructive features of industrial-urban technology, they run the risk of accelerating that desert-breeding sequence of negative feedbacks on the ecosystem which has been rendering portions of the earth's surface uninhabitable since the second millennium B.C.

Underlying the social and ecological dilemmas of both high- and low-income countries is the contemporary formulation of the Victorian concept of progress. This idea took hold as a small island nation—with little more than one percent of world population—embarked upon an industrial transformation four or five decades in advance of any other country. Within little more than a century, the technological and organizational forms embodying the transformation had spread to include one-fifth of a greatly enlarged world population. Since the close of Victoria's reign advocates of progress have generally assumed that the economic and social benefits to be derived from this great alteration in occupational and residential patterns far outweighed any social costs entailed. Until recently the ecological costs were ignored altogether since most adherents of progress were unaware that human populations were part of a human ecosystem.

Thus the intellectual framework devised for the study of industrial-urban development tended to become extremely narrow. Certain concomitants of the transformation were adduced to explain and rationalize the material changes involved. Attention was focused on *measurable* inputs and outputs. Larger net differences in real values of inputs and outputs are conventionally reckoned a more efficient use of scarce resources; rising productivity in the output and utilization of resources is attributed to the more intangible, but no less benign, influences of technology and organization. To the extent that net product and income grow faster than population, almost without regard to their actual distribution, the average level of living is said to be raised, real incomes enlarged, and a country's welfare enhanced. By the same entelechy, sectional and class antagonisms are progressively resolved by urbanization, upward mobility, and increased consumption of goods and services. All but the technical aspects of social problems are thus solved by the process itself.

This intellectual framework is none the less a hastily improvised structure designed to meet the exigencies of contemporary history. It represents a rapid translation of the Victorian idea of economic progress into the mid-twentieth-century idea of economic growth. While the inherited liberal and socialist systems of thought still differ on the desirability and extent of conscious public intervention in the socio-economic transformation, they are alike convinced of the transformation's necessity and virtue. Despite a brief flurry of disquiet concerning the need 'to conserve' natural resources, and a throb of neo-Malthusian alarm about the technical elasticity of the food supply in a period of rising prices before the First World War, this faith in progressive economic solutions to what others had mistakenly conceived as political, social, or even moral questions has remained unabashed.

It is the contemporary idea of 'growth,' albeit managed growth, that inspires the 20 percent of world population in high-income countries to recommend a parallel and more expeditious transformation to the less affluent 80 percent of mankind. The identification of economic and social progress with rising G.N.P. *per capita*, and a corollary belief that problems of production and consumption are solvable for all but a minority of social misfits and intellectual intransigents, are common ground between liberal and socialist growth managers competing in today's urbanizing world. The faith that, on a firm foundation of economic growth, social and all but the most profound human problems are manageable is the meaning of the Victorian urban-industrial transformation projected into contemporary history.

From an ecological perspective, the growth framework is inadequate and potentially calamitous. Even from the economic standpoint the apparatus of theory and measurement must be judged incomplete in so far as it reduces the complexity of men's relationships with their social and physical environments to the formal simplicity of an ideal market-place. The utility functions employed by economists are by definition only associated with voluntary exchanges between two parties: buyers and sellers. Waste products and other side effects of normal transactions are not taken into account as goods and services. Yet 'bads' and 'disservices' arise in the course of such exchanges, regardless of whether either party wants them or not. Before the automobile, for example, gasoline or petrol was largely a 'waste' by-product of kerosene manufacture; it was customarily dumped into the rivers and streams adjacent to refineries. Thus neither the full product nor the full cost of business decisions is entered in a firm's ledgers or even in a country's income and product accounts. Such products and costs are absorbed by either the social or the physical environment.[73]

In respect of human environments, the rationality of the market has always been highly dubious. Economists have long recognized that population concentration gives rise to productivity increments which are independent of the operational decisions of firms which locate at such points. The economies of concentration and urbanization are essentially various types of scale economies. But just as part of the economies which are independent of the operations of firms nevertheless accrue to those firms, as well as to the larger economy, so do the *diseconomies* of concentration. Most of the diseconomies that arise, whether from concentration or from the operations of individual firms and industries, are by accounting-practice kept 'external' to those firms. Some of these costs fall on other firms, for example those connected with traffic congestion or water pollution, and are duly accounted as internal costs of production. Still others are borne by households in such forms as poisonous air, noxious drains, sooty window-sills, or insufferable noise. Householders must clean up such products at their own expense, adapt themselves to a degraded or unhealthy environment, which probably entails a capital loss, or complain to the local authority. If they can afford it, householders are free to remove to another site the costs of which, if not actually lower than at the present one, will at least be 'voluntarily' incurred. Thus optimizing behavior by one unit in the economy is almost always achieved by coerced sub-optimizing of other units and by uncompensated damage to the environment.

Society stands as a cushion between the economy and the ecosystem. The balance of externalized and unrequited costs redounds to society in the form of 'urban' or 'social' problems. Municipalities or other authorities eventually charge back a portion of these costs to households and enterprises in the form of tax bills; the residuum passes into the environment as an ecosystem cost. Ecological costs are virtually disregarded by all practical decision-making units except perhaps as they sometimes reappear in the rising prices of raw material inputs. Since the socialist countries have the same system of economic belief as liberal-capitalist countries and differ only in respect of 'ecclesiastical' control over assets, their awareness of the effects of externalities on the ecosystem is no more sensitive than that of their political antagonists. Indeed, in so far as state enterprises create external diseconomies and state authorities 'plan' to pass such wastes and side effects into the people's environment, their decisions might be judged, by outsiders at least, the more culpable and coercive.

Historically, political adjustments in the form of regulation and taxation have moderated some of the socially more dysfunctional effects of the urban-industrial transformation. More recently, governmental decisions affecting the social and physical environments have been subjected to a welfare-accounting technique which is thought to provide a more comprehensive 'cost-benefit' analysis than conventional accounting practice. The procedure involves itemizing all the foreseeable consequences of a proposal—such as building a motor highway or extending a rapid transit system—and estimating the full costs and benefits of alternative actions. Since costs and benefits are expressed in money values, it is comparatively easy to make the rational choice in favor of the particular proposal which maximizes benefit-values relative to costs. By such means, economic decisions made in the public sector are brought into conformity with the ultimate good of Gross National Product. In liberal societies, progress is further safeguarded by the requirement that no decision be taken in the public sector which could not be more efficiently made in the private sector. The comparative efficiencies of the two sectors are likewise judged in terms of cost-benefit analyses.

This recent innovation in social accounting is in part a response to rising criticism of the products of affluent societies. But even with the heightened social and ecological sensitivities of the 1970s, there is much that is dubious about the 'higher rationality' of policy-science. Are all consequences of decisions in fact foreseen? Do the money-value estimates attached to consequences which are foreseen really measure the full costs and benefits? Can ecosystem costs really be requited in a 'growth'-traumatized system? Can political decision-makers realize and accept the full costs of their actions any more than private decision-makers? Under the combined pressures of commercial and political advertising, is the public likely to be more aware of real issues today than in the past? Undoubtedly the techniques of welfare analysis will be improved. It potentially offers a more intelligent appraisal of alternative futures than either laissez faire or arbitrary decree. On the other hand, the primacy which cost-benefit analysis attaches to short-run gain, the intangible nature of so many real social values, and the ultimate weight it attaches to the most 'economical' solution, tend to narrow the range of social choices which technocratic decision-making leaves open to the future. In default of social vision, it will make not for a greater variety of urban environments but for the most uniformly 'efficient' one. To the extent that neither welfare nor growth frameworks take any account of fundamental inequalities in the distribution of wealth or income, nothing is changed very radically from the past.

Applied to the human ecosystem, cost-benefit analysis tends rather to build into policy-making much of the conventional 'growth' wisdom than to open up new patterns of life and livelihood which might embody the environmental wisdom we already possess. It is something, perhaps, that the costs of enforcing antipollution laws, many of which have rested on the statute books for more than half a century, are likely to be passed on to the consumer in the form of taxes or higher prices; this will at least reduce the amount of income available to be spent on unnecessary things. Nevertheless, to import moon dust at an admitted cost of $100,000 a pound, while reducing appropriations to prevent the unwanted production of earth dust, suggests that criteria other than welfare govern the decisions of at least one of the two largest industrial-urban polluters in the contemporary world: Cost-benefit calculations seem merely to confirm the existing order of social priorities.[74] This not only bodes ill for the actual calculations that are made regarding the relative private and social rates of return in the immediate future, but also almost ensures that the larger exploration of resource-uses will, from an ecosystem viewpoint, be suboptimal. While this situation is obviously critical in the case of non-renewable resources, it also indicates that in the longer run we are more likely to achieve the quantitative expansion of industrial-urban civilization, whose end John Stuart Mill once described as 'a stationary state,' than a planned 'steady state' of near-zero population growth, stable *per capita* energy-consumption, and effective recycling of resources called for by an ecological moderate like René Dubos.

A third possibility, that conditions for human life will rapidly become untenable and *pari passu* the chances of provoking nuclear disaster increased, cannot entirely be ruled out. The scenario has already been written in the apocalyptic message of the biologist, Paul Ehrlich.[75] In light of critical currents loose in the contemporary world, it is no less far-fetched to postulate the achievement of telesis: an intelligent direction of natural and social forces toward a benign end. As the future unfolding between these extremes becomes more random, historians of the Victorian age can only turn back to one of its prophets, Patrick Geddes, who lived long enough into this century to mark off the progress of the city along its course:[76]

> In all the great cities—especially the great capitals—you have in progress the history of Rome in its decline and fall. Beginning as Polis, the city, it developed into Metro-polis, the capital; but this into Megalo-polis, the city overgrown, whence megalomania. Next, with its ample supply of 'bread and shows' (nowadays called 'budget') it was Parasitopolis, with degeneration accordingly. Thus, all manner of diseases, bodily, mental, moral: hence Patholo-polis, and finally, in due time Necro-polis—the city of the dead, as its long-buried monuments survive to show.

By the 1970s, at a conservative estimate, the Victorian city is already a well-advanced Megalopolis. In the contemporary ambience, it is still too early to say whether it will have even a surviving monument.

### Notes

1  G. Barraclough, *An Introduction to Contemporary History* (1965), pp. 1–35.
2  Data from A. F. Weber, *The Growth of Cities in the Nineteenth Century: A study in statistics* (New York, 1899), pp. 20–154.

3   E. E. Lampard, 'Historical Contours of Contemporary Urban Society:
    A Comparative View,' *Journal of Contemporary History*, iv (1969), 3–10.

4   W. C. Taylor, *Natural History of Society in the Barbarous and Civilized State* (1840);
    *Notes of a Tour in the Manufacturing Districts of Lancashire* (2nd edn, 1842).
    Taylor expressed the view, nevertheless, that some critics had exaggerated the
    dangers from the 'new element of society' hoping to destroy it 'instead of regulating
    its courses.'

5   A. de Tocqueville, *Democracy in America* (ed. P. Bradley, New York, 1945), I,
    pp. 299–300; J. S. Mackenzie, *An Introduction to Social Philosophy* (Glasgow, 1890),
    pp. 101–4.

6   J. B. Priestley, *English Journey* (1934), *passim;* P.E.P., *Report on the Location of Industry
    in Great Britain* (1939), pp. 294–8.

7   Weber, op. cit., p. 1.

8   United Nations Department of Economic and Social Affairs, *Report on the World
    Social Situation 1957—Including Studies of Urbanization in Underdeveloped Areas*
    (New York, 1957), pp. 111–12. Unless otherwise indicated, *level* of urbanization, u/p,
    in this study refers to the proportion of total population resident in agglomerations
    with 20,000 or more inhabitants. The terms 'rate of urbanization' and 'rate of
    concentration' are used interchangeably throughout as a measure of *absolute* structural
    change in the residential distribution of total population between urban
    agglomerations, $\geq 20{,}000$, and small town and rural areas, $\leq 20{,}000$. The 'rate' is
    simply $\delta(u/p)$ over a given time interval and is usually expressed as a percentage
    point shift. N.B. The size threshold $\geq 20{,}000$ tends to underestimate the level of
    urbanization given by most national census definitions of 'urban' population:
    see Table 1.5.

9   Sen Dou Chang, 'The Million City of Mainland China,' *Pacific Viewpoint*, ix (1968),
    128–53, and S. R. Rein, 'The World's Great Cities: Evolution or Devolution,'
    *Population Bulletin*, xvi, no. 6, 109–30.

10  Demographic and economic data in the text from B. R. Mitchell and P. Deane,
    *Abstract of British Historical Statistics* (Cambridge, 1962). Comparisons of Table 3,
    columns 2 and 3, 4 and 5, 7 and 8, indicate that in certain decades (1830s, 1860s through
    1890, in England and Wales; the 1860s and 1880s in the U.S.) the growth of the
    labor force outside of agriculture was chiefly in the service sector and not the
    manufacturing-mining-and-construction sector.

11  An extreme example of this dependence on migration is provided by London in the
    eighteenth century. The crude death-rate, 1701–50, averaged 49 per 1,000
    while the rate for England and Wales averaged only 33 per 1,000. Since the crude
    birth-rate in London, 1701–50, averaged 38 per 1,000, the average rate of natural
    increase for the capital area was *negative*, $-11$ per 1,000, while for the country as a
    whole an average birth-rate of 34 per 1,000 assured a slight positive increase.
    Both the natural deficit and the net increment (which may have reached 125,000 over
    the fifty-year span) were made up by migration of people from other, mostly
    rural, parts of England and Wales. Even if London had not grown rapidly, net
    migration must have been considerable, merely to have maintained the existing
    population. E. A. Wrigley estimates a net in-migration of 8,000 to 10,000 a year
    'to make good the burial surplus and allow the city to continue to grow';

*Population and History* (1969), p. 150. See also R. Mols, *Introduction à la démographie historique des villes d'Europe du xiv<sup>e</sup> au xviii<sup>e</sup> siècle* (Louvain, 1955), II, Bk IV.

12 Weber, op. cit., p. 236; H. A. Shannon, 'Migration and the Growth of London, 1841–91,' *Economic History Review*, v (1935), 79–86; A. K. Cairncross, 'Internal Migration in Victorian England,' *Manchester School*, xvii (1949), Table VII. The early surplus of London births cited by Weber is clearly a calculation based upon place of birth and death and not upon place of residence.

13 *Statistisches Jahrbuch der Stadt Berlin*, xix (1892), 94–5. The adjustment for Liverpool annexations is based on Mitchell and Deane, op. cit., pp. 25–7, note (e). City-born children of migrants are counted in the city's increase.

14 E. Levasseur, *La Population française* (Paris, 1889–92), II, p. 386; R. Boeckh in *Statistisches Jahrbuch Berlin*, 1892; I. B. Taeuber, 'Urbanization and Population Change in the Development of Modern Japan,' *Economic Development and Cultural Change*, ix (1960), Part 1, 4–14; Weber, op. cit., p. 240.

15 The Massachusetts census for 1895 makes this point clear. Over the preceding decade the population of the thirty-two incorporated cities of 1895 increased by 38 percent, or 38 per 1,000 for one year; but since the annual excess of urban births was averaging about 7 per 1,000 and the political process of annexation becoming more difficult by the year, the bulk of the urban increase must actually have been of foreign birth. In 1880 Boston, with 31·6 percent of its population foreign-born, ranked ninth among the nation's large cities by this measure but by 1910, with 35·9 percent, it ranked second; 74·2 percent of its population was foreign or had one or both parents born abroad.
See Massachusetts *State Census of 1895*, I, pp. 49, 220; *49th Registration Report*, 1890, pp. 156, 372, 374; F. S. Crum, 'The Birth Rate in Massachusetts, 1850–90,' *Quarterly Journal of Economics*, xi (1897), 259; *Summary of the Vital Statistics of the New England States*, 1892, p. 56; *10th U. S. Census, 1880, Population*, pp. 538–41; *13th U. S. Census, 1910, Population*, I, pp. 178, 826–8, 1007.

16 C. Booth, 'On the Occupations of the People of the United Kingdom, 1801–81,' *Journal of the Royal Statistical Society (JRSS)*, xlix (1886), 329; G. B. Longstaff, *Studies in Statistics: Social, political, and medical* (1891), p. 25. Supplement to the Swedish Census of 1890, *Befolkningsstatistik*, n.s. xxxii, no. 1, cited by Weber, op. cit., p. 237.

17 W. F. Willcox, 'The Federal Census,' American Economic Association *Publications*, no. 2 (March, 1899), 24; E. G. Ravenstein, 'The Laws of Migration,' *JRSS*, xlviii (1885), 167–235; Weber, op. cit., Table CXXI, pp. 249, 264–5.

18 The 'rural population' here is that portion given in the *Census of England and Wales* as 'rural districts and towns under 2,000.' See also, G. B. Longstaff, 'Rural Depopulation,' *JRSS*, lviii (1895), and more generally J. Guillou, *L'Émigration des campagnes vers les villes* (Paris, 1905), pp. 143–295.

19 Weber, op. cit., Table CXXI; *Historical Statistics of the U. S., Colonial Times to 1957* (U.S. Bureau of the Census, 1960), Ser. C, pp. 2–3; H. Llewellyn Smith, 'Influx of Population,' in *Life and Labour of the People in London*, C. Booth, ed. (1892–7), III, chs 2 and 3; H. Rauchberg, 'Der Zug nach der Stadt,' *Statistische Monatsschrift*, xix (1893), 125–71. W. Köllmann, 'The Process of Urbanization in Germany at the Height of the Industrialization Period,' *J. Contemp. Hist.*, iv (1969), 59–76.

20   Weber, op. cit., pp. 287–8; *11th U.S. Census, 1890, Vital Statistics of Cities*, p. 13;
     W. F. Willcox, 'Distribution of the Sexes in the US,' *American Journal of Sociology*,
     i (1896), 732.

21   Since registration data from a number of countries indicated a smaller preponderance
     of male births in large cities than in the countryside, the heavier infant mortality in
     the cities contributed to the urban female surplus as well as the in-migration
     differential: see data in M. A. Legoyt, *Du Progrès des agglomérations urbaines et de
     l'émigration rurale* (Paris, 1870), p. 69; Weber, op. cit., pp. 298–9; Massachusetts State
     Board of Health, *28th Annual Report, 1896*, p. 753. Also C. Walford, 'On the Number
     of Deaths from Accident, Negligence, Violence and Misadventure,' *JRSS*,
     xliv (1881), 28.

22   P. Meuriot, *Des Agglomérations urbaines dans l'Europe contemporaine* (Paris, 1897),
     gives an illuminating graphic representation of the age and sex structures of the
     populations of Paris and France respectively. *11th U.S. Census, 1890, Vital Statistics of
     Cities*, p. 16. R. Kuczynski, *Der Zug nach der Stadt* (Munich, 1897).

23   Booth, *Life and Labour*, III, p. 139; N. Brückner, 'Die Entwickelung der grossstädtischen
     Bevölkerung im Gebiete des Deutschen Reiches,' *Allgemeines Statistisches Archiv*, i
     (1899), 632–50. Also, A. J. Coale, 'How a Population Ages or Grows Younger,' in
     *Population: The Vital Revolution*, R. Freedman, ed. (Chicago, 1965), pp. 47–58.

24   Weber, op. cit., p. 324; W. Ogle, 'On Marriage-Rates and Marriage-Ages,' *JRSS*,
     liii (1890), 253, 267.

25   Mass. St. Bd of Health, *28th Annual Report, 1896*, p. 826; F. S. Crum,
     'The Marriage Rate in Massachusetts,' American Statistical Society *Publications*,
     iv (1895), 338. *11th U.S. Census, 1890, Population*, I, pp. clxxxvi, 851, 858.

26   M. Rubin and H. Westergaard, *Statistik der Ehen* (Jena, 1890); Rauchberg, *Stat.
     Monatsschrift*, XIX, pp. 136–7; Brückner, *Allg. Stat. Archiv*, i, 640–1; Weber,
     op. cit., p. 320. E. A. Wrigley, *Industrial Growth and Population Change* (1961), pp.
     143–5.

27   *Zeitschrift des K. Sächsischen Stat. Bureaus*, 1885, cited by Weber, op. cit., p. 333.
     J. E. Wappäus, *Die allgemeine Bevölkerungsstatistik* (Leipzig, 1861), II, pp. 481–4;
     Levasseur, op. cit., II, pp. 77–81, 390–8.

28   *11th U.S. Census, 1890, Population*, I, p. cxc; Crum, 'The Birth Rate,' p. 259.
     H. Bleicher, 'Die Eigenthümlichkeiten der städtischen Natalitäts und
     Mortalitätsverhältnisse,' 8th International Congress of Hygiene and Demography,
     *Proceedings*, Budapest (1894), VII, p. 468.

29   Weber, op. cit., p. 337. There is, of course, much evidence to confirm the fact that
     rural fertility exceeds urban fertility and even that the refined birth-rate tends to vary
     inversely with size of city: see W. S. Thompson, *Ratio of Children to Women 1920*
     (Washington, D.C., 1931) p. 142, and A. J. Jaffe, 'Urbanization and Fertility,' *Amer. J.
     Sociology*, xlviii (1942). Nevertheless, an analysis of U.S. data by states in B. Okun,
     *Trends in Birth Rates in the United States since 1870* (Baltimore, 1958), pp. 52–101,
     shows that neither cityward migration nor resulting size and density are *per se*
     explanations of lower urban fertility. Socio-economic class structure and what Okun
     calls 'urbanism,' the spread of middle-class 'urban' ideas and attitudes among
     lower classes and to segments of the rural population, are more directly related
     to the fall in fertility. Significantly, 'rural birth ratios are lowest in the most

urbanized and industrialized states.' Some of the remaining confusion in the literature about urbanization and fertility probably arises because some scholars employ *structural* or *behavioral* definitions of 'urbanization': on this point, see E. E. Lampard, 'Historical Aspects of Urbanization,' in *The Study of Urbanization*, P. M. Hauser and L. F. Schnore, eds (New York, 1965), pp. 519–20.

30 *55th Annual Report of the Registrar General for England and Wales*, 1893, *Supplement*, Pt I, p. xlvii, Pt II, p. cxvii. *11th U.S. Census, 1890, Report on Vital and Social Statistics*, Pt I, pp. 17–19. In 1890 the census registration states were: N.H., Vt., Mass., R.I., Conn., N.Y., N.J., Del., and D.C. The 'urban' segment is that population resident in incorporated places ≥ 5,000; the 'metropolitan district' of New York includes New York, Kings, Queens, Richmond, and Westchester counties in N.Y., Hudson and Essex counties in N.J., and the cities of Paterson and Passaic (ibid., appendix). Weber, op. cit., p. 346.

31 Data from *Encyclopaedia Britannica* (11th edn), XVI, p. 946. If changes in mortality are easier to interpret than changes in fertility they nevertheless remain very hard to measure precisely; apparent differences between town and country and among towns should be treated with due caution in light of D.V. Glass, 'Some Indicators of Differences between Urban and Rural Mortality in England and Wales and Scotland,' *Population Studies*, xvii (1964), 263–7.

32 See A. Shadwell, *The London Water Supply* (1899); G. P. Bevan, *The Statistical Atlas of England, Scotland, and Ireland* (Edinburgh, 1882), pp. 65–8; London County Council, *London Statistics*, xix, 1909, map. Also N. M. Blake, *Water for the Cities: A History of the Urban Water Supply Problem in the United States* (Syracuse, 1956).

33 E. R. Dewsnup, *The Housing Problem in England, Its Statistics, Legislation, and Policy* (Manchester, 1907); A. Newsholme, *The Elements of Vital Statistics* (3rd edn, 1899), pp. 140, 155.

34 Data from Dewsnup, op. cit.

35 A. Shadwell, 'Housing,' *Encycl. Brit.* (11th edn), XIII, pp. 819–20. Also D. Ward, 'A Comparative Historical Geography of Streetcar Suburbs in Boston, Mass. and Leeds, England, 1850–1920,' *Annals of the Association of American Geographers*, liv (1964), 477–89.

36 *51st Annual Report of the R.G., 1891*, p. lvii; *55th Annual Report of the R.G., 1893, Supplement*, Pt II, p. cxi. In addition to the seven types of milieu noted in the text, the report also covered *dockyard towns* and *London*. Also E. B. Collett, 'The Extent and Effects of Industrial Employment of Women,' *JRSS*, lxi (1898), 219–60.

37 *55th Annual Report of the R.G., 1893, Supplement*, Pt II, p. cx; T. A. Welton, 'Local Death-Rates in England,' *JRSS*, lx (1897), 65–6. Infant mortality data from Mitchell and Deane, op. cit., pp. 36–7. But note D. V. Glass, 'Some Indicators of Differences,' cited above, note 31.

38 F. von Juraschek, 'Die Sterblichkeit in den Oesterreichischen Städten,' 8th Int. Congr. of Hyg. and Dem. *Proceedings*, VII, pp. 491, 502; Bleicher, 'Die Eigenthümlichkeiten,' ibid., p. 477. On the German housing problem, see J. Faucher, 'Die Bewegung für Wohnungsreform,' *Vierteljahrschrift für Volkswirtschaft und Kulturgeschichte*, 3rd Year, iv (1865), 127–99; Verein für Socialpolitik, *Die Wohnungsnoth der ärmeren Klassen in Deutschen Grossstädten* (Leipzig, 1886), 2 vols; T. C. Horsfall, *The Improvement of the Dwellings and Surroundings of the*

*People: The Example of Germany* (Manchester, 1904), pp. 21–7, 138–61; A. Skalweit, 'Die Wohnungszustände in den Deutschen Grossstädten und die Möglichkeit ihrer Reform,' *Städtebauliche Vorträge aus dem Seminar für Stadtleben*, J. Brix and F. Genzmer, eds, VI, no. 6 (Berlin, 1913); Kuczynski, op. cit., p. 199.

39  W. Thompson, *Housing Up-to-Date* (London, 1907) gives details of housing conditions and public programs from correspondents in a number of countries. Weber, op. cit., p. 362.

40  New York Board of Health, *Report for the Year ending December 31, 1896* (New York, 1897), p. 1; Milwaukee Commissioner of Health, *Annual Report, 1908*, p. 18; Crum, 'The Birth Rate,' p. 259. Infant mortality in *all* Prussia, nevertheless, remained well above Massachusetts levels in prewar years.

41  C. D. Wright, *The Slums of Baltimore, Chicago, New York, and Philadelphia* (U.S. Commissioner of Labor, *Special Report No. 7*, 1894); *11th U.S. Census, 1890, Abstract*, p. 223; G. K. Holmes, 'Tenancy in the United States,' *Quart. J. Econ.*, x (1895), 37; N.Y. Tenement House Committee, *Report*, 1894, pp. 23–5; Weber, op. cit., pp. 460–2. Also R. Lubove, *The Progressives and the Slums: Tenement house reform in New York City, 1890–1917* (Pittsburgh, 1962).

42  *Historical Statistics of the U.S.*, pp. 18, 25–6. On the problem of the pure milk supply in the U.S.: E. E. Lampard, *The Rise of the Dairy Industry in Wisconsin, 1820–1920* (Madison, 1963), pp. 227–36.

43  Milwaukee Commissioner of Health, *Annual Report, 1908*, p. 18; Shadwell, *Encycl. Brit.*, XIII, p. 827. Strictly speaking, international comparisons of crude mortality are misleading owing to possible differences in sex-age composition of the populations involved, hence the greater emphasis given here to infant mortality which is not affected by age-composition; close comparisons among crude mortality-rates of individual cities, of course, are subject to the same shortcomings.

44  Weber, op. cit., p. 341n.; T. H. C. Stevenson, 'The Fertility of Various Social Classes in England and Wales from the Middle of the 19th Century to 1911,' *JRSS*, lxxiv (1911). Class differences in fertility were not a novelty of the late-Victorian era. A population's birth-rate is always an average of the fertility of different groups comprising the population. From the standpoint of interpretation, the critical question is the *basis* for differentiating people into groups; thus one can compare the fertility of different age-cohorts, communities by size, occupational groups, etc. as well as socio-economic classes. It is revealing that urban professional and business classes, as well as members of the older landed interest, deplored the relative fecundity of the lower strata of large cities once the heavy toll of their mortality was lessened. Concern was also expressed in different countries about the sectarian, 'biological,' and 'psychological' characteristics of the urban masses. Compare D. H. Wrong, 'Class Fertility Differentials Before 1850,' *Social Research*, xxv (1958), 70–86.

45  A. Smith, *An Inquiry into the Nature and Causes of the Wealth of Nations* (1776), Bk V, ch. 1.

46  J. A. Hobson, *The Evolution of Modern Capitalism: A study of machine production* (1894), pp. 340–2. Hobson removed some of these strictures on town populations from later editions of his classic study.

47  W. Z. Ripley, 'The Racial Geography of Europe,' *Popular Science Monthly*, lii

(1893–4), 479–80; A. T. Hadley, *Economics—An Account of the Relations between Private Property and Public Welfare* (New York, 1896), pp. 48–9.

48    Cited by Weber, op. cit., p. 474. C. Kingsley, *Miscellanies* (1860), II, pp. 318–45; A. J. Downing, *Cottage Residences* (New York, 1842).

49    S. J. Low, 'The Rise of Suburbs,' *Contemporary Review*, lx (1891), 545–58; 'London . . . surrounds itself, suburb clinging to suburb, like onions fifty on a rope'; J. F. Murray, *The World of London* (1843), cited by D. A. Reeder, 'A Theatre of Suburbs: Some Patterns of Development in West London, 1801–1911,' in *The Study of Urban History*, H. J. Dyos, ed. (1968), pp. 253–71. H. Herzfeld, ed., *Berlin und die Provinz Brandenburg im 19. und 20. Jahrhundert* (Veröffentlichung der Historischen Kommission zu Berlin, xxv, 1968) contains an extended account of organizations and interests proposing and opposing annexation of areas around the spreading capital. In the United States political annexation of peripheral areas around the major cities had slackened by the 1890s, giving rise to 'metropolitan suburbs and satellites': American Municipal Association *Report No. 127*, 'Changes in Municipal Boundaries Through Annexation, Detachment, and Consolidation,' (Chicago, 1939), and L. F. Schnore, 'The Timing of Metropolitan Decentralization,' *Journal of American Institute of Planners*, xxv (1959), 200–6.

50    A. Marshall, *Principles of Economics* (3rd edn), pp. 263–85, 305n.; Marshall, 'The Housing of the London Poor. Where to House Them,' *Contemporary Review*, xlv (1884), 226–9; H. Solly, *Industrial Villages: A remedy for crowded towns and deserted fields* (1884).

51    *Garden Cities of Tomorrow* (ed. F. J. Osborne, 1945), introductory essay by L. Mumford, p. 35 (italics in original). For the development of the town- and country-planning movement after Howard, see W. Ashworth, *The Genesis of Modern British Town Planning* (1954), pp. 167–237. The issue underlying Howard's plan for a trust to buy and control land, as distinct from taxing the 'economic rent,' was broadly anticipated by the German movement to control land uses and structures: R. Baumeister, *Stadt-Erweiterungen in technischer, baupolizeilicher, und wirtschaftlicher Beziehung* (Berlin, 1876).

52    P. Geddes, *City Development*, pp. 221–2; *Cities in Evolution, An Introduction to the Town Planning Movement and to the Study of Civics* (1915), p. 258. P. Mairet, *Pioneer of Sociology: The Life and Letters of Patrick Geddes* (1957). Geddes' spirit infuses the remarkable M. Safdie, *Beyond Habitat* (ed. J. Kettle, Cambridge, Mass., 1970). H. W. S. Cleveland, *Landscape Architecture, as Applied to the Wants of the West, 1873*, ed. R. Lubove (Pittsburgh, 1965), is a pioneering American contribution.

53    On the metropolitan phase of the urban transformation: T. W. Freeman, *The Conurbations of Great Britain* (Manchester, 1959), pp. 3–15; A. H. Hawley, *The Changing Shape of Metropolitan America: Deconcentration since 1920* (Chicago, 1956), pp. 1–33; L. O. Stone, *Urban Development in Canada* (Ottawa, 1967), pp. 127–42; J. R. Scobie, *Argentina: A city and a nation* (New York, 1964), pp. 160–88.

54    Rates based on recent U.N. data. The rate of urban population growth is $\delta(u/u)$ as distinct from the rate of concentration, $\delta(u/p)$. Annual rates of urban population growth of from 3 to 4 percent involve doubling urban population every seventeen to twenty-four years.

55    At the outset of the urban demographic transition in late-Victorian times, fertility

was already stable or falling when mortality began to fall rapidly. In the newly urbanizing countries mortality has recently fallen without as yet a corresponding reduction in fertility. See G. J. Stolnitz, 'Comparisons Between Some Recent Mortality Trends in Underdeveloped Areas and Historical Trends in the West,' *Trends and Differentials in Mortality*, Millbank Memorial Fund (New York, 1956), p. 34. On ecological 'backfire' from predator control programs, see R. Rudd, *Pesticides and the Living Landscape* (Madison, 1964).

56 Data drawn from P. M. Hauser, ed., *Urbanization in Asia and the Far East* (UNESCO: Calcutta, 1957), pp. 123–7, Appendix Tables A–F. Consistent with the emphasis on the *infant* death-rate above, George C. Whipple terms it 'the most sensitive index of social welfare and of sanitary improvements which we possess': cited by T. L. Smith, *Fundamentals of Population Study* (New York, 1960), p. 352.

57 In addition to low vital rates and infant mortality shown in Table 1.7, the *absolute* size of rural and small-town population in Japan fell by an estimated 1·6 millions in 1950–70. These three movements were cited earlier as indicators of the urban demographic transition. The gross reproduction rate was already below unity. On the 'economic miracle' in Japan since 1945, see W. W. Lockwood, ed., *The State and Economic Enterprise in Japan* (Princeton, 1965), Pt III.

58 Data in these paragraphs principally from P. M. Hauser, ed., *Urbanization in Latin America* (UNESCO: Paris, 1961), ch. 3. In N. America the negative association between fertility and size of community was said to indicate structural and behavioral change rather than urbanization of population as such: note 29 above. More generally, T. L. Smith, 'Urbanization in Latin America,' *International Journal of Comparative Sociology*, iv (1963), 127–42. The six countries mentioned are Argentina, Brazil, Chile, Cuba, Mexico, Venezuela.

59 Hauser, ed., *Urbanization in Asia*, pp. 130–3. While rejecting the notion of 'over-urbanization,' J. Friedmann and T. Lackington, 'Hyperurbanization and National Development in Chile: Some Hypotheses,' *Urban Affairs Quarterly*, ii (1967), 3–29, argue, nevertheless, that prolonged discrepancy between rates of urbanization and *per capita* income generates a socio-political 'crisis of inclusion.' P. W. Amato, 'Elitism and Settlement Patterns in the Latin American City,' *J. Amer. Inst. of Planners*, xxxvi (1970), 96 argues that slums are developing in the core of certain Latin American cities as well as on the perimeters and that the 'upper classes' are now fleeing to the suburbs; thus the traditional settlement pattern has already collapsed.

60 E. E. Lampard and L. F. Schnore, 'Urbanization Problems,' *Research Needs for Development Assistance Programs* (Brookings Foreign Policy Studies Program: Washington, D.C., 1961), pp. 28–31; B. Harris, 'Urbanization Policy in India,' Regional Science Association *Papers and Proceedings*, v (1959), 196.

61 Data from Weber, op. cit., ch. 2; Mitchell and Deane, op. cit., pp. 25, 27. Also, R. Murphey, 'New Capitals of Asia,' *Econ. Dev. & Cult. Change*, v (1957), 216–43; and S. K. Mehta, 'Some Demographic and Economic Correlates of Primate Cities: A Case for Reevaluation,' *Demography*, i (1964), 136–47.

62 See B. J. L. Berry, 'City Size Distributions and Economic Development,' *Econ. Dev. & Cult. Change*, ix (1961), 573–88. Nevertheless, as of 1955–60 there was no country with *per capita* G.N.P. above $750 with any marked degree of primacy in its

urban structure, with possible exceptions of Denmark and France; there were many countries with *per capita* G.N.P. below $250 with both high and low degrees of primacy.

63  See, for example, H. Jacob, *German Administration since Bismarck: Central Authority versus Local Authority* (New Haven, 1963); E. Lavoie, 'La Décentralisation en France au xix^e siècle: une étude bibliographique et sémantique,' *Canadian Journal of History*, v (1970), 43–70.

64  R. Morse, 'Trends and Issues in Latin American Urban Research, 1965–70,' unpublished paper, Faculty Seminar on Comparative Urban Societies, Yale University, spring 1970, 81–8. Also E. E. Lampard, 'Historical Aspects of Urbanization,' *The Study of Urbanization*, Hauser and Schnore, eds, pp. 531–42.

65  E. E. Lampard, 'The Evolving System of Cities in the U.S.: Urbanization and Economic Development,' in *Issues in Urban Economics*, H. S. Perloff and L. Wingo, eds (Baltimore, 1968), pp. 81–139. E. Juillard, 'L'Urbanisation des campagnes en Europe occidentale,' *Études Rurales*, i (1961), 18–33, provides a closely reasoned analysis of urban-rural relations during industrialization. Also, W. Christaller, 'Die Hierarchie der Städte,' I.G.U. Symposium in Urban Geography *Proceedings* (Lund Studies in Geog. Series B, Human Geography no. 24, Lund, 1962), 3–11.

66  E. E. Lampard, 'Urbanization and Social Change,' in *The Historian and the City*, O. Handlin and J. Burchard, eds (Cambridge, Mass., 1963), pp. 234–8. F. Adickes and R. Baumeister, *Die unterschiedliche Behandlung der Bauordnungen für das Innere, die Aussenbezirke, und die Umgebung von Städten* (Brunswick, 1893) is one of the first studies to advocate social controls over differential building and land uses in *and around* large cities. H. Hoyt, *The Structure and Growth of Residential Neighborhoods in American Cities* (Washington, D.C., 1939). On the relation of 'modern mentality' to the spread of the vital revolution among all classes, see R. von Ungern-Sternberg, 'Die Ursachen des Geburtenrückganges im westeuropäischen Kulturkreis während des 19. und 20. Jahrhunderts,' *Congrès International de la Population 1937*, vii (Paris, 1938), 16–34; N. E. Himes, 'Contraceptive History and Current Population Policy,' ibid., 200–10, on successive waves of alarm concerning population growth or decline. Also, E. Lewis-Faning, *Family Limitation and Its Influence on Human Fertility During the Past Fifty Years* (Papers of the Royal Commission on Population), I, (HMSO, 1948), 10, and D. H. Wrong, 'Trends in Class Fertility in Western Nations,' *Canadian Journal of Economics & Political Science*, xxiv (1958), 216–29. On the persistence of other differences in class-related behavior and urban life styles, see M. Young and P. Willmott, *Family and Kinship in East London* (1959) and B. M. Berger, *Working-class Suburb* (Berkeley, 1963).

67  T. Yaziki, *The Japanese City: A sociological analysis* (Rutland, Vt., trans., 1963), ch. 3; C. D. Harris, *Cities of the Soviet Union: Studies in their functions, size, density, and growth* (Chicago, 1970), ch. 8; A. Bose, 'Six Decades of Urbanization in India,' *Indian Economic & Social History Review*, ii (1965), 23–41; Q. Azad, 'Indian Cities— Characteristics and Correlates,' University of Chicago, *Dept. of Geography Research Paper No. 102* (Chicago, 1965); T. O. Wilkinson, 'Patterns of Korean Urban Growth,' *Rural Sociology*, xix (1954).

68  S. Kuznets, *Modern Economic Growth: Rate, structure, and spread* (New Haven, 1966), Table 5.7, Table 8.1, lines 83–110.

69   Ibid., Table 8.2. G. Ohlin, *Population Control and Economic Development* (Paris, 1967), is a model treatment of this problem. Also Lord Boyd-Orr, 'Food Enough for Everyone,' *New York Times*, 17 December 1970.

70   Statement of G. H. Brown, Director U.S. Census Bureau, reported *New York Times*, 8 October 1970. President Richard Nixon hailed the U.S. trillion dollar G.N.P. as now giving the nation the means of making social improvements 'that no other country in the world' can match. The *New York Times*, 17 December 1970, commented editorially on this silly boast, that only minute quantities of resources consumed annually in the U.S. are used for social purposes and less for maintenance of the environment: 'these resources go overwhelmingly into a luxurious private consumption such as the world has never known issuing ultimately in a waste such as the world has never imagined: 7 million cars junked a year, 20 million tons of paper, 48 billion cans and the like—all costing close to $3 billion a year just to dispose of.'

71   R. J. Dubos, *So Human an Animal* (New York, 1968), passim; G. D. Bell, ed., *The Environmental Handbook* (New York, 1970), passim.

72   See R. A. Bryson, 'Climatic Effects of Atmosphere Pollution,' paper delivered at Amer. Assn for the Advancement of Science Meeting, 1968; 'All other Factors being Constant,' *Weatherwise*, xxi (1968), 56–61; G. R. Taylor, 'Trends in Pollution,' *Futures*, ii (1970), 105–13; J. K. Page, 'Possible Developments in the Urban Environment,' *Futures*, ii (1970), 215–21. Also, S. F. Singer, ed., *Global Effects of Environmental Pollution* (Amer. Assn Adv. Science, 1970).

73   E. J. Mishan, *Costs of Economic Growth* (1967) for a general critique of the G.N.P. accounting framework. J. Breslaw, 'Economics and Eco-systems,' *Environmental Handbook*, Bell, ed., pp. 102–12; S. Tsuru, 'The Economic Significance of Cities,' *The Historian and the City*, Handlin and Burchard, eds, pp. 44–55.

74   The inherent limitations of economics as the 'science of control' are indicated by P. A. Samuelson: 'Economics cannot tell us what to believe; it can help us to sort out the costs and benefits of various arrangements, as those costs and benefits are defined by the ethical value systems that we bring to economics,' *New York Times*, 26 December 1970. Also K. E. Boulding, 'The City as an Element in the International System,' *Daedalus*, xcvii (1968), 1111–23.

75   P. Ehrlich, *The Population Bomb* (New York, 1968).

76   Cited by Mairet, op. cit., pp. 125–6.

# 2    Voices from Within

## Paul Thompson

The daily life of the Victorian city seems superficially so remote that we can too easily assume it irrecoverable: as dead as the eighteenth century. Yet it survives among us in the minds of the old, who can often remember their nineteenth-century childhood with astonishing clarity. It is still possible to discover, through asking them, answers to some of the questions which interest us but which contemporaries did not think worth recording; and more important, since the great majority of the population do not write autobiographies, these old people's stories can convey real experiences and provide imaginative insights from points of view rarely found in documents.

If, for example, we want to define more precisely the extent and strength of the late Victorian labour aristocracy, we can still ask how they themselves drew the line —if they did—between the rough and the respectable working classes. We can at the same time discover their family occupational patterns and thus compare subjective views of social class with objective social situations. Similarly, we can supplement existing reports of the very poor and the criminal classes (which mostly come from the police or from paternalistic social workers) with their own accounts. Or if we wish to know whether urbanization in the nineteenth century produced a distinct way of life not simply explicable in terms of occupation and social class, we can examine leisure habits, relations between neighbours, eating, and religious behaviour of different social classes, and see how they vary with the move from village to small town, from large town to conurbation, from suburb to inner city. We can also compare migrants from the countryside with those born in the cities.

Inevitably this fresh evidence as often alters the social historian's question as answers it. In contrast to the changing forms of adult leisure, for example, one is more impressed by the uniformity and persistence of children's games in the face both of Victorian urbanization and the spread of cheap manufactured toys. The chief exceptions are found in one of two situations: either where children were deliberately isolated by the refusal of their parents to allow them to play outside their own house and garden, or in the intense poverty and overcrowding of inner slum districts where a child might be more concerned with feeding itself than with playing. Such inner districts were also exceptional in not being within walking distance of open fields. Since 1900, while fewer children are no doubt kept from traditional play by sheer hunger, perhaps the appearance of motor traffic in the streets, the distancing of the countryside, and the spread of lower middle-class notions of respectability have resulted in more isolated childhoods. Thus we move from the straightforward assessment of 'Urbanism as a Way of Life' to more complex—and more real—problems.

Similarly, when, in order to test the assumption that parents seventy years ago were harsh, distant, and frequently violent, one listens to descriptions of real families by their own members, it is less the change than the continuity which is striking. There is a timeless quality in many of the emotional relationships which emerge. Interviews can demonstrate conclusively that, rather than a wholesale revolution in parent–child relationships since 1900, there have been gradual changes in distribution of the various types which then, as now, may be found.

Interviews, if collected on a sample basis, can also be used to estimate the scale of this kind of change. The descriptions of city life which follow are in fact taken from a national survey of family, work, and the community before 1918, which is based upon a quota sample of occupations derived from the 1911 census.* At the time of writing it is not, however, complete. In any case, although the descriptions which follow relate entirely to the years before 1900, it is designed to be representative of the Edwardian rather than the late-Victorian period. As it happens, the seventeen interviews used here, which are those completed first, present quite a typical range. Eight are from London, two from an old cathedral city, and seven from the north. Of the heads of the families in which these childhoods were spent, two were professional, four were in trade, one was a clerk, ten were working-class; five were in serious poverty. Nevertheless, it would be misleading to treat them other than as a series of individual cases. At this stage of the work they are simply presented for their intrinsic interest.

Let us begin with two working-class families from a pre-industrial city, a cathedral and market town. City life here was still entangled with that of the countryside,

* The survey is supported by a grant from the Social Science Research Council, and is described more fully in *SSRC Newsletter*, June 1969. It was preceded by pilot interviewing, aided by the Nuffield Foundation and the University of Essex. The respondents quoted here were all born before 1892, and the oldest in 1873. I should like to acknowledge them and their interviewers by name, but in order to preserve confidentiality they must remain anonymous. Personal names and some place names have been altered, but the quotations are otherwise as far as possible literal transcriptions, except for the elimination of some repetitions and hesitations. The recordings of the interviews are to be preserved as an archive.

so that these families provide a good point of departure for our movement towards the inner districts of the great cities. They also bring us directly to the issue of respectability, subjective and objective.

Both families were relatively poor. With the *Pococks* this was because the father, although a skilled man, was old. He had been a railway guard, but was now reduced to casual work such as window cleaning and carpet beating. To make ends meet, Mrs Pocock took in tailoring work: 'mother was always at the machine . . . right into the night sometimes.' They remained nevertheless a proud family. 'You used to get the rough people as well you know, and we were told of course not to mix with those people . . . Well, my father used to say we don't owe anyone anything so therefore we can walk about with a free head. High head.' They were active churchgoers, observed the sabbath, said grace at meals. Perhaps one sign of demoralization was that Mr Pocock began to drink more as he aged, but his main response to the family's difficulty was to help more in the house, even doing all the cooking. This may be why some meals, in characteristically urban fashion, were fetched from a nearby restaurant which served meals on to the customers' own plates 'and that was put in the oven ready for the boys when they came in.' But in many ways the family's food was distinctly rural. Rabbits, crayfish and pheasants poached from a nearby ducal estate by an uncle were roasted on the open fire. There were wild mushrooms. Fresh milk came from the cattle market: 'all the beasts were brought in by road, walking in . . . They needed milking before they could go back and we were sent with a big jug and for twopence we had a big jug of milk straight from the cow. You see the farmers were glad to relieve the cows of it.' Similarly, fresh fruit was easy to get if you lived near 'a man who worked on the railway, an engine driver or something like that, and they had the run through to Evesham: they could buy what they called a pot of plums which was . . . a big basket which held 40 pounds . . . They would share them with their neighbours and sell them.' And again, in the children's play, urban and rural pleasures were juxtaposed: fishing in the river with jam-jars, the traditional autumn fair, the theatre, bicycling to country pubs for cider, and playing in a pub yard where the bargees' horses from the canal were stabled. 'They had a big rough yard with a nice big loft up above, you know. We used to think that was wonderful.'

Similar pleasures also mitigated the poverty of the *Bell* family: fishing again, playing in the fields, and sometimes on Sundays an outing to a riverside pub. But for the Bells poverty was absolute, rather than in contrast to earlier prosperity. Of fourteen children, six died in childhood. They could only afford to buy pieces of meat, the leftovers, and relied for bread on the cast-offs of a Co-operative bakery. Mr Bell was a bricklayer's labourer, quite a young man. 'He used to get 4d. an hour for carrying bricks up a ladder and keeping three bricklayers supplied, and he was only a little man too. He gloried in it too, seeing how much he could do.' Although Mrs Bell worked two days a week as a washerwoman to supplement his earnings, he would not help at all with the house, or with the children, unless to 'shut you up, with a good clout perhaps'. He was illiterate, and regarded education as 'just a waste of time . . .

"Ah well, my boy, I'm all right." ' His attitude to wealth was also defiant. 'He hated the sights of motor cars and being in the building trade, you see, he had plenty of nails, and he used to stand on the pavement when they used to come down the bridge just over here . . . and he used to chuck all these nails so they'd get punctures. He was very bitter that way.'

Although he was a rough man, this did not mean that Mr Bell did not expect strict standards of behaviour in the family. For example, at meals 'Mother used to keep a cane where she sat at the head of the table and if you started talking, you had a smack across the arms. Oh, we had no chance to talk.' They were punished for lies in the same way. Sunday was observed strictly: no playing football in the street, but instead 'three times on Sundays we used to go in the choir. And then that was a farthing a time, and if you misbehaved yourself when you was in the chancel the old vicar used to say, when we got down, "Sixpence off your money, Bell, for talking." So I didn't get much money when it came to the end of the year.' On weekday evenings they were sent to a boys' club, where there was boxing to keep them out of mischief.

Despite these precautions, less respectable forms of fighting remained favourite pastimes. Boys from another neighbourhood 'used to call us the St James's Bulldogs and we used to call them the Thorney Arabs and throw stones at one another up the lane there.' And on quarter days, when army pensions were paid, they could be sure of a good fight to watch among adults. 'You could see them come down the yard, out of the pub they'd come. Course we enjoyed it . . . We boys at school, "Come on, it's pension day today, kids, come and see some fights," out we used to come.' On the other hand, it is apparent that the district was much quieter than it had been in his father's youth. At that time the police had not dared enter it and the vicar had been thrown in the ditch. 'They were rough and ready, I mean. They'd got no discipline, no nothing. They were just ignorant.' Without protection from the police, a man had to be more self-reliant. 'My great-uncle he had . . . a well known pub, the Blue Boar . . . and great-uncle used to keep his double-barrel . . . a muzzle loader . . . loaded in the bar, because of the customers here . . . And if he had any trouble with his customers, which there was plenty, he'd get his gun down, and say, "Look, if you don't get out of here, I'll shoot your legs off." He'd ha' done it too, ooh.'

Here, as elsewhere, it is noticeable that schools did not provide a lead which might help to explain this gradual quietening of a rough district. On the contrary, they stood out as examples of institutionalized violence.

I was a bit of a rip when I was a boy, high spirits . . . slap a boy's face in class for one thing . . . The master says to me, 'Bell, come out, stand on that form,' so I stood on the form, and the form used to go round the back, the windows was here . . . horses and carts would go by . . . He gets his cane and he slashes me all across the legs, and he never stops, so, I had a very powerful voice, and at the top of my voice I screamed 'Murder!' He stopped . . . 'None of that!' That's how he hit us.

It is a far distance to move from this childhood to that of a middle-class child in a suburb of Liverpool. 'I liked school very much . . . and I liked the teachers, and they were very fond of me.' For Katherine *Bowie* and her two sisters, in fact, school was almost her only experience of the world outside her home. Her father was a ship's officer, away most of the year; Mrs Bowie ran the house without any servants. Being Scottish, she felt 'she didn't understand the people round about her', and made no friends among them. The children were taken shopping, and sometimes in the evening to the park. There was the annual Sunday School picnic, and sometimes a summer holiday in Scotland with her father when 'oh, we just absolutely ran about wild. Go down to the shore and, you know, bathe, and . . . out in the small boats, and the fishing boats, and oh, it was lovely. And then go up to the hills to the farms . . . to help with the haymaking.' But, at home, they were not allowed into other people's houses, or to play in the street. She did not play games with other children, or wander, or have pocket-money, or go to the theatre. Only when Mr Bowie was at home were guests entertained in the house. And of all these days of isolation,

> Sunday was the quietest day on earth. We weren't allowed to do anything.
> Everything was done on Saturday and there wasn't a dish washed on Sunday.
> No. We got up in the morning and we had, as I said, we had prayers in the
> morning, everyone of us knelt down by the chairs. And we got our
> breakfast . . . And then go at 11 o'clock out to the morning service, come
> home, and the dinner was all ready cooked the day before, except for a few
> potatoes being put on. We'd have that and then go back to the Sunday
> School . . .

For this family, the city in which they lived remained as remote as if their mother had never left the Scottish countryside. Liverpool's cultural and social diversity was beyond their experience. The social system, for example, was conceived by them simply in terms of those who were 'nice people', and those who were not. Apart from school teachers, the music teacher and the dressmaker were 'nice people. My mother wouldn't allow us to be with, you know, people that wasn't nice. We had to speak properly.' These improper others were represented by 'people that would come round, the coal man and the bin men and people like that. You'd hear swear words and things like that.' And Katherine's world, even when she grew up, remained a tiny hedged garden, for she married her father's image, another ship's officer. 'When I was introduced to him, of course, it was the brass buttons that took my eye. My father had brass buttons.'

The second professional family was in some ways similar: suburban, religious, few visitors allowed to the house, and no living-in servants. 'Mother didn't want people to help with the children, she didn't like interference in that way.' But the *Lindsells* were artistic and this made a great difference. The family would perform plays, black minstrel shows, music on the piano, clarinet, mandolin, and banjo: 'we all played something.' Occasionally they were taken to the theatre and 'we did sometimes go to cinemas if the programme was suitable, you see, if father went to see what they were like first of all.' They would play tennis, and go out cycling with their father on Saturday afternoons. There were plenty of books to read in the house, and the girls were also very happy at school.

Nevertheless, the children had their anxieties. Not so much owing to discipline, for this chiefly took the form of strong moral pressure. For example, food 'had to be finished. We were told of all the children who hadn't enough to eat and that sort of thing—and I say one day, "Well couldn't we give it to the children who haven't enough to eat?" They told me to be quiet and get on with my meal.' But it was less easy for the child to handle her fear of divine wrath, and she suffered from constant nightmares. 'I was a mischievous child and I was terribly afraid of going to sleep in case I burnt up. I suppose, you know, I was brought up in the old way of the hell fire.'

Her parents, moreover, had definite psychological problems. 'Mother . . . would have made a marvellous actress, you see, but she just married and had a domestic life and—but she used to be very gay very often and sing, we used to sing operatics and she'd sing, be gay. But she was very frustrated and sometimes very bitter . . . She found it very difficult to show affection. Father was better.' He was, in fact, 'a very sociable man, father; he would have liked a much more sociable life.' But he was unwilling to bring his friends to the house, because they could have no drink there. 'Mother wouldn't allow it in the house, because she was afraid that if father took to it, you see he would drink too much.' For in the background Mrs Lindsell always held the haunting memory of her own parents' broken marriage. 'Grandmother was a very delightful woman but she made the wrong marriage . . . She'd got long dark ringlets —and she was so lovely.' She started to drink, perhaps because her husband's career took him away too much, but more likely because she couldn't stand him when he was at home. 'Grandfather would never drink tea or coffee—he believed in water— "God's ale," as he called it. He was a natural vegetarian. He didn't believe in killing anything.' But these high principles did not protect him from infidelity, or grandmother from drinking herself to death.

There must, of course, have been few Victorian middle-class families completely free of moral fears of Armageddon, drink, sex, or other sins. They can be discerned in the first of our lower middle-class families, who were again strongly religious supporters of a mission chapel. Mr *Barrett* was a London master chimneysweep, employing up to twenty men each night. The Barretts belonged to a Temperance Club; but at one point Mrs Barrett started to drink. There was again a memory in the family, of a great-grandmother, deserted by a ship's captain, who 'died with a broken heart'. The girl's own fears were that the 'end of the world was coming. Oh, I thought myself, I'm not going out tonight, not leave my mother and father.'

If such feelings left little mark on the Barretts, this may be because their economic situation drew them closer together. Mr Barrett expected the children to help with his chickens and garden, and he ran his business from his home. There were also advantages in living in a less isolated house. The children were allowed to play in the street, and, later on, even to get parts in a pantomime. Although guests were rare and the house door was firmly locked at ten o'clock, there was plenty to look at from the bedroom window. 'We used to watch the children over this park . . . There was a stall, fish stall, and then on each side was these shops, and afterwards they didn't shut till . . . 12 o'clock at night, and the poor little children from Kensal Town they used to have no socks or shoes on, terrible, and they used to pick all the stuff out and eat it, they were so hungry.'

For the two publicans' families, there was of course no escape from contact with poverty and drink: it was part of their business. In one the father was himself an unemployed alcoholic, drinking himself to an early death. Mr *Venables* had been a newspaper lawyer, but after persuading a capable widow who ran her own pub to marry him, he gave up work. 'He never did a thing, never did a stroke, only sit with the customers, drinking and enjoying himself. He was no use.' His only contribution to the household was to keep pigeons and bantam cocks and hens, mainly so that he could watch them fight, but sometimes for use as pigeon pie. He would invite the boy in to show him off to the customers—'put the tip of my head on one chair and the tip of my feet on the other and I would be stiff'—and then send him away so that he could tell some smutty jokes. Although their standard of living was comfortable, with good food, and the services of a maid, charwoman, and seamstress, 'there's no family life, really.' They did not eat together, and there were no family games or music. The parents kept apart although there were occasional fights—and the father was left behind when they attended church, and went on their annual holiday. The boy was not really close to his mother either: she 'was always attentive and looking after me, you know; but there was no loving or anything like that shown . . . She had her own troubles, I think . . . with the bar and the barmaids and probably they'd be pilfering . . . drinking the stock or something like that.'

Consequently the boy spent much of his time in the street, although the pub was in a very mixed district near the Liverpool docks. One of his playmates, for example, was a Chinese girl. Mrs Venables had 'a lot of poorer customers, but they were always treated. They could say what they wanted and buy a pint and have their dinner out of the bread and cheese basket for nothing . . . That was put on the counters, and in the evenings probably small plates of peas and beans or something like that. Given free.' And as so often, the roughness of the area was formalized with peculiar nastiness in the school, where the headmaster kept his personal torture instrument in his study—'a train window flap strap—slit, you know—and rap you on the knuckles.'

In the other publican's family, the *Glanvilles*, the boy also mixed with poor children in the streets, sharing their warfare with the policeman. Here too the adults kept on the right side of the police by knowing when to send over the barman with a pint of beer. But in other ways family life was a complete contrast: family meals with grace, games, magic-lanterns, and the piano, and no violence—even punishment was never severer than being sent to bed. Such gentle discipline may seem remarkable from a father who was a prize-fighter as well as a publican, and was to die as the result of a punch on the kidneys. Mr Glanville, however, seems to have been a man of unusual talents. London born, he had been brought up in Scotland, and joined a Scottish cavalry regiment. He then returned to London, first as a dairyman in Hoxton, keeping fifteen cows under his shop. He then ran an antique-furniture business, and finally a public-house. He was an amateur lawyer. 'He'd jump his own height: very fine swordsman, good runner, good jumper, good swimmer . . . Very light on his feet too. He was a Highland Fling dancer.'

Apparently he was as respected in the community as in his family. He was a churchwarden (although perhaps this was simply because the vicar was a very regular customer). There would be banquets, supervised by Mrs Glanville: 'lovely glasses she had, all colours, like a long stem and a yellow top, a blue top, a fawn top—made a nice show.' There would be elaborate flower decorations, and a menu of 'sucking pigs, H-bone of beef, shoulder of lamb, lobsters—oh, a lovely dinner.' And for the poor of the district, he organized a soup-kitchen. When the London cabmen went on strike, 'they were allowed to come to our house and have a glass of stout and bread and cheese every day they were on strike. Well, when my father died there was 95 empty cabs followed the funeral and the wreath they sent was as large as a hansom cab was . . . It was a procession. They had a Salvation Army Band, East Bloomsbury Radical Club Band . . . from City Road to Old Street, right down Old Street to Shoreditch.'

The father of the last of the four tradesmen's families was, by comparison, unenterprising, for both Mr *Timbs* and his wife came from shopkeepers' families. One grandfather kept pigs in the country and sold them in his city shop, and the other also had a shop in the city centre.

Compared with his grandparents he was not, however, a successful tradesman, and he eventually abandoned his grocer's and baker's shop to become an insurance agent. Resentment at her declining social standing may partly account for Mrs Timbs's harshness to her five children. She even burnt the girls' books to remove a distraction from household chores, and, although a charwoman was employed, the girls were made to empty bedroom slops during the school lunch hour. She was in fact a paradigm of frigidity, as cold to her husband as to her children. 'I remember once seeing my father at Christmas put his arm round my mother and she did this— she brought her hands together. You know, she almost froze. Eh dear, my mother never taught us any affection—never, never, never. It was always right and wrong and how much work you could do.' The effect of this example on the girls proved disastrous. One sister rebelled, stole, became promiscuous, and then lived with a married businessman until she had a child by him, which she handed over to her parents to bring up. The younger sister was obedient, but as unaffectionate as her mother, and when she later found a husband, she was unable to hold him.

As it happens, the father of the one clerical family had made the same move out of trade: Mr *Enfield* had been a country grocer before his appointment as a senior railway clerk. But he was a much more successful man, later becoming a station-master, and there is, compared with the Timbs, a general buoyancy in the family atmosphere. The children were allowed out in the street skipping, spinning tops, and running iron hoops until the evening meal. Life in the suburbs included pleasant walks to fetch eggs 'through the buttercup fields over Highbury Rise'. Friends were made welcome, there was family singing, reading aloud and plenty of books. The children were encouraged at school ('Dad would always help me with my sums in the evenings') and a favourite school teacher 'used to walk home with two or three of us hanging on her arm and have . . . a cup of tea and a piece of cake.'

The family were keenly religious, although far from fanatical, and on Sundays went to church three times. They regarded themselves as 'upper working-class' rather than middle-class, and had chosen a select artisan estate for their home. On Sundays their neighbours could see visible proof of their respectability: Mr Enfield in 'his frock coat and silk hat and mother with her silk cape . . . and little bonnet'. Mr Enfield was particularly proud of a fancy blue waistcoat of Chinese silk, with crocheting and braiding, which 'was looked upon as a little bit of gold dust'. Yet their main contact with the poorer working class, none of whom lived on the estate, was through the church, which had a 'sunshine committee'. The members made clothes for poor children, took them on a summer outing, bought them boots, and gave them a January tea-party with coconut ice.

It is hardly surprising, although we now cross the boundary between manual and non-manual workers, that a skilled manual worker's family can easily be found whose way of life was essentially similar to that of the 'upper working-class' but non-manual Enfields. The *Towlers*, craftsmen prosperous enough to employ a regular dressmaker, in fact thought of themselves as middle-class. Basketmakers, they made cradles, pushcarts, fancy chairs, and tables, 'and all of us used to work in it . . . We was a united family.' Mrs Towler came from a middle-class London French family, and before marriage had given public readings of Dickens's works. 'They all used to pay a penny to go and the halls were always full . . . She was a wonderful reader. And a speller too.' Mr Towler, who worked all hours, was from a humbler background, but 'aristocratic looking, with the goat's beard . . . And he was very gentle and very intellectual.' They appear to have been obliged to move a number of times because of difficulties with rent, and for about six years they gave up basketmaking and took a house with a large garden and greenhouses 'and the whole family worked in the gardens.' With their own meat, vegetables, and fruit, fresh or preserved, they ate well. At this time they 'used to employ a woman from the union to do the washing . . . and she was allowed a pint of beer and bread and cheese for dinner.'

The children clearly imbibed a strong sense of respectability. At school, for example, 'there was two girls, used to come from the fried-fish shop, and they'd hang their clothes up and we'd all rush round and take our clothes from the pegs as far as we could from them.' Another incident, however, revealed that others too might have their pride. The children had always thought of a navvy working in a gang of roadmen as 'someone different. But when I spoke to his daughter . . . she said, that nobody could do his job. It was a high skilled job to keep that hammer going on that top of that knob, you know how—five—one after the other banging. She said it was the most skilled job that was going. So they were proud of that job, see, and thought nobody was so good as them.'

Religion once more served to emphasize the special standing of their own family. The Towlers were undenominational 'Peculiar People', and at one time held services in their own house, which were attended by neighbours and children and a few other supporters. Both parents also went visiting, the mother reading to the gypsies in an encampment opposite the house, the father calling on the poor, 'cheering them up', and sometimes if they were ill staying the night. He organized a soup kitchen for the poor in his house, with the help of local butchers and corn chandlers and their own vegetables. Tickets would be sent for distribution to the Board School 'for the children to get a pint of pea soup'.

Another artisan family, although less prosperous themselves, also organized charity for the poorer working classes. The *Whitworths* lived in central Salford. Mr Whitworth was a Corporation horsekeeper, living next to the stable yard, where 'he went day and night—sat up all night sometimes with a sick horse.' The family were well fed themselves, with hens kept in the cellar, and special advantages from the father's position.

> Me father got plenty of things given to him . . . It was the farmers that supplied the Corporation with hay and corn and stuff for the horses, and they always sent . . . a hamper every Christmas with perhaps a turkey in and a goose and onions, apples, sage, parsley all round, right big hampers, you know. And then the vet that was with . . . the horses, he always sent a big round of beef.

The children, too, profited from their situation, and organized macabre tea parties.

> Me brother had two or three lads, friends, but on Saturday our Albert he used to get some bricks and cover them with bird lime to catch sparrows . . . and he'd pluck them, clean them, him and me together, I helped him.
> Me dad had a little room like he called his surgery where he kept all his horse medicines and things and he used to let us play in there. And our Albert and me, we used to clean these sparrows and then we'd get me mother's roasting tin, big lump of dripping in it. And in this surgery there was a big range . . . and our Albert'd make a fire and get the oven hot and we used to cook them . . . and me mother'd make a big jug of tea for us and we had a tea party.

The facilities of the yard also proved useful when it came to helping to feed the poor.

> I can remember one winter and it was a very long cold winter . . . and there was a lot of poverty about. And me father, he went to different shopkeepers on Charlotte Road and he got promises of scrapmeat, bacon, bones, you know, lamb bones, and all sorts of things, peas, beans, and of

course he had carrots and turnips and . . . he got some oatmeal promised him
and a baker promised him some bread . . . Me father had a very big iron
boiler . . . that he used to make gruel for horses and he cleaned it all out and
they made soup in this big boiler and I can remember seeing the people come.
They had to come on a certain time at a certain day twice a week. They came
for two or three weeks that winter. They had . . . to bring their own jugs . . .
They was that hungry and . . . the children running about barefoot,
even in the cold.

Hunger had its effect, at a distance, even with this well-fed family. The girl
found her mother cold. 'I don't think she wanted me. I don't think she did. Well she'd
had four boys. And I don't think she wanted any more because they weren't well
off.' Her brother had passed on the story of an exchange with a neighbour at the
time of her birth, who had asked, ' "Aren't thou pleased that thee's got a little
sister?" He said, "We could have done without her. It's only another mouth to
feed".'

Mr Whitworth, however, was a more affectionate man who helped a lot with the
children; for example, he would bath them. It was a gentle home, in which punishment of any kind was rare. The children could enjoy the entertainments of the city,
such as a round-the-world panorama shown in the Free Trade Hall, as well as
outings into the nearby countryside. It was walking down a country lane one evening
that the girl met her husband; he was a young Co-operative shop assistant out on a
bicycling excursion, who stopped to ask her the way to the inn.

Both of them were city people, strangers in the countryside, although her
father had started work on a farm. The distance which her family had travelled in
moving to the city was indicated by an incident when the grandmother came to stay.
'Me mother persuaded dad to take her to the pantomime. So me dad worked to
persuade her to go.' She had never been to the theatre, and as a Particular Baptist,
was very suspicious of it.

Anyway, he got a cab and he took her, and it was Bo-Peep, Little Bo-Peep.
Well it started and when the ballet came on and there were dancing girls,
and they'd be in tights, she says to me dad, she said, 'William, take me
home.' She said, 'Take me home.' He said, 'It's only just started mother.'
She said, 'Take me home. I'm not sitting here watching them dancing and
kicking their legs about . . .' she says. 'And wagging their fat tails behind
them,' she says, 'the brazen hussies.'

The great gulf between city and country as well as between the generations was
also felt by a boy from central London who went in 1897 to stay for a holiday with his
grandfather in an Essex village. Tom *Farrow* took a friend with him, also a post-
office telegraph boy. 'We paid him, of course, the old man was just on his own.' They
were amazed by the 'old cronies' whom they found at the village pub.

They'd sit round smoking, and gossiping—best part of 'em couldn't read. They'd have a pot and they'd keep passing it round and—one pot—they'd keep passing it round and having a sip out of it, see. When it was empty somebody else'd pay for the next pot, and so on . . . We'd buy a bottle of lemonade for a penny . . . and we'd sit there among them and read the newspaper. Read to them out of a newspaper and you know they'd sit there going 'Ah, ah.' Well they didn't know anything much . . . We were always having little wars at some place such as little African places . . . and of course, they'd not heard about this. Some of 'em hadn't heard of the Crimea war you know—and of course they'd all be people who was alive then.

One can imagine how far this village pub must have seemed from the Victoria Palace music-hall where 'when I was young I'd take a girl friend . . . A shilling each for the seats and there was always a waiter hopping about, you know; if you wanted a drink they'd fetch you one.' Inevitably, living where he did, Tom Farrow saw something of the extremes of social life. One nearby street 'was such a rough place [the police'd] go down there four at a time. If one went down there, he'd get a good hiding.' At work he also got to know the seamier side of upper-class life. One of his workmates was an allowance man—

a nuisance and the families used to pay 'em, make an allowance, three or four pounds a week to keep away. [This allowance man] was a gentleman born. And he used to go to church on Sundays and he went to St Peter's Eaton Square. He'd have a tall hat, frock coat and gloves and all the rest of it, see. People didn't recognize him you know because in the week he'd just be wearing the postman's uniform. And, anyway, this particular Sunday morning he went to church. As he walked into church and took his tall hat off, he—he—he'd inadvertently got a postman's hat under it . . . It was a by-word all round the office.

Tom Farrow was also introduced through work to the servants of the rich. The night boys at the post office could not go out much in the evenings, so

in the morning in the summer time we'd go to Battersea Park to have a game of cricket. We used to find kindred souls like ourselves. There was a club; we called ourselves The Owls. They called themselves The Early Birds. And they were composed of footmen and butlers and gentlemen's servants generally. Well, then, they'd turn out and meet us perhaps at 5 o'clock in the morning.

There was also contact through courting. 'Course when I was single I used to know a lot of maids . . . Probably they had one day a week or something and take 'em for a walk in the park . . . They had to be home by nine or something like that . . . If you popped down the area steps you might get in.' You could then enjoy gossip with the other servants about their employers—'they'd all generally got some spicy little tale to tell you and—"Here, Postie," so, see . . .' He suspected some of the maids were wearing their mistress's clothes when he took them out. He also observed how the cook would enter extra milk in the account book, which the milkman would not deliver. Not that the milkman swindled only the rich. 'They always used to give you "a little drop over", so they said. But what used to happen was this. They [were] what they called "quick on the handle"... They wouldn't pour all of it out.' Similarly, but in a more straightforward fashion, at the local brawn shop 'they never bothered to weigh it, they just cut it off.'

He had direct experience of shopkeeping, for although Mr Farrow was a postman the family kept an umbrella shop. 'It was quite a paying business . . . Mother used to do the sewing work . . . I had to do a lot of running about for the shop, you know. Go to school and take a note to be let out at four o'clock and then I had to rush off to the City, see, warehouse, for something or other. Or else I'd have to go over to the Borough for a walking stick.'

With his own family, however, it was not shop practices which induced cynicism. More relevant was his parents' attitude to religion. They never went to church, but taught him prayers and sent him to Sunday school. 'That went on for a time but I mean it was never serious . . . The local vicar came round . . . and had a chat with mother but . . . I mean, it petered out. They were never very serious on these things.' The children were also sent to the Wesleyan chapel when there was something to be had there. 'Once a year we used to have a service and a tea there and after the tea we had to spend the evening in this church . . . I know we was always glad to get out.' And although the parents were not churchgoers they insisted on Sunday suits, Sunday boots, 'and you mustn't have a ball or read a paper nor have a comic or anything like on a Sunday, no.'

Some of their other demonstrations of respectability were equally hollow, even if they may not have been atypical of artisan culture. In the parlour above the shop, which was reserved for week-end use when relatives came, a piano was kept, 'but nobody could play it, see.' One might have thought that in a house with nowhere to hang clothes, 'not an inch of back yard', the room could have been better used. Certainly 'so far as working people were concerned we were tolerably comfortable', with meat most days cooked on the gas-stove, and in the evenings perhaps fish bought from the fried-fish shop, or shrimps or winkles from a barrow. Food, indeed, had to be just right: when an aunt served suet pudding before the Sunday joint in the old fashion, 'we just looked at it and they got on. "Come on then—get on." "No, no, we'll wait till we have it all together." So we wouldn't touch it till we got the rest.'

With purchases, it was always 'cash down and we never owed.' But the Farrows let their attitude to money go to extremes. Tom was never allowed to accept money for running an errand, yet he was worked exceptionally hard at home, not merely having to clean the knives and boots and do other housework but being responsible for the younger children. 'I had very little leisure . . . because I was always in charge of the younger ones. See? I used to have one pal, and occasionally I'd be allowed to go out with him.' When his parents went out at night he had to baby-sit, 'scared stiff' they would wake and interrupt his reading in the kitchen. His parents also 'made all sorts of promises . . . "When you get married we'll give you a house to live in and the deeds of it", you know. But it didn't happen.' The worst deception, however, was the double trick of the money box.

> I had a money box and I was taught as a small boy not to accept anything from anybody, see. I used to [say] 'No thankyou. Father's got some', see. But of course I had to have a money box but I was never allowed to spend any and never had any pocket money . . . I know some children used to get a Saturday penny but I never did. No . . . I can see that blessed thing now, mahogany affair, see. And then one day it disappeared. And it turned up a few days after tied up with string and sealing-wax and all the rest of it. And of course, opened in front of me—'Oh, let's see what this is'—and that'd been to the baby shop to buy me a new sister. And that was that . . . That's where the money went.

This incident must have occurred in the 1880s. Nevertheless, it is striking to find that ten years later Dan *Shaw*, a Liverpool dock carter who had none of these pretensions, gave his daughter Annie threepence pocket money a week—'that was a penny for morning service, a penny afternoon service and penny night.' Himself no churchgoer, he was proud of his daughter's singing and if she practised at the piano with her choir book 'he'd say, "Huh, singing on Sunday, wench? I'm going to church." And he'd come to church that Sunday. Yes he'd come to the mission hall that Sunday.'

The Shaw family regarded themselves as 'just ordinary working class', and their life was indeed typical of a group which is under-represented in this set of interviews. In the district 'we were all pretty well of the same living—just carters and cotton porters and all like that . . . Very, very few on the rough side . . . all pretty well respectable.' The children played in the street, although certain companions from bad homes were forbidden, at games such as 'skipping rope, hop scotch, shuttlecocks, rounders . . . kick the can . . . blind man's buff . . . and Jacks and Hollies—four jacks and a holly, kneeling on the floor.' Relationships with neighbours were warm but limited. Mrs Shaw was 'very well liked. And no matter what went wrong in the street—if anybody died—"Go tell Mrs Shaw and she'll lend you the sheets".' Similarly, when she was ill a neighbour would come in to 'do a few messages or any hard jobs'. But Annie's parents did not regard neighbours as friends. 'No they just kept to themselves—just was sociable with all the neighbours and that but that was all . . . Mother always taught us to keep neighbours outside.'

The family's standard of living was reasonable. Clothes were new, and there was meat most days. Nevertheless, there was not always enough to go round, and Mrs Shaw would often go short. When the father's earnings were down, 'she used to do a day's washing . . . at home. The neighbours used to bring it up to her. It was only neighbours she did it for.' As a dock carter Mr Shaw had a very irregular income.

He was more out of work in my early years than he was in work . . . You had to go and stand on the corner . . . You'd be glad to see the chap coming along and you'd be praying he'd say, 'Come on, come on, come on, I want you, you, you'—you'd be glad to be among the five he'd picked. And if you didn't get picked your heart'd be in your boots . . . You had to come home and go on the corner next day.

Under favourable circumstances it was possible for a family considerably poorer than this to maintain quite respectable standards of behaviour—for example, the *Ranns*, a family of nine children who lived in a London mews. Mr Rann was a navvy, illiterate but independent-minded, and 'out of work very often . . . He was a man that wouldn't be shown his work . . . He knew his work and he wouldn't be shown.' Mrs Rann couldn't read either, and they refused to allow books or newspapers in the house, no doubt regarding them as a threat to their authority. Their poverty was severe. The children were sent out to 'pick up firewood'. Apart from some chickens they were able to keep in an empty stable, they could only afford pieces of meat or pork-rind soup. Similarly, they bought fish pieces and for bread 'you used to go to the baker's and get 3d. worth of stale bread . . . if there was any there, mind you.' Often the boy, Sidney, would miss breakfast, for he had to do a milk-round before school, to earn money; and, if he was in time, there would be just bread and dripping. He also earned money in the evenings, running errands or cleaning boots or silver for the wealthy. On Saturdays he was again expected to 'find a job some-where . . . Perhaps go and help a baker on his round.' In some ways it was best to be out of the house, which was desperately overcrowded.

Nevertheless, Mrs Rann was clearly of some local standing, for she worked as a midwife until uniforms were demanded. The children were brought up to 'raise the hat to the ladies'. They were dressed in new clothes. Bedtime was strictly imposed. Grace was said at meals 'and we weren't allowed to talk over the table . . . You had to sit right and you had to hold your knife and fork right.' Cards were not allowed in the house, and although Sidney had to fetch drinks for his parents from the pub, his father 'would never take us in the public house . . . he always used to say, "Nobody'll ever say I learned my children to drink".' In the same way, although not themselves interested in church, 'they saw that *we* went.' On some evenings the Band of Hope would hold outdoor services: 'we used to go to the bottom of the mews here and sing . . . If the cabmen were here, in the week, they used to join in . . . We was all one happy family.' Later, indeed, when he married, it was to a girl from the same mews.

In a hostile environment it was difficult to maintain such standards of behaviour, even when financial poverty was less acute. A smaller family, the *Doyles* with four children, lived in Blackgate, a central slum district in Salford. Although clearly poor, they could always afford some kind of meat every day, and on Saturdays with the week's pay in hand would often buy a chicken from a 'Chicken Ann' who toured the streets with her push cart. Mrs Doyle had worked as a weaver 'until several of the children were born'. She now was a respected figure in the district, 'a little stout old lady' in middle age. 'She was a marvel . . . She couldn't read or write, but she was a good woman . . . [It] was a pretty tough neighbourhood and the people in trouble, it didn't matter how bad they were, she'd go and try to help 'em . . . She didn't believe there were bad people, I don't believe.' Her particular friends, however, were undoubtedly from the elite of the district. She used to go out some evenings to an 'old-fashioned pub' to chat with the lady publican, a tobacconist, and a tripe shop-keeper. Occasionally the four ladies would go out into the countryside on a picnic together.

Mr Doyle was semi-skilled, an iron fettler at a foundry, and his income regular, for he was only unemployed when, about once in every five years, he decided to break out of the routine of his existence. 'He used to occasionally get fed up with the job and he purposely used to stop off and have a bit of a booze and get the sack. Then he'd be some time getting a job.' Even during these lapses he maintained appearances by drinking in some other part of the city. His privacy was fiercely maintained. 'A neighbour daresn't step in the house. They daresn't come past the partition. If they put their nose past the partition he'd say, "What do you want?" '

The rough standards of the neighbourhood had, however, affected him more than he would have liked to recognize. He was harsh with the children, never playing with them and reluctant even to talk. 'He expected you to obey his look, never mind his order . . . He was a bit of a savage.' Meals were silent, although parents were not 'dressed up over the etiquette . . . We had to have a knife and fork mind you.' Afterwards they would sit round the hearth. 'There wasn't much room . . . and he used to get in front of the fire with his chair and you try to get near and he'd say, "You shouldn't be cold".' His evening slippers were discarded iron moulds which he brought back from the foundry. 'When I wanted chastizing he used to call me over and say, "Turn round", and he was a giant and he used to hit you on the back with this shoe and it'd knock you across the kitchen . . . Very strict man—he used to swear a bit and you weren't to swear though.'

In the house he was no help at all. He expected the boys to fetch beer for him and read to him, because he was illiterate, but he tried to prevent them helping their mother. 'A lad hadn't to do anything. We had flag floors and we musn't clean the floor and "They're not going to make a girl of my lad"—that was his idea. Ignorance, really. But anyway I took no notice of him: I used to help my mother.'

Because of the atmosphere at home when his father was about, the boy 'didn't spend a lot of time in the house. He was too tough.' But the entertainments he could find outside were quite as savage. A particular pleasure, for example, was observing at the slaughter house—'Oh aye, I've seen them slaughter them all and cut them up.' Nor was it much more edifying to watch some of the neighbours. For although they were all poor, he felt strongly the distinctions between them.

> Our class was a respectable working man's class. But on the poor side . . .
> Some of them . . . couldn't even keep their houses decent. They used to call
> our street 'good husbands' street' because they cleaned the flags . . .

Crompton Street was one standard poor. Lyme Street [the next street] was,
oh it was awful, much lower than normal. They were living under a horrible
condition. Broken windows. Really you couldn't believe the difference
in two streets. Mixed up with Jews and thieves. Crompton Street they weren't
too bad . . . They were very hard worked anyway. They didn't all work in
Lyme Street . . . They lived like chip choppers . . . chopping chips and
selling them in bundles [for] firewood . . . children going round with them.
They were a better type of people in Crompton Street. Although as I say there
was a criminal opposite to us. The lady that her husband was in jail and she
had another pal. Oh, she had more than one. Smart woman too. But that
was the way of life I understand with these people. My mother used to warn
me against her.

Round the corner, however, such people were typical.

A family named O'Brien had the first house in Lyme Street . . . He was a
high-class tailor. They hadn't a stick in the house . . . Nice man, Mr O'Brien.
Their children were no good. And the mother . . . used to take several
policemen to lock her up and they always had to take her on a hand cart.
That was Lyme Street. And O'Brien the poor fellow, he put up with it.

The Stacey family were still worse.

Everybody knew them. They were downright villains. They were thieves.
The women were bad women, real bad women. One eloped with a doctor.
The doctor must have been mad. And they were barmaids some of them till
they got a bit older and then they went to lob. Went to bed. Lob—made love.
The eldest son, I think it was Paddy, he was always in and out of prison.
Violence and drunkenness . . . He died from head injuries in the prison . . .
Saw him one day in Chapel Street, walking, drunk, talking to himself with a
brick in his hand. He used to throw bricks through pub windows . . . I saw
another criminal drop dead out of a pub. Paddy Talman. He was a villain . . .
He lived off Blackgate, married to a fine young woman and I was coming
home from work and I saw this fellow. I'd a bit of a truckle with him once,
I was glad they'd got rid of him . . . Doctor came, he was dead, shot through
the heart. Now what had happened—the publican said that he'd raised a
stool up to hit him and this revolver—well he might have done, I don't
know. But there was one of the Stacey girls mixed up with him in the pub
in that.

In a district where, to a boy, the police were 'brutes', collusion was probably
the best form of protection from the criminals. One incident reveals something of the
nature of this protection, and the organization of the criminal world.

The decent people in Blackgate was safe from the roughs. Safe from the
criminals . . . Well I used to come home early and go and stand on the

corner of Gravel Lane and I could see my mother come out of the Bull's Head. I was watching for her safety come home. No local'd interfere with her but a stranger might. Well a chap comes out of the pub and he offered me a handkerchief. I didn't know him, so I knew he was a stranger. Something like this—'Give me five bob for this.' And he started edging towards me. Well, the only way for me to stop him was to hit him or something. I'd no intention of giving him five shillings. And a woman came along. I'd never spoken to her in my life but she was known—as a few things. It was doubtful whether she was in touch with the police to give criminals away . . . She had a shop down some cellars, a big place. The thieves used to deal with her . . . She had a daughter that was a thief . . . and her husband they called a megs man [confidence man] . . . And she said, 'What's to do?' So I said, 'He wants five shillings for this.' And another criminal, schoolboy same time as me, came out of the pub. He'd had penal servitude—Freddy Barnes. And she said to Freddy Barnes, 'Give him a good hiding. He's trying to get five shillings off Dicky Doyle'. . . Freddy Barnes he wiped the floor with this fellow. And she said to him, 'If you're in Blackgate tomorrow morning you'll know about it. Get out tonight.'

The territorial arrangements of the adult criminal world were probably particularly well defined, but there were parallel struggles taking place in other spheres. Jews, for example, were as far as possible kept out of the district by systematic window-breaking. There were also the territorial bases for the various youth gangs of the district, known as the 'Scuttlers'. 'Gangs used to meet and fire bottles at one another, and belts with buckles on . . . There was the Savoy gang—Red Shelley was the leader of them. And Johnny Hoddy was the leader of the Blackgate mob—the King Street mob it was.' These two gangs apparently differed, the Savoy gang being more likely young criminals, the King Street mob simply a street-corner group, whose leader 'anybody could have blown down with a feather. He was only the leader because he happened to be the oldest . . . married to quite a nice girl.'

Of the two Doyle boys, one seems to have been engulfed by the way of life of this rough district, but Dicky proved more successful than his parents. He was sent to the Roman Catholic school in Blackgate, where he experienced savage caning. The school's one advantage was that he was able to make friends in a more respectable district, and go there to play, although there were penalties involved in this too. The local boys 'used to think I was stuck up . . . I had to fight my way through. Now if I got a good hiding outside [my father]'d give me another one for getting a good hiding.'

The real turning point came when he started work with a portmanteau worker in 1895. It was here, rather than at school, that he felt he learnt manners, especially from 'the man I served my time under'. Even during the first few months when he was an errand boy, buying cigars and delivering love letters for the manager, new worlds were opened to him. Once he was sent out into the country to deliver some engraved cutlery. 'Oh, she was a lovely lady. She sat in the hall. And she had a lot of money there. She give me a sovereign—"That's for you. Put it away." So I put it in my pocket—six shillings was the most I'd ever had. I was in my element. Anything to help me mother. I was happy.' After a few months his father insisted that he should be properly apprenticed (although normally only sons of portmanteau workers were accepted) so that he was trained in the skills of fancy leather work—'crocodile, seal skin, Russian skin . . . The boys used to have to sit down at a bench and stitch for a week. Oh, I can stitch real—I think I can stitch with my eyes shut . . . You gradually learnt to do other things . . . Oh, I loved it.'

Once Dicky Doyle had become a journeyman he very quickly became prominent in the craftsmen's union. The trade was already in decline, its standards undermined by competition from sweaters, and the union had an appropriately moribund air. The delegates 'used to wait with tall hats and frock coats and they hadn't tuppence . . . They used to borrow money to go and have a drink in the pub . . . [and] come drunk to the meeting.' At the age of twenty-two he found himself elected president of the union. His father at any rate was forced to recognize his new status. Dicky refused to continue 'going for free beer for him . . . I said, "You're finished." I told him, I said, "You telling me what to do"—and I told him what I had accomplished at my age—"You've not accomplished nothing, not a heap . . . And I'm not going to read for you," I said, "and Nelly's not going to read for you." But she used to when I was out . . .'

This boy's rise was matched by the descent of others into the semi-criminal world. The *Colliers* lived in a district close to Blackgate. There were seven children, and the household was in most ways exceptionally rough. Neither Mr Collier, who was a blacksmith's striker, nor the children were expected to help in the house. They spent their time 'fighting with one another' while he would belt them (if he was not at the pub) for causing damage. 'He'd knock us about terrible you know . . . We deserved it, you see.' He was entirely illiterate, so that he could not even recognize the names on a ballot paper—he would just vote blind. 'He just put [the cross] down. He didn't know what there was.' None of the family ever went to church or to Sunday school. The children bathed in a canal, warmed by discharges from the boilers of a factory, rather than at home. Their patched trousers were 'hanging out at the back' from fights. If they had any decent clothes, for most of the week they would be in pawn. They had no underwear—'just our shirts and our trousers. That's all we had . . . Went to school in winter in bare feet. We'd no clogs to put on, until about Sunday.'

Their meals were eaten without knives and forks, and the children were allowed to chatter and even to read comics while they were eating. The diet was extremely meagre, with scarcely any meat. Bread, tea, and kippers were the staple, with potato pie the Sunday special. Because there were so many children the youngest were forced to eat from a ledge underneath the table, while their parents and elder brothers sat above. 'I'll never forget—I think I've got the mark yet—my father was having his dinner and I put me hand under his knee like that and I took a piece of meat off his plate. Well, he didn't see me first time. So the next time I comes again, but he had the knife, and he chopped me fingers—he nearly chopped me three fingers off.'

The children got into the habit of petty thieving when money was short. 'We couldn't see the old woman short . . . We two or three others we'd go together . . . outside the shops . . . We'd perhaps take a couple of taters out of that bag . . . and get onions, you know, where there was onions. We'd get a dinner that way and take it to the old woman and let her stew it up. She'd know where it came from.' It is hardly surprising that the children should think of this when they were out on the streets, continually being chased by the police for playing football, bathing in the canal, shouting in the streets at night, or trying to sell papers on Sundays. 'My mother was sick and tired of policemen coming to door.'

The children's regular pleasures included watching the police fish drowned men from the canal, and 'every morning we used to go to the police station to see if anybody was been locked up—the drunks.' Drunken women, even with children in arms, were a familiar sight. 'They used to feed 'em with the breast at one time . . . sit there in the pub with their babies.' There was also the pathetic example of Neddy Tattler who used to steal clothes 'when the washing was out in the entry', and pawn them for cash. 'The detective says, "He's the cheekiest fellow that ever we knew," he says. "He's even come back for pegs," he says. "That's how he got caught".' Even the sixpenny doctor found when he was called out that his patient was incapable, probably drunk, and the call was at his own expense. ' "I've come down for sixpence to see a fellow what's looney," he said, "and he's not got sixpence to pay, and they've stolen my dog while I've come." '

The dog, like other stolen goods, would be quickly taken to the local receiver. Also, as in Blackgate, there were gangs of Scuttlers who 'always wore belts . . . with brass buckles on . . . I knew a lot of them. One called Red Heriots. He was one of the leaders. Wore a jersey which said "Red Heriots" on it and "King of the Scuttlers". Aye, they stabbed a fellow on Oak Street Bridge . . . It was over the girls, jealousy with one another, you see.'

Another regular battle was with the landlord. If the rent was in arrears he would come round himself, and he'd say, 'Spent?'

> That's the way they'd say to him, you know—'bills'. And in question, 'Just bets and spending on horses?' And he'd get taking his coat off to have a fight, you know, for your rent. Aye, he did one person down there. He couldn't get no rent off him so he went and got a fellow . . . [to] go and put a slate on top of chimney so he try and smoke him out . . . Well them days we used to flit from one house to another . . . If there was a house empty you used to go to the woman and give her a shilling for the key . . . and keep missing rent there you see until he was going to throw them out, so they got another one, going, perhaps . . . only next street.

The short distances involved in these moves no doubt help to explain why despite the transience of many neighbours, 'in the street we knew every one of each others, you see, what they did and everything.' When the family was in trouble 'they'd come in and do any mortal thing for you.' Mrs Collier had, in fact, a rather special role in the street, for people 'used to come to her' to hear their fortunes. She knew a few primitive rituals. If a young woman had been deserted by her suitor, she would buy dragon's blood from a chemist, and put it in a frying-pan. As she turned it over above the fire, she would say:

> It is not this dragon's blood I wish to burn,
> It is my lover's heart I wish to turn.
> May he never eat or sleep until he returns to me.

After one success, her reputation spread. But the children remained cynical. 'We used to kid me mother over it.'

In spite of their shoplifting, none of the Collier children was ever caught stealing by the police. One brother even had a short rise towards respectability as a shop-keeper himself, selling greengrocery. 'He'd start with a basket and he'd go round with a basket on his head. About two or three months after that he'd have a donkey and cart. And then he'd get to a pony and cart.' Eventually he had three shops—until he ran away with Dublin Ginny, a prostitute, who robbed him.

Two of the boys started as miners. The younger, himself, went down the pit when he was thirteen and gave up at seventeen when he married a girl from the same street. 'We was young then like and we wanted a bit of pleasure.' For many years he worked on the roads with a steam-roller and they lived in a caravan, travelling the country. Before that, however, he had nearly been forced to travel in a less independent way. In 1900, when he was still working in the pit, he had been sent up the street 'for some sugar for me mother . . . And I'm going up the street, up Hesketh Street to the top and the lads are stood at the corner, you see. Well when they sees [the police] coming they flew away.' So that he was arrested instead, for loitering. He preferred going to prison for three days to paying a fine. The next time he was sent for seven days. The third time the magistrate said, 'I think you've got a lot of bad pals . . . Will you go in the Navy if I let you go?'

He joined a ship in Scotland. It seemed far tougher than the mine—'up aloft at four o'clock in the morning with weather, you know, bare feet, and you had to do knots and splices, bends and hitches, rope pulling, swimming . . . with your clothes on in the sea.' After a fortnight he was birched in front of the ship's company for smoking—'they sound the bell on ship to let them see me getting flogged.' So Bill ran away home to go back to the pit. He was caught, brought back, and flogged again, but this time he was so badly cut that he had to go to hospital where a kindly doctor arranged for his release. ' "I think you'll be best away." So he put me down for the discharge. "Unfit".'

He was lucky, for it was families like his own that fed the armed forces. We conclude with another very rough family, this time Londoners. Of the nine *Burns* children, two were to go to sea and a third into the army. Mr Burns, who was Scots, had also been a soldier, and had a good job as a foreman packer, but, since both parents drank heavily, life was only slightly worse for the children after he died. He was a rough man who did nothing for his family. 'I think if he'd ever took me out he'd have threw me in the canal.' They lived in two rooms in central London, sleeping five in a bed. They had no regular baths, no shoes, no new clothes. 'We wore one another's cast-offs. Oh, we wore practically nothing.' The clothes were ragged, not even well patched, and 'we were never clean.' There were no regular meals, and 'we was all hungry—always hungry.' They relied on bacon bones, pieces of leavings of meat, and 'pick-ups' of fruit from Covent Garden. They also made use of a nearby soup-kitchen. Only the parents sat on chairs. The children sat on the floor and ate their food with their fingers. 'I don't remember using a knife and fork as a youngster. Me Mum used to say, "Fingers before forks".'

With no chairs to sit on, guests could not be invited in. But a home which 'only had a few sticks in it' was easier to move. 'We shifted so many times . . . Some place, sometimes, we had to move quick—couldn't pay the rent.' The parents did not trouble much over school attendance. 'I was always one for running away from school. I didn't like school at all. I detested it. I . . . didn't go school any day if I got the chance.' To stop him 'hopping the wag', the headmaster would tie him to the radiator. Nor was he sent to church or Sunday school. His parents never went to church, unless something useful such as free coal was offered. Even so, his father seems to have been pleased by an occasional call from a missionary visitor who 'used to say, "Mr Burns, you'd be a fine Christian and you're a real gentleman." It was a good thing you know.'

There were no family outings or holidays, no games or sing-songs. In fact, the family did nothing together. 'We was all gone poles apart. We all used to go our own way.' For the children, this meant out into the street, dodging the policemen, cheering motor cars, picking up food from shops. 'I used to steal sweets . . . Used to be a little shop . . . I used to go in there and buy something for me mother and me hand used to creep up and steal a lump of coconut cake and she told me mother. Mother belted the living daylights out of me for it.' They would be sent out to beg, however. 'We used to go to different coffee shops and stand outside with a bag waiting for the girl who was in the serving or something to call us in and give us the leavings. Collect the leavings.' Or just to wander aimlessly, seeing what might be picked up from the gutter. 'We used to walk the streets all night at times . . . miles and miles and miles all along Tottenham Court Road, Oxford Street, all along the gutters . . . We used to walk from King's Cross to Hampstead Heath. And it was fun of the fair in happy Hampstead in those days.'

Fun the boy might watch, but could not afford to join. So we end with a child who saw the wealth and pleasure of the Victorian metropolis from a position of utter deprivation. Yet he noticed other children, whose voices are unrepresented here, in a state still worse than his own. There was a foundling hospital nearby, and 'every morning the people that was in the foundling hospital there, they used to come out and put fresh straw round the door and women used to leave their unwanted babies there.' And at night, a few hundred yards from the crowded main street with its gas-lamps and gin-palaces, a dedicated figure could be seen on his round. It was the Salvation Army man, who 'used to go down the mewses and stables and lift up the tarpaulins to see if there was any derelict children under.'

# II  Numbers of People

# 3    The Human Aggregate

## Asa Briggs

To understand the nature of Victorian civilization it is necessary to understand Victorian cities—visually, through their forms and formlessness; socially, through their structures and the chronology of their processes of change, planned and unplanned; symbolically, in literature and the arts, through their features and images; together for the light they throw on the processes of urbanization; separately and comparatively in order to understand particularity and the sense of place. The world of Victorian cities was fragmented, intricate, eclectic, messy; and no single approach to their understanding provides us with all the right questions and answers or leads us to all the right available evidence.

In studying such complex questions there is a danger in following singly one or other of two different kinds of approach, which all too seldom are considered together —the approach through 'qualitative' evidence derived from a wide range of sources, documentary and non-documentary, public and private, and the approach through the accumulation and analysis of 'quantitative' evidence—the vast store of measurable data which the men of the nineteenth century produced in greater and greater quantities. It is important that the two approaches should be considered together since there already tends to be a gulf between them. On one side are the literary historians and the architects, on the other side the historical demographers and the economists. A few social and economic historians and a few general historians straddle the divide. The dangers of this situation do not lie simply in failures of interdisciplinary communication: they prevent us from understanding many problems which are key problems in Victorian studies.

The fact that the quantitative approach is now becoming increasingly feasible and increasingly fashionable is of the utmost significance in this context. There is obviously much that we can find out quantitatively—in general and in detail—not least about the 'quality of urban life' that has not been found out before. By the intelligent use of social indicators, by the employment of a retrospective cost-benefit-analysis approach, by an analysis, with the help of modern statistical techniques, of factual material which the Victorians collected simply for immediate purposes, and by asking questions which for various reasons the Victorians did not themselves ask, at least in precise form, about their own society and culture, we can go some way towards 'measuring' the quality of life in nineteenth-century cities.

Before exploiting our own approaches, it is as wise to turn back to the attitudes of the Victorians themselves as it would be in studying the history of vocabularies or of tastes and styles. There is little doubt that throughout the whole period they approached the growth of their cities first and foremost in terms of *numbers*. They were aware—either with fear or with pride—that they were living through a period of change of scale—change in the size of industrial plant, change in the size of social organization, change, above all, in the size of towns and cities. They liked to collect facts about all these phenomena—sometimes for reasons of curiosity, sometimes for reasons of what we would now call 'social control'—and they developed machinery for doing so. The facts which they collected were set out in trade directories and brochures for local Chambers of Commerce as well as in the national Census reports and Blue Books: alongside successive editions of vast treatises like George Porter's *Progress of the Nation* (1836) or J. R. McCulloch's *Descriptive and Statistical Account of the British Empire* (1837) (against which Dickens reacted so sharply when he wrote *Hard Times*), there were detailed guides, heavy with statistics concerning what were often called 'the large towns and populous districts'.

Some of the facts were crude indicators of what the Victorians themselves thought of as 'material progress', aggregates derived from the success stories of economic individualism. Other facts dealt with the unplanned collective problem areas—with fertility—or mortality-rates for example, with crime, or with the supply of houses and schools. Others were far wider in scope, relating demography to social class, to economic structure, or to moral behaviour.[1] From the outset the facts were collected because many of the social statisticians were anxious not merely to present information but to propound a message, sometimes a gospel. Even when they were employed by the government as inspectors or servants of commissioners, they were seldom merely agents of the state. Moral instructors like Charles Kingsley eagerly translated the facts into the language of the sermon and the lecture. For example, in his lecture on 'Great Cities and their Influence for Good and Evil' delivered at Bristol in October 1857, Kingsley deliberately crossed the frontier between statistical and non-statistical methodology, stating that 'the moral state of a city depends—how far I know not, but frightfully, to an extent as yet uncalculated, and perhaps incalculable—on the

84

physical state of that city; on the food, water, air, and lodging of its inhabitants.'[2]

As I have argued in *Victorian Cities*, there was no agreement on the implications, moral or social, either of the acknowledged facts or of the general laws which Victorians liked to derive from them.[3] In the most general terms, on the one side was fear—fear of a change in the pattern of social relationships associated with change in the scale of the city; fear of the emergence and of the mounting pressure of new social forces which were difficult to interpret, even more difficult to control; fear about the capacity of society to deal quickly enough with urgent urban problems before the social fabric was torn apart. On the other side was pride—pride in achievement through self-help and, through self-help, in economic growth; pride in local success through rivalry with other places, not only in the tokens of wealth and in the symbols of prestige but also in the means of control—mileage of sewers, number of water-taps or water-closets, number of school places or of policemen.

There was sometimes no give-and-take in this clash of values: the chimneys spoke for themselves. Yet there was usually ambivalence, with the ambivalence stretching to the statistical method itself. Dickens was not attacking all statistics in *Hard Times*, but rather a naïve reliance on certain kinds of statistics and on nothing more.[4] *Punch* made fun of statistics, particularly 'useless' statistical research, on many occasions, but recognized that the great utility of some kinds of research and calculation was so very obvious that it need not point out the value of the labours of contemporary statisticians. Wordsworth, of all people, wrote to H. S. Tremenheere, the 'classic' Victorian inspector, that 'we must not only have knowledge, but the means of wielding it, and that is done infinitely more through the imaginative faculty assisting both in the collection and application of facts than is generally believed.'[5]

Given such ambivalence, much of which pivots on the Victorian idea of 'fact' itself, it is necessary to explore the growth of statistics as a mode of enquiry and a means to reform, not to take the mode and the means for granted. More work has recently been carried out on 'literacy', albeit still an under-developed subject, than on 'numeracy'. It may be true that 'statistics is to industrialism what written language was to earlier civilization.'[6] Yet it was in the pre-industrial seventeenth and eighteenth centuries that the origins of statistical preoccupation are to be found. 'Great cities', J. C. Lettsom had written in 1774, 'are like painted sepulchres; their public avenues, and stately edifices, seem to preclude the very possibility of distress and poverty: but if we pass beyond this superficial veil, the scene will be reversed.'[7] Statistics pierced the veil, and throughout the last decades of the eighteenth century there were as many statistical enquiries into living-conditions in pre-industrial communities (Chester or Carlisle, for example) as there were into those in the new English industrial cities.[8] Although 'abstract' classical political economy, as developed in the early nineteenth century by Ricardo, was by its very nature (like the developing natural sciences) non-statistical, this does not mean that political economists were uninterested in statistics. Ricardo himself agreed that 'speculation' had to be submitted to the 'test of fact', and the first Fellows of the Statistical Society of London, founded in 1834, included Nassau Senior, Malthus, and McCulloch.[9]

They were doubtless as sceptical as Dickens concerning the proposition that everything could be reduced to 'Two and Two are Four', 'Simple Arithmetic', or 'A Mere Question of Figures', the possible titles for *Hard Times*, although by 1838 some of their number were expressing the hope that 'the study of Statistics will, ere long, rescue Political Economy from all the uncertainty in which it is now enveloped.'[10]

The purposes which the Statistical Society of London was established to serve were set forth in a prospectus as 'procuring, arranging, and publishing "Facts calculated to illustrate the Condition and Prospects of Society".'[11] Its provincial counterpart, founded in the same year in Manchester, a city of unbridled economic individualism, certainly had from the start a distinct social leaning.[12] Businessmen might be concerned in their daily affairs with the statistics of the counting-house, but the little formative group of people, related by kinship and religion as well as by common interest, who created the Manchester Society were from the beginning preoccupied with the statistics of social relevance. They were anxious above all to show that Manchester was being misrepresented in official reports. The first complete available paper (1834) of the Society, was entitled 'An Analysis of the Evidence taken before the Factory Commissioners, as far as it Relates to the Population of Manchester and the Vicinity Engaged in the Cotton Trade.' The paper, prepared by the Greg brothers—one of whom was to clash with Mrs Gaskell on her interpretation of the texture of social relationships in Manchester[13]—was a secondary analysis of data gathered earlier by a parliamentary committee. It had five sections dealing, not with 'the facts of progress' as registered in profits and wages, but with health, fatigue, alleged cruelty towards factory children, education, morals, and poor-rates. The first completely original survey produced by the Society dealt with the provision of education,[14] and the first annual report of the Society spoke of 'a strong desire felt by its projectors to assist in promoting the progress of social improvement in the manufacturing population by which they are surrounded.'[15]

In the case of some of the other early statistical societies, all of them expressions of the great burst of provincial intellectual and social energy during the 1830s and 1840s, the purposive emphasis was even more marked.[16] The full title of the Birmingham Society was 'The Birmingham Statistical Society for the Improvement of Education'; the Glasgow Society spoke of collecting 'facts illustrative of the condition and prospects' of the community 'with a view to the improvement of mankind'. The London Society itself referred to the 'careful collection, arrangement, discussion and publication of facts bearing on and illustrating the complex relations of modern society in its social, economical, and political aspects', with the adjective 'social' being placed first. By 1838 the fourth annual report of its Council noted that 'the spirit of the present age has an evident tendency to confront the figures of speech with the figures of arithmetic; it being impossible not to observe a growing *a priori* assumption that, in the business of social science, the principles are valid for application only inasmuch as they are legitimate deductions from facts accurately observed and methodically classified'.[17]

Such a statement was at the opposite end of the scale from romantic styles of social criticism; it was at some distance, too, both from generalized Owenite social science and Benthamite reasoning. Yet the Owenites sometimes used statistics. Bentham argued powerfully that the systematic collection and annual publication of returns would furnish data for the legislator to work on, and the political economy of Edwin Chadwick, unlike that of J. S. Mill, needed to be fed on a diet of statistics. Chadwick, indeed, was an energetic member of the Statistical Society of London, even if the limitations of his statistical methods were to be emphasized later in the century.[18] He told the Political Economy Club in 1845 that of two types of economists —'the hypothesists' who reasoned deductively from 'principles' and those who believed in 'the school of facts' and worked inductively—he belonged to the second.[19] Nor was he alone. By the time of the tenth report of the Statistical Society of London in 1844, the Council was claiming that 'the pursuit of statistical enquiries has already made such progress . . . as henceforth to be a necessity of the age, and one of its most honourable characteristics.'

The statistical method was deliberately employed during the 1830s and 1840s to identify 'problems', to spread 'knowledge of social facts', and to educate 'opinion'. It was because the pioneering statisticians of this period were thought of as explorers of society—and, particularly, of urban society within which the statistical societies were created—that they were able to influence both the collective will and the individual literary imagination. Their chief merit seemed to be that they discovered 'facts' at first hand, and Mill deferred to Chadwick on the grounds that Chadwick got his information direct while he (Mill) 'could only get it second hand or from books.'[20] The notion of 'exploration' which recurs time and time again in the imagery of early urban studies carried with it a sense of adventure. It also carried with it the sense that nineteenth-century cities, in particular, were 'mysterious places' where one section of the community knew very little directly about the rest. 'Why is it, my friends,' the great American preacher W. E. Channing asked in Boston in 1841—in a sermon in which he anticipated Disraeli in speaking of 'two nations coexisting side by side in the same community'—'that we are brought so near to one another in cities? It is, that nearness should awaken sympathy; that multiplying wants should knit us more closely together; that we should understand one another's perils and sufferings; that we should act perpetually on one another for good.'[21] In reality, however, the nineteenth-century city, with all its varieties of experience, did not permit this intuitive understanding. There was a striking contrast between *ought* and *is* which the statistician could expose. At his best, indeed, he could be a mediator as well as an explorer, not dwelling on the 'mystery' of the city—or exploiting it, as G. M. W. Reynolds and some of the purveyors of romantic fiction did—but rather on the dissipating of it.

Beyond a certain point it was clearly impossible to talk of 'numbers', the starting point of urban exegesis, without also talking about 'relationships', social and geographical. Most pre-industrial cities had been places which were small enough and for all their complexities, simple enough to generalize about or about which to moralize as 'wholes' or to satirize in terms of galleries of urban 'types'. It was far more difficult, in socially and geographically segregated cities with unequal spatial densities and with manifestly unequal conditions of 'class', segregated district by district, to grasp the idea of the city as a whole and to identify its 'problems' except through the collection and deployment of statistics. Doctors, who were particularly prominent in the deliberations of the Manchester Statistical Society, might be in a more favourable position than most to move easily from one area to another, relying on knowing directly rather than knowing at second-hand. So also might at least an active minority of ministers of religion. Yet with the separation of work-place and home, the growth of single-class living areas and the decline in what later urban sociologists were to call primary or 'face-to-face' relationships, statistics as a mode of enquiry easily came into its own.[22]

It was because 'numbers' could be used not simply for the purpose of rhetoric but for purposes of disclosure—exposure in many cases is not too strong a word— that journalists as well as 'men of good will' were deeply concerned with statistics— the famous articles in the *Morning Chronicle* in 1849 and 1850, written in the aftermath of Chartism and in the alarming presence of cholera, provide the outstanding example[23]—or that novelists also used statistics when they presented social comment in fictional form during the 1840s. As Arnold Kettle has pointed out, they were often addressing 'the downright factual ignorance of the middle class'.[24] 'The facts— the facts are all in all; for they are facts', wrote the reviewer of Mrs Gaskell's *Mary Barton* in *Fraser's Magazine* in 1849.[25]

There were obvious difficulties when 'disclosure' was extended to 'analysis' and 'analysis' was related to 'action'. First, despite Mill's comment on Chadwick, there was a problem of knowledge. The statisticians were observers who often started their enquiries not only in ignorance of what facts they would find but also with different values from those of the people they were observing. At best, they were able to display the need for sympathy which Channing emphasized. At worst, they were handicapped by their lack of the kind of personal knowledge that Mrs Gaskell, for instance, possessed, whatever the social limitations which restricted her approach, of how working-class families thought and felt.

Henry Mayhew, who throughout his work deliberately interposed individual vignettes and statistics (many of his statistics related to people whom he was not directly describing—employers, customers, and clients), sometimes seemed to be trying to move one or two steps beyond the position of an observer. He took the trouble, for example, to provide written answers to queries he received from individuals mentioned in his surveys, and he was willing to hold public meetings. He also appeared freer from many of the stifling inhibitions and restraining 'value frames' which limited the social comment of most of his contemporaries. Yet even in Mayhew's case, as E. P. Thompson has remarked, it would be 'ludicrous' to suggest that he 'discovered Victorian poverty'. 'The poor had long before discovered themselves, and the *Northern Star* contained a part of their own testament.'[26] Their testament, moreover, necessarily had policy implications written into it which diverged from the policy implications of social statisticians like Chadwick.[27] The work of the statisticians was important, in Mayhew's opinion, in that it encouraged a questioning of untested middle-class assumptions and prejudices, and he complained bitterly, if a little too comprehensively, that 'economists, from Adam Smith down, have shown the same aversion to collect facts as mad dogs for the touch of water.'[28]

There was more, however, to the question of 'values' than this. Not every middle-class critic of society was impressed by statistical exposure or by the conclusions which statisticians were prone to reach about the viability of the 'social system' and its inherent possibilities for 'improvement'. The kind of people who turned for guidance to Thomas Carlyle, the prophet of his age, spurned statistics, as Ruskin was to spurn them. What could be more 'general' than the opening sentences of Carlyle's *Past and Present* (1843)—'England is full of wealth, of multifarious produce, of supply for human want in every kind' or Ruskin's remark in *Unto this Last* (1862) that 'our cities are a wilderness of spinning wheels . . . yet the people have not clothes . . . Our harbours are a forest of merchant ships, and the people die of hunger'? 'Where men formerly expended their energy on scholastic quibbles,' a writer in the *Edinburgh Review* complained during the late 1850s, 'they now compile statistics, evincing a mental disease, which may be termed the colliquative diarrhoea of the intellect, indicating a strong appetite and a weak digestion.'[29]

The preference for 'generality' was reinforced by the feeling, first that statistics was something of a 'fad', second that there could be more evasion and misrepresentation than disclosure in the work of statisticians, and third that individuals counted for more than 'averages'. 'It is astonishing', *Punch* wrote in 1848,[30] having regularly satirized such pursuits,

> what Statistics may be made to do by a judicious and artist-like grouping of the figures; for though they appear to begin with a limited application to one subject, there is no end to the mass of topics that may be dragged in collaterally on all sides. A few facts on mendicancy, introduced by one of the members [of the British Association for the Advancement of Science] became the cue for an elaborate calculation of how many meals had been given to Irish beggars in the last twenty years; and this was very near leading to a division of the meals into mouthfuls, with a table showing the number of teeth, subtracting the molars and taking out the canine, employed in the mastication of these twenty years' returns of meals.

There are innumerable satirical references to statistics in *Punch*, where the quality of life in London was a subject of frequent pictorial comment, but it was the novelist, in particular—and given the educational and social patterning of the time, perhaps the woman novelist even more than the rest—who made the most of the inadequacies of 'averages'. There appeared to be something misleading as well as arid in constructing systems of classification and statistical tables. One man's death was more 'real' than a statistic in a bill of mortality or what Mr Gradgrind called 'the laws which govern lives in the aggregate'. The preacher shared this same preoccupation with the individual (real-life even more than fictional) and the plot.

'We may choose to look at the masses in the gross, as subjects for statistics,' wrote Kingsley in 1849, 'and, of course, where possible [he went on characteristically], of profits.' Yet there was 'One above who knows every thirst and ache, and sorrow, and temptation of each slattern, and gin-drinker, and street boy. The day will come when He will require an account of these neglects of ours not in the gross.'[31] For Kingsley and those who thought like him, 'the Sanitary Idea' might depend for its ammunition on statistics relating to the unhealthy environment, but its force as a 'gospel' rested on an appeal to deeper forces within the individual, through the operations of the conscience, and, possibly unconsciously, through psychological pressures which the men of the nineteenth century did not understand. It is interesting to compare Elizabeth Barrett Browning with Kingsley when she wrote in her verse-novel, *Aurora Leigh* (1856),[32] the lines

> A red-haired child
> Sick in a fever, if you touch him once,
> Though but so little as with a finger-tip
> Will set you weeping; but a million sick . . .
> You could as soon weep for the rule of three
> Or compound fractions.

Ruskin went far beyond 'the Sanitary Idea' in his writings on political economy, drawing an explicit general distinction between questions of quality and quantity: it was not the sum of products but the quality of a people's happiness which constituted the wealth of the community, he argued. 'But taken as a whole,' he wrote, throwing statistics to the winds, 'I perceive that Manchester can produce no good art, and no good literature; it is falling off even in the quality of its cotton.'[33]

In any discussion of the approach of statisticians and the response of contemporaries to their methods and conclusions it is important to bear in mind that there were changes in statistical preoccupations from one part of the century to another. The earliest statistical surveys of city populations, some of which were based on questionnaires or what Kay-Shuttleworth called 'tabular queries', were already giving way in the late 1840s to less controversial analyses of more narrowly defined specific questions, with at least one precocious pre-Le Play essay on family budgets, pointing the way forward to new modes of enquiry.[34] By the 1850s and 1860s, substantial city surveys based on original exploration had been almost completely replaced by social-science essays concerned with secondary material: they were being debated by the members of the National Association for the Promotion of Social Science, founded in 1857,[35] with the aged Brougham, a link with Bentham, as first president, but they received far less widespread public attention from contemporaries than the surveys of ten to fifteen years before. The title of the Statistical Section of the British Association, which had been created in 1833, was changed to 'Statistical Science' in 1857 and in 1863 to 'Economic and Statistical Science', and the proportion of papers devoted to economics increased significantly. During the late nineteenth century, the social survey was to come into its own again, but by then some of the older provincial statistical societies had disappeared, the Royal Statistical Society had acquired its prestigious adjective (in 1875), and statisticians had developed an embryonic professional sense. 'We have learned', William Newmarch was once quoted as saying, 'that in all questions relating to human society . . . the only sound basis on which we can found doctrines . . . is not hypothetical deductions, however ingenious and subtle, but conclusions and reasoning, supported by the largest and most careful investigation of facts.'[36]

The middle years of the century belonged to the National Association for the Promotion of Social Science which, on its visit to Manchester in 1866, inspired the *Manchester Examiner and Times* to comment that 'the mass of miseries which afflict, disturb or torment mankind have their origin in preventable causes. They can be classified just as drugs are classified and they may be employed with almost the same certainty of operation. It is to social science that we are indebted for a knowledge of their character, and it is to its progress we must look for the amelioration of our home miseries.'[37] On the same occasion the *Manchester Guardian* noted how social science thrived in a city atmosphere just because of the multiplicity of urban problems. 'Nowhere are the social changes which are now in progress and which are viewed with hope or fear according to the temper of the observer, more manifest than among the teeming population of which this city is the centre and metropolis.'[38]

Characteristic of the new style of 'learned' paper in 'social science' was Dr William Ogle's fascinating piece on 'Marriage-Rates and Marriage-Ages with special reference to the Growth of Population', read before the Royal Statistical Society in 1890.[39] This paper, which neatly sets out a problem—why had the nineteenth-century marriage-rate fluctuated in 'a very irregular manner'?—first disposed of a fallacy propounded by, amongst others, J. S. Mill and Henry Fawcett, who had not bothered to give the actual figures on which their statements were based, that the marriage-rate varied inversely with the price of wheat. Second, it went on with the aid of graphs to correlate the marriage-rate with the value of exports per head of the population. Third, it explored the relationship between export data and the very patchy trade-union statistics relating to employment and unemployment. Fourth, it developed a fascinating theory on the basis of the statistical evidence, explaining why there were marked variations of marriage-rates in different registration counties (arguing that marriages were more numerous in those counties where women earned independent wages). Fifth, it looked at age and occupation structure. Sixth, it related historical evidence to anticipations of the future. The limitations of statistical method were noted, even if they were not fully or critically investigated. This kind of article needed ingenuity and skills of the highest order, far removed from Dickens's 'Simple Arithmetic', and Dr Ogle certainly could not be placed in the camp of those who saw 'figures and averages and nothing else'.

There is still much to sort out in relation to the detailed history of the use of statistics. As late as 1887 Wynnard Hooper, the writer on Statistics in the ninth edition of the *Encyclopaedia Britannica*,[40] had to devote much of his limited space to the dispute between those who believed that there was a science of statistics—with its own specific content—and those who believed that there was only a statistical method, a convenient aid to investigation in the majority of sciences. The former group was still of strategic significance—not surprisingly so, perhaps, when thinking in the natural sciences remained for the most part non-statistical. It had moved from political to social arithmetic, with some of its members following Maurice Block and anticipating Louis Chevalier in giving a new name to their branch of study—'demography'. The President of the Royal Statistical Society argued boldly and passionately at the jubilee meeting in 1885 that statistics was superior in method to social science or sociology and that it amounted to 'the science of human society in all its relations'. Statistics *was* sociology.[41]

Hooper was more cautious, as he had every right to be when the map of both natural and social sciences was changing as significantly as it was at that time. After noting—and how common a note it was becoming in so many areas of English life—that there had unfortunately so far been 'no attempt in England to deal with the subject . . . in a systematic way', though 'the practice of statistical inquiry of scope and method has been carried on in England with a high degree of success'—he refused to identify all sociology with statistics.

> The statistical method is essentially a mathematical procedure, attempting to give a quantitative expression to certain facts; and the resolution of differences of quality into differences of quantity has not yet been effected even in chemical science. In sociological science the importance of differences of quality is enormous, and the effect of these differences on the conclusions to be drawn from figures is sometimes neglected, or insufficiently recognized, even by men of unquestionable ability and good faith.

The term 'values' was not used in this context. 'Society is an aggregate', wrote Hooper, 'or rather a congeries of aggregates.' And he went on to draw an 'expert' conclusion, concerned solely with statistical techniques—a conclusion which was sharply different from that current in the statistical societies during the pioneer amateur phase of the 1830s and 40s before the rise of professionalism: 'the majority of politicians, social "reformers" and amateur hoarders of statistics generally were in the habit of drawing the conclusions that seem good to them from such figures as they may obtain, merely by treating as homogeneous and comparable qualities which are not comparable. Even to the conscientious and intelligent inquirer the difficulty of avoiding mistakes in using statistics prepared by other persons is very great.'[42]

This cautious conclusion, set out two years after Charles Booth had started his huge statistical enquiries by challenging Hyndman's simple, unsophisticated, and politically orientated figures of London poverty, should be set alongside Booth's ambition, far-reaching in scope, to prepare a detached and impartial presentation of the social situation through the use of statistics. 'A framework can be built out of a big theory and facts and statistics run in to fit it, but what I want to see instead is a large statistical framework which is built to receive accumulations of facts.'[43] Seebohm Rowntree likewise turned to statistics because they provided a less 'sentimental' foundation for policy recommendations than straight appeals to human feeling or to political prejudice.[44] It was Mrs Webb who wrote of Booth's study that 'prior to this enquiry, neither the individualist nor the Socialist could state with any approach to accuracy what exactly was the condition of the people of England. Hence the unreality of their controversy.'[45]

The problem of relating quantity to quality, which Booth never tried to baulk in the same way as he baulked most questions of theory, could be tackled, he said, 'given sociological imagination'. 'The statistical method was needed to give bearings to the results of personal observation and personal observation to give life to statistics ... It is this relative character, or the proportion of facts to each other, to us, to society at large, and to possible remedies, that must be introduced if they are to be of any value at all in social diagnosis. Both single facts, and strings of statistics *may* be true, and demonstrably true, and yet entirely misleading in the way they are used.'[46] Booth added to the list of questions for full quantitative examination those relating to poverty, seeking 'to connect poverty and well-being with conditions of employment'. And, in this attempt to connect, he was to query (like Rowntree later) and with the blessing of the great neo-classical political economist of late-Victorian England, Alfred Marshall, the non-quantitative basis of much of earlier nineteenth-century political economy. It was not only sociology that had to be statistical. Economics had to be statistical, too, as it had been for Porter earlier in the century and as it was at the time for Robert Giffen.[47]

However great the changes in mood and context, in one important respect Booth followed directly in tradition from writers of the 1830s and 1840s. He never concerned himself very much with the state. The city was still *the* place to study if you wished to understand society. 'It is not in country', he wrote in a famous passage,[48]

> but in town that 'terra incognita' needs to be written on our social map. In the country the machinery of human life is plainly to be seen and easily recognized: personal relations bind the whole together. The equipoise on which existing order rests, whether satisfactory or not, is palpable and evident. It is far otherwise with cities, where as to these questions we live in darkness, with doubting hearts and ignorant unnecessary fears, or place our trust with rather dangerous consequences in the teachings of empiric economic law.

Booth's own preferences—subjected to searching self-criticism and criticism— quickened the enquiry. London was a stage, not a laboratory: it had its drama, and the drama was perpetually interesting, as it was for Henry James who, while complaining of London's 'horrible numerosity', none the less concluded that it offered 'on the whole the most possible form of life'.[49] H. L. Smith, one of Booth's assistants, emphasized that among the attractions of London was 'the contagion of numbers' and that, taking into account all the problems of the city, it was 'the sense of something going on . . . the difference between the Mile End fair on a Saturday night, and a dark and muddy country lane' which drew the young in particular into the 'vortex'.[50] Number and quality were being related in a more sophisticated way. 'New York's the place for me,' Booth himself once wrote to his wife. 'There seems something subtle, an essence, pervading great metropolitan cities and altering everything so that life seems more lively, busier, larger, the individual less, the community more. I like it. It does me good. But I know it has another aspect and I am not surprised when people feel crushed by the wickedness of it, the ruthlessness, heartlessness of its grinding mill, as you did in Paris.'[51]

By the end of Queen Victoria's reign, very much in English life had been measured. The great official enquiries into environment at the beginning of the reign —in the name of 'the Sanitary Idea'—had their counterpart at the end of the reign in the great unofficial enquiries into poverty. In between, while the cities grew, as did the proportions of the population who were city-dwellers, the collection of many of the relevant statistics ceased to be a major exercise in difficult and uncharted social investigation and became, like so much else in Victorian life, an institutionalized routine with decennial census reports, annual medical officer of health reports, financial returns, and so on. There were still big gaps in relation to both economic statistics (including the statistics of employment) and cultural statistics, but there were now statistical experts who were taking over or seeking to take over previously debatable areas of policy and administration. From its inception in 1889 the London County Council appointed a full-time statistical officer to collect such data for the use of its various committees.[52] As for the dedicated non-experts, they were moving again from urban detail to more general schemes of social regeneration, to the nature of what Sir John Simon had called earlier in the century the 'underframework of society',[53] from issues related to municipal action within the particular city to national welfare policy which would iron out some of the differences between cities.

It is interesting in the light of this story that the writer on the history of statistical method in *The International Encyclopaedia of the Social Sciences* states that 'if we have to choose a date at which the modern theory of statistics began, we may put it, somewhat arbitrarily, at 1890.' Pointing to the work of F. Y. Edgeworth, Karl Pearson, Walter Weldon, and G. U. Yule, he notes also that this was the birth year of R. A. Fisher. 'Life was as mysterious as ever,' he goes on, 'but it was found to obey laws. Human society was seen as subject to statistical enquiry, as an evolutionary entity under human control.'[54] This realization, as we have seen, came earlier in studies of the city, but the refinements of statistical analysis came later. Full sophistication was a twentieth-century achievement.

Before turning briefly from what the Victorians themselves did or failed to do with their limited techniques and the quantitative evidence at their disposal to what we in the twentieth century can and should do with statistics in our interpretation of the past, it is important to make two basic points. The first concerns the rates of measurable change in relation to qualitative evidence offered by or available to the Victorians themselves. The second concerns the relationship between facts and theories centred specifically on the city, and facts and theories relating to the constitution and development of society as a whole.

On the first point, it is obvious from the history, particularly, of urban public health that the noisiest and most exciting periods of debate did not necessarily coincide with the periods of greatest demographic and social change. Because rates of measurable progress did not reflect the power of language or of argument, qualitative evidence by itself may often be misleading. The fierce debates in the 'age of Chadwick' did little to force down crude death-rates which did not fall substantially until the 1870s when, on the whole, questions of public health stirred contemporaries less. What William Farr, the statistical genius behind the mid-Victorian censuses, described as 'one of the most important series of facts relating to the life of a nation ever published' was the revelation that the annual mortality for all ages in the population had scarcely altered throughout the period 1838–71.[55] The infant mortality-rate, rightly considered in the twentieth century to be one of the critical indices of social control, remained more or less constant around 150 per thousand live births until the twentieth century.

Earlier historians of public health concentrated on the study of qualitative materials relating to 'the age of Chadwick'. Confronted with the mid-Victorian inability to bring down death-rates and infant mortality-rates, the social historian with quantitative interests may now seek to explain the statistics in one or all of four ways: (1) qualitatively by pointing to the fact that it was not until the 1870s that advances in bacteriology began to produce results and that the limitations of 'environmentalism' were overcome in an age of increasing concern for personal health and housing; (2) qualitatively by examining those changes in the economy, in the 'administrative system', and in society which distinguished late-Victorian from early-Victorian England and permitted effective 'amelioration'; (3) quantitatively by breaking down national aggregate-rates within short periods and examining, as best he can, the pattern of death-rates in particular places, for particular groups or for particular diseases; (4) counter-factually, as is now beginning to be common in the new quantitative economic history,[56] by seeking to analyse what would have happened if there had been no health legislation, local or national, during the 1840s and 1850s.

There is little doubt that in this field quantitatively based urban history enables us to know far more and to understand what we do know far more clearly and in greater depth than if we rely, as did whole generations of historians, on the colourful and rhetorical Victorian discussion of sanitary matters, from the propaganda of the Health of Towns Association to an article by the Bishop of Bedford on 'Urban Populations' in the *Fortnightly Review* of 1893 which did not give one single precise statistic.[57] It forces attention to local variations in the period from the 1830s to the 1870s, gives new interest to the late-Victorian years when rates actually did fall, and provides the basis for a not unfavourable assessment of the mid-Victorian achievement. 'Stable death rates', it has been argued, 'conceal a considerable victory; for by holding in check the powerful forces against health which swiftly growing population and rapid urban agglomeration naturally generated, the sanitary pioneers could congratulate themselves on a valuable, if negative achievement.'[58] Finally it leads to a new evaluation (but not to a dismissal) of the qualitative evidence itself. The early language of 'civic economics', the kind of language Chadwick talked naturally—and some of it was couched almost in terms of cost-benefit analysis[59]—gave way to the specialist language of doctors, engineers, and housing economists. At the same time, the fervour of the first novelists and poets when they took up 'the Sanitary Idea' disappears, and with it the sense of drama.

The second important point is related to the first. The local element in initiative for health improvement during the mid-Victorian years, which sometimes led to fierce battles between 'clean' and 'dirty' parties at the city level, changed in relative significance from 1870 onwards as the demand for a 'national' health policy gained in strength. Statistical information was a necessary, and, as time went by, an uncontroversial instrument in the reforms achieved through legislation and administration between 1869 and the foundation of the Ministry of Health at the end of the First World War. Indeed, it was through a detailed consideration of health statistics (along with statistics of education) that the balance between local and national action began to change. The significance of what was happening can be well illustrated also from a brilliant review of Seebohm Rowntree's *Poverty* by C. F. G. Masterman, who was to make his reputation as author of the Edwardian classic, *The Condition of England*. Masterman, who was a master of qualitative argument and a brilliant coiner of original phrases which still stick, was forced by Rowntree's bleak and ungarnished statistics on poverty in York to this conclusion. 'The social reformer, oppressed with the sense of the . . . poverty of London,' Masterman pointed out, 'is apt to turn with envy towards the ideal of some flourishing provincial town.' What better town than York, he might ask, an ancient community revitalized by the railway in recent Victorian history, a community contrasting in every way with the 'homogeneous matrix' and 'sheer immensity of the aggregation' of London? Would it not be desirable, he might go on, to break up the giant city of six millions into sixty cities of 100,000 each, 'not too large to cause congestion nor too small to prevent the intertwining of varied industries necessary for permanent stability'?

Such an approach, Masterman concluded, was quite wrong. Rowntree's demonstration that the proportion of primary poverty in York was the same as in Booth's London proportion was a devastating answer—'a thunder-clap', Masterman called it—to such social reformers. A national policy was needed to tackle poverty, not a series of local urban expedients, however enlightened. From this angle Masterman found Rowntree's detailed statistical work far more persuasive than Booth's, for at the end of reading Booth's 'nine bulky volumes, mazes of statistics ordered and classified, maps of picturesque bewilderment of colour, infinite detail of streets and houses and family lives' what was left was 'a general impression . . . of something monstrous, grotesque, inane: something beyond the power of individual synthesis; a chaos resisting all attempts to reduce it to orderly law.'[60] Rowntree's 'definite and limited material' was manageable enough and comprehensible enough to guide policy —and, we can add in retrospect, to guide it towards the peculiarly English twentieth-century balance between the urban and the national.

There are more than administrative implications to this second important point. It is easy for writers on the Victorian city or for that matter on Victorian urbanization to concentrate so much on the city or on what happened in all cities that they forget that urbanization is a 'societal' process which not only precedes the formation of particular cities but also shapes their role as agencies in a developing society.[61] Quantitative analysts have rightly pointed to other implications of this, relating changes in cities to changes in the countryside—this was beginning to be a favourite late-Victorian theme, very dear, it may be noted, to Rowntree—or to the map of world trade. They have also qualified conceptions of urban causality by looking more closely at the components of class behaviour and at the logic of industrialization.[62] In this context, it is not strange that studies which begin with the Victorian city end with the twentieth-century state. Quantitative investigation—concerning rates of change and differentials between cities, about the balance between urban and national finance, and about shifts in politics and communications—is a necessary element in the approach to a fuller understanding of this range of issues which cannot easily be grasped in terms of qualitative evidence or argument taken by itself.

Any account of the Victorians' approach to statistics and the way in which they handled quantitative evidence must be qualified and supplemented in the light of recent historical scholarship. Yet the wisest of the Victorians themselves knew that their evidence was in places incomplete and in other places defective. Some of them even anticipated recent social scientists who have argued that 'both quality and quantity are misconceived when they are taken to be antithetical or even alternative. Quantities are *of* qualities and a measured quality has just the magnitude expressed in its measure.'[63] In Britain, as in France, current research, in Louis Chevalier's words, is 'a continuation of earlier interpretative efforts which have gone on as long as urbanization itself'.

Different kinds of quantitative enquiry are being carried out in Britain at the present time, though perhaps less ambitiously than in several other countries. First, historical demographers are relating data about birthplace and migration to occupational data, family size, and varieties of environment within the same urban community, with W. A. Armstrong, for example, using enumerators' books for nineteenth-century censuses to explore urban social structure through 'still glimpses of a moving picture'. Following in the footsteps of Rowntree in exploring York, he is explicitly concerned not with the social pathology of the city—the subject which has always captured most attention, qualitative and quantitative—but with 'normal' communities and classes. He is also interested in the relationship at the family base between experience in Victorian urban society and what had gone before.[64]

Second, H. J. Dyos, with the assistance of computers, is seeking to define and explain the social changes which occurred in the making of Camberwell, a suburb of Victorian London. His interest is not in 'still glimpses' but in processes—'how particular neighbourhoods came to be occupied, held, or vacated by different social classes, and just what kinds of communities these were in terms of the structure of families and households'—and he suggests cautiously that 'quantitative techniques can give precision to history, but they do not seem capable of formulating new hypotheses, much less of bringing to it objectivity.'[65]

Third, J. R. Kellett, who has made the most of urban railway statistics, has, in fact, advanced new hypotheses as a result of his detailed studies, pointing out on the way how the techniques of enquiry into the social effects of railway building on the urban way of life became far more sophisticated by the beginning of the twentieth century than they had been during the 1840s. His study is useful also in underlining that even in twentieth-century cost-benefit studies 'the most adequate and detailed statistical analysis tends to become only one of several factors moulding final decisions.'[66]

Fourth, in relation to political decision-making in nineteenth-century cities, where studies of city 'personalities' and attempts at 'city biography' have hitherto dominated a largely underdeveloped field, J. R. Vincent has directed attention to the analysis of poll-book material, making generalizations on the way about political statistics and the political motivation which lies behind them. A number of other writers have collected statistics about the social composition of town councils— here, as in occupational studies, there are very real difficulties in categorization—in an effort to relate leadership to class and occupational structure.[67] Other studies have focused on minority groups and sub-cultures. So far, however, it is obvious that the note of caution sounded by H. J. Dyos is particularly necessary in any consideration of 'the behavioural aspects of urban communities', and L. F. Schnore has even argued that quantitative studies are 'practically impossible'. 'We shall have to continue depending', he concludes, 'upon impressionistic accounts concerning the attitudes and values of our urban forebears.'[68]

Finally, on one subject where quantitative approaches seem possible and inevitable, very little statistical work has been carried out on local finance, where there are complicated issues centring on rateable values and annual rates in the pound (there were for long, of course, whole clusters of urban rates) and the relation of rating statistics to land values, building, and economic activity. What work has been started points to the difficulty of making even simple comparisons.

How far is it feasible to go beyond all these individual studies and produce a Victorian counterpart for the useful study of C. A. Moser and W. Scott, *British Towns: A statistical study of their social and economic differences* (1961)? In *Victorian Cities* I suggested that 'a whole Victorian urban typology could be constructed on these lines.' In pursuing the matter a little further—and some historians should pursue it a lot further—it is useful to start with Moser and Scott's conclusion about 'the striking diversity' of the 157 English towns with a population of more than 50,000 in the middle of the twentieth century. Some are more or less self-contained towns with rural districts at their limits: others are grouped together, with no obvious boundaries, in the tangle of conurbations. 'Between the extremes . . . lie every variety of urban species both simple and complex' so that 'no single formula can describe them all.' The statistical diversity even after decades of national social policy-making was extremely striking: one household in five in Gateshead lived in overcrowded conditions, for example, as against one in sixty in Coulsdon: infant mortality-rates in Rochdale were three times as high as in Merton and Morden.

Moser and Scott followed eight main lines of statistical enquiry—into population size and structure; demographic change over twenty years; households and housing; economic characteristics; social class; voting; health; and education. What they left out was just as interesting as what they put in—local government finance, on the grounds that it 'needed more detailed treatment' than they 'had time to give'; employment statistics, on the grounds that these were collected from different units; all cultural data, because the statistics were too patchy; all information on crime, religion, and 'the physical characteristics of the town and its amenities'.[69] Given the superiority of twentieth-century statistical sources over those of the nineteenth century, the omissions look discouraging to the historian.

Indeed, the historian of Victorian cities, fascinated as he would be by the diversity of his communities—there were twenty-one of them (plus London) in 1901—would not be happy on historical grounds about most of these exclusions or with the authors' statement that while 'the change of population between 1931 and 1951 is, on the whole, an inadequate index of the age of a town' they did not feel that they could delve further back into history. As a minimum he would wish to introduce chronological tables setting out the timetables of change in different cities as far, at least, as the creation of new institutions or activities was concerned, and more ambitiously he would want to go on to relate classificatory systems to urban 'profiles' or 'images'.[70] He could, none the less, experiment happily with schemes of urban classification both in terms of Moser and Scott's list of primary variables, and, if he had the skill, with component analysis.

It is apparent at the outset that there are fascinating contrasts of experience between the nineteenth and twentieth centuries, with no Victorian town ever containing, as Worthing did in the period covered by Moser and Scott, 58·8 percent of its population over the age of sixty-five. Bradford, for instance, never had more than 4 percent at any census between 1841 and 1901, while the town with the lowest proportion in Moser and Scott's account—Dagenham—had 4·9 percent in 1951. Middlesbrough had 36 percent of its population below the age of fifteen in 1841 and 1901, a significantly higher figure than the English town with the highest 1951 figure—31·1 percent—Huyton-with-Ruby. Bradford had as high a figure as 45 percent in 1841. The male/female ratio is also particularly interesting to compare. Middlesbrough, with more males than females both in 1851 and 1901, stood out in this connection as much as in its remarkable statistics of growth, a matter of civic rhetoric and one of the topics covered qualitatively in my *Victorian Cities*. It was, in fact, described in 1885 by the statistician E. G. Ravenstein as a town which by 'its rapid growth, the heterogeneous composition of its population, and the preponderance of the male sex, recalls features generally credited only to the towns of the American west.'[71] Statistical series of many of Moser and Scott's social indicators are missing for the nineteenth century, but far more can be done with the nineteenth-century 'mix' of the population and the relationship between 'native' and 'extraneous' elements than they have tried to do. There would be value, too, through econometric and other network studies in relating recent urban experience to that of the nineteenth century. Of Moser and Scott's urban groups 1, 2, and 3 in 1951—mainly resorts, administrative, and commercial towns—five out of thirty-seven were already towns of over 50,000 in 1851 and thirteen in 1901; whereas of their groups 4, 5, 6, 7 and 8—mainly industrial towns—sixteen out of sixty-seven were in the 1851 list and forty-seven in that of 1901. Of the fifty-one towns in their groups 9, 10, 11, 12, 13 and 14—suburbs and suburban-type towns—there were no towns in the 1851 list and only seven in 1901.

Much of the history of Victorian urbanization can be studied in such terms, although full explanations of historical change depend on relating statistics to evidence of a qualitative kind derived from impressions of particular places as seen by inhabitants, visitors and 'experts'. Such evidence must be accumulated from a wide variety of sources, local and national. No urban history can afford to neglect the 'sense of place' which must be a main theme of all studies of Victorian cities, or fail to consider the distinctive and the 'unusual' as well as the general and the commonplace. It was Henry James, writing of London, who commented aptly that 'when a social product is so vast and various, it may be approached on a thousand different sides, and liked and disliked for a thousand different reasons.'[72] All such visions illuminate the city as it actually is or was. In the famous third chapter of Macaulay's *History of England* (1848), the historian drew an unforgettable picture of seventeenth-century London which relied heavily, through contrast, on the character of mid-Victorian London. 'The town did not, as now, fade by imperceptible degrees into the country. No long avenues of villas, embowered in lilacs and laburnums, extended from the great centre of wealth and civilization almost to the boundaries of Middlesex and far into the heart of Kent and Surrey.' By the middle of the nineteenth century 'the fireside, the nursery, the social table' were no longer in the City of London: 'the chiefs of the mercantile interest are no longer citizens.' The use of space had changed. 'He who then rambled to what is now the gayest and most crowded part of Regent Street found himself in a solitude, and was sometimes so fortunate as to have shot at a woodcock.' Relations had changed, too, along with the ecology. Unimproved London was less socially segregated: 'In Covent Garden a filthy and noisy market was held close to the dwellings of the great.' At the same time, there was a more absolute difference between the metropolitan and the Londoner. 'A Cockney in a rural village was stared at as much as if he had intruded into a Kraal of the Hottentots. On the other hand when the Lord of a Lincolnshire or Shropshire manor appeared in Fleet

Street, he was as easily distinguished from the resident population as a Turk or a Lascar.'

Macaulay had little to say about statistics—far less, for instance, than Mayhew, writing soon afterwards, or Henry Buckle—yet his picture holds and illuminates. He set out less to explain or to interpret than to describe and to evoke. Quantitative approaches to social history do not destroy the value of this kind of writing. What they do, indeed, is to sharpen the appeal of the artist's vision, enabling us to relate special experience or special ways of viewing common experience to common experience itself.

## Notes

1   See, for example, R. W. Rawson, 'An Enquiry into the Statistics of Crime in England and Wales', *Journal of the Statistical Society of London (JSS)*, ii (1839–40), 316–45, and J. Fletcher, 'Moral and Educational Statistics of England and Wales', ibid., xii (1847), 151–76.

2   The address is printed in Charles Kingsley, *Sanitary and Social Lectures and Essays* (1880), pp. 187–222.

3   *Victorian Cities* (1963), pp. 57–8.

4   'My satire is against those who see figures and averages, and nothing else . . . the addled heads who would . . . comfort the labourer in travelling twelve miles a day to and from his work, by telling him that the average distance of one inhabited place from another in the whole area of England, is not more than four miles.'
    From a letter to Charles Knight, 30 January 1855, quoted in the Norton Critical Edition of *Hard Times*, ed. George Ford and Sylvère Monod (1966), p. 277.
    Dickens admired H. T. Buckle's *History of Civilization in England* (2 vols, 1857–61) with its statistical preoccupations.

5   His letter of 16 December 1845 is quoted in H. S. Tremenheere, *I Was There: Memoirs*, ed. E. L. and O. P. Edmonds (1965), p. 54.

6   Harold Perkin, *The Origins of Modern English Society 1780–1880* (1969), p. 326.

7   J. C. Lettsom, *Medical Memoirs of the General Dispensary in London* (1774), p. x.

8   See M. W. Flinn's admirable introduction to his recent edition of *Report on The Sanitary Condition of the Labouring Population of Great Britain, 1842*, by Edwin Chadwick (1965), pp. 21 ff.

9   M. Blaug, *Ricardian Economics* (1958), pp. 182–3. See also J. A. Schumpeter, *History of Economic Analysis* (1954), p. 524.

10  Review of *An Address Explanatory of the Objects and Advantages of Statistical Enquiries* by J. E. Portlock, F.R.S., *JSS*, i (1838–9), 317.

11  See [James Bonar and Henry W. Macrosty], *Annals of the Royal Statistical Society, 1834–1934* (1934), p. 22. The first meeting, in the convening of which the Rev. T. R. Malthus played a leading part, took place on 15 March 1834.

12  Its story is well told in T. S. Ashton, *Economic and Social Investigations in Manchester, 1833–1933* (1934).

13  W. R. Greg (1809–81) critically reviewed *Mary Barton* in the *Edinburgh Review* in April 1849 (lxxxix, 402–35) as being unfair to the mill-owners. Mrs Gaskell in

her preface had stated that she was concerned to show how things *seemed* to the poor. See A. Pollard, *Mrs Gaskell, Novelist and Biographer* (1965), pp. 59–60, and E. Wright, *Mrs Gaskell* (1965), pp. 231–2.

14  *Report of Committee of the Manchester Statistical Society on the State of Education in the Borough of Manchester, in 1834* (1835). The Committee comprised seventeen men, and the main object of the report was to show that Parliament had underestimated the number of schools in Manchester. A second edition containing 'a more minute classification' appeared in the same year.

15  Quoted in Ashton, op. cit., p. 13.

16  See 'Provincial Statistical Societies in the United Kingdom', *JSS*, i (1838–9), 48–50, 115–17; ii (1839–40), 132–3.

17  See also B. Kirkman Gray, *Philanthropy and the State, or Social Politics* (1908), Appendix to ch. 2: 'The Origin of the Royal Statistical Society'.

18  See A. Newsholme, *The Elements of Vital Statistics* (1889), pp. 111–12.

19  MS. draft, June 1845, quoted in R. A. Lewis, *Edwin Chadwick and the Public Health Movement 1832–54* (1952), p. 12.

20  Quoted in Lewis, op. cit., p. 15.

21  William E. Channing, *A Discourse on the Life and Character of the Rev. Joseph Tuckerman, D.D.* (Boston, 1841), p. 4. For Dickens's view of Channing, see *American Notes* (1842), ch. 3.

22  For the classic statement, widely reprinted, of urban sociology in terms of numbers and relationships, see Louis Wirth, 'Urbanism as a Way of Life', in *American Journal of Sociology*, xliv (1938), 1–24, and its critique by R. N. Morris, *Urban Sociology* (1968). See also R. E. Park, E. W. Burgess and R. D. McKenzie, *The City* (1925).

23  The first *Morning Chronicle* article by Mayhew on what was later incorporated in his *London Labour and the London Poor* (1861–2) appeared in October 1849.

24  Arnold Kettle, 'The Early Victorian Social Problem Novel', in Boris Ford, ed., *The Pelican Guide to English Literature*, vi. *The Nineteenth Century* (1958), p. 171. For the novel as a favourite form of social commentary during the 1840s, see Kathleen Tillotson, *Novels of the Eighteen-Forties* (1954).

25  *Fraser's Magazine*, xxxix (1849), 430.

26  E. P. Thompson, 'The Political Education of Henry Mayhew', *Victorian Studies*, xi, no. 1 (September 1967), 43–62.

27  For Chartist attacks on Chadwick, see, for example, *Charter*, 28 April and 23 June 1839. Yet in 1848 Chadwick wrote to the Bishop of London that he did not see 'how any one could get up in the Commons and contend that where there was a heavy infantile slaughter, or where the working classes are ravaged by epidemics, there shall be no intervention except on the initiation of the middle classes.' (Quoted in Lewis, op. cit., p. 170.)

28  Henry Mayhew, *Answers*, July 1851, quoted in Thompson, loc. cit., p. 56.

29  Quoted in Ashton, op. cit., p. 51.

30  *Punch*, xv (1848), 92: it added, more succinctly, a misquotation of Pope's line from his 'Epistle to Dr Arbuthnot': 'They lisped in numbers, for the numbers came.'

31  *Charles Kingsley. His letters and memories of his life*, edited by his wife (1892 edn), p. 88. Compare the speech by Dickens with that of Lord Carlisle at a Festival of the Metropolitan Sanitary Association in 1851 as described in the *Illustrated London News*, 7 May 1851: K. J. Fielding, ed., *The Speeches of Charles Dickens* (1960), pp. 127–32;

the occasion is briefly described in Humphry House, *The Dickens World* (1942 edn), pp. 195–6. See also the account of the implications of Tom-all-Alone's 'filth and slime', with its retribution theme, in *Bleak House* (1853).

32  Book II.

33  John Ruskin, *Fors Clavigera*, Library edn, xxix (1905), p. 224.

34  Henry Ashworth, 'Statistics of the Present Depression of Trade at Bolton', *JSS*, iv-v (1842-3), 74–81. See also T. C. Barker, D. J. Oddy and J. Yudkin, *The Dietary Surveys of Dr. Edward Smith, 1862–3* (1970).

35  See Brian Rodgers, 'The Social Science Association, 1857–1886', *Manchester School of Economics & Social Studies*, xx, no. 3 (September 1952), 283–310.

36  Frederic J. Mouat, 'History of the Statistical Society of London', *JRSS*, Jubilee vol. (1885), 50.

37  *Manchester Examiner and Times*, 5 October 1866.

38  *Manchester Guardian*, 1 October 1866.

39  *JRSS*, liii (1890), 253–80.

40  Vol. XXII, pp. 461–6.

41  Sir Rawson W. Rawson, *JRSS*, Jubilee vol. (1885), 8–10.

42  *Encyclopaedia Britannica*, loc. cit.

43  Quoted in T. S. Simey and M. B. Simey, *Charles Booth, Social Scientist* (1960), p. 77.

44  B. Seebohm Rowntree, *Poverty, A Study of Town Life* (1901), pp. 133–4. For the method and its implications, see Asa Briggs, *Social Thought and Social Action: A study of the work of Seebohm Rowntree* (1961), ch. 2.

45  Beatrice Webb, *My Apprenticeship* (1926), p. 216.

46  T. S. Simey and M. B. Simey, op. cit., p. 78.

47  T. W. Hutchison, *Review of Economic Doctrines, 1870–1929* (1953), p. 426. See also Alfred Marshall, *Principles of Economics* (1920 edn), p. 492: 'No doubt statistics can be easily misinterpreted, and are often very misleading when first applied to new problems. But many of the worst fallacies involved in the misapplications of statistics are definite and can be definitely exposed, till at last no-one ventures to repeat them even when addressing an uninterested audience.'

48  Charles Booth, *Life and Labour of the People in London*, 2nd series: *Industry* (1903), I, p. 18.

49  *The Notebooks of Henry James*, ed. F. O. Matthiessen and Kenneth B. Murdock (New York, 1961), pp. 27–8. He wrote this in a Boston hotel in 1881.

50  H. Llewellyn Smith, 'Influx of Population', in Charles Booth, ed., *Life and Labour of the People in London* (1892), III, p. 75. There is something of the same sense in Ruskin's *Praeterita* (1886).

51  T. S. Simey and M. B. Simey, op. cit., p. 80.

52  See *London Statistics*, 1889 onwards.

53  *City Reports* (1849), pp. 44–57, quoted in Royston Lambert, *Sir John Simon* (1963), p. 150.

54  M. G. Kendall, 'The History of Statistical Method', in *The International Encyclopaedia of the Social Sciences* (1968 edn), XV, p. 227.

55  That for males was 23·3 per 1,000 for 1838–54 and precisely the same for the whole period 1838–71, and for females 21·6 and 21·5, respectively. See William Farr, *Vital Statistics* (1885), p. 183.

56  See R. W. Fogel, 'The New Economic History, its Findings and Methods',

*Economic History Review*, 2nd series, xix (1966), 642–56. See also D. K. Rowney and J. Q. Graham, eds, *Quantitative History* (1969).

57  *Fortnightly Review*, liii, new series (1893), 388–93.

58  Lambert, op. cit., p. 602.

59  See, for example, Morpeth's speech in the debate on the Public Health Act of 1848 in Hansard, xcvi, cols 385–428, and Asa Briggs, *Public Opinion and Public Health in the Age of Chadwick* (Chadwick Trust, 1946).

60  C. F. G. Masterman, 'The Social Abyss', *Contemporary Review*, lxxi (January 1902), 23–35.

61  See Eric E. Lampard, 'Historical Aspects of Urbanization', in Philip M. Hauser and Leo F. Schnore, eds, *The Study of Urbanization* (1965), pp. 519–54.

62  A. Kaplan, 'Measurement in Behavioral Science' from *The Conduct of Inquiry* (1964), reprinted in M. Brodbeck, ed., *Readings in the Philosophy of the Social Sciences* (1968), pp. 601–8.

63  Louis Chevalier, *Classes laborieuses et classes dangereuses à Paris pendant la première moitié du xix$^e$ siècle* (1958). See also his article 'A Reactionary View of Urban History' in *The Times Literary Supplement*, 8 September 1966.

64  See W. A. Armstrong, 'Social Structure from the Early Census Returns', in E. A. Wrigley, ed., *An Introduction to English Historical Demography* (1966), pp. 209–38, and 'The Interpretation of the Census Enumerators' Books for Victorian Towns', in H. J. Dyos, ed., *The Study of Urban History* (1968), pp. 67–85.

65  H. J. Dyos and A. B. M. Baker, 'The Possibilities of Computerising Census Data', in ibid., pp. 87–112. See also H. J. Dyos, *Victorian Suburb: A study of the growth of Camberwell* (1961).

66  J. R. Kellett, *The Impact of Railways on Victorian Cities* (1969). See also A. R. Prest and R. Turvey, 'Cost Benefit Analysis, A Survey', *Economic Journal*, lxxv (1965), 683–735.

67  J. R. Vincent, *Poll Books: how Victorians voted* (1967); E. P. Hennock, 'The Social Composition of Borough Councils in Two Large Cities,' in H. J. Dyos, ed., *The Study of Urban History*, pp. 315–37.

68  Leo F. Schnore, 'Problems of Quantitative Study', in ibid., pp. 189–208.

69  C. A. Moser and W. Scott, *British Towns: A statistical study of their social and economic differences* (1961), p. 8.

70  See A. L. Strauss, *The American City: A source book of urban imagery* (1968); Kevin Lynch, *The Image of the City* (1960).

71  See Asa Briggs, 'The Sense of Place' in Smithsonian Annual, II, *The Fitness of Man's Environment* (1968), pp. 77–99.

72  Henry James, *English Hours* (1963 edn), p. 10. The article first appeared in 1888.

# 4    The Contagion of Numbers

## J. A. Banks

Between 1841 and 1901 the population of England and Wales more than doubled, rising from 15,914,148 to 32,527,843 persons.[1] Inevitably this growth was not distributed evenly throughout the country. By 1841 the agricultural and industrial changes of the previous century had already made their impact on the social life of the people in the form of a great expansion of town dwelling, yet over half the population still lived in what for convenience may be loosely termed 'rural' as compared with 'urban' districts. By 1901 this proportion had fallen to about one-fifth, and it has remained more or less at this level ever since.[2] The last fifty years or so of the nineteenth century, that is to say, saw the consolidation of a process of urbanization in what had been at the beginning of the century an agrarian society. Towns of over 100,000 inhabitants increased from six in 1841 to thirty in 1901—only London had been so large in 1801. Towns of 50,000 to 100,000 inhabitants, of which there had been five in 1801, increased from twenty-two in 1841 to forty-nine in 1901.[3] Many rural areas, whole counties even, became depopulated in the sense that by 1901 their populations were smaller than they had been in 1851.[4] A simple graph or histogram showing the expansion of urbanism should, therefore, be interpreted as indicating rather more than a mere change in the proportions living in urban as opposed to rural districts.[5] Behind the steady advance of the town lies a history of movement into and out of the countryside, although with the balance always in favour of urban growth.[6]

To the Victorians this pattern of rural-urban migration and the accompanying growth of town life was probably more obvious in England and Wales than might have been the case had the island been geographically much larger. A journey across

105

the north of England from Liverpool to Leeds, for example, could pass through two other major cities, Manchester and Sheffield, and not one of these is more than forty miles from the next. Sheffield, moreover, is at the northern end of another such journey, less than forty miles from Nottingham, which is less than fifty miles from Birmingham. Of course, all these towns were large for their time in 1801, having more than 20,000 inhabitants, but by 1901 even the laggard amongst them was over six times as big. In such a relatively small total area the growth of population rapidly made the English a nation of townspeople. The Victorians, indeed, created a new civilization 'so thoroughly of the town' that it has been said to be the first of its kind in human history.[7] The task of this chapter is to attempt an analysis of what this notion of such a civilization entails, especially as a sociologist sees it in its demographic aspects, with particular emphasis on the patterns of migration.

The differences in the quality of town life as contrasted with that of the countryside have often been attributed to population growth and the increase in density. The movement into the towns in the nineteenth century inevitably meant that more people lived in the same space. Thus London, always in the vanguard, already housed 20·9 persons to the acre in 1801, but even London doubled this number over the hundred years. 112 other towns with populations of 4,000 persons and over in 1801 had increased their densities from 12·5 to 22·9 to the acre by 1891. 170 towns of from 2,000 to 3,999 inhabitants in 1801 increased from 5·8 to 13·5 over the same period, while 224 towns of from 1,000 to 1,999 inhabitants increased from 3·0 to 10·6.[8] A growth in size was accompanied by an increase in density—and such figures have regularly been interpreted by social historians as the background cause to much of the misery, squalor, and vice which were found in the Victorian cities at this time. Thus Kitson Clark has written of them that they were 'singularly ill prepared' to receive the millions who went into them.[9]

> Suitable housing did not exist and the additional numbers were crammed into every nook and cranny from attic to cellar of old decaying property, or into cottages run up hastily in confined spaces with little or no access to light and air . . . Water and sanitation were often not provided at all, and where they were provided there was often a judicious mingling of cesspools and wells with an occasional overstocked graveyard or active slaughter house to add to the richness of the mixture . . . Since many industrial processes now needed coal furnaces, and by this time probably most domestic fires burned coal, from many towns, particularly in winter, a heavy sulphurous smoke cloud was emitted to combine with other atmospheric conditions to make the fogs which were such a feature of Victorian England, and which probably slew their thousands.
>
> Such conditions were not new, nor probably were they inherently worse than what had existed before . . . But as numbers increased so these

evils increased in the area they affected, and probably certain factors in them, as for instance, the problems of the provision of water and the disposal of sewage, came to be less manageable and more pregnant with danger.

Or again, Ashworth has put the beginning of town-planning in Britain into the context of growing public recognition, or at least middle-class recognition, that the towns of the 1840s constituted a social problem of considerable magnitude.[10]

> Even if he were not his brother's keeper every man of property was affected by the multiplication of thieves; everyone who valued his life felt it desirable not to have a mass of carriers of virulent diseases too close at hand . . . It was morality (or, more exactly, criminality) and disease that were causing concern. Overcrowding and congestion, poverty, crime, ill health and heavy mortality were shown to be conditions commonly found together . . . there was nothing new in the existence of congested criminal quarters. In this as in other matters it was the changed scale of things that gave to an old problem the appearance of something new.

The growing density of the population in the cities produced acute over-crowding which in its turn was the cause of social evils, growing awareness of which led to the rudiments of a Welfare State.[11]

The implication of such quotations and of the argument underlying them is that the quality of mid-nineteenth-century urban living was as a matter of fact inferior to that of earlier periods, and even, perhaps, inferior to that of the areas from which the migrants to the towns had come. The impact of urbanization on these people, indeed, has been summed up[12] as a

> grave social damage. A family dwelling in an industrial town found itself not only divorced from nature and from the particular place of its origin, but cut off from other families. To isolation were added serious stresses within the family. Not all its members were engaged, as formerly, as a group, doing essential farming tasks, and sharing the benefits on the basis of a family communism administered by the senior members. Instead, the members of the family might well be employed in different occupations, with a premium placed by the wages system upon youth and vigour, so that the rights and authority by which the older generation traditionally maintained their status and self-respect into old age were impaired or destroyed. The new mobility made possible by the railway operated to disperse families as their more enterprising members sought new opportunities. Many of these became lodgers in the houses of others, or servants living in dingy conditions in the lesser middle-class families. So there developed an element of the population with a kind of sub-status, neither heads of families nor true members. Others of the unassimilated were the growing

hordes of homeless children, the street-arabs who became a kind of nomad class in the heart of the great cities.

Thus, although it may be legitimately concluded, with Hobsbawm, that in recent years the 'pessimistic' and the 'optimistic' schools have become overshadowed by 'agnostics' in the long-continued debate over the impact of the Industrial Revolution on the level of living of the working class at this time,[13] a residue of this controversy has been the assumption that the 'deprivations', if not definitely economic, were harmful in their influence on the 'personality'.[14] This assumption will not be considered in quite this form here, largely because of the difficulty of deciding how to deal with such an elusive concept when the reference is to large numbers of people over a generation or so. What will be challenged, nevertheless, is the view that the people concerned *felt* the hardships of town life so acutely, as compared with life in the countryside. The sociologist is bound to ask why it was that people continued to move into towns if conditions there were so manifestly worse than elsewhere. Undoubtedly it was the case that some of the worst urban areas were inhabited by the Irish, and it was also true that Irish vagrants constituted a large proportion of those figures of the migrant unemployed which Hobsbawm has used with such telling effect in his presentation of the anti-optimistic point of view;[15] but the further interesting fact about the Irish was their preference for an urban rather than for a rural alternative to the life they had left behind them in their country of origin. In the United States, for example, where throughout the nineteenth century and especially after the Homestead Act of 1862 a policy was deliberately fostered to make it easy for immigrants to settle on the land,[16] the Irish were notorious for remaining in the commercial and manufacturing centres, and it has been estimated that although some 80 percent of the Irish immigrants were of rural origin, no more than about 6 percent in all settled permanently on the land in that country. No doubt, as Mac-Donagh has pointed out, most emigrants from Ireland, during the period of the famines at least, were cottiers or squatters accustomed to living in close communities rather than in rural isolation.[17] Nevertheless it would be hazardous to claim that the concentration of Irish in the urban areas of England and Wales was a simple consequence of their failure to find work on the land at some distance from the cities, although it is true that the decline in agricultural employment could have made settlement on the land extremely difficult for those Irishmen who would have preferred to live in the countryside.

The alternative, therefore, must be to explore the possibility that the movement into the towns was a direct response to some feature of town life which was attractive to the rural population of the nineteenth century. Economic opportunities, clearly, there must have been, since the Industrial Revolution was an urban rather than a rural phenomenon; but such opportunities should not be interpreted as implying that the economic state of the rural areas was necessarily consistently worse than that of the urban and hence drove people into the towns in search of work. One assessment of migration patterns in Victorian England has concluded that 'both in

North and South the rise and fall in the movement of population from the rural areas had little to do with agricultural prosperity and depression',[18] although there is other evidence that emigration abroad was related to long-term economic decline in the rural areas of Cornwall and Gloucestershire.[19] A sociologist might thereupon suggest that some attempt should be made to examine the quality of town life to determine whether it was superior to that in the countryside, not so much perhaps in terms of material levels as in terms of those social relations, which in this context the eminent French sociologist, Émile Durkheim, called in 1893, a 'dynamic or moral density' (*densité dynamique ou morale*). Indeed, one implication of this position is that it would tend to make the series of changes which we call the Industrial Revolution a result of urbanization, in the sense that the rate of growth of industry, as well as its initial establishment in the towns, would seem to be dependent upon the social attractiveness of town life. Stripped of its other nuances, this was essentially Durkheim's claim. Eager to refute the assumption of his day that the division of labour was the driving force behind social change, he put forward a sociological plea for considering 'moral' density to be intimately connected with physical density (*densité matérielle*), each influencing the other and both responsible for the growth of specialization and the division of labour in society. In a series of deductions from the assumption that individuals possess a need for as intimate a social contact with one another as they can find, he demonstrated that a denser population increases the possibility of greater intimacy and also makes possible a diversification of interests and functions in social life. The outcome is that such diversification, as a matter of fact, occurs in the form of economic, political, and social specialization.[20]

Empirical justification for this point of view, is, to be sure, very difficult to obtain except in a very broad sense. Thus, although the Registrar-General's 'dictionary' of occupations is not altogether a reliable guide, because of variations in linguistic usage in different parts of the country at different times, it is the best guide we have, and it identified about 15,000 distinct occupations in 1901 as compared with only 7,000 in 1851.[21] The population had doubled and the number of occupations had more than doubled in fifty years. The overwhelming number of new occupations, it can be safely assumed, were urban occupations, and urban densities had grown much faster than rural densities,[22] some of which had certainly declined. Such figures, taken together, suggest that there is at least a tenuous relationship between specialization and density, although of themselves they do not indicate which is the cause and which is the effect. In any case there is no hint here of any measure of that elusive concept, '*densité morale*'. Durkheim, indeed, spent the rest of his professional life wrestling unsuccessfully with the attempt to get a clearer understanding of what is implied in the idea and others like it,[23] and, it must be admitted, sociologists and social anthropologists studying urban-rural phenomena have added little to what he achieved. But, for all that, there appears to exist a general consensus amongst them that the urban and the rural differ in important respects in the nature of the social relationships which they display.[24]

Durkheim's *Division of Labour in Society* is perhaps best understood in the present context as a contribution to a discussion of social relationships in terms of what has been called 'unquestionably the most distinctive development in nineteenth-century social thought, a development that extends well beyond sociological theory to such areas as philosophy, history and theology to become indeed one of the major themes of imaginative writing in the century'. The characteristic feature of this development was the 'rediscovery of community', that is, the rediscovery of 'forms of relationship which are characterized by a high degree of personal intimacy, emotional depth, moral commitment, social cohesion, and continuity in time'. [25] Among sociologists Auguste Comte, Frederic Le Play, and even Karl Marx had some part to play in the discussion, but the man whose name is still most closely associated with the notion of a marked contrast between rural and urban ways of life in this respect was Ferdinand Tönnies, whose book, *Gemeinschaft und Gesellschaft*, published in 1887, gave to sociology the two words of its title as distinctive terms by which to refer to the contrast. Tönnies, it is true, did not draw the line of distinction between the village and the town as such, but rather between the town and the city; yet his description of the latter as 'essentially a commercial town and, in so far as commerce dominates its productive labour, a factory town' makes plain that the kind of town which emerged in Britain in the nineteenth century was a city in his sense and hence 'typical of *Gesellschaft* in general'.[26]

The word *Gesellschaft* in this context largely eludes translation, for Tönnies regarded it essentially as a negation of *Gemeinschaft* which can easily be replaced by 'community' as described above. What Tönnies had in mind was what he conceived to be an

> artificial construction of an aggregate of human beings which superficially resembles the *Gemeinschaft* in so far as the individuals live and dwell together peacefully. However, in the *Gemeinschaft* they remain essentially united in spite of all separating factors, whereas in the *Gesellschaft* they are essentially separated in spite of all uniting factors . . . everybody is by himself and isolated and there exists a condition of tension against all others . . . nobody wants to grant and produce anything for another individual, nor will he be inclined to give ungrudgingly to another individual, if it be not in exchange for a gift or labour equivalent that he considers at least equal to what he has given.

Thus the sharp contrast is between 'all intimate, private, and exclusive living together' as in the family, and the 'mere co-existence of people independent of each other' as in the joint-stock company. City life for Tönnies was dominated by the latter spirit, although of course, because people lived in families even in the cities, *gemeinschaftlich* relationships were not unknown there. Nevertheless,[27]

> in the city . . . and especially in the metropolis, family life is decaying . . .
> In the village the household is independent and strong, also in the town
> the household is preserved and has a certain beauty; only in the city does

the household become sterile, narrow, empty, and debased to fit the conception of a mere living place which can be obtained everywhere in equal form for money. As such it is nothing but shelter for those on a journey through the world.

From such passages and others it is quite clear that Tönnies saw nineteenth-century city life as dominated largely by relationships that were impersonal, cold, morally indifferent, socially alienated, and transient, and the whole tenor of his book indicates that he associated himself with those who praised rural life with the claim that 'the *Gemeinschaft* among people is stronger there and more alive: it is the lasting and genuine form of living together.'[28] The lack of authenticity in town life which is central to this theme was directly challenged by Durkheim, although without specific reference to Tönnies. 'Cities', he wrote, 'always result from the need of individuals to put themselves in very intimate contact with others. They are so many points where the social mass is contracted more strongly than elsewhere. They can multiply and extend only if the moral density is raised.'[29] Of course, Durkheim did not attempt to argue that the high moral density of cities was characterized by that kind of community which Tönnies attributed to the village. Rather did he point to the stifling effect which *Gemeinschaft* could have on individual initiative and to the contrast between this and 'the free expression of individual variations' which obtained in large urban areas.[30]

> To assure ourselves of this it is sufficient to compare great cities with small. In the latter, whoever seeks to free himself from accepted customs meets with resistance which is sometimes very acute. Every attempt at independence is an object of public scandal, and the general reprobation attached is of such a nature as to discourage all imitators. On the contrary, in large cities, the individual is a great deal freer of collective bonds.

Tönnies had called *Gemeinschaft* 'a living organism' and *Gesellschaft* 'a mechanical aggregate and artefact'.[31] Durkheim referred to the same kind of evolution from the former to the latter as a movement from mechanical to organic solidarity; that is, from relationships which constrained people to behave in similar ways to those which united them in different but complementary roles. In this sense each type of solidarity was as genuine and authentic a form of co-operation as the other. Thus, if Tönnies was inclined to romanticize the past in his critique of the present,[32] Durkheim underplayed the element of repression in modern society in order to redress the balance,[33] concluding that[34]

> great cities are the uncontested homes of progress; it is in them that ideas, fashions, customs, new needs are elaborated and then spread over the rest of the country. When society changes, it is generally after them and in imitation. Temperaments are so mobile that everything that comes from the past is somewhat suspect. On the contrary, innovations, whatever they may be, enjoy a prestige there almost equal to the one the customs of

111

ancestors formerly enjoyed. Minds naturally are there oriented to the future. Consequently, life is there transformed with extraordinary rapidity; beliefs, tastes, passions, are in perpetual evolution. No ground is more favourable to evolution of all sorts. That is because the collective life cannot have continuity there, where different layers of social units, summoned to replace one another, are discontinuous.

Durkheim, it should be understood, saw the growth of cities as dependent materially on migration. 'Far from owing their existence and progress to the normal preponderance of births over deaths, they present, from this point of view, a general deficiency. It is, then, from without that they receive the elements to which they owe their daily increase.' But why do people move from the countryside to the town? Because 'it is inevitable that the greatest centres, those where life is most intense, exercise an attraction for the others proportionate to their importance.' This is hardly illuminating as it stands, although it becomes clearer if seen against Durkheim's view that the traditions of societies dominated by relationships of 'mechanical' solidarity were perpetuated by old people who could exercise authority over their children. Migrants to cities, he argued, were mainly people 'who, on becoming adult, have left their homes and been freed from the action of the old'; and this is because 'the prime of youth' is 'the time when men are most impatient of all restraint and most eager for change'.[35] Durkheim was relying here on what Weber referred to as a matter of 'common observation' in the nineteenth century, namely that the migrants to the cities were 'chiefly young people'.[36] The statistical evidence in support of this observation is, as a matter of fact, not altogether so strong as Weber (and Durkheim) seem to have thought, since there were cases of marked losses from rural areas of women aged over thirty-five in the period 1881–1901.[37]

Nevertheless, it does seem to have been generally true that girls of from fifteen to twenty and men of from twenty to thirty-five formed the great bulk of migrants from the countryside at this time, and probably earlier. Economic explanations were usually put forward to account for this movement, although the emphasis therein was not necessarily placed on destitution on the part of the migrants. Thus, H. L. Smith's discussion for Charles Booth of the influx into London asserted that 'the countrymen drawn in are mainly the cream of the youth of the villages, travelling not so often vaguely in search of work as definitely to seek a known economic advantage.' Moreover, even here there was an emphasis on an attraction in London beyond what he called the 'gigantic lottery of prizes'. What brought them to live in the city was 'the contagion of numbers, the sense of something going on, the theatres and the music halls, the brightly lighted streets and busy crowds—all, in short, that makes the difference between the Mile End fair on a Saturday night, and a dark and muddy country lane, with no glimmer of gas and with nothing to do. Who could wonder that men are drawn into such a vortex, even were the penalty heavier than it is?'[38] Possibly such a 'contagion of numbers' and the lure of 'busy crowds' were what Durkheim had in mind when he wrote of the intensity of city life in the context of 'moral density'.

Of course, as the Claphams pointed out, 'until the forties, neither the man of business nor the clerks or operatives who worked for him had much leisure in the factory towns';[39] or rather, until the Ten Hours Act was amended in 1850 to create the 'normal' working day with much of Saturday afternoon free,[40] working people had few opportunities to take advantage of the public pleasures of town life when they were fully employed, and when they were unemployed they could hardly afford to. Nevertheless, in these respects they were no worse off than the country-dwellers who, indeed, along with shop assistants still at the end of the century had no weekly half-holiday.[41] On the other hand, so long as the towns were physically small it was possible for their inhabitants to continue the inexpensive leisure-time pursuits to which they had become accustomed in their villages of origin. Thus, the Leicester Domestic Mission Society reported in 1846 that 'groups of ten or twelve men of the very poorest classes would get out of their alleys and back streets to roam the fields near the town and perhaps poach a little.'[42] For those who could read, twenty-five towns had opened *free* public libraries by 1860[43] and Co-operative Societies, following the practice of the Rochdale Pioneers, often put aside some of their funds for educational purposes, opening reading-rooms and lending-libraries for their members.[44] Undoubtedly, only a very small number of persons took advantage of such opportunities, or of the excursions arranged by Mechanics' Institutes, which gave Thomas Cook the idea of the excursion train in the 1840s;[45] and it is likely that most of the new, urban activities of the second half of the century—rowing, sailing, cricket, musical concerts, and drama—in the industrial towns of the Midlands and the North, were patronized by the middle classes rather than by the rest of society.[46] However, it is clear that the opportunity for a richer, fuller life lay in the future development of the town, rather than in the countryside. Although as the towns grew in size and outdoor pursuits had perforce to be confined to suburbia, the impression grew that these were poor substitutes for the changing pleasures of Arcadia, denied to those 'whom cruel fate prevents from living in the real country'.[47]

For women, one of the attractions may have been marriage, and indeed the fact that women were more likely than men to be short-distance migrants was explained categorically in terms of 'the marriages which take women into a neighbouring town'. Presumably this is meant to imply that some countrywomen married town-dwellers, possibly following men who had moved earlier from their village; but there may have been a marriage attraction in the town from the possibility that, in spite of the more unfavourable sex-ratio there,[48] a woman's chances of marriage may have been better, because both men and women married at younger ages in the town than in the country and a larger proportion of them altogether married. Again, an economic explanation has been put forward for this, namely 'the degree to which women find industrial occupations' which was claimed to be 'one very powerful factor in determining the marriage-rate'.[49] It is open to question, however, whether economic opportunity in the case of women, especially when linked with migration from home, might better be interpreted as a means of independence from the often severe restraints on behaviour inherent in rural family life, dominated by the Victorian paterfamilias. Young women copied the example of the young men, becoming lodgers in the factory towns nearby, or fending wholly for themselves, where they did not marry early.

As early as the 1830s, it should be noted, observers had been commenting on the growing economic independence of children in urban, working-class families,[50] and Engels in 1844 referred to the practice on their part of paying their parents a fixed sum for board and lodging, keeping the rest of the wages for themselves. Occasionally they moved out from their parental home to set up houses for themselves, either alone or with a friend.[51] Charles Booth, at the end of the century, wrote similarly of the 'weakening of family ties between parents and children' which he thought had occurred during the twenty years previous to his survey. 'Nowadays the home tie is broken early . . . The growing independence on the part of the children is frequently spoken of.'[52] In all, this economic opportunity *may* be seen as a determining factor but an alternative possibility is to regard it as influential mainly in the sense that it made possible the children's independence from parents. That some sections of the population migrated in search of the new jobs has been taken here to indicate that they were attracted as much by the freedom from traditional family ties as by the opportunities of employment.

The demographic consequences of this development are also of some significance. With a relatively younger population marrying earlier, and with a larger proportion of the population marrying, the Victorian towns might have been expected to show a higher birth-rate and a larger completed family than prevailed in the countryside. On the whole, however, the opposite was the case,[53] and in certain comparisons the difference was marked.[54] This is particularly noticeable when the analysis is conducted in occupational, rather than in urban-rural terms. Amongst the working class the highest fertility, as demonstrated by the 1911 Family Census data, occurred in mining families, with those engaged in agriculture second. Both groups were engaged in rural pursuits and both had a higher fertility than the average for unskilled workers taken as a whole. Textile families, on the other hand, were low in fertility, below the average for skilled workers, taken as a whole. A movement of women from the countryside into the textile towns might hence be seen as involving a transition to a type of family life which was very different from that of their family of origin, and this was all the more emphasized once people began to restrict the size of their families; for in the 1860s the practice began first in the towns, or at least amongst urban occupations, and proceeded much further there.

Of course, as is well known, this vital revolution was started initially and proceeded in the nineteenth century most rapidly amongst the upper and middle classes. It was only later that it was adopted by the working class. However, even amongst the middle classes it was an urban rather than a rural phenomenon, the 1911 census showing that farmers and graziers had larger families throughout the period 1861–86 than any other section of the middle class. Indeed, their families were larger than those of the working-class textile workers.[55] Thus, the distinction existed independent of social class, and, however much later developments in the country-side may have invalidated many more recent urban-rural comparisons,[56] it can hardly be denied that the formative years of British urban civilization witnessed a change in the character of the evaluation of children in the family, which has been revolutionary in its impact on the position of married women in society and hence on society generally.

For present purposes it is not necessary to go into the factors responsible for the inception and spread of family limitation. What is rather more to the point is that one facilitating means appears to have been the comparisons which members of the middle class were able to make of their own levels of living at different times with those of their immediate neighbours and acquaintances.[57] Hence what Himes called 'the democratization' of birth-control might possibly be explained, not so much by the publicity which was given to the Bradlaugh–Besant trial and which he thought to be important,[58] as by the comparisons which members of the urban working class were able to make of their situation with that of their wealthier neighbours. This may also have been related to the pattern of migration into the town, to the degree that many of the young girls from the country originally went into domestic service, and it is possible that the very great growth in the demand for such servants on the part of the middle class between 1851 and 1871[59] provided an economic opportunity for migration at the time. Later, it is true, the supply of domestic servants declined, especially amongst girls under twenty.[60] However, by that time the lesson had been learned, at least in the sense that some of the middle-class standards and aspirations had been adopted by the working class. It is not suggested here that they learned to use birth-control from being employed in the middle-class families. So far as it is possible to tell, working-class birth-control is a twentieth-century practice, on the whole; and there seems to have been a 'conspiracy of silence' on the issue on their part long after the Victorian age had come to an end. Nevertheless, there can hardly be any doubt that by the end of the century working-class women were expressing a need for relief from the burden of too frequent childbearing, as their letters to the Women's Co-operative Guild showed,[61] and in this respect the demand for emancipation on the part of working-class women followed a generation later than that made by the wives and mothers in the middle class.

Thus, Hobsbawm's argument for the earlier period—'on a gloomy interpretation, the popular discontent of the early nineteenth century makes sense; and on an optimistic interpretation it is almost inexplicable'[62]—is a clear *non sequitur*. The discontent of women with their traditional lot of childbearing and child-rearing, in families of an average size of at least six children, arose not because they had now become worse off than their mothers and grandmothers had been, but because they saw themselves worse off than they *might* be. It is, of course, true that such discontent did not manifest itself in the kind of collective organization intent on reform that Hobsbawm may be presumed to have had in mind, but it seems equally true that the feminist movement as such was organized to claim equal rights with men in the educational, occupational, and political fields, in response to social changes which made manifest that there was a large section of the population for whom such rights were essential. There is no question that they were claiming rights which had once been theirs and had latterly been lost. The issue, indeed, centred round a demographic fact, namely that throughout the nineteenth century there was a great growth of 'surplus' women. Already by 1841 there were 358,976 more women than men in England and Wales. By 1901 this number had increased to 1,070,015, and the sex-ratio had risen over sixty years from 1·046 to 1·068 women to each man.[63] Although about one-third of these were below the customary age for marrying, the number who could never marry while monogamy lasted was large and grew disproportionately throughout the century.

A traditional agricultural society could possibly cope with such a problem in that there is always productive work in and around the homestead for an unmarried woman to do and so to augment the family's worldly goods; but the kind of pecuniary calculations which is typical of urban industrialization effectively separates home and work for the middle and working class alike, making home activities overwhelmingly a form of consumption and work a form of family-income earning. The problem of the surplus woman, accordingly, was that of finding some place for her in such a civilization; and the feminist movement obtained its greatest impetus from the need to find for spinsters and widows, especially of middle-class origins, outlets for their energies which would also be remunerative.[64] For working-class women the factories already existed, and where there were no factories they could find employment as dressmakers, admittedly at very low wages. The danger here was that they might easily drift into prostitution, the great social evil of the Victorian era, and there was always a section of the feminist movement which saw its task, ideologically speaking, as that of a struggle of woman versus man. Hence, although organized feminism was led by middle-class women it was never a class movement, and some of the issues it adopted, such as the abolition of the Contagious Diseases Acts and the ending of the double standard of sexual morality, were clearly not of direct advantage to middle-class women.[65] It is, that is to say, an error to regard social protest as indicative of deterioration in the situation of those who mount it. Urban life, by bringing ever larger numbers of people in close proximity to one another, increased the possibility of invidious comparisons, and it was this which produced social movements aimed at an even better future for all.

Again, it is to be expected that towns might differ in such respects according to the degree to which the sex-ratio, for example, and the numbers of surplus women varied markedly from the national average. Thus, Middlesbrough was selected for special mention by Ravenstein in 1885 on the ground that 'its rapid growth, the heterogeneous composition of its population, and the preponderance of the male sex, recall features generally credited only to the towns of the American West.'[66] Does this mean that, in the face of aggressive masculinity, feminism was a movement which found it difficult to take roots there? Historians have apparently found no reason to comment on this point,[67] and clearly a much more intensive study of such questions than has been presented here would be necessary to decide the issue. In so far as a town like Middlesbrough could be shown to display characteristics of 'moral density' distinct from what obtained generally, and more like what was typical of the American frontier, added emphasis would be given to the analysis of urban life in Durkheimian terms. Thus, although Durkheim's notions cannot claim to have been rigorously tested here, sufficient illustrative material has been presented to support the general argument that the analysis of the process of urbanization in terms of growing social solidarity makes good historical and sociological sense.

The thesis that the quality of social life in cities attracted migrants to them from the countryside, in spite of the greater morbidity and mortality associated with over-crowding, should not be interpreted as implying that there were no disadvantages to be discerned in so far as social solidarity was concerned. Durkheim, indeed, proffered an explanation of the fact that 'suicide, like insanity, is commoner in cities than in the country', in terms of a direct relationship between 'voluntary deaths' and the *intensity* of social life. Individuals who, for one reason or another, find themselves isolated from strongly integrated groups are more prone to suicide,[68] so that the stranger in the town can be especially vulnerable. The basis of this situation, as another sociologist put it about this time, is 'reserve'.[69]

> If so many inner reactions were responses to the continuous external contacts with innumerable people as are those in the small town, where one knows almost everybody one meets and where one has a positive relation to almost everyone, one would be completely atomized internally and come to an unimaginable psychic state. Partly this psychological fact, partly the right to distrust which men have in the face of the touch-and-go elements of metropolitan life, necessitates our reserve.

Hence the warmth of social relationships with friends in the city is matched by what appears to be coldness in relationships with mere acquaintances, and a man who cannot find or make friends is in some peril.

This point should not be laboured unduly. After all, most migration was over short distances. Ravenstein, who was probably the first to emphasize this fact, asserted that even long-distance migration was undertaken in stages. Among the Irish, for example, he said, 'some of them landed at Liverpool, and gradually worked their way through Cheshire, Stafford, Warwick, Northampton, and Birmingham, whilst another stream, and perhaps the more voluminous one, passed through Plymouth, Hampshire and Surrey.'[70] The concept of short distance is, of course, meant to be comparative. Some migrants went a long way, even further when railway traffic became commonplace, although the general effect of the railways on the pattern of migration was negligible in this respect, since their greatest effect was that many more people moved a short way. Thus, most migrants were never very far from their villages of origin and could maintain some contact with their families and perhaps with friends, even where economic circumstances made it difficult for them to return home for long or permanently. The element of strangeness would in any case be small for those who had not moved very far. Local dialects would probably not have presented the kind of communication problem that existed for long-distance migrants and this was probably also true of cultural differences generally. It seems reasonable to assume, therefore, that the rural hinterland for most towns provided a population more easily assimilated into urban life than likely to remain aloof and apart. When they moved, moreover, they probably went to those parts of the town where people from their villages already lived, as a recent study of Preston has shown.[71] In this sense the adjustment to the new way of life could be made gradually.

Occasionally this clustering resulted in some part of the town perpetuating distinguishing features and even influencing the life of the rest, although this seems to have been rare. For example, Liverpool in 1881 contained only 81 percent English-born inhabitants, as compared with West Bromwich, Norwich, Ipswich, Leicester, and Nottingham with over 98 percent English-born; and 12·8 percent of the Liverpudlians were Irish.[72] The existence of a relatively large Roman Catholic 'enclave'[73] in a predominantly Protestant area gave Liverpool a characteristic ethos which has set it off as different even to the present day. At a time when working-class attendance at church was minimal, the fact that the Irish continued the habit of going to church regularly gave it an influence in the life of the city. Possibly 'worship with their fellows, led perhaps by an Irish priest, was one of the few familiar and comforting things available to them in ugly industrial England';[74] but the effect was to maintain a sense of community, of having interests in common which were different from those of their neighbours, and which influenced not merely their religious but also their political life. The only Irish Nationalist candidate ever elected to Parliament from an English constituency, T. P. O'Connor, was returned for the Scotland Division of Liverpool in 1885 and held the seat until 1929.[75] What the example of Liverpool emphasizes, however, is that it was exceptional for migrants to carry their way of life into a town, in the sense of it remaining an abiding source of strength and separateness. Rather was it that the town's way of life became theirs. Thus, the kind of social solidarity which Durkheim had in mind as characteristic of rural life was to some extent perpetuated in local pockets within the new urban areas; but the overall character of urban life in this new civilization invented in nineteenth-century England was one of integration through the co-operation of people of diverse sorts— a truly new way of life graphically labelled by him as organic solidarity.

## Notes

1   United Kingdom Registrar-General, Census 1961, *England and Wales Preliminary Report*, HMSO (1961), Table 6, p. 75.
2   John Saville, *Rural Depopulation in England and Wales, 1851–1951* (1957), Table VI, p. 61.
3   Details obtained from B. R. Mitchell, 'Population and Vital Statistics 8,

Population of the Principal Towns of the United Kingdom, 1801–1951', *Abstract of British Historical Statistics* (Cambridge, 1962), pp. 24–7.

4  Details obtained from Mitchell, 'Population and Vital Statistics 7, Population of the Counties of the British Isles 1801–1951', pp. 20, 22; cases of county decline in England were Cornwall, Huntingdonshire, Rutland, Somerset; in Wales, Anglesey, Breconshire, Cardiganshire, Montgomeryshire, and Radnorshire. See also Saville, op. cit., Table V, pp. 56–7. For details of rural decline in two counties of growing population, see Richard Lawton, 'Population Trends in Lancashire and Cheshire from 1801', *Trans. Historic Society of Lancashire and Cheshire*, cxiv (1962), 197–201, and Figure 20. A detailed analysis of areas smaller than the county is to be found in Richard Lawton, 'Population Changes in England and Wales in the later Nineteenth Century: an Analysis of Trends by Registration Districts', *Trans. Institute of British Geographers*, no. 44 (1968), Figure 1, 59.

5  See, for example, Mary P. Newton and James R. Jeffery, *Internal Migration: Some aspects of population movements within England and Wales*, General Register Office Studies in Medical and Population Subjects, no. 5, HMSO (1951), histogram on p. 9.

6  Richard Lawton, 'Rural Depopulation in Nineteenth-Century England', in Robert W. Steel and R. Lawton, eds, *Liverpool Essays in Geography* (1967), pp. 233–47.

7  Thomas W. Freeman, *The Conurbations of Great Britain* (Manchester, 1959), p. 1.

8  Thomas A. Welton, 'On the Distribution of Population in England and Wales, and its Progress in the Period of Ninety Years from 1801 to 1891', *JRSS*, lxiii (1900), 529, 533.

9  G. Kitson Clark, *The Making of Victorian England* (1965), p. 79. The implication is that this covers the period 1821–51. For a sample of contemporary documents of the 1840s see 'A Gazateer of Disgusting Places' in E. Royston Pike, *Human Documents of the Industrial Revolution in Britain* (1966), pp. 305–35.

10  William Ashworth, *The Genesis of Modern British Town Planning* (1954), pp. 47–8.

11  David Roberts, *Victorian Origins of the British Welfare State* (New Haven, 1960), ch. 1. Notice that Asa Briggs does not mention the population issue in his 'The Welfare State in Historical Perspective', *European Journal of Sociology*, ii (1961), 221–258.

12  Sydney G. Checkland, *The Rise of Industrial Society in England, 1815–1885* (1964), pp. 263–4. See also John L. and Barbara Hammond, *The Town Labourer, 1760–1832. The new civilization* (1917), ch. 3.

13  Eric Hobsbawm, *Labouring Men: Studies in the history of labour* (1964), pp. 64, 121. Although he concludes that the 'negative case is now pretty generally accepted', and although he himself has contributed to it in the tradition of the pessimistic school, chapters 5, 6, and 7 of this book comprise an excellent and fair survey of the debate.

14  Checkland, op. cit., ch. 7. Section 9 of this chapter is entitled: 'The Impact on Personality' and begins with the sentence: 'Even more fundamental to happiness than monetary rewards and living conditions was the state of mind of men, women and children who needed to be able to find comfort and even pride in their relations with one another and with the productive tasks upon which their livelihood depended' (p. 263).

15  Hobsbawm, op. cit., pp. 78–9.

16  Stanley C. Johnson, *A History of Emigration from the United Kingdom to North America, 1763–1912* (1913), pp. 203–7.

17  Oliver MacDonagh, 'Irish Emigration to the United States of America and the British Colonies During the Famine', in R. Dudley Edwards and T. Desmond Williams, eds, *The Great Famine: Studies in Irish history 1845–52* (New York, 1957), pp. 383–4. See also Johnson, op. cit., p. 183, n. 2, for details of the numbers of Irish in the farming and industrial states in 1880.

18  A. K. Cairncross, *Home and Foreign Investment 1870–1913* (1953), p. 75.

19  Ross Duncan, 'Case Studies in Emigration: Cornwall, Gloucestershire, and New South Wales, 1877–1886', *Economic History Review* (second series), xvi (1963–4), 1.

20  Émile Durkheim, *De la division du travail social*, 3rd edn (Paris, 1911), p. 238.

21  Interdepartmental Committee on Social and Economic Research, *Guide to Official Sources, No. 2: Census Reports of Great Britain, 1801–1931*, HMSO (1951), pp. 31, 34.

22  Welton, op. cit., Summaries 1 and 2, pp. 529, 533.

23  Talcott Parsons, *The Structure of Social Action*, 2nd edn (Chicago, 1949), chs 8–11, and ch. 18, pp. 708–14. A very careful and accurate survey of Durkheim's position on moral density is given in Leo F. Schnore, 'Social Morphology and Human Ecology', *American Journal of Sociology*, lxiii (1957–8), 620–34. See also Harry Alpert, *Émile Durkheim and his Sociology* (New York, 1961 edn), pp. 91–3.

24  See the useful summary in Ronald Frankenberg, *Communities in Britain: Social life in town and country* (Penguin, 1966), pp. 286–92.

25  Ronald A. Nisbet, *The Sociological Tradition* (New York, 1966), p. 47.

26  Ferdinand Tönnies, *Community and Association*, trans. and ed. Charles P. Loomis (London and New York, 1955 and 1963), p. 227 (page references are to the New York edition).

27  Ibid., pp. 64–5, 33–4, 229, 162.

28  Ibid., p. 35: 'Gemeinschaft ist das dauernde und echte Zusammenleben, Gesellschaft nur ein vorübergehendes und scheinbares.'

29  Durkheim, op. cit., p. 239. Cf. English translation by George Simpson with the title, *The Division of Labor in Society* (New York, 1933), p. 258.

30  Ibid., English version, pp. 297–8.

31  Tönnies, op. cit., p. 35.

32  Rudolf Heberle, 'The Sociological System of Ferdinand Tönnies: "Community" and "Society"', in Harry E. Barnes, ed., *An Introduction to the History of Sociology* (Chicago, 1948), pp. 242–3.

33  Alpert, op. cit., p. 185.

34  Durkheim, op. cit., p. 296.

35  Ibid., pp. 342 and 295.

36  Adna F. Weber, *The Growth of Cities in the Nineteenth Century: A study in statistics* (New York, 1899), p. 280.

37  See the summary conclusion in Thomas A. Welton, *England's Recent Progress. An investigation of the statistics of Migrations, Mortality, &c.* (1911), p. 9.

38  H. Llewellyn Smith, 'Influx of Population', in Charles Booth, ed., *Life and Labour of the People in London* (1892), III, pp. 75, 120.

39  J. H. Clapham and M. H. Clapham, 'Life in the New Towns', in G. M. Young, ed., *Early Victorian England, 1830–1865* (1934), I, pp. 230–1.

40  Frank Tillyard, *The Worker and the State* (1922), pp. 111–12; Barbara L. Hutchins and A. Harrison, *A History of Factory Legislation*, 3rd edn (1926), pp. 105–7.

41  J. A. R. Pimlott, *The Englishman's Holiday* (1947), p. 142.

42  Page 12 of the Report quoted in A. Temple Patterson, *Radical Leicester: A history of Leicester, 1780–1850* (Leicester, 1954), p. 378, n. 8.

43  E. L. Woodward, *The Age of Reform, 1815–1870* (Oxford, 1949 edn), p. 475, n. 1.

44  G. D. H. Cole, *A Century of Co-operation* (Manchester, 1944), pp. 227–32. For a description of the social aspects of a Co-operative Store on a Saturday evening see George J. Holyoake, *The History of the Rochdale Pioneers* (1900 edn), p. 39.

45  John Pudney, *The Thomas Cook Story* (1953), pp. 53–9.

46  Clapham and Clapham, op. cit., pp. 237–44.

47  Mrs C. S. Peel, *The New Home* (1898), quoted in H. J. Dyos, *Victorian Suburb* (Leicester, 1961), p. 26.

48  Weber, op. cit., pp. 278, 286.

49  William Ogle, 'On Marriage-Rates and Marriage-Ages, with special reference to the growth of population', *JRSS*, liii (1890), 268.

50  See the evidence cited in Ivy Pinchbeck, *Women Workers and the Industrial Revolution, 1750–1850* (1930), p. 313.

51  Friedrich Engels, *The Condition of the Working Class in England*, trans. and ed. W. O. Henderson and W. H. Chaloner (Oxford, 1958), pp. 164–5. Notice that Harriet in Disraeli's *Sybil* (1845) left her parents to set up lodgings with a friend because she was tired of supporting her family.

52  Charles Booth, 'Notes on Social Influences and Conclusion', *Life and Labour of the People in London* (1903), final volume, p. 43.

53  David V. Glass, 'Changes in Fertility in England and Wales, 1851 to 1931', in Lancelot Hogben, ed., *Political Arithmetic, a Symposium of Population Studies* (1938), pp. 161–212.

54  Francis Galton, 'The Relative Supplies from Town and Country Families to the Population of Future Generations', *JSS*, xxxvi (1873), 19–26.

55  John W. Innes, *Class Fertility Trends in England and Wales, 1876–1934* (Cambridge, 1938), Table XIII, p. 42.

56  See the useful discussion in Peter H. Mann, *An Approach to Urban Sociology* (1965), pp. 96–105.

57  J. A. Banks, *Prosperity and Parenthood: A study of family planning among the Victorian middle classes* (1954), ch. 9.

58  Norman E. Himes, *Medical History of Contraception* (Baltimore, 1936), pp. 239–45. For an alternative assessment of the effect of the trial see J. A. and Olive Banks, 'The Bradlaugh–Besant Trial and the English Newspapers', *Population Studies*, viii (1954), 22–34.

59  Banks, *Prosperity and Parenthood*, ch. 9 and pp. 83–4.

60  United Kingdom Registrar-General, *Census of England and Wales, 1901: General Report with Appendices*, HMSO (1904), pp. 95–6.

61  *Maternity: Letters from working-women collected by the Women's Co-operative Guild* (1915), pp. 18–190.

62  Hobsbawm, op. cit., p. 241.

63  United Kingdom Registrar-General, Census 1961, p. 75.

64 J. A. and Olive Banks, *Feminism and Family Planning in Victorian England* (Liverpool, 1964), ch. 3.

65 J. A. and Olive Banks, 'Feminism and Social Change—A Case Study of a Social Movement', in George K. Zollschan and Walter Hirsch, eds, *Explorations in Social Change* (Boston, 1964), pp. 552–4.

66 E. G. Ravenstein, 'The Laws of Migration', *JRSS*, xlviii (1885), 215.

67 Cf. Asa Briggs, *Victorian Cities* (1963), ch. 6.

68 Émile Durkheim, *Suicide: A study in sociology*, trans. J. A. Spaulding and G. Simpson (1952), pp. 70, 121–2, 208–16. *Suicide* was first published in French in 1897.

69 Georg Simmel, 'Die Grossstädte und das Geistesleben', in Karl Bücher *et al.*, *Die Grossstadt* (Dresden, 1903), trans. Kurt H. Wolff, *The Sociology of Georg Simmel* (Chicago, 1950), p. 415.

70 Ravenstein, op. cit., p. 183. See also Weber, op. cit., and Arthur Redford, *Labour Migration in England, 1800–1850* (Manchester, 1962).

71 Michael Anderson, *Family Structure in Nineteenth Century Lancashire* (Cambridge, 1971), pp. 152–8.

72 Ravenstein, op. cit., pp. 173, 176.

73 Twenty-three percent of Roman Catholic places of worship in England and Wales in 1851 and 1861 were found to be in Lancashire. See William G. Lumley, 'The Statistics of the Roman Catholics in England and Wales', *JSS*, xxvii (1864), 183.

74 K. S. Inglis, *Churches and the Working Classes in Victorian England* (1963), p. 121.

75 John A. Jackson, *The Irish in Britain* (1963), p. 122.

# 5    Comers and Goers

## Raphael Samuel

The 'migrating classes', as they were called by the promoters of the Leicester Square Soup Kitchen in 1850,[1] have left remarkably few traces of their existence, even in the places which once served them as town lairs. No railway hotels mark the terminal point of their journeyings. No imposing clubs stand as memorials to the seasons they spent in town. The back-street lodging houses where many of them put up have long since been swept away, though not their forbidding institutional successors—the 'Free Dormitories' and 'Night Shelters' promoted and endowed by late Victorian philanthropy. The no-man's-land where the travelling showmen drew up their caravans and the gypsies encamped—the wasteland edge of the nineteenth-century town—has been built over by houses and streets. It is not easy to imagine a time when men slept rough in the shadows of the gas-works, the warmth of the brick-kilns, and the dark recesses of places like London Bridge; or lined up in their hundreds with tin cans or basins at Ham Yard, Soho, or the midnight soup-kitchens of White-chapel and Drury Lane.[2] Perhaps the most complete change has been on the water-front, which has been robbed of all its life. There is no Scandinavian settlement in Rotherhithe, no Tiger Bay in Cardiff. Rambling down Ratcliffe Highway, the curious observer is likely to find himself alone, flanked by derelict land and a low brick wall instead of the crowded dancing-saloons and rifle galleries, photographers' booths and boarding-houses of a hundred years ago. Then it was a great night-time pleasure strip, drawing sailors of all nations—red-shirted Americans, 'chewing indefatigably', Chinamen and Lascars, 'smoking Trichinopoly cheroots', 'shivering' Italians, 'piratical-looking' Greeks.[3]

Travellers in nineteenth-century England played a much greater part in industrial and social life than they do today. Among them were to be found some of the country's major occupational groups, as well as many hundreds of miscellaneous callings and trades. On the canals there were the boatmen and their families, who remained an important element in the carrying trade long after the coming of the railways—a half-gypsy population who owed their very existence to the Industrial Revolution. Tens of thousands of navvies followed in the track of Victorian 'improvement' and the great public works, a class of men 'very fond of change', and forever on the move, especially the more skilled among them.[4] The building trades were chronically migratory, with men moving constantly from job to job, sometimes covering very great distances in the tramp for work. (Some hundreds of stonemasons emigrated seasonally to the United States, leaving in the early spring and returning in the fall.)[5] The summer harvests depended to a considerable degree upon travelling labourers, most of them recruited from the countryside, but some coming out from the towns. James Greenwood met one of these on the road to Hitchin:[6]

> He seemed to be a decent sort of man, and, for a wonder, was not an Irishman. He lived and worked, all the winter, at the Potteries at Shepherd's Bush, he told me, and every June set out on tramp, working his way at any kind of field labour, and winding up with the Northern late corn harvests, when he returned home with a pound or so in his pocket, besides what he was able to send, from time to time, to keep his old woman.

At the heart of the wayfaring constituency were those whom Mayhew called the 'wandering tribes'; people who had been either born and bred to a roving life (like the gypsies and travelling showmen) or forced into it when settled occupations failed them, like the travelling Irish, who came over each year for the harvest, or the old soldiers and army reserve men, who lived as trampers on the road, and were said to constitute 'probably not less than one-fourth or one-fifth of the whole class of destitute homeless persons.'[7] It is possible to distinguish four different classes among them. First there were the habitual wanderers, who flitted about from place to place, with no regular settlement at all. Second there were those who spent the greater part of the year in the country, but kept regular winter quarters in the town. Third there were the 'fair weather' travellers, who went out on 'summer tours', but for the rest of the year stayed in one place. Finally there were those who made frequent short turns into the country, but never moved far from their home base. Examples of these types could be found in each of the wandering tribes. Amongst the packmen and dealers, for instance, there were some who followed a weekly itinerary, 'pitching it' in town on Saturday-night markets, and going on country rounds during the week;[8] there were others who turned out only for special occasions, like the army of free-lance hucksters who made an annual appearance on Derby Day at Epsom Downs; and yet others who left home for months at a time, like the 'muggers' and 'potters' who dealt in cheap crockery and earthenware,[9] and the cheap-jacks, whose yearly round began in February and often did not end until November.[10] 'I used to go round the country—to Margate, Brighton, Portsmouth—I mostly travelled by the coast, calling at all the sea-port towns', a cutlery seller told Mayhew; 'I went away every Spring time, and came to London again at the fall of the year.'[11] Similarly among the gypsies there were comers and goers within every migration range, including the most limited (the Battersea gypsies kept very close to London, and a few of them remained encamped all the year round).[12] Race-meetings and fairs attracted both short- and long-distance migrants, some following them round as part of a regular circuit, others going out on individual expeditions, with a basket, or a show, or with a tray suspended from the neck.

Wayfaring life had a definite place in the moral topography of the nineteenth-century town. Railway stations always attracted a floating population to the vicinity; so did the wholesale markets, especially those frequented by the drovers. Brickfields, on the outskirts of town, were regular dossing-places, along with gasworks, railway bridges, and viaducts. There were Irish quarters in every centre of industry and trade, 'Little Irelands', whose inhabitants remained notoriously migratory in their habits, 'exceedingly fluctuating and unsettled'.[13] The Irish were among the first to settle in the boom towns of mid-Victorian England (Middlesbrough, Barrow-in-Furness, West Ham). They were among the first to leave when there was a depression.[14] 'Our population is rather a floating one . . . following the up and down . . . of industry', wrote a Catholic priest of his Irish flock at Sunderland. 'St. Patrick's mission is not like many other ones.'[15] In the summer many of the Irish went off to 'counthry' work. A few of the York Irish were still doing this in Rowntree's time,[16] while in London the Cockney Irish constituted a lasting element in the annual exodus of hop-pickers.[17] Waterfront districts, too, always bore a peculiarly migratory character, not only in the big sea-ports, where there were fully-fledged sailortowns, but also inland, wherever there were wharves or docks. 'The quarters of every town that lie near the wharves and banks always seem to deteriorate', wrote Lady Bell, in her book about Middlesbrough. 'There is something in the intercourse of sailors from other ports who come and go, nomadic, unvouched for, who appear and disappear, with no responsibility for their words or their deeds, that seems to bring to the whole world a kinship of lawlessness and disorder.'[18] Quite apart from the native sailors—perennial comers and goers—there were the sailors from other ports, an even more nomadic element. At Shields, for instance, it was computed that besides the 15,000 sailors belonging to the port there were no less than 40,000 seamen from other places who annually visited the port.[19] On the Middlesbrough waterfront there were 'many . . . foreigners'. 'Almost daily we come in contact with Germans, Greeks, Swedes, Danes, Norwegians, Arabians, Chinese, Lascars and Spaniards', remarked a chaplain to the seamen in 1892.[20] Sailors were not only more numerous and varied than their counterparts today; they were also more visible, spending far more time ashore, especially in winter.

Regular 'trampers'—'comers and goers who . . . prefer darkness to light'—had their own peculiar lairs. An example in Nottingham is Narrow Marsh ('this provincial Whitechapel') where J. Flanagan, the Bermondsey evangelist, once spent eighteen months in rescue work 'chiefly among the crimps, outcasts and tramps, who were ever turning up'.[21] Another provincial example is Angel Meadow ('the lowest, most filthy, most unhealthy and most wicked locality in Manchester') whose inhabitants were accounted for by the *Morning Chronicle* special correspondent as 'prostitutes . . . bullies, thieves, cadgers, vagrants, tramps and . . . those unhappy wretches, the "low Irish"'.[22] In Merthyr Tydfil there was 'China', a maze of courts and tortuous lanes which the Education Commissioners of 1847 described as 'a sort of Welsh Alsatia'. It was, they said, 'a mere sink of thieves and prostitutes such as unhappily constitutes an appendage to every large town'.[23] There was a little enclave of this kind even in a sleepy place like Hitchin. James Greenwood came upon it in 1872, a long, narrow street which he describes as 'evidently the headquarters of the tramping fraternity':[24]

> It is like a slice from the backslums of Whitechapel, or Kent Street in the Borough. As, in the delectable localities named, at least one house in a half-dozen throughout its length is a lodging house for travellers— travellers, however, who are not so worn-out and leg-weary but they prefer, on a sultry night in June, to sprawl in the house passages and on the steps . . .

London had a number of little enclaves of this kind. Some of them were ancient haunts of the travelling fraternities (St Giles; Tothill Fields, Westminster; the Mint, Southwark); others were the accompaniment of the city's nineteenth-century growth. One of the newer tramp quarters was in Mill Lane, Deptford and its environs, 'known to tramps and low-class prostitutes throughout London', according to Booth.[25] Another was in the Arpley Road area of Anerley and Penge, 'a resting place for tramps entering London from the South'.[26] In the north there was Campbell Road, Islington, the occasion of much police and clerical disquiet.[27] To the south-east there was the 'Dust Hole', Woolwich, the subject of Canon Horsley's anti-vice campaign in the 1890s.[28] Booth wrote that it was a 'house of call' for tramps passing in and out of London on the high road to Kent, and a regular junction for the outer London tramp circuit. 'Policemen from Notting Dale', it was said, 'find old friends in Rope-yard Rails. The casual loafer floats between the two.'[29] Notting Dale, 'the resting place for tramps entering London from the North or West',[30] was the largest of these new 'tramp' districts. It was first settled by some refugee pig-keepers from Marble Arch, in flight from the sanitary authorities, and they were soon followed by gypsies, brickmakers, and (in later years) lodging-house keepers. Bangor Street, the most frequently noticed of its streets, was occupied by lodging-houses from end to end, and we are fortunate to have a good account of how a tramping family made its way there in the 1890s. It comes from the autobiography of Sam Shaw, a little boy of ten at the time. The family had set out from Birmingham 'without any fixed stopping places or definite . . . sleeping places':[31]

126

Father told us that we were going on the road to a big place where matches and newspapers sold better than in Birmingham. So 'on the road' we went . . . For weeks we tramped . . . each stage was from workhouse to workhouse where we were provided with bed and breakfast. If we arrived too late for admittance then we begged a shelter in a barn . . . or slept under the stars . . . Day after day, begging our way . . . We reached Edgware . . . and . . . spent the night in a workhouse . . . reaching London . . . next day . . . While we children played in one of London's parks our parents searched for a room . . . Bangor Street, Notting Hill Gate, eventually provided us with a home . . . It consisted of only one room and was furnished with two beds and two rickety chairs which were all the family exchequer could afford. Those who hadn't chairs to sit on sat on the bed.

Within such quarters, and scattered on all the tramp routes of the country, were the common lodging-houses, the night-time haven of the wandering tribes, or at least of the better off portion among them, hawkers and travelling labourers especially. Travelling people used them as regular staging posts, and laid up in them for the winter when the season's journeyings came to an end. There were few towns without a street or two largely given over to them. Around mid-century (a time when they were the subject of much anxious investigation) Gloucester's lodging-houses were concentrated in Leather-Bottle Lane;[32] Banbury's in Rag Row (a back street of the proletarian suburb of Neithrop);[33] Huddersfield's in the narrow courts off Kirkgate and Castlegate (the Irish ones in Windsor Court);[34] Doncaster's in Skinner's Yard, Far St Sepulchre Gate;[35] Brighton's in 'those bad streets' Egremont Street and Nottingham Street.[36] In Derby they were in Walker Lane, 'the St Giles of Derby'.[37] At Ashton-under-Lyne the twopenny lodging-houses were in Crab Street and the twopenny-halfpenny ones in Duncan Street.[38] London, of course, was full of them—no fewer than 988 were registered in 1889, with accommodation for over 33,964 people, quite apart from the coffee-shops which offered twopenny and three-penny beds, and the rooming-houses.[39] There were great numbers of them, too, in Liverpool, not only the sailors' boarding-houses of the waterfront, but also the 'emigrant houses' where travellers put up while waiting to make the transatlantic passage.

Common lodging-houses were condemned by sanitary reformers on account of the 'promiscuous' mixing of the sexes, and the crowded, impromptu conditions in which the inmates ate and slept. But to the footsore wanderer they offered warmth and a cheerful shelter. The kitchen was the hub of lodging-house life; it was usually to be found in the basement and served as a drying-room, a workplace (for those with a basket of merchandise to prepare), an eating room, and sometimes (though illegally) as a place to sleep. In the evening, when travellers returned from their rounds, it was turned into a common-room, thick with the fumes of coke cooking and tobacco, and warmed by huge, blazing fires. Even hostile observers had sometimes to admit that the atmosphere was companionable. 'The night being wet, enormous fires blazed in both rooms', wrote Dr Coulthart, investigating one of the low lodging-houses of Ashton-under-Lyne:[40]

> Groups of evidently abandoned creatures of both sexes, many of them dripping with rain, were drying themselves before the fires; while others, more jovial than the rest, were doing ample justice to the merits of ale, porter, porridge, beefsteaks, cow-paunch &c., nearer the door. Among the numbers was a woolly-haired negro who, the police officer with me said, had been driven from the streets a few hours before for ballad-singing. In vacant corners were hawkers' baskets, pedlars' boxes, musical instruments, and beggars' crutches.

Lodging-houses offered cheap overnight accommodation for prices ranging at mid-century from a penny to threepence, and in later years from fourpence to sixpence. Even so, they were expensive for travellers of the poorer class, who were able to use them only when they were 'flush'. There was a good deal of interchange between the lodging-houses, on the one hand, where accommodation had to be paid for, and the Casual Wards and Refuges, on the other, where it was free.

Men who slept rough (by no means only tramps) had an easy time of it in the country, when they made their summer rounds, and could pick and choose their places to sleep al fresco. Things were more difficult when winter drove them to the towns, and they were subject to a good deal of police harassment. But they were never without refuge. Police supervision was slight on the ragged peripheries of town, where many of them made a halt. The kilns on the Brent Brickfields at Willesden were an overnight stopping-place for men who tramped up to London. 'The cavities . . . afford warmth and shelter,' says a police report, 'hence the . . . numbers'.[41] Outside Manchester, too, 'the numerous brickfields on the outskirts of the city' were frequently resorted to by tramps.[42] In town itself there were certain places where men could escape the glare of the bull's-eye lantern: empty or ruinous buildings, shop doorways, omnibus depots, railway stables, coal-holes and boiler-rooms, cul-de-sacs and covered passageways, impromptu shelters arising, as it were, within the crevices of city life. In London, the wholesale markets were always a draw to tramps, partly because of the all-night coffee-shops and stalls, partly because they provided odd jobs, but also because of the shelter: any corner might be used for a kip—even the water-closets at Covent Garden.[43] There were certain other places, too, where tramps could assemble together more or less undisturbed. The Thames bridges served them for many years as 'Dry Arch' hotels, 'open houses for the houseless wayfarer'.[44] As late as 1869 Daniel Joseph Kirwan came upon a dozen people who had made their home in the underground recesses of London Bridge, and were burning driftwood for their fire: he called it a 'perfect gypsy encampment'.[45] The most sensational of these shelters in inner London were the Adelphi Arches off the Strand, a series of underground chambers and vaults 'running here and there like the intricacies of catacombs'. Thomas Miller described them as a 'little subterranean city'[46] and in the 1860s (according to one excited account) 'no sane person would have ventured to explore them without an armed escort'.[47]

Victorian 'improvement' swept away many of these nooks and crannies, but it created others in their stead. Street lamps yielded the homeless wanderer a certain starveling warmth; so did the boiler-rooms of the factories, the newspaper offices, and (in later years) the big hotels. Model dwellings, with their open landings, stairways and passages gave a rudimentary shelter to sleepers-out.[48] The colonnade of St George's Hall ('our great municipal building') sheltered so many of Liverpool's homeless that it was described in 1890 as the 'lodging-house' of the destitute.[49] The Thames Embankment, the most spectacular of mid-Victorian 'improvements' in inner London, very soon became a by-word for the number of its tramps, some of whom filled the seats beneath the plane trees ('No. 2 bench' was recommended to Duckworth by a former *habitué*),[50] and others of whom used it as an all-night promenade. Its character was reinforced by the Shelters built at either end (the Salvation Army's 'Penny Sit-Up' at Blackfriars, and the *Morning Post*'s 'Embankment Home' on Millbank); by charitable distributions of food (such as the Eustace Miles Food Barrow at Cleopatra's Needle); and by the nightly distribution of relief tickets underneath the Craven Street arches (2,000 men were assembling there nightly in October 1908).[51] The 'lynx eyed metropolitan police' (as they were described by General Booth),[52] after attempting to drive the tramps away, were by 1910 treating the Embankment as a 'kind of corral' where large numbers of tramps were conveniently assembled under the direct observation of law and order.[53]

Railway arches—both brick viaducts and iron bridges—were by far the most frequented of these new al fresco shelters, and they were resorted to by the homeless from their earliest days.[54] The Craven Street Arches at Charing Cross were a nightly assembly point for trampdom; so was Byker Bridge at Newcastle and (in later years, at least) the 'Highlanders' Meet' along Argyle Street in Glasgow. In Croydon the Windmill Bridge of the London & Brighton railway was a night-time resort for sleepers-out;[55] in Spitalfields the Wheler Street arches of the Great Eastern railway (a long, low, tunnel-like bridge) were used by some forty to sixty people a night, according to a police report; at Rotherhithe there were the 500 arches of the South Eastern and the London & Brighton railways, whose night-time *habitués* were not deterred by occasional prosecutions before the local magistrates.[56] The building of the Overhead Railway along the docks was a late addition to tramp facilities in Liverpool, skirting the seven-mile length of the waterfront and open to all comers— it became locally known as 'the Docker's Umbrella'.[57]

Gypsies made their encampments on the outer edge of town, where streets and houses gave way to waste. The Everton gypsies pitched their tents on a piece of waste ground near Walton Breck; in 1879 they were summoned before the magistrates for having failed to supply themselves with water 'as required by the Public Health Act', but the camp was still flourishing seven years later.[58] The Smethwick gypsies occupied a piece of waste ground near to the Navigation Inn.[59] At Charlton the local gypsies occupied an open space near Riverside—with six travelling-vans and a number of tents.[60] At Plumstead they camped out in the marshes—a stretch of land drained by deep ditches 'like the fen country' and used as a shooting range; their tents were made of old skirts 'stretched over hurdles'.[61] In west London one of their camps was by Latimer Road, 'the ugliest place . . . in the neighbourhood of London . . . half torn up for brickfield clay, half consisting of fields laid waste in expectation of the house-builder';[62] another was in West Kensington (in the days before it was overrun by the bourgeoisie) close to the market-gardens and the brickfields, between Gloucester Road and Earls Court.[63] In north-east London the chief gypsy settlement was at Hackney Wick, 'where the marsh-meadows of the River Lea, unsuitable for building land, seems to forbid the extension of town streets and blocks of brick and stuccoed terraces';[64] there was a smaller settlement near Finsbury Park, in the dust-heaps at the bottom of Hermitage Road.[65] The Battersea gypsies camped in Donovan's Yard, a plot of ground near the South-Western railway, 'commanding an unpicturesque prospect of palings, walls, and arches'. The encampment, in 1900, was occupied for about six months every year, 'from October till the flat-racing season'. It was made up of two long lines of wagons 'broken here and there by a firewood-dealer's hut'. The horses had been sold off 'to save the cost of keeping them in idleness during the cold months'. T. W. Wilkinson, writing about the camp,[66] remarked on the

> curious air of domesticity: . . . women, most of them stamped with their
> tribal characteristics, sit on the steps of the waggons, some at needlework,
> some merely gossiping. Other housewives are engaged on the family wash.
> Bent over tubs and buckets in close proximity to the fire, on which
> clothes are boiling briskly, they are rubbing and rinsing with a will, now
> and again going off for more water to a tap at one end of the ground.

This 'domesticity' was less extraordinary than Wilkinson implies. However far they travelled, the gypsies, like others of the wandering tribes, usually retained a base to which they regularly returned. The larger gypsy-colonies were well established. At Notting Dale a nucleus of families (most of them Hearnes) remained in occupation all the year round. Thomas Hearne, the father of the community, and a chair-bottomer, had converted his van into a makeshift cottage, with an old tin pail serving for a chimney, and a signboard announcing his trade.[67] The Wandsworth gypsies were also well entrenched. 'The houses are many of them owned by the richer members of the clan; and room is found for vans, with wheels or without, in which the poorer members crowd. The gypsies regard their quarter as their castle.'[68] They had been subject to some harassment in the 1870s, when they were driven from the Common by the Metropolitan Board of Works, and later on were hauled up before the local magistrates on account of the 'intolerable nuisance' of their tents, hovels, and vans. But a gypsy capitalist called Penfold had bought up cottages and lands in the vicinity, and twenty years later the colony was flourishing undisturbed, '3 families to a house'.[69] The Battersea colony, too, had acquired the status of semi-permanent residents when Booth enquired about them: 'These people,

living in their vans, come and go, travelling in the country part of every year . . .
They move about a good deal within the London area as well as outside, but are
usually anchored fast all winter, and throughout the summer one or another always
occupies the pitch.'[70]

The ebb and flow of wayfaring life in nineteenth-century England was strongly
influenced by the weather. The months from March to October were the time when
travelling people were to be found on the roads, and when they were joined by every
class of occasional itinerant. With the approach of cold weather, in October and
November, the season of journeyings came to an end and the wandering tribes
returned to town. Spring was the time when long-distance travellers left town.
Country labourers, who wintered in the metropolitan Night Refuges, were said to
'fly off' about March.[71] So did the men who sailed in the Greenland whalers, as one
of their songs reminds us:[72]

> Twas eighteen hundred and twenty four,
> On March the eighteenth day,
> We hoist our colours to the top of the mast,
> And to Greenland bore away, brave boys,
> And to Greenland bore away.

The trampers' London season ended when the Night Refuges closed down:[73]

> The winter is the homeless man's London season; and most of the refuges,
> especially the larger ones, are open only four or five months in the year,
> from November or December till about April. In mid-winter they are most
> crowded, by April they are usually comparatively empty. Still, even to the
> last there is a substantial number at the large refuges. What becomes of
> them when turned out is not very clear. Probably the majority go . . .
> into the country.

Travelling showmen began to leave town quite early in the spring. The peep-
show caravans (Mayhew tells us) generally left London between March and April
'because some fairs begin at that time', and were seldom seen again until October,
'after the fairs is over'.[74] Some showmen had already travelled considerable distances by the time of the Easter Fairs. Manchester showmen turned up regularly at
Blackburn for the annual fair which opened on Easter Monday: on one occasion
there was even a troupe of strolling players from London.[75] Travelling circuses began
their tenting tours in March.[76] Old Joe Baker's Circus, which wintered in the Bristol
slums, had 'taken to the road for the Easter Fairs', and had already reached Worcester
when the young Ben Tillett caught up with them.[77] David Prince Miller, 'weather-
bound' one winter in Carlisle, began the next year's season with a February fair at
Dumfries, then doubled back to Carlisle, and worked his way over to Newcastle upon
Tyne for the Easter Monday 'hopping'. Another year he had an indoor engagement

in Birmingham, which kept him for the winter, and then proceeded to Manchester in the spring, to take part in Knott Mill Fair, 'the great Manchester carnival'.[78] Broadly speaking one may say that the showman's season began with the Easter fairs, but the starting-point was different on certain circuits. In East Anglia the season opened with the great Charter Fair at King's Lynn, which began on 14 February and lasted six days. It was here that Batty, the circus proprietor, began the 'outdoor business' of the season, after putting on a Christmas show indoors; here too, according to one of Mayhew's informants, cheap-jacks started their rounds.[79] In the Thames valley, when 'Lord' George Sanger was a boy, the season opened with the May-Day Fair at Reading. 'Showmen of all descriptions moved out of their winter quarters to attend it', Sanger recalls. Among them was his own father, who travelled the fairs with a peep-show during the summer months, and in the winter returned to his carrying-business in Newbury.[80]

All through the spring men were beginning to move from indoor to outdoor jobs, sometimes taking the step of exchanging a fixed occupation for a roving one. Gas-stokers ('regular winter men')[81] were giving in their notices—or getting the sack—as early as February and March, when the retort-houses began to close down. Only about a third of them were employed all the year round. 'What becomes of the extra men who are employed in the winter?' an official of the Gas, Light & Coke Company was asked by the Labour Commissioners in 1893, and he replied, 'They are only too ready to leave us in the spring.'[82] At the South Metropolitan Gas Works the bulk of them went bricking. 'Our best stokers, at any rate, do', a Charity Organisation Society enquirer was told. 'They give us notice early in the year . . . and then they go to the brickfields in the summer.'[83] The chimney-sweeper's town season ended in May, and both masters and journeymen were thrown out of employment. 'Some turn coster-mongers, others tinkers, knife-grinders &c., and others migrate to the country and get a job at hay making or any other kind of unskilled labour', wrote Mayhew.[84] Those who still worked in the trade went on country rounds, travelling from job to job, and making up their money by the country sale of soot.[85] The maltings season in the breweries ended about the same time, and some thousands of country lab-ourers, who had come up to town for the winter, and spent seven or eight months at the work, returned to their native villages. 'We used to finish at the maltings towards the end of May,' a Suffolk labourer told George Ewart Evans, 'but before you went home you had to have a new suit. You dussn't come home from Burton wearing the suit you went up in . . .'[86]

The spring migration out of London occurred in stages; it began with an outward drift from the city to the suburbs rather than with a single clean break. Regular trampers hung about town as long as they could after the Night Refuges closed down, 'tiring out' the London and suburban workhouses (as one of Mayhew's tramp informants put it) before finally cutting adrift.[87]

The outward movement of the London gypsies only became general in May, and those who gained their living as itinerant agriculturalists moved out even more slowly: 'Christians who wish for opportunities of doing good to the Gipsies in and about London will find many of them in the suburbs in . . . April, May, and June, when they generally find work in the market gardens. In . . . July and August they move into Sussex and Kent, and are engaged in the harvest.'[88] Showmen also frequently spent a month or two in the suburbs before 'pitching it' out in the shires. Stepney Fair ('then the biggest gathering of the kind in England') was the first place where the Sangers pitched, when they wintered in Mile End, and they followed it up with King's Cross Fair, one of the new impromptu fairs which had grown up on the wasteland edge of the city.[89] In later years (when the city extended outwards), the Easter Fair on Wanstead Flats took its place: it was known as the 'Gypsy Fair' from the number of them who made it the first 'gathering' of their season.[90]

By the beginning of June a fresh series of migrations was under way. Gangs of mowers moved about the country, and haymakers followed in their wake. Later on in the summer the corn harvest set up a demand for extra helpers on all sides. At Kenilworth the extra men who came to do the work were from 'Coventry, Ireland, Buckingham and Berkshire'.[91] At Holbeach, Lincolnshire, they included numbers of Irishmen from the big towns of the Midlands—'English Irish' as they were called locally; at Godstone in Surrey there was an immigration from London, Croydon and elsewhere—'frequently travellers on their way to the hop-picking in Kent.'[92] Some of this movement took place within a short migration-range, the surplus labour of the towns being absorbed in the fields of the immediately surrounding countryside. But some of it occurred over longer distances. A town missionary who boarded a steamer at London Bridge in August 1860 found that a 'considerable number' of the 300 passengers were labourers from the southern counties 'going to Yorkshire for the harvest' (the steamer was bound for Hull).[93]

During the summer months there was big money to be earned in the fields, for the man who was prepared to rough it, and to try his luck on tramp. Early in July 1872, for instance, wages were said to have risen as high as eight to ten shillings a day in some of the suburban hayfields of Middlesex.[94] Harvest rates could be nearly as high, even in a low-wage county like Oxfordshire: in August 1872 two builders' labourers at Woodstock were demanding seven-and-six a day to dig the site of a new gasholder 'because the harvest was about to begin'. When the rate was refused as 'exorbitant' they went off to find work as harvesters instead.[95] For a few brief months industrial and agricultural employments faced one another as direct competitors, and the worker who was disgruntled, or ill-paid, or out on strike, was not slow to take advantage of the situation. Those who worked in the 'dangerous' trades, for example— the lowest class of Victorian town labour—had a chance to escape from the wretched conditions in which they worked. 'It is surprising to me how persons can breathe here', a factory inspector wrote of a London enameller. 'One man is sensibly affected; he goes away each year hop picking, for the purpose (as he says) of cleaning himself from chalk.'[96] Amongst London fur-pullers the escape into hopping was general. 'The work, disagreeable at best, is unendurable in hot weather, and when hop or fruit picking in the country offers as an alternative, it is gladly accepted.'[97] There was a similar efflux of labour from some of the white-lead factories, with their dust-laden, poisonous atmosphere. At H. & G. Grace's, Bethnal Green, for example, as many as a third of the employees were said to go off hopping, even though there was no summer shortage of work.[98] Similarly, at the Millwall Lead Company, 'All of them go hopping in the autumn for a month or two, that is one of their chief occupations, but of course that lasts only a short time; and they hawk fruit about if they can; but when they have nothing of that kind to do, then they come back to the white lead works.'[99] In the Brough Lead Works, Sheffield, haymaking rather than hopping provided a seasonal escape. 'Have you any difficulty in getting men to come here?' the manager was asked by the Labour Commission in 1893; 'only just in the summer time', he replied, 'in the middle of the summer, when there is hay harvest and other jobs.'[100]

The summer harvests prompted a whole series of different itineraries. Some labourers followed the harvests round—haymaking in June, turnip-hoeing or pea-picking in July, corn-harvesting in August, hop-picking or fruit-picking in September. Others went out only for a single crop or relied upon the odd jobs in the countryside to support them on the road. Those who went for one harvest sometimes stayed for two, either because the work was available or because they had given up their lodgings in town. Others alternated between town and country. Even those who followed the 'long' harvest were by no means all of one type, and there seems to have been a broad division between those who visited a variety of *places*, travelling from county to county, and those who did a variety of *jobs*, all of them within a single district. In Lincolnshire and the East Riding, for instance, migrant labourers were divided between those who worked the country in regular rounds, 'beginning further south and working northwards as the harvests successively ripen', and others, 'less migratory than this' who came into a district at hay harvest 'and manage to find sufficient work at odd jobs in the same district to keep them till corn harvest commences.' Both, it may be added, hailed from the Midland manufacturing towns.[101]

Haymaking was the starting point for many of these summer rounds. Cobbett called it the 'first haul' of the 'perambulating' labourer,[102] and the London tramp regarded it as 'just the proper season' for leaving town. 'Down I strolled into Sussex, towards the border of Hampshire, and soon got a job', one of Thor Fredur's informants told him, 'half-a-crown a day, my food, a corner of a barn with clean straw to lie at night, as much beer as I would drink while at work . . . I . . . always begin with a spell at haymaking.'[103] The Irish came over for it *en masse*, leaving the mowing for native-born labourers, but following closely behind them. Haymaking in the nearby countryside was one of the resources which enabled the Padiham weavers to support themselves during the long strike of 1859.[104] It was still a standby for out-of-work labourers in York when Rowntree and Lasker made their study for *Unemployment*, along with 'carting', 'droving', 'farm work', 'snow sweeping'; the weekly itinerary of an unemployed grocer's assistant shows the way in which it was dovetailed into the local network of odd jobs:[105]

*Monday*—Called on . . . [grocer] in answer to an advertisement. Was told I

134

had been too long out of the trade. Then searched advertisement in the
Library.

*Tuesday*—Got job of digging up sand at boat landing-place (having drawn
owner's attention to need for the job).

*Wednesday*—Same.

*Thursday*—Worked for boat owner. Earned 3s. 6d.

*Friday*—Library for advertisement.

*Saturday*—Applied for work at stores and for horse clipping at . . . without
success. Spent afternoon outside the town looking for a job haymaking.

*Monday*—Started at 4 a.m. seeking haymaking job at three villages
[named]: got work at 9 a.m. Came home early owing to rain. Earned 3s.

Market-gardens, too, drew upon migrant labour from the towns. The London Irish
were prominent amongst them, and according to 'A Wandering Celt', writing in the
*Labour News* for 1874, did most of the pea- and fruit-picking for the London market.
'Young Irish women, who in London during the winter are fruit-sellers or working in
dust-yards, pickle-factories, sack-making, etc., go into the market-gardens for the
summer.'[106] In Essex there was a regular influx of Londoners in June and July—
most of them rough women from the East End, who took on summer employment as
market-garden hands, and then crossed over to Kent, in time for the start of the
hopping. James Greenwood came upon a little colony of them at Rainham in 1881,
'browner by many shades than gipsies'. 'There ain't no men among 'em,' a local told
him, 'only women, and girls, and a few lads.' The work (chiefly pea-picking) lasted
from eight to ten weeks, and was paid at a flat rate of eighteenpence a day. But much
of the work could be done piece-work, which suited a woman with children to work
alongside her: 'in fine weather and at certain work—onion-pulling for instance—
some families earned as much as four shillings a day.'[107]

Summer was the height of the travelling season. There were more navvies on the
road, moving from job to job,[108] more tramps, more travelling hawkers and dealers.
Street-arabs left London in shoals, traversing the country in every direction, and
trading (or thieving) as they tramped: 'they sometimes sleep in low lodging-houses . . .
frequently "skipper it" in the open air . . . and occasionally in barns or outhouses.'[109]
Vagrants, too, preferred to spend the summer out of town, and 'seasoned it' al
fresco, or staged their way across the country with the aid of the Casual Wards. In
the workshop trades the tramping artisan, who trudged along under his oil-skin
knapsack, was a familiar figure at this time, as Thomas Wright, the journeyman
engineer, reminds us. According to him, it was a 'frequent practice' for men on
tramp to do their travelling by night (when the weather was hot) and to have their
sleep by day, in an orchard or a field 'conveniently near the roadside'.[110]

The wayfaring constituency was further enlarged by summer newcomers. There
was a seasonal influx of Italians, for example. Some seven or eight hundred of them
crossed over to England every year for the ice-cream trade. 'Each spring brings a
contingent', wrote Ernest Aves, in his notes on the Italian colony in Clerkenwell.

'They come in small parties from all parts of Italy, travel slowly, take their food with them and when autumn comes go back to their wives and their vineyards.'[111] The organ-grinders arrived a little later. 'June July Aug. Sept, are the busiest months, when a great number migrate and travel the country through visiting Birmingham Bradford, even Scotland, Wales & most seaside resorts . . . It is then that a great number of fresh arrivals are seen, but as winter arrives they gradually depart.'[112] On a larger scale there was the annual influx of harvesters from Ireland who began to arrive in large numbers at the end of May and followed the harvests round. The coming of really warm weather, in May and June, also tempted a weaker and more occasional class of traveller to venture out of town. Some hundreds of sandwich-board men, for instance, took to the roads at this time, most of them army pensioners and 'beyond middle life'; 'in the summer . . . numbers of them go into the country and by pea, hop or fruit-picking, or in some other way, obtain a livelihood until September or October, when they return to their old haunts.'[113] Even in the workhouse there was a class of inmate who had their summer 'tour'—old men and women, who laid up in the 'house' for most of the year, but enjoyed a brief spell of freedom when conditions outside allowed it. Booth came upon some of them in Stepney Union workhouse.[114]

| Male | Married | 69 | Carpenter | Wife left him and went to her son's. Man goes on tramp during summer months. |
| Male | Married | 56 | General labourer | Man was doing casual work when relief was first given . . . admitted in 1886 . . . Only out for short periods in the summer since. |
| Female | Married | 63 | | Woman had medicines in 1882. She goes out nursing or fruit picking in summer, and winters in workhouse. |
| Female | Widow | 60 | Washing | Husband died (1849). Woman had out-relief, but it was stopped. Goes hopping with daughter. |

The largest movement out of town took place in August and September. It was the season both for feasts and fairs ('Wakes' weeks in the Potteries and Lancashire), and for holidays on the sands. All kinds of opportunities opened up for those who followed the track of holiday-spending, and the regular showmen were joined by a whole army of itinerant hucksters ministering to the pleasure-goers' needs. It was also, in a different branch of summer activity, the height of the harvest season. The corn harvests which began in August and which lasted (until the coming of the mechanical reaper and binder) for up to six weeks, set up an enormous demand for extra hands and, as in the case of haymaking, some of this was supplied from the towns. Fruit-picking and hopping, the September harvests, offered a choice of less strenuous opportunities.

The late summer exodus corresponded to a general slackness in town employment. August and September were the 'dead months' of the year in many of the indoor trades (especially those which depended upon the world of rank and fashion), in heavy industry (on account of the heat), and in certain branches of factory work. During the 'Long Vacation' even the occasional law-writer was said to go off hopping.[115] In the London docks 'very many men' found work elsewhere in the months from July to September, 'the time of the harvest, and . . . the militia . . . in training'.[116] The same was true in the coalfields, an important source of harvest labour in the Midlands and South Wales. In the Black Country many smithies were closed up when the inhabitants took themselves off *en masse* to the fruit-picking in the Vale of Evesham, and the hopping in Herefordshire. Women and girls found work particularly hard to come by at this time. A 'little army'[117] of ironers and laundresses was thrown out of work when the middle class went off on holiday (some followed them to the sea-side);[118] the tailoring trade was invariably dull at the end of the London season, and the number of women and girls thrown out of employment was said to be 'incredible'.[119] Factory work was also scarce. At Allen & Hanbury's, Bethnal Green, one of the biggest factories in the East End, something like a quarter of the girls were sacked every summer;[120] the same was true of the match-factory girls (some found alternative employment in the jam factories, others went hop-picking or fruit-picking in Kent),[121] and in the bundlewood yards on the Surrey side of the Thames: 'Nothing is made up for stock . . . the women go fruit and hop picking, and the men find casual employment as best they can.'[122]

This is no doubt one of the reasons why women and girls figure so largely in the late-summer movements out of town. Another was that the work was of a kind which gave them a positive advantage over men—work for the nimble-fingered. Hopping was often undertaken by family groups with a woman in command and the husband (if he existed) elsewhere. It was piece-work, and children could make as great a contribution to earnings as grown-ups. Fruit-picking seems to have been largely in the hands of itinerant girl labourers. London work girls who went 'fruiting' in the orchards of West Middlesex were joined by others who had come south from Staffordshire and Lancashire: there is a good description of them in Pask's *Eyes of the Thames* (1889):[123]

> the North Country girls . . . look forward to this fruit harvest ten miles from London to find them the means to form a little nest-egg to help them through the coming winter. Their work, when they choose to take over-time, which they generally do, is, in the early summer, from half-past three in the morning until eight at night. By this custom, they can always, if they choose, earn over eighteen shillings a week, doing piece-work, or, as it is termed in market-garden parlance, 'great' work . . . In their short print dresses and with their red cotton handkerchiefs tied over their heads, the girls look well enough to form a pretty study for any follower of the Fred Walker school. Still, despite rosy cheeks, blue eyes, and agile forms,

the romance is soon broken when they open their mouths. If ever a rival could be found for Billingsgate, it would be some London market-orchard. Even the Irish girls, who can boast a far higher standard of morality, are as foul-tongued as a lighterman working on the Pool.

The September hop-picking was the jamboree of the wandering tribes. Mayhew called it the 'grand rendezvous for the vagrancy of England and Ireland.'[124] Gypsies came to it from every part of southern England—'nearly all the gypsies in England', according to one inflationary account.[125] In London the common lodging-houses were said to be 'almost deserted' on account of it, 'the Bohemian inmates having betaken themselves *en masse* to the pleasant fields of Kent'.[126] Even the workhouse population was notably affected.[127] The Irish poor had a 'positive mania' for hopping, and the 'wild unrestrained kind of life' which it allowed;[128] for those who travelled the harvests it was the climax of the summer's round; for many more it was the one departure of the year from town: 'It is no uncommon thing for the houses of rooms to be shut up and for whole families to go off together', wrote Denvir. 'In the season of 1891 as many as eight hundred, chiefly Irish, went from Poplar alone, and it is the same among our poorer fellow-countrymen in other parts of London.'[129] Trampers were moving off to the hop-fields fully a month before the picking season began. 'They are gone for about two months and then we have another rush', Mr Duffus, the Superintendent of St Giles workhouse, told an enquirer in 1891.[130] In September they 'infested'[131] the hopping counties of Hereford and Kent, a ragged army of followers, some of them quite indigent: when an inspection was made of the casual ward at Hollingbourne in 1868, only two of the 289 inmates ('all hoppers') had a sum of money amounting to twopence on them. 'The great majority had nothing, and were partly without clothing.'[132]

The social composition of the migrant picking-force gradually changed in the course of the nineteenth century, partly because of the greatly increased demand for hopping-labour, partly because of improved methods of cultivation (which shortened the season to as little as three weeks) and partly because of the cheap trains promoted by the railway companies which put the hop-fields within reach of the proletarian family group, instead of only its more able-bodied members. In earlier times the French, the Welsh, and later on the Irish migrant labourers had been prominent: in the second half of the nineteenth century the hopping became increasingly an affair of women and children from the towns. Long-distance migration did not cease (a man from Warrington who went hopping in Kent in 1893 found himself working alongside two Yorkshire colliers who were out on strike)[133] but most recruitment was from nearer localities. At Martley in Worcestershire the extra hands were reported as coming from 'Stourbridge, Dudley and the mining districts',[134] those at Bromyard in Herefordshire were from Cradley Heath.[135] In East Kent many of the hoppers came from the Sussex villages and the seaport towns.[136] In mid-Kent and west Kent the immigration was more Cockney, being drawn from the Medway Towns (2,000 hoppers came from Gravesend in 1876),[137] from Croydon, and, above all from Inner

London (according to one account, Poplar sent to East Farleigh, Bermondsey to Wateringbury, Shadwell to Paddock Wood).[138] The Farnham hoppers in Surrey (said to number about 5,000 in 1887) were attributed by Sturt to 'the slums of Reading and West London',[139] in earlier years they had come from Portsmouth and the south-coast towns.[140] There were slum districts in which something like a general turn-out took place as hop-picking approached. Ellen Chase, one of Octavia Hill's property managers, says that 'exciting rumours' of the size of the hop harvest filled her Deptford street for weeks beforehand;[141] and George Meek, who went hopping in Mayfield, Sussex, in 1883, remarks on the 'rough lot from the purlieus of Edward Street Brighton' whom he found there.[142] Many of the hoppers travelled down together in family and neighbourhood groups, and worked together for the same farmer in their own companies. The frequency of hop-pickers' strikes, one of the more affecting if least noticed features of this seasonal migration, may be partly accounted for by the fact that many of them were already closely knit together.

After the harvests the movement from town to country was reversed. Country occupations began to grow scarce, while in the towns, on the other hand, there was a general revival of trade. The season of journeyings came to an end, and with the approach of cold weather the wandering tribes returned to town 'with the instinct which sends some birds of passage southwards at the same season'.[143] 'I like the tramping life well enough in summer', a girl tramp told Mayhew, ''cause there's plenty of victuals to be had then . . . it's the winter . . . we can't stand. Then we generally come to London.' Her sentiments were echoed by another of Mayhew's informants—a girl who passed the winter in the Metropolitan Asylum for the Houseless Poor. 'I do like to be in the country in the summer-time', she told him. 'I like hay making and hopping, because that's a good bit of fun . . . It's the winter that sickens me.'[144] Travelling in winter was 'an unusual thing for the gipsies':[145] it was very little practised by vagrants,[146] or by tramping artisans.[147] Even the regular tramper, who moved about for the sake of keeping on the move, rather than with any particular destination in mind, deserted the roads.

Travelling people began to drift back to town in October, and by November the movement was general. 'All over England', wrote an observer in 1861, 'a characteristic migration sets in . . . tens and hundreds of thousands . . . driven by necessity . . . swarm into the towns.'[148] The largest movement, and certainly the most frequently commented on, was in the direction of London, the winter Mecca of the wandering tribes. But it had its counterpart in a whole series of local migrations from country to town, and in a general change-about, which continued right through the autumn, from outdoor to indoor jobs, and from summer to winter trades. General labourers took their navvying skills into the gas-works. Travelling sawyers exchanged the saw-pit and the woodland clearing for a workshop bench ('towards winter time . . . a roof over their heads became desirable').[149] Migratory thieves, who conducted their summer business al fresco, at the race-grounds and the fairs, turned to a spell of safe-cracking or burglary in town aided by the long dark nights. (November, according to Manby Smith, was the month when many of them came back to London.[150]) Cheap-jacks rented shops and conducted mock auctions from their own premises instead of from temporary pitches in the open air.[151] Not all the exchanges were as regular or predictable as this: Booth gives us a glimpse of one or two in the street notes which he collected from London School Board visitors: 'Punch and Judy show in summer and makes iron clamps in winter'; 'Works at watercress beds in season, and sweeps chimneys in winter.'[152]

A first wave of travellers returned to London immediately after the hop-picking. 'Within a few days' (according to one account) some of the gypsies were back in town: 'hopping over, they go, almost *en masse* . . . to buy French and German baskets . . . in Houndsditch.'[153] In the Kentish suburbs (Gravesend, Woolwich, Greenwich) there was 'always' an influx of unskilled labourers at this time, 'men who . . . resort to the casual labour afforded by the revolution of the seasons.'[154] Some of them found local employment as rubbish-carters and scavengers, others drifted on into town. In Notting Dale, the common lodging-houses, 'comparatively empty' during hay-making, hop-picking, and fruit-picking, filled up with returning travellers:[155] Bangor Street ('one of the most dangerous streets in London') was said to be inhabited 'almost entirely by' them. St Giles, '*le quartier général des vagabonds*', was very soon packed: tenements, closed up for the summer, were once again re-occupied, as the inhabitants returned with their summer earnings from Kent; the lodging-houses took on their winter complement of sandwich-men, loafers, and touts; and the casual ward of the workhouse was crammed with travellers (many of them country labourers) making their way back home.[156] The Holborn Irish returned home in mid-October, much to the dismay of the local Medical Officer of Health, who complained of 'crowds of squalid Irish people . . . returning from the country to their winter haunts in the Courts and Alleys.'[157] Even on the London waterfront the end of hopping made itself felt: 'I never saw so many callers', wrote a correspondent of the *Labour News* in October 1874, 'the dock labourers having returned from the hop gardens . . . seem to have grown in number.'[158]

Not all the travelling harvesters returned at this time. Some of them jobbed about the country until the frosts came, or worked their way home in stages. Potato-lifting kept some of them out of town until November—the West Ham Irish[159] in the early nineteenth century, for example, and the travelling Irish of York in later years.[160] Trade tramps, too, sometimes delayed their arrival in town. Travelling coopers had a mid-autumn season at Lowestoft and Yarmouth, where they were employed in the herring trade.[161] In the Northampton shoemaking trade there was a 'very large influx' of travellers a little before Christmas, 'when the better sort of work is more brisk, and when there are generally more orders in the "bespoke" department'.[162] Cheap-jacks and showmen were among the latecomers. Many of them followed the autumn fairs, such as the great autumn cattle fairs, and the Michaelmas and Martinmas 'Hirings', or wound up their season by 'pitching' at the late town fairs. Some showmen delayed their wintering almost till Christmas, when the 'World's

Fair' ('the great event in the showmen's year') opened at Islington and van-dwellers from all parts of the country made a winter camp in the yard of the Agricultural Hall.[163]

'Wintering in town' was a regular part of the showmen's round, and the difficulty of making it pay was one which cost them much ingenuity. Some, it seems, let out their shows, and lived upon the proceeds, like the little 'half gypsy' colony whom Hollingshead came upon in Owen's Yard, Lambeth, settled in the midst of dust-heaps and factories.[164] The more enterprising adapted themselves to the conditions of town life by hiring temporary premises and putting on their shows indoors (the penny sideshows and 'gaffs' which figure so largely in descriptions of nineteenth-century street-life were often promoted in this way). 'Lord' George Sanger, who seems to have been very successful in making wintering pay, has left an excellent account of his repertory. One winter he went in for *poses plastiques* and conjuring, and hired a warehouse in Bethnal Green Road where the crowd sometimes was so great 'that we had to square the policeman not to interfere'. Another year he took on an empty chapel in Clare Market, and fitted it up as an impromptu theatre, playing a round of pieces, 'gaff fashion', and for Christmas put on a pantomime. Wintering in Liverpool, during the Crimean winter of 1854–5, he took on a large piece of ground near 'Paddy's Market' ('the lowest part of Liverpool'), and built a board and canvas theatre, with admission charges of a penny:[165]

> Here we had a semi-dramatic-cum-circus sort of entertainment that
> exactly suited the neighbourhood . . . what we mostly did was acting on the
> gaff principle, and there was nothing we were afraid to tackle in the
> dramatic line, from Shakespeare downwards . . . One of our best and most
> popular actors . . . was Bill Matthews. He . . . made a big hit . . . by his
> impersonation of Paddy Kelly, an Irishman who had distinguished himself
> as a soldier at the Alma, news of which battle, fought on September 20th,
> had thrilled the nation. Well, Matthews did a riding act, 'Paddy Kelly,
> the hero of the Russian war', and in his uniform, slashing at the enemy
> with a sword and plentiful dabs from a sponge of rose-pink, excited the
> audience to frenzy.

Trampers 'led by an instinct somewhat analogous to that of . . . animals who lurk in holes from the inclemency of the season',[166] came up to town for the shelter and the warmth. In London, according to Mayhew, they turned up each year 'as regularly as noblemen' to season it in town.[167] 'In the winter season', the Chief Constable of Manchester complained,[168]

> tramps flock to large towns such as Manchester, where they can obtain
> warm sleeping-quarters in the various brick-yards, boiler-houses, and
> different buildings connected with factories and workshops; also they can
> generally obtain free meals, which are provided by the various philan-
> thropic societies in Manchester during the cold season. In the summer

> months they migrate to the country . . . sleeping out in the open when the
> weather is good.

Night Refuges ('strawyards' as they were known to *habitués*)[169] brought many of
them to town. In London, critics alleged, there was an immediate increase in vagrancy when they opened up for the winter (usually in November, but the precise date
depended on the state of the weather).[170] 'A great number of persons come to London
in November, when the refuges are generally opened', an officer of the Mendicity
Society complained. 'It is not an unfrequent answer, when they are asked, "How
is it you have come to London again? You were here last year". "Oh, I thought the
Houseless was open".'[171] Night Refuges (which were financed by private subscrip-
tion) were much more popular with travellers than the workhouse, and, while they
were open, slept many more people than the metropolitan Casual Wards.[172] The
regime, though spartan, was comparatively kindly. The stranger was offered warmth
and shelter without any of the humiliations and restraints associated with the Poor
Law. Inmates could stay for as long as a month at a time (in the Casual Wards the
rule was two nights only), and they were allowed to go out when they liked (in the
Casual Wards shelter had to be paid for by hard labour and forcible detention for a
day). At the Playhouse Yard Asylum, Cripplegate, the oldest and largest of the
metropolitan asylums (it later removed to Banner Street) the dormitories were
kept 'always . . . heated', and there was a gigantic communal fire. 'As these are
lighted some time before the hour of opening, the place has a warmth and cosiness
which must be very grateful to those who have encountered the cold air all the day,
and perhaps the night before.'[173] Night Refuges existed in a number of the larger
towns: Manchester, Birmingham, and Edinburgh each had one; in London there
were seven (more, when the Salvation Army embarked on its social work), quite
apart from such specialized institutions as the Destitute Sailors' Asylum, in Well
Street, Ratcliffe Highway, and critics may well have been right to hold them responsible for so many homeless men making London their winter retreat.[174]

The autumn migrations, like those of the spring, took place in stages, and once
again it was the outskirts and environs of the town which felt them first. Vagrants,
it seems, made their way into London sideways, circling the outer ring of the metropolis, and testing the hospitality of the brickfields—or the suburban Casual Wards—
before making their way into town. Travelling prostitutes seem also to have arrived
back in this way, with preliminary comings and goings. 'They travel round the
country in summer and come into London in November', an officer of the Mendicity
Society told an enquiry in 1846. 'If they come before the refuge is open they go to
Peckham, then they go to St Olave's, and then to Greenwich, and other unions.'[175]
Gypsies ended their autumn journeys on the outer peripheries of town ('as close as
you please to the skirts of civilization'),[176] but as the weather grew more severe some
of them moved further in, and went to live in rooms. 'They leave the country, and
suburban districts of London', wrote a City Missionary in 1860, '. . . and make their
dwelling in some low court . . . 2 and 3 families . . . in one small room.'[177] George

Smith came upon a little colony of this kind when he visited Canning Town in the winter of 1879–80, seventeen families crowding together in two small cottages, where they had crept 'for . . . the winter'.[178] Families like this occasionally visited Deptford. Ellen Chase recalls that they would 'tide over the rough weather' by renting temporary accommodation. 'The walls would remain as bare as they found them . . . young and old sat upon upturned boxes about the small grate, as contented as if it were a camp fire.'[179]

As well as the travellers, returning to base, the towns received a large winter influx of refugees. Some came for the charities and shelter. Many were winter out-of-works, who came up to town (sometimes unwillingly) when every other resource had failed them. 'It was when the snow set in . . . I thought I would come to London', an inmate at the Houseless Poor Asylum told Mayhew:[180]

> The last job I had was six weeks before Christmas, at Boston, in Lincolnshire. I couldn't make 1s. 6d. a day on account of the weather. I had 13s., however, to start with, and I went on the road . . . going where I heard there was a chance of a job, up or down anywhere, here or there, but there was always the same answer, 'Nobody wanted—no work for their own constant men'. I was so beat out as soon as my money was done—it lasted ten days—that I parted with my things one by one. First my waistcoat, then my stockings (three pair of them), then three shirts . . . After I left Boston, I got into Leicestershire, and was at Cambridge and Wisbeach, and Lynn, and Norwich; and I heard of a job among brickmakers at Low Easthrop, in Suffolk, but it was no go. The weather was against it, too. It was when the snow set in. And then I thought I would come to London, as God in his goodness might send me something to do.

London was full of such winter refugees, caricatured, and yet in some sense truly represented, by the 'froze out gardeners', who regularly appeared in winter as beggars, or buskers, about the city streets. Night Refuges ('the outcast's haven') catered largely for men of this class. 'Travelling tradesmen' were said to compose the bulk of the inmates of the Ham Yard Hospice—trade tramps who had been reduced to a state of complete destitution, and could not afford even the price of a lodging-house bed; country labourers figured largely at Banner Street, 'a very rough class of men, who will work if they can get it . . . digging among fruit trees and market-garden work—in the fields'.[181]

A certain number of farm labourers, turned off after harvest, drifted into the towns, and they were joined by others as country employment grew scarcer and the weather more severe. In Norfolk and Suffolk there was a class of freelance labourers, known as 'joskins', who went off after harvest to Lowestoft and Yarmouth and got work in the autumn fishings (October and November were the height of the East Anglian herring season); another class migrated to the breweries of Burton-on-Trent.[182] Farm labourers in Monmouthshire and Nottinghamshire took up winter employment in the pits;[183] in Carmarthenshire, at mid-century, some of them went off to the ironworks ('in the summer they return home or go to England for the harvest').[184] In Sussex, according to a report of 1895, 'the more helpless class' made for Brighton and Hove, 'large towns . . . where there are many charities'.[185] Most of these migrants disappeared, for the season, into obscurity—mere 'birds of passage' in the town—and the historian is fortunate when he comes upon an individual case, like the one recorded by Steel-Maitland and Miss Squire in Jenner's Row, Birmingham:[186]

> Mr. J. and his wife, in third floor front, were occupied in making straw-baskets, which they sell to some of the family shops. Mr. J. about fifty, seemed a superior type of man. He said he should not take to regular home-life now. For the last twenty years he had tramped from town to town. During the winter he and his wife took a furnished room, and in the summer they walked into Herefordshire, where he did apple-pulling, and other odd jobs at the cider harvest, for a farmer. They were allowed to lock up a few pots and pans and a bed in a shed on the farm, and to this they returned every summer. Mr. J. said he had wintered in Plymouth, Manchester, Bristol and in London. They generally reckoned to be in the country for about five months of the year. If times were good, 'The missus' might perhaps go by train, but he always walked . . . He thought he should go to Cardiff next winter, if all was well . . . He had found Birmingham an expensive place, and did not think he would return. (This was his first visit.)

One of the most enduring of these autumn migrations was that which brought many hundreds of country labourers to work in the breweries. It has been vividly documented from oral tradition by George Ewart Evans, and his account can be supplemented by documentary references from earlier years. Maltsters were usually taken on at the beginning of October and continued till about the latter end of May, 'being about seven months of the year'.[187] The great majority of them were drawn from the country—'big-framed men, strong enough to handle the comb-sacks (sixteen stones each) of barley'. At Hertford and Ware, according to a *Morning Chronicle* account in 1850, 'nearly the whole of them are employed as agricultural labourers when not engaged in malting.'[188] At Newark, where 460 maltsters were employed in the 1890s, only about a third of the men were engaged all the year round, 'the rest go into the kilns in September, and remain till May or June.'[189] Farm labourers in Derbyshire went up to Burton-on-Trent. 'The winter employment in Burton helps to keep wages up', the Agricultural Employment Commissioners were told in 1868, 'especially for the hired single men.' 'A good many men go to Burton in the winter, where they get 13s a week and beer . . . many of them would be out of work in winter if they didn't.'[190] The catchment area for Burton was very wide indeed. In the later nineteenth century it extended as far as East Anglia, and George Ewart Evans has collected some remarkably detailed testimonies from labourers who made the last of these autumn journeys in the years 1900–30. He has also recovered a

Burton labour list for 1890–1 which shows the extent of the East Anglian hirings. It is taken from the records of Messrs Bass, Ratcliff & Gretton. Here are the first twelve entries.[191]

| Name of worker | Home village | Nearest railway station |
| --- | --- | --- |
| ADDISON, George | Melton | Woodbridge |
| ASHEN, Henry | Flempton | Bury St. Edmunds |
| ASHEN, William | Flempton | Bury St. Edmunds |
| BALDWIN, William | Aldburgh | Harleston |
| BARBER, Walter | Martlesham | Woodbridge |
| BEAUMONT, Peter | Baylham | Ipswich |
| BETTS, Arthur | St. Cross | Harleston |
| BACKHOUSE, Jesse | Sutton | Woodbridge |
| BLOOMFIELD, Richard | St. Lawrence | Harleston |
| BRAGG, John | Bardwell | Bury St. Edmunds |
| BRETT, Charles | Martlesham | Woodbridge |
| BROOKS, Alfred | Pakenham | Bury St. Edmunds |

Building-workers flocked up to town when the frosts put a stop to the country trade. In London they figured very largely among the winter refugees—pick and shovel men, who tramped the metropolitan building-sites looking for work ('*bona fide* navvies, up to "Lunnun" in search of a job'); country craftsmen like the 'strong and handy carpenter' whom the roving correspondent of the *Labour News* met in Greek Street, a 'most desponding' man who had left Watford just after Christmas, and tramped it inside and outside the town, without finding himself a place; painters and decorators 'calling at every job, and offering, in many instances, to work at half-starvation wages'. 'Outside the heavy jobs on hand', he writes in January 1873 '. . . may be seen building hands and labourers . . . asking the foreman to put them on, and the reply is that they have already too many men.'[192] Painters were particularly badly placed, and are often singled out for attention in distress reports. At the Newport Market Refuge for instance, they were by far the most numerous group of inmates—57 of the 644 men admitted in 1889.[193]

The months from November to February were always a bad time in the building trade, but it was only in the country and suburban branches of the trade that the stand-still was complete.[194] In the towns there were big contract jobs where work continued in all but the worst of weather. Stonemasons, 'though apt to be severely hit by a really hard winter', stood a fair chance of getting work; so did navvies. The ordinary builders' labourers were less well placed, but some got employment with the vestries, some went into the gas-works, and there was always a chance of employment wherever there was a heavy job in hand. In the mid-Victorian years 'no end of work' was provided (even in winter) by town improvement schemes, by the building of Board Schools and Model Dwellings, churches and chapels, town halls and commercial offices, by extension work on the railway terminals and the docks; by road-widening work, tramways and the laying out of drainage works and sewers.[195] In

London such great undertakings as the building of the Metropolitan Railway (where the writer of the *Reminiscences of a Stonemason* was taken on for tunnelling work in January 1866),[196] the Thames Embankment, and the Law Courts, were a continuing source of winter employment.[197] Cubitt's, one of the largest London builders, seem actually to have put on extra men in winter: 'when the summer comes they go brickmaking', a branch manager told an enquiry in the 1890s, 'the Brick men are very good workers, and we always give them a job. They come and go.'[198] It was the same in some of the big provincial towns, to judge from a trade report which appeared in January 1882.[199]

> LIVERPOOL . . . the works in hand are of almost unexampled importance and magnitude. The City Corporation is proceeding actively with its immense operations for supplementing the present water supply with water from the Vyrnwy reservoir. Each of the railway companies having a terminus at Liverpool is making extensions. The Mersey Docks and Harbour Board is engaged in improving at various points its vast system of docks. The scheme for tunnelling the Mersey is being pushed forward actively. A new university is being erected. New commercial and trading edifices are springing up in all directions.
>
> MANCHESTER. In this district the building trade is fairly active so far as heavy work for public and business purposes is concerned but in house-building, either of the cottage, or in the better class of dwellings, there is comparatively little doing . . . The Manchester Corporation have several important works in hand. A new free library and reading-room with the basement occupied by shops . . . recently erected on the old Knott Mill Fair ground, are on the point of completion . . . New baths are . . . being erected by the Corporation for the Rochdale Road district . . . the contractor . . . Mr. James Hind . . . has also in hand for the Corporation the erection of women's swimming baths, as an addition to the present Leaf Street baths . . . Amongst other important work at present in hand . . . is a new General Post Office, a new railway station for the London and North Western Railway Company, and new business premises for the proprietors of the *Manchester Guardian* . . .

Perhaps sailors might be classed among the winter refugees. There were many more of them on shore in winter than in summer, weather-bound or without a berth. Some found shore-going occupations for the season—for instance as dock labourers or as shipwrights—but most of them swelled the ranks of the unemployed: at the Destitute Sailors' Asylum, Well Street, London, established in 1827 to supply shelter, food and clothing to distressed seamen, 'and to keep them until they can obtain employment', winter admissions were more than double those of the summer months.[200] The months of December, January and February 'usually' found the shipping trade at its lowest point in the West Coast ports—at Fleetwood in Lancashire, for example,[201] at Liverpool (where the emigrant traffic seasonally collapsed), and at Milford Haven, where a great number of vessels, 'large and small', and manned by men of many nations, sheltered for the winter.[202] Many thousands of sailors were shored up in the East Coast ports, when the Sound froze over and the Baltic trade came to a stop. The period of this winter standstill varied from year to year, depending on the state of the weather: in 1895 it was causing unemployment among the seamen of North Shields and Grimsby as late as May;[203] in mild winters it could be quite brief. Bagshawe has left a vivid description of the winter scene at Whitby when the Baltic traders laid up:[204]

> The old quays were thronged with . . . lads . . . home from long cruises . . .
> Grave old skippers stood in knots at the Bridge-end and fought their
> battles with gales and bad holding-ground over again, and discussed the
> chances of good freights in the coming spring, when the ice should loosen
> its hold on the northern waters, and each of them would strive to be the
> first of the year to break into the silent fiords and gulfs.

For the man who was looking for work, October was a good time for coming up to town. Vestries were beginning to recruit sweepers and street orderlies, in anticipation of the late autumnal muds; extra men were taken on at the public parks for end-of-season gravelling and repairs.[205] The gas-works were making up their winter labour force; the breweries were beginning their 'regular busy season' (in London the biggest brewings took place in October, immediately following the arrival of the hops).[206] In the building industry there was a late burst of employment—'an early covering-in process seems to be the one thing aimed at', wrote the *Labour News* in October 1876.[207] Some of the workshop trades enjoyed a 'second season' in mid-autumn (hatters and brushmakers, for example);[208] in others it was the peak period of the year, notably amongst the journeymen coopers,[209] the bookbinders, and in the printing trades, where the production of Christmas numbers, almanacks, and the 'great variety of . . . literary productions that usually crop up about this season of the year', kept 'grass hands' in full work.[210]

A certain amount of extra employment became seasonally available on the waterfront. In the Liverpool docks some 2,500 extra porters were taken on when the cotton season began: 'A certain number of these are men who systematically follow another trade in one season or go to sea and come back for the busy period between October and March.'[211] In the London docks there were more men employed in December than at any other time of the year. Waterfront industries too were seasonally brisk, notably the oil mills at Hull, 'the largest seed-crushing centre in the United Kingdom',[212] and cotton-picking at Liverpool. There was a steadily increasing volume of work at the riggers, the sail-makers, and the shipwrights as the weather grew more severe. Winter was the height of the repairing season, with many ships laid up for the purpose of dry docking, or put on the slip to have their bottoms caulked, coal-tarred, and blackleaded. At Whitby, when the Baltic traders laid up, the town presented a 'stirring scene', with the ships moored in tiers across the upper harbour, and many men at work. 'The caulking mallets rang merrily in half-a-dozen shipyards; rope-walks and sail-lofts worked overtime, and the air was redolent of pitch-kettles and new timber.'[213] Deep-sea ships continued to be treated in this way in the days of steam: the *Great Eastern* was put on the gridiron after its first transatlantic crossing, and laid up at Milford Haven for the winter.[214] The winter harvest of wrecks brought more work to the repairing yards as well as providing salvage men (such as the Yarmouth beachmen) with a full-time occupation. 'Seamen seem more abundant than berths, but not more so than is usual at this season', wrote the West of England correspondent of the *Labour News* in January 1873, 'the many shipping casualties having found temporary employment for many of them, and abundant work for the shipwrights and sail makers.'[215]

Industrial employment was less open to the wayfarer, but a limited amount of it became seasonally available. For example, oil mills ('very warm work') recruited their winter labour force from those who followed the summer trades.[216] So did some of the coal-mines. Both steel-smelting, which was slackest in June and July, and iron-puddling, which was at full stretch in November, were to a certain extent winter trades,[217] with extra jobs at times for the rough class of general labourer. Gas-works were by far the most frequent employers of this class of labour. They began putting on extra men 'about the latter end of August'[218] and took in many more in midwinter, when the 'dark . . . days of fog and cold' drew in. The work (stoking and firing) was intensely laborious (there was said to be no other trade in England where a man lost weight and size more quickly),[219] and the hours were incredibly long (a seventy-eight hour week was quite normal in 1882).[220] But it was very well paid. Winter 'so much dreaded by others', was hailed by gas-stokers as an old friend (wrote an observer) 'the harbinger of . . . plenty'.[221] Winter hands at the gas-works were largely recruited from migrant labourers who spent the summer out of town, brickmakers especially, but also a 'good proportion' of builders' labourers, navvies, and 'many . . . who . . . go into the country for farming work in the summer'.[222] Will Thorne, who went navvying and brick-loading in the spring and summer, has left a very good account of the way men tramped up to town for the work:[223]

> I had always wanted to go to London, and my desire . . . was stimulated by letters from an old workmate . . . who was now working at the Old Kent Road Gas Works . . . I finally decided to go . . . in November, 1881. With two friends I started out to walk the journey, filled with the hope that we would be able to obtain employment, when we got there, with the kind assistance of my friend . . . We had little money when we started, not enough to pay for our food and lodgings each night until we arrived in London. Some days we walked as much as twenty miles, and other days less. Our money was gone at the end of the third day . . . For two nights we slept out—once under a haystack, and once in an old farm shed . . . On arrival in London we tried to find . . . my friend . . . but . . . were unsuccessful. Our money was all gone, so there was nothing for us to do but to walk around until late at night, and then try to find some place to sleep.

We found an old building and slept in it that night. The next day, Sunday, late in the afternoon, we got to the Old Kent Road Gas Works, and applied for work. To my great surprise, the man we had been looking for was working at the time. He spoke to the foreman and I was given a job.

Quite apart from the regular winter trades, such as gas-stoking and cotton-portering, there was a multitude of chance occupations and residuary employments which the migrant classes were well-placed to take up. Street-trading was a major resource to which many of them turned during their winter stay in town. Gypsies hawked their clothes-pegs and basketry about the suburbs, canvassing from door to door; and they turned up in force on Fridays for market day at the Caledonian Road. Travelling Italians took up position, with tin cans and braziers, outside the pubs, selling roast potatoes or hot chestnuts; organ-grinders perambulated the streets. The migrant Irish often turned trader for the season when winter drove them back to town. The street trade in cutlery, which was particularly brisk in winter, seems to have been largely in the hands of those who went on summer rounds, like 'Showman George', the man who makes a brief appearance in *The Life and Adventures of a Cheap Jack*, 'a big, stout, free-spoken, and rather jolly fellow, who kept a large drinking-booth at the fairs and races during the summer months, and in the winter hawked butchers' cutlery.'[224] So was the winter sale of nuts and oranges, which in London was the special province of the Irish. 'When we got to London', one of Mayhew's informants told him,'. . . we got to work at peas-picking, my wife and me, in the gardens about. That is for the summer. In the winter we sold oranges in the street, while she lived, and we had nothing from the parishes.'[225] The development of Christmas as a great spending holiday increased the possibility of impromptu sales, and produced its own fugitive callings, such as the kerbstone trade in novelties and toys (especially penny toys), the crying of almanacks and Christmas numbers, and the street-sale of holly and mistletoe. Christmas also helped to loosen the purse-strings of the rich, and made life temporarily easier for the 'griddlers' and 'chaunters'. As children were taught in the nursery:

> Christmas is coming
> The goose is getting fat
> Please put a penny in the old man's hat.

London in the weeks before Christmas was a paradise of odd jobs. Extra hands were taken on at the Post Office, to cope with Christmas deliveries; at Covent Garden, where there was a 'second season' in fresh fruit and flowers; at the railway stations; and at the docks. The Christmas pantomime season gave temporary employment to a whole army of 'extras'—scene-shifters, stage-hands, ballet-girls and 'supers'.[226] Christmas was the height of the advertising season, and men of the lodging-house class were widely employed in delivery work on tradesmen's hand-bills (a winter refugee from Stockton, lodging in St Giles, was earning 2s. 6d. a day for this in November and December 1877);[227] also hand-bill distribution at the street corners, and board-carrying.

In London something like six or seven thousand men were employed as board-carriers at this time, more than twice as many as at other times of the year, 'the extra contingent being provided by those who have spent their summer months in agricultural pursuits.'[228] The work was paid for at rates varying from one shilling to one-and-eightpence, the 'highflyers' (who carried over-head boards) being paid at a somewhat higher rate than the others ('except for theatrical & publisher's work which is always the worse paid').[229] Some of this work was done on a casual basis, but Nagle's, one of the leading London contractors, employed men for as long as a month at a time,[230] and according to Booth's investigators, a man, if known to the contractors, might reckon on employment 'throughout the season'. The chief employment office for the West End boardmen was at Ham Yard, Leicester Square, where an enterprising contractor had established himself next door to the soup-kitchen. In the early morning it served as the sandwich-board equivalent of the dock-gate call. A forest of grimy hands shot up for each of the jobs, and little knots of the chosen came forward from the throng. At night a 'Doré-like' group of figures were to be seen, 'camping . . as near as they can to the office which doles them out their jobs'.[231] On 29 January 1904, when the L.C.C. enumerators of the homeless counted forty-nine of them, they were sleeping out (or making themselves comfortable for the night) by the air vents of the Palace Theatre 'on account of the heat coming from the boilers through the grating'.[232]

Christmas was the winter harvest of the wandering tribes. When it was over things changed for the worse. January and February were bad months for the working man, and especially for the poor and insecure. Almost every trade experienced a lull after the Christmas rush of work, and unemployment became widespread as the weather grew more severe. Even so, the balance of advantage, from the point of view of the homeless, remained overwhelmingly on the side of the town—in fact it was after Christmas that the last of the migrations to town took place. There was warmth and shelter in the town, even if work was impossible to come by, soup to be obtained at public kitchens, open to all comers, Night Refuges and Asylums in place of the workhouse, public works (always started up by the vestries when the season was particularly severe) in place of the humiliations of the parish stoneyard.[233]

Bad weather itself, in the conditions of town life, was a prolific source of occasional opportunities. Wintry weather added urgency to the street beggar's cry. Rainy days were a godsend to the cab touts who loitered about the railway stations and the theatres, and to the crossing-sweeper, who levied a small tribute on the wealthier passer-by. After a big snow thousands of hard-up opportunists took to the streets. Augustus Mayhew noticed how 'The whole town seems to swarm with . . . sweepers, who go about from house to house, knocking at the doors, and offering to clear the pavement before the dwelling, according to the Act of Parliament, for twopence.'[234] Frosts, too, had their collateral advantages for the wide awake. In London the 'ice harvest' on the northern heights brought some hundreds of men foraging, with ice-carts and shallows, to Finchley Common and Hampstead Heath,[235] while at the frost fairs which sprang up in the public parks, the hard-up could earn

1 *above* Sailors' Home in the East End, from *Illustrated London News*, lxiii (1873), 600.

2 *below* The Strangers' Home, Limehouse, from *Illustrated London News*, lvi (1870), 253.

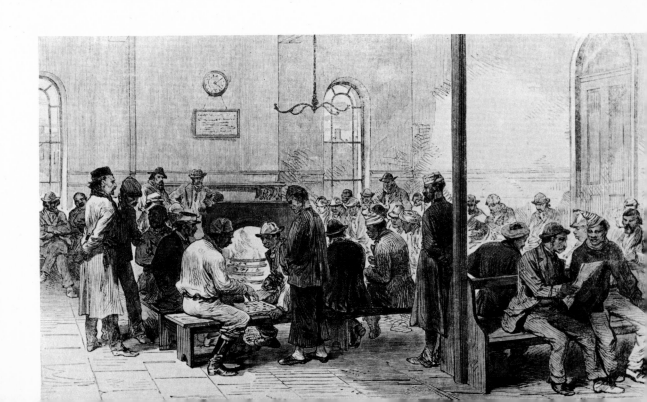

**3** *above left* The Bull's-Eye, from Gustave Doré and Blanchard Jerrold, *London. A Pilgrimage* (1872), facing p. 144.

**4** *left* Gypsy encampment in Notting Dale, from *Illustrated London News*, lxxv (1879), 504.

**5** *above* A gypsy bivouac on Epsom Downs before the Derby. Not less than 1,500 'trampers, gypsies, and one sort or another' camped here overnight but many more arrived by morning. From *Illustrated London News*, xxxii (1858), 513.

## 'OUT OF THE PARISH'

SIR GILES OVERREACH. 'NOW, THEN, MY MAN! YOUR WORK'S DONE, SO BE OFF OUT OF THIS PARISH.' AGRICULTURAL LABOURER. 'AH! SIR GILES! IT BE BETTER NOR FOUR MILE TO T'TOWN.' SIR GILES OVERREACH. 'CAN'T HELP THAT! NO "UNION CHARGEABILITY" FOR ME.'

**6** *above*  From *Punch*, xlviii (1865), 213.

**7** *above right*  'All the way from Manchester, and got no work to do-o-o.' London out-door music, from *Illustrated London News*, xxxiv (1859), 13.

**8** *right*  Sale of spring herrings at Yarmouth, from *Illustrated London News*, xxviii (1856), 373.

'ALL THE WAY FROM MANCHESTER, AND GOT NO WORK TO DO-O-O.'

**9** *above left*  New ward for casual poor at Marylebone workhouse, from *Illustrated London News*, li (1867), 353.

**10** *below left*  Labour-yard of the Bethnal Green Employment Association, from *Illustrated London News*, lii (1868), 156.

**11** *above right*  Frost fair in St James's Park, from *Illustrated London News*, xxxviii (1861), 63.

**12** *below right*  A thaw in the streets of London, from *Illustrated London News*, xlvi (1865), 184.

**13** *above right* London gypsies, from
[John Thomson and Adolphe Smith],
*Street Life in London* (1877), facing p. 1.
*Guildhall Library*

**14** *right* Moved on by the police: St
James's Park, December 1873, from
*Illustrated London News*, lxiii (1873), 601.

**15** *above far right* On the tramp, from
J. H. Crawford, *The Autobiography of a
Tramp* (1900), facing p. 104.

**16** *below far right* Van-dwellers at the
Agricultural Hall, London, from
George R. Sims, ed., *Living London*
(1901), III, p. 321.

**17** *left*  A sandwich-board man, from [John Thomson and Adolphe Smith], *Street Incidents* (1881), p. 21.
*Guildhall Library*

**18** *above right*  Italian street musicians in London, from [John Thomson and Adolphe Smith], *Street Life in London* (1877), opposite p. 85.
*Guildhall Library*

**19** *right*  A mobile circus in a London street, from a lantern slide, *c*.1890.
*David Francis*

**20** *below* Suffolk maltsters at Burton-on-Trent, *c.*1906, from George Ewart Evans, *Where Beards Wag All* (1970), facing p.145.

**21** *right* Navvies at the Crystal Palace, Sydenham, 1854.
*Mansell Collection*

**22** Hop-pickers, September 1875.
*Mansell Collection*

**23**   Fishermen in Whitby harbour, from a lantern slide.
*Photo: Frank Sutcliffe*
*David Francis*

24  A Dundee whaler putting to sea about 1900, from Basil Lubbock, *The Arctic Whalers* (1937), facing p. 406.

odd pennies by sweeping the ice for the skaters, putting on and hiring out skates, or by trading in comforters and sweets.[236] 'Lord' George Sanger, wintering in London one year during the 1840s, found this a profitable line:[237]

> A terrible winter it was, with an unusually hard, long spell of hard frost. Our funds in hand were not very heavy, and seeing all our cash going out and none coming in made me very unhappy. At last, however, I struck a new line with considerable success. Wandering on to Bow Common and Hackney Marshes I found numbers of people sliding and skating on the large ponds there. They were trying to keep warm in the bitter weather, and I noticed that, despite the crowds gathered there, nothing was being sold or hawked. That gave me an idea.
>
> I knew how to make rock and toffee, such as was sold at the fairs, for I had assisted in the process many times. Here was my chance. I went and bought about ten pounds of coarse moist sugar, at that time seven-pence a pound, and some oil of peppermint, borrowed some pans to boil it in, and very soon had a nice little stock of strong, good-looking peppermint rock. Then I took it to Hackney Marshes near the biggest piece of ice, and at a penny a lump it sold like wildfire. I was cleaned out in an hour, and had made several shillings profit.
>
> I could see I had hit on a good thing, and at once went to work on a bigger scale. I borrowed what little money my brothers William and John had saved, added my stock to it, and then went and purchased a big parcel of sugar from a grocer in the Whitechapel Road and more oil of peppermint. This I boiled into rock, which was cut into penny lumps, and having pressed my brothers William and John into the service we started out. The rock sale proved as brisk as ever, and we came home with our pockets loaded with coppers and silver, having made over two pounds profit.
>
> The problem of how to live through the winter in London without trenching on the savings from the summer show business, savings that were always needed to give a good start to the caravans when the time came for the road again, was solved.

With the return of spring the wandering tribes began to stir. Sailors, no longer weather-bound, signed on at the Registry Offices. Showmen put their caravans in harness, and set off for the early fairs. Cheap-jacks and packmen resumed their country rounds. By March the emigrant traffic, almost at a standstill in the three winter months, was moving to the first of its seasonal peaks. In the workshop trades the 'regular roadster'—the congenital nomad—showed signs of restlessness as soon as the sun began to rise higher in the sky. Such a man was Dominic Macarthy, the travelling compositor affectionately recalled in W. E. Adams' *Memoirs of a Social Atom*.[238] Every winter he came to London and supported himself as best he could by getting an occasional job as a 'grass hand'. In the spring his wandering life was resumed. He was a good workman, Adams tells us, but incurably nomadic, 'whenever the proper season came round'. George Acorn, recalling his childhood in Bethnal Green, describes a similar type, a tramp shoemaker called 'Old Bill', who turned up in the neighbourhood every winter, 'bronzed and tattered', and left again in the spring. He was employed at 'The Little Wonder', a back-street cobbler's shop, and while winter lasted, and the nights were long, he would sit contentedly at his bench, heel-balling or sewing 'as patiently as anybody':[239]

> But as soon as the sap began to rise, and the buds to burst in the trees, he would get fidgety, would rise from his stool, and, going to the door, would look at the sky, with his hand shading his eyes.
> 'Weather breaking, eh?' Jordan commented.
> 'Yes', the old cobbler would reply, as if a new spirit had entered into him.
> 'Want to be off?' His employer took a delight in putting these leading questions to him.
> 'Not just yet', 'Old Bill' replied, 'but very soon, very soon.'
> As the days lengthened his eyes fairly glowed with anticipation, his restiveness increased.
> One evening I called in at Jordan's to find a vacant chair.
> 'Where's Old Bill?' I inquired.
> 'God knows', was the reply. 'Somewhere in the country by now, getting fresh air, and seeing things.'
> 'Does he go away every year?' I asked.
> 'He has, ever since I've known him, George. He's got the wandering spirit, and when he sees the green leaves a-coming on the trees he has to go out and taste the country air; it would kill him to stop here all the year round . . .'

The wandering tribes found their place in the underlife of the nineteenth-century town, and it is not easy to log their comings and goings with precision. Their circuits were innumerable, their settlements obscure, and their interconnections with more settled lives can often only be conjectured. Numbers are difficult, perhaps impossible, to arrive at, since they varied with the changing of the seasons and the ups and downs of trade. Nor is it easy to define the boundaries of each individual group. The way-faring constituency was in a constant state of flux. The tramp, the navvy, and the pedlar might be one and the same person at different stages of life, or even at different seasons of the year; the 'gaff' proprietor might spend his summer on the roads; the free-lance labourer turn to busking, or board-carrying, or gas-stoking, when winter drove him into town. The distinction between the nomadic life and the settled one was by no means hard and fast. Tramping was not the prerogative of the social out-cast, as it is today; it was a normal phase in the life of entirely respectable classes of working men; it was a frequent resort of the out-of-works; and it was a very prin-ciple of existence for those who followed the itinerant callings and trades. Within the

152

wandering tribes themselves the nomadic phase and the settled were often inter-twined, with men and women exchanging a fixed occupation for a roving one when-ever conditions were favourable.

One thing at least is clear. The wandering tribes (like other nomadic peoples) followed well-established circuits, and journeyed according to a definite plan. There were comparatively few who moved about the country simply for the sake of keeping on the move, or who travelled hither and thither, as the spirit moved them, without a springboard, a haven, or regular ports-of-call. Some kept a foothold in town all the year round; many of them wintered there, and turned up again 'as regularly as noblemen' when the long nights drew in. Their comings and goings were closely bound up with the social economy of the town, and the openness (or otherwise) of its employment and its trades. The wandering tribes were often the object of hostile legislation, whether to bring their lodging-houses under inspection and control, to bar them from using city wastes, or to harass them from pursuing their callings about the city streets. Their children, after 1870, were subject to the eager ministrations of the School Board Visitors; the camping sites of those who lived in moveable dwellings fell one by one to the enterprise of the speculative builder, or the railinged enclosure of the public parks. But it was economic change, in the later Victorian years, which really undermined them—the growth of more regular employment, especially for the unskilled, and the decline of the 'reserve army of labour' in both the country and the towns; the mechanization of harvest work, and the displacement of travelling labourers by regular farm servants;[240] the rise of the fixed holiday resort in place of the perambulating round of wakes and feasts and fairs; the extension of shops to branches of trade which previously had been in the hands of itinerant packmen and dealers. Towards the end of the century the towns began more thoroughly to absorb their extra population, and to wall them in all the year round.

## Notes

1   *A Plan for Preventing Destitution and Mendicancy in the British Metropolis* (1850), p. 6.
2   Public Record Office (P.R.O.), Home Office Papers (H.O.) 45/10499/117669/10.
3   *Household Words*, 6 December 1851; Richard Rowe, *Jack Afloat and Ashore* (1875), p. 74.
4   On the Settle–Carlisle railway, which was building in the early 1870s, more than 33,000 men found employment on a single section of the line, although the greatest number of men employed at any one time was never more than 2,000: F. S. Williams, *The Midland Railway* (1876), p. 522.
5   R. T. Berthoff, *British Immigration in Industrial America* (Cambridge, Mass., 1953), pp. 82–3. For a parallel migration of stonecutters see 50 Cong. 1, Misc. Doc. 572, part 11, Dip. and Consular Reps. on Immigration, p. 10; 51 Cong. 2, Rep. No. 3472, Select Committee (S.C.) on Immigration, pp. 301, 305, 352, 870.
6   James Greenwood, *On the Tramp* (1872), p. 26.
7   Charity Organisation Society (C.O.S.), *Report on the Homeless Poor* (1891), p. xx.

8   For an example, see *Sir James Sexton, Agitator, An autobiography* (1936), pp. 21–2.

9   F. Groome, *In Gypsy Tents* (Edinburgh, 1880), p. 286.

10   Charles Hindley, ed., *The Life and Adventures of a Cheap Jack* (1881 edn), passim.

11   Henry Mayhew, *London Labour and the London Poor* (1861), I, p. 339.

12   Charles Booth, *Life and Labour of the People in London* (1902–4), 3rd series, V, p. 157.

13   Lancashire Record Office, RCLv, Visitation Records, 1865.

14   John Denvir, *The Irish in Britain* (2nd edn, 1894), p. 411.

15   'St. Patrick's Church Sunderland', notes in the possession of the Rev. Vincent Smith; for a similar situation at Warrington, 'a large thoroughfare for Irish people', see P.R.O., H.O. 129/466, St Alban's, Warrington.

16   B. S. Rowntree, *Poverty* (2nd edn, n.d.), pp. 31–2; for earlier references to the travels of the York Irish, see *Parliamentary Papers (P.P.)*, 1867–8, XVII, Royal Commission (R.C.) on Employment of Children, Young Persons, and Women in Agriculture, 1st Report: Appendix Pt II (4068–I), pp. 255, 258.

17   Denvir, op. cit., p. 400.

18   Lady Bell, *At the Works* (1907), p. 8.

19   *The Word on the Waters*, i (December 1858), 258.

20   Ibid. (April 1892), 332.

21   J. Flanagan, *Scenes from My Life* (1907), p. 36.

22   *Morning Chronicle*, 4 January 1850. Sixty years later, Angel Meadow still bore a 'peculiar reputation' on account of its common lodging-house. See *P.P.*, 1909, XLIII, R.C. on the Poor Laws, Reports on the Relation of Industrial and Sanitary Conditions to Pauperism (Cd. 4653), App. XVI, p. 102.

23   *Morning Chronicle*, 29 April 1850; *P.P.*, 1847, XXVII–Pt 1, R.C. on Education in Wales (870), p. 304.

24   Greenwood, op. cit., pp. 27–8.

25   Booth, op. cit., 3rd series, V, p. 75; cf. London Mendicity Society, 76th Annual Report (1894), p. xiii; Mayhew, op. cit., I, p. 337.

26   Booth, op. cit., 3rd series, VI, p. 136.

27   London School of Economics, Booth MSS., B. 267, pp. 145–9; Booth, op. cit., 3rd series, I, p. 138.

28   Booth MSS., B.281, pp. 83–5; B.371, pp. 117–29, 143–61; John W. Horsley, *I Remember* (1911), pp. 125–31; Booth, op. cit., 3rd series, V, pp. 90–1.

29   Booth, op. cit., 3rd series, V, pp. 90–1.

30   Ibid., III, pp. 151–2.

31   Sam Shaw, *Guttersnipe* (1946), p. 29.

32   *P.P.*, 1842, XXVI, Report of the Poor Law Commissioners on an Inquiry into the Sanitary Condition of the Labouring Population of Great Britain: Appendix.

33   T. W. Rammell, *Report to the Board of Health: . . . Banbury* (1854), p. 11. There is an excellent description of Rag Row in Barrie S. Trinder, *Banbury's Poor in 1850* (Banbury, 1966).

34   P.R.O., H.O. 107, Census Returns; Huddersfield Ref. Lib., Lodging House Committee M.B., 1 May 1854 and *passim*.

35   W. C. E. Ranger, *Report to the Board of Health: . . . Doncaster* (1850), p. 38.

36   Sanitary Condition of the Labouring Population, Local Reports, pp. 63–5, 78.

37  Ibid., p. 174; E. Cresy, *Report to the Board of Health . . . Derby* (1849), pp. 13–15.

38  J. R. Coulthart, *Report on Ashton-under-Lyne*, in *P.P.*, 1844, XVII, R.C. on the State of Large Towns and Populous Districts: 1st Report (572), Appendix, p. 84.

39  C.O.S., op. cit., p. xvi.

40  Coulthart, op. cit., pp. 36–7.

41  P.R.O., Metropolitan Police (Mepol.), 2/1490.

42  *P.P.*, 1906, CIII, Departmental Committee on Vagrancy (Cd. 2891), II, QQ. 7768, 7947; ibid. (Cd. 2892),Report on Vagrancy, III, App. XXXII; Mary Higgs, *Glimpses into the Abyss* (1906), p. 51; S. and B. Webb, *The Public Organisation of the Labour Market* (1909), pp. 81, 83.

43  Bishopsgate Library, Mansion House Committee on the Unemployed in London (1885), transcript of proceedings, fol. 10$^r$.

44  John Fisher Murray, *The World of London* (1844), I, p. 247.

45  Daniel Joseph Kirwan, *Palace and Hovel* (1963 edn), pp. 64–70.

46  Thomas Miller, *Picturesque Sketches of London* (1852), p. 207.

47  *London in the Sixties, by One of the Old Brigade* (1914 edn), pp. 61–2.

48  P.R.O., H.O. 45/10499/117669; Booth, op. cit., 1st series, I, p. 68; 3rd series, II, p. 244; *The Times*, 28 August 1894.

49  *Liverpool Review*, 19 April 1890.

50  Booth MSS., B. 152, p. 104.

51  P.R.O., Mepol. 2/645, Mepol. 2/1068, Mepol. 2/1425, Mepol. 2/1490; H.O. 14571/ 20236; T. W. Wilkinson, 'London's Homes for the Homeless', in G. R. Sims, ed., *Living London* (1903), I, p. 337.

52  General Booth, *In Darkest England and The Way Out* (1891), p. 25.

53  P.R.O., Mepol. 2/1068.

54  Terry Coleman, *The Railway Navvies* (1965), p. 49; John R. Kellett, *The Impact of Railways on Victorian Cities* (1969), p. 346.

55  *Surrey Gazette*, 10 November 1863.

56  P.R.O., H.O. 45/10499/117669; Mepol. 2/1490.

57  Stan Hugill, *Sailortown* (1967), p. 112; Rowland Kenney, *Westering* (1938), p. 82.

58  *Porcupine*, xxi (1879), 409; George Smith, *Incidents in a Gipsy's Life* (Liverpool, 1886), p. 11.

59  *Labour Press and Miners' and Workmen's Examiner*, 15 August 1874.

60  Booth MSS., B. 371, p. 55.

61  Ibid., p. 239.

62  *Illustrated London News*, lxxv (1879), 503.

63  Reginald Blunt, *Red Anchor Pieces* (1928), p. 110.

64  *Illustrated London News*, lxxvi (1880), 11; Booth MSS., B. 346, pp. 165, 231; George Smith, *Our Gipsies and their Children* (1880), p. 267.

65  Booth MSS., B. 348, p. 97.

66  T. W. Wilkinson, 'Van Dwelling London', *Living London*, III, pp. 321–2.

67  Henry Woodcock, *The Gipsies* (1865), pp. 144–7; V. Morwood, *Our Gipsies in City, Tent, Van* (1885), pp. 338–40; George Sims, *Off the Track in London* (1911), pp. 36–7.

68  Booth, op. cit., 3rd series, V, p. 206.

69  J. J. Sexby, *Municipal Parks* (1898), pp. 237–8; British Museum, Leland Collection, newspaper cutting, 2 January 1879; Booth MSS., B. 298, pp. 91–7.

70  Booth, op. cit., 3rd series, V, p. 157; cf. Booth MSS., B. 366, pp. 183–5, 190; *Building Trade News*, December 1894.

71  C.O.S., op. cit., QQ. 1892–4.

72  'The Greenland Whale Fishery', in R. Vaughan Williams and A. L. Lloyd, eds, *The Penguin Book of English Folk Songs* (1968), pp. 50–1; in 'The Whale-catchers', ibid., p. 100, the date is 23 March. For the spring departure of the whalers at Dundee, see G. N. Barnes, *From Workshop to War Cabinet* (1924), pp. 14–15; for Hull, see *Autobiography of Thomas Wilkinson Wallis* (Louth, 1899), pp. 14–15.

73  C.O.S., op. cit., pp. xv–xvi.

74  Mayhew, op. cit., III, p. 88.

75  P. A. Whittle, *Blackburn as It Is* (Preston, 1852), pp. 31–2; Hindley, op. cit., pp. 280–1.

76  James Lloyd, *My Circus Life* (1925).

77  Ben Tillett, *Memories and Reflections* (1931), pp. 33, 37, 38.

78  David Prince Miller, *The Life of a Showman* (1849), pp. 65, 67, 83–4, 86; *Free Lance*, viii (1873), 125; Hindley, op. cit., p. 149.

79  [C. Thomson], *The Autobiography of an Artisan* (1847), pp. 240–1; Mayhew, op. cit., I, p. 329.

80  'Lord' George Sanger, *Seventy Years a Showman* (1952 edn), pp. 42–4, 66.

81  C.O.S., *Report on Unskilled Labour* (1890), Q. 885.

82  *P.P.*, 1893–4, XXXIV, R.C. on Labour: Minutes of Evidence (Group 'C') (C. 6894–IX), Q.26,435.

83  C.O.S., *Unskilled Labour*, Q.282; cf. Frank Popplewell, 'The Gas Industry', in A. Freeman and S. Webb, eds, *The Seasonal Trades* (1912), pp. 168–71; Booth MSS., A.3 fol. 209; Will Thorne, *My Life's Battles* (1925), p. 36.

84  Mayhew, op. cit., II, p. 375.

85  G. Elson, *The Last of the Climbing Boys* (1900), p. 199.

86  George Ewart Evans, *Where Beards Wag All* (1970), p. 266.

87  Mayhew, op. cit., III, p. 399.

88  B.M., Leland Coll., cutting, 16 May 1872; J. Crabb, *The Gipsies' Advocate* (1831), pp. 136–7.

89  Sanger, op. cit., pp. 141, 147, 195.

90  George Smith, *I've Been a-Gipsying* (1883), pp. 39–59.

91  *P.P.*, 1868–9, XIII, R.C. on Children in Agriculture, 2nd Report (4202–I), App. II, A.i, p. 61.

92  *P.P.*, 1893–4, XXXV, R.C. on Labour: The Agricultural Labourer, Assistant Commissioners' District Reports (C. 6894–VI), B.–VI [Holbeach], para. 12; ibid. (C. 6894–V), B.–VII [Godstone], para. 10.

93  *Seaman's and Fisherman's Friendly Visitor*, iii (1860), pp. 111, 126.

94  *Labour News*, 13 July 1872.

95  *Jackson's Oxford Journal*, 3 August 1872.  (I am grateful to David Morgan for this excellent reference.)

96  *P.P.*, 1880, XIV, Factory Inspectors' Report for 1879 (C. 2489), p. 54.

97  Booth, op. cit., 2nd series, II, p. 140.

98   Booth MSS., B. 93, fol. 88.

99   *P.P.*, 1893–4, XVII, Departmental Committee on Conditions of Labour in Lead Industries (C. 7239–I), p. 181. (I am grateful to Anna Davin for this excellent reference, as also for the refugee London enameller.)

100  Ibid., Q.5216.

101  R.C. on Labour: Agricultural Labourer, Summary Report (C. 6894–VI), para. 20.

102  William Cobbett, *Rural Rides* (Everyman edn) I, p. 84.

103  Thor Fredur, *Sketches from Shady Places* (1879), p. 24.

104  William A. Jevons, 'The Weavers' Strike at Padiham in 1859', National Association for the Promotion of Social Science, *Trade Societies and Strikes* (1860), pp. 468–9.

105  B. S. Rowntree and B. Lasker, *Unemployment* (1911), p. 63; cf. pp. 30, 99, 152, 160.

106  'The Irish in England, III', *Labour News*, 14 March 1874.

107  'Whitechapel Villagers' in *Toilers in London by One of the Crowd* (1883), pp. 99–101; for some Essex evidence, see G. A. Cuttle, *The Legacy of the Rural Guardians* (Cambridge, 1934), pp. 267, 273; for Irish pea-pickers at Stoke Poges, *P.P.* 1867–8, XVII, R.C. on Children in Agriculture, 1st Report: App. Pt II, p. 539; for a Bloomsbury pea-picker, see P.R.O., N.H. 13/268, paper dated 2.4.1851.

108  Thomas Fayers, *Labour among the Navvies* (Kendal, 1862), p. 12.

109  Mayhew, op. cit., I, p. 478.

110  Thomas Wright, *The Great Unwashed* (1868), pp. 261–2.

111  Booth MSS., B.210, pp. 1–3.

112  Booth MSS., A.28.

113  Booth, op. cit., 2nd series, II, pp. 277–8.

114  Ibid., 2nd series, IV, App. B.

115  Booth MSS., B.152, p. 104.

116  Booth, op. cit., 2nd series, III, p. 411.

117  *Labour News*, 20 September 1873.

118  A. M. Anderson, *Women in the Factory* (1922), p. 38. (I am grateful to Anna Davin for this reference.)

119  *Labour News*, 20 September 1873.

120  Booth MSS., B.93, fol. 69.

121  Booth, op. cit., 1st series, IV, pp. 286, 313–14, 324.

122  Ibid., 2nd series, I, p. 220.

123  A. T. Pask, *Eyes of the Thames* (1889), pp. 148–9.

124  Mayhew, op. cit., II, p. 299.

125  'The Irish in England, II', *Labour News*, 28 February 1874.

126  Denvir, op. cit., p. 400; *P.P.*, 1906, CIII, Report on Vagrancy (2891) II, QQ. 5820–2; J. Ewing Ritchie, *Crying for the Light* (1895), p. 123.

127  *Indoor Pauper, by One of Them* (1885), pp. 54–5.

128  'The Irish in England', *Dublin Review* (1856), 508.

129  Denvir, op. cit., p. 401.

130  C.O.S., *Homeless Poor*, Q. 398; P.R.O., Mepol. 2/1490, 1 August 1913.

131  Report on Vagrancy, II, Q. 4180.

132  R.C. on Children in Agriculture, 2nd Report, App. Pt. II, p. 139.

133   *Runcorn Examiner*, 30 September 1893.

134   R.C. on Children in Agriculture, 2nd Report, App. Pt II, Ai, p. 135.

135   R.C. on Labour: Agricultural Labourer, District Reports (C. 6894–IV), B.–V [Bromyard], para. 9; Cf. Stourbridge Observer, 10 September 1881.

136   R.C. on Children in Agriculture, 2nd Report, App. Pt II, G, p. 43.

137   *Labour News*, September 1876.

138   'Three Weeks with the Hop-Pickers', *Fraser's Magazine*, n.s., xvi (1877), 635.

139   George Sturt, *A Small Boy in the Sixties* (Cambridge, 1923), p. 76; R.C. on Children in Agriculture, 2nd Report, App. Pt II, C, p. 4.

140   William Marshall, *The Rural Economy of the Southern Counties* (1798), II, p. 69.

141   Ellen Chase, *Tenant Friends in Deptford* (1929), pp. 102–3.

142   George Meek, *Bath Chair Man* (1910), p. 55.

143   'Shelter for the Homeless', *Leisure Hour* (1865), p. 11.

144   Mayhew, op. cit., III, pp. 405, 406.

145   Alexander Somerville, *The Autobiography of a Working Man* (1848), p. 56.

146   *P.P.*, 1895, VIII, S.C. on Distress from Want of Employment, 2nd Report (253): App., p. 33.

147   'Trade Tramps', *Leisure Hour* (1868), 358.

148   *London City Mission Magazine*, 2 December 1861.

149   George Sturt, *The Wheelwright's Shop* (Cambridge, 1963 edn), p. 29.

150   Charles Manby Smith, *The Little World of London* (1857), p. 143.

151   Mayhew, op. cit., I, p. 329; Hindley, op. cit., p. 209.

152   Booth MSS., B.50, p. 58; B.82, p. 14.

153   B.M., Leland Collection, undated cutting [1879?].

154   Mayhew, op. cit., II, p. 335.

155   C.O.S., *Homeless Poor*, Q.1,498; Sir Henry Smith, *From Constable to Commissioner* (1910), p. 165.

156   L.N.R. [Mrs Ellen Ranyard], *The Missing Link* (1859), pp. 29–30, 51; *P.P.*, 1833, XVI, S.C. on Irish Vagrants (394), pp. 175, 193; Mayhew, op. cit., IV, p. 297.

157   Holborn Board of Works M.B., Report of Septimus Gibbon, 6 October 1856 (Holborn Reference Library).

158   *Labour News*, 10 October 1874.

159   Edward G. Howarth and Mona Wilson, *West Ham* (1907), pp. 306–7.

160   R.C. on Children in Agriculture, 2nd Report, Appendix.

161   Verbal communication from Charles Connor.

162   *Morning Chronicle*, 23 January 1851.

163   T. W. Wilkinson, 'Van Dwelling London', in Sims, op. cit., III, pp. 319–20; according to J. Howard Swinstead, *A Parish on Wheels* (1897), p. 194, the Drill Hall, Portsmouth, seems to have served a similar winter function.

164   John Hollingshead, *Ragged London in 1861* (1861), pp. 181–2.

165   Sanger, op. cit., pp. 135–6, 175, 204–5.

166   *London City Mission Magazine*, 2 December 1861.

167   Mayhew, op. cit., III, p. 407.

168   Report on Vagrancy, App. XXXII.

169   Mayhew, op. cit., III, p. 381.

170   26th Report of the Mendicity Society (1844), pp. 13–14.

171   *P.P.*, 1846, VII, Report on District Asylums (368), Q.1903.

172    *P.P.*, 1914–16, XXXII, Report of the Metropolitan Poor Law Inspectors' Advisory
Committee on the Homeless Poor (Cd. 7840), p. 7.

173    C.O.S., *Homeless Poor*, p. xiv; Report on District Asylums, Q.1812; Mayhew,
op. cit., III, p. 410.

174    For some venomous attacks, see C. E. Trevelyan, *Three Letters . . . on London
Pauperism* (1870); C.O.S., *Conference . . . on Night Refuges* (1870).

175    Report on District Asylums, Q.1909.

176    James Greenwood, *Low Life Deeps* (1876), p. 212.

177    *London City Mission Magazine*, 2 January 1860.

178    George Smith, *Our Canal, Gipsy Van and other Travelling Children* (1883), pp. 17–18.

179    Chase, op. cit., p. 96.

180    Mayhew, op. cit., III, p. 412.

181    C.O.S., *Homeless Poor*, QQ.2, 141–2.

182    Evans, op. cit., pp. 235–6.

183    R.C. on Labour: Agricultural Labourer, District Reports (C. 6894–IV), B.–V
[Bromyard], paras 8, 9.

184    A. H. John, *The Industrial Revolution in South Wales* (Cardiff, 1950), p. 66.

185    S.C. on Distress from Want of Employment, 2nd Report, App., p. 53.

186    R.C. on the Poor Laws, Reports on Relation of Industrial and Sanitary Conditions
to Pauperism p. 364.

187    Evans, op. cit., p. 243; cf. Leone Levi, *Wages and Earnings* (1885), pp. 112–13.

188    *Morning Chronicle*, 8 May 1850.

189    R.C. on Labour, Agricultural Labourer, District Reports (C. 6894–VI), B–V, 62.

190    R.C. on Children in Agriculture, 2nd Report, Aj2, 33, 36ᵇ, 37ᵃ, 38.

191    Evans, op. cit., Appendix I.

192    *Labour News*, 19 October and 30 November 1872; 18 January 1873.

193    C.O.S., *Homeless Poor*, p. xxii.

194    N. B. Dearle, *Unemployment in the London Building Trades* (1908), p. 80.

195    *Labour News*, 5 December 1874 and *passim*.

196    *Reminiscences of a Stonemason*, by A Working Man (1908), p. 75.

197    51st Report of the Mendicity Society (1869), p. 11; *Labour News*, passim.

198    C.O.S., *Unskilled Labour*, QQ. 1722–3.

199    *Building and Engineering Times*, 7 January 1882.

200    *Fisherman's Friendly Visitor and Mariner's Companion*, March 1844, p. 27; cf.
*Morning Chronicle*, 19 April 1850.

201    S.C. on Distress from Want of Employment, 2nd Report, App., p. 159.

202    G. Holden Pike, *Among the Sailors* (1897), p. 127; *The Word on the Waters*, iii
(1860), 270.

203    *Labour Gazette*, 11 May 1894.

204    J. R. Bagshawe, *The Wooden Ships of Whitby* (Whitby, 1933), pp. 84–5.

205    *Labour News*, 14 October 1876.

206    Booth MSS., B. 122, fol. 63.

207    *Labour News*, 21 October 1876.

208    Webb, op. cit., p. 256.

209    *Labour News*, 1 November, 1873; Booth MSS., B. 84, fols 2, 9, 18, 25, 65.

210    Ibid., *passim*; Booth MSS., B. 104, fols 12, 26, B.101, fol. 75; *P.P.*, 1876, XXX,
Factories and Workshops, Q. 4604.

211 R. Williams, *The Liverpool Docks Problem* (Liverpool, 1912), p. 42; and 'The First Year's Working of the Liverpool Docks Scheme', *Trans. Liverpool Economic and Statistical Society* (1913–14), p. 99.

212 R.C. on Labour: Minutes of Evidence (C. 6894–IX), QQ. 31,598; 31,616; 31,501; *The Port of Hull* (Hull, 1907), p. 189.

213 Bagshawe, op. cit., pp. 84–5.

214 *The Diaries of Sir Daniel Gooch* (1892), p. 78.

215 *Labour News*, 25 January 1873.

216 *Paddy the Cope, My Story* (1935), p. 61; R.C. on Labour, QQ. 31,501; 31,598; 31,616; Booth MSS., B. 94, fols 5,14; B.117, fols 1,18.

217 Webb, op. cit., pp. 256, 257.

218 R.C. on Labour, Q. 26,439.

219 'The Irish in England', *Labour News*, 28 March 1874.

220 *Labour Standard*, 15 April 1882.

221 *Labour News*, 4 November 1876.

222 'The Irish in England', *Labour News*, 28 March 1874.

223 Thorne, op. cit., pp. 49–50.

224 Hindley, op. cit., pp. 188–9; Mayhew, op. cit., I, p. 338.

225 Mayhew, op. cit., I, p. 104, 105; III, p. 413.

226 Ibid., III, p. 94; *Labour News*, 8 January 1876; Booth, op. cit., 1st series, I, p. 211; 2nd series, IV, p. 130; Webb, op. cit., p. 257.

227 C.O.S., *Report on Soup Kitchens* (1877), p. 13.

228 T. Camden Pratt, *Unknown London* (1897), p. 32.

229 Booth MSS., A. 17 part A, fol. 82.

230 C.O.S., *Homeless Poor*, Q. 1,871.

231 Alsager Hay Hill, *The Unemployed in Great Cities with suggestions for the better organisation of labourers . . .* (1877), p. 15; Wilkinson, in Sims, op. cit., I, p. 332; J. B. Booth, *London Town* (1929), pp. 302–3.

232 P.R.O., H.O. 45/10499/117669; Mepol. 2/1490.

233 C.O.S., *Exceptional Distress* (1886) and, for a hostile scrutiny, *Winter out-of-Work, 1892–3* (1893). Booth wrote that the vestries, were 'the principal extra source of casual employment during the winter' (op. cit., 2nd series, IV, p. 40).

234 Mayhew, op. cit., p. 6.

235 Ibid., p. 6; Greenwood, op. cit., pp. 152–6.

236 Walter Besant and James Rice, *The Seamy Side* (1880), p. 10; *Labour News*, 8 November 1873; Booth, op. cit., 2nd series, I, pp. 94, 131.

237 Sanger, op. cit., pp. 128–9.

238 W. E. Adams, *Memoirs of a Social Atom* (1893), I, pp. 304–7.

239 George Acorn, *One of the Multitude* (1911), pp. 92–4.

240 David Morgan, 'The place of harvesters in nineteenth-century village life', in Raphael Samuel, ed., *Work: Industrial work groups and workers' control in nineteenth-century England* (forthcoming).

# 6   Pubs

## Brian Harrison

Comparison in urban history is best conducted at the level of particular institutions within the town, rather than between towns as a whole.[1] The pub and the temperance society, which can be found in most Victorian towns, demand such an approach. Vigorously competing for the attention of the new urban masses, they symbolized alternative styles of urban life. They had not always been rivals. In a predominantly rural society, the pub complemented the church; vestry meetings and Sunday schools were often held in the pub, parsons promoted church-ales, and church-goers from a distance took a dram before they prayed. Vicars of Wakefield had long been exhorting 'the married men to temperance, and the bachelors to matrimony', but only after the 1820s did they begin to attack pubs as such. Teetotallers before the 1830s were isolated eccentrics, and it was only with the launching of the anti-spirits and teetotal movements in 1829–34 that formal associations of abstainers appeared.

Throughout the nineteenth century, the temperance movement remained a predominantly urban movement, and in its early years attracted those urban and nonconformist personalities who supported the Anti-Corn Law League, the Liberation Society, and the Chartist movement. Total abstinence gradually became a passport to social respectability. In a society relatively starved of recreation, working men had to choose the life of the pub and the music-hall or the life of the temperance society, mutual improvement society, and chapel: there was nowhere else to go. The steady extension of temperance ideas to the countryside throughout the century helped to advance the Liberal Party's rural frontier; and, given the striking success of the Church of England Temperance Society in the 1870s, there was nothing to prevent even rural communities from polarizing round pub and temperance society. Whereas in the early nineteenth century the Protestant Dissenting Deputies' watch-dog committee met regularly at the King's Head Tavern in the Poultry, such a venue would have been inconceivable by the 1870s; and whereas temperance in the 1830s was a politically neutral issue, by the 1890s it lay at the heart of party politics.

The survival of two drink maps, for 1887 and 1899, enables us to study London's pub geography in some detail; similar analyses could in principle be conducted for other Victorian towns, and London is prominent in the subsequent discussion only because information about its pubs is so readily accessible. Temperance societies will receive rather less attention, because London temperance geography was never mapped out, though maps could perhaps be created from temperance society sub-scription-lists. In 1896 London had 393 persons per pub—a lower pub density than that of any other major English city: Leeds had 345 persons per pub, Liverpool 279, Birmingham 215, Sheffield 176, and Manchester 168. Pub density was lower than in London in only nine of the 235 boroughs outside London. But London's pub geography clearly reveals the pub's three major roles in nineteenth-century society: transport centre, recreation centre, and meeting place.[2]

As transport centre, the pub's role strikingly diminished during the nineteenth century, because railways greatly reduced the quantity of long-distance road travel. Until the 1830s, the great London coaching-inns were the equivalents of railway termini: one of the most famous, the Bull and Mouth in St Martin's-le-Grand, had underground stables for 400 horses. Passengers loaded up in the great backyards, for in stage-coach days the whole inn was oriented round a galleried rear-courtyard. Coaches entered and left through a large archway into the main road—the most impressive of these being the Bull and Mouth's classical arch rebuilt in 1823. Only after the pub had lost its special connection with horse-drawn transport did the street façade become overwhelmingly important. Regular timetables were issued, and, at public-house stops between the termini, passengers waited in the large glazed front rooms for the coach to arrive (Plates 25 and 26). The great transport-inns clustered together—in Borough High Street, Bishopsgate, Piccadilly, and the inner suburbs of the City—and competed for custom. It is not surprising that pubs are so prominent in a book like *Pickwick Papers*: as B. W. Matz put it, 'the book . . . opens in an hotel and ends in one'.[3]

The railway completely upset this pattern, for by speeding up travel and in-creasing its comfort, the railway reduced the need for refreshment on the journey. Railway companies did not at first perceive these implications, and provided generous drinking facilities at their stations. One of the earliest London termini, the London & Croydon Railway's Bricklayers' Arms, actually took the name of a pub, and two of the company's earliest stations—the Dartmouth Arms and the Jolly Sailor—were not renamed Forest Hill and Norwood Junction till 1845. Temperance reformers, who eagerly invested in the early railways and saw them as instruments of progress, fought to alter this policy; in 1881 they prevented even Gladstone from allowing the sale of drink on the train to railway passengers.[4] The pub's billeting function declined for the same reason: railways enabled soldiers to travel faster and to lodge at their own specialized version of the hotel—the barracks.

In towns, pubs suffered partly from the rerouting of transport (which lent attractions to station-hotels as against the old coaching-inns), but also from the sheer volume of railway travel. Hotel-keeping grew up as a trade in its own right, where drink accounted for a smaller proportion of the profits. The old coaching-inns had to adapt; the Bull and Mouth converted its great archway into a front entrance and became a hotel (Plate 27), and a London travel guide in 1871 claimed that the coaching-inns had 'all become comfortable middle-class hotels, with railway booking-offices attached'.[5] The less enterprising among them decayed until they were pulled down: the Green Dragon, last of the great coaching-inns in the Gracechurch Street/Bishopsgate complex, was torn down in 1877. Nevertheless, the 1899 map shows the persistence of the link between pubs and railway travel; there were three pubs actually on the station premises at St Pancras, and two each at King's Cross, Euston, and London Bridge. Several Waterloo Road pubs faced the passenger as he left Waterloo station, and of the thirty-five railway stations on Booth's map, twenty-six had pubs on or immediately outside the premises.

Publicans are resilient creatures: they may suffer by some social changes, but they take care to profit by others. Long-distance railway travel, by greatly increasing the amount of short-distance road travel (particularly in London, where through-journeys by rail could not be made), enabled the urban publican to recoup some of his losses. Furthermore, the railways were slow to cater for suburban commuters: roadside pubs therefore gained from the consequent growth of bus and tramway systems which linked suburbs to city-centre. All five of the pioneer tram-routes out of Leeds city-centre launched under the Leeds Tramways Order of 1871 terminated at suburban pubs; London Transport's maps still advertise the Royal Oak, the Angel, Swiss Cottage, and Elephant and Castle. But although the increased speed and utilization of urban road transport benefited some urban roadside pubs, it reduced pedestrian travel and thereby reduced passengers' opportunities for drinking while travelling. Hence John Dunlop's comment in 1839: 'we have known the establishment of a coach or omnibus on some road, abolish public-houses along its line'.[6]

The mark of the commuter lies heavily upon late-Victorian London's pub geography. The 1887 map shows pubs concentrated far more closely in the city-centre than in the suburbs; in 1896 the number of persons per pub ranged all the way from 116 in St James's to 727 in Edmonton. Unfortunately we have no figures to reveal contrasts in pub density *within* provincial towns; it is therefore impossible to see whether St James's high concentration of 0·7 acres per pub was a record for the country as a whole. But the figure certainly represents a pub concentration far greater than in any other complete town in 1896; the City (1·0 acres per pub) and the Strand (2·0) followed close behind. With fifty persons per pub in 1896, the City of London had a pub density greater than any other of the 235 boroughs. Yet the City

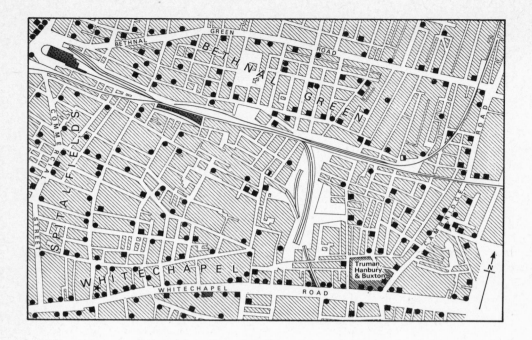

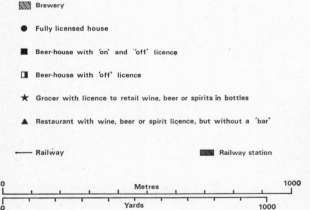

Brewery

● Fully licensed house

■ Beer-house with 'on' and 'off' licence

▯ Beer-house with 'off' licence

★ Grocer with licence to retail wine, beer or spirits in bottles

▲ Restaurant with wine, beer or spirit licence, but without a 'bar'

—— Railway      Railway station

**I** Licensed premises, Bethnal Green and Spitalfields, 1899. This is an area of small-scale manufactures and of working-class housing. Whitechapel Road, as a major east–west thoroughfare, attracted many pubs. There were only two grocers' licences in the whole area, but many beer-shops and a famous brewery. Note the siting of the pubs on street-corners. Source (as for II–IV): Charles Booth, *Life and Labour of the People in London*, final volume (1903), 'London, 1899–1900'.

pubs were really catering for ten times as many people, resident in the suburbs; if these are allowed for, its pub density was low—479 persons per pub.[7]

Commuter travel is also reflected in the long lines of pubs which straddle the major east–west routes and, to a lesser extent, the north–south routes. Until the eighteenth century, London's east–west transport axis had been waterborne as well as landborne, but by the Victorian period river transport had markedly declined, and relatively few riverside pubs survived. In the nineteenth century, imported goods, after being unloaded, were moved west across London by road to be sold or consumed: much of the labour force—particularly after the late-Victorian slum clearance at St Giles—lived in the east, but moved westwards for most of its working day. Before the large popular restaurants appeared, strategically-placed pubs provided the working man with breakfast on his journey to work, and with refreshment on his journey home. In the one mile of Whitechapel Road from Commercial Street to Stepney Green, there were in 1899 no less than forty-eight drinking-places: in the three-quarter mile stretch of the Strand from Trafalgar Square to St Clement's there were forty-six (Maps I and II). Drinking-places also clustered along the major north–south axes: Bishopsgate/Shoreditch/Borough High Street and Tottenham Court Road/Waterloo Road. At both ends of the London river bridges, pubs closed in on

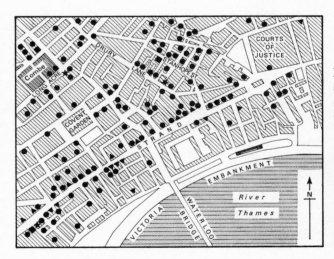

**II** Licensed premises in the Strand, 1899. Drinking facilities clustered along the Strand's major east–west route, but they have been excluded from the Victoria Embankment. Gladstone's refreshment-house licences accommodated the many middle-class commuters who staffed the shops and offices in the area. But poverty lurked in the back-streets, and in the Stanhope Street area Booth found 55·5 percent of the population in poverty; the 'large proportion of Irish, many rough characters' there ensured that pubs clustered in the locality. But for the Duke of Bedford's policy, the Covent Garden porters would have ensured a more impressive cluster further south.

*Key and scale as for Map I*

165

the passer-by, as they also did at the major road-junctions—there were six at Elephant and Castle, five at Cambridge Circus, four at St George's Circus.

Many of the West London pubs were therefore catering, not for the privileged classes, but for working people resident in East London, or for the personal servants of the well-to-do. Areas of working-class employment in the west—the Wellington and Knightsbridge Barracks and Covent Garden (Map II), for example—were well supplied with pubs. The 1899 map also shows a remarkable concentration outside the Mint, and in dockside areas like Shadwell High Street and West India Dock Road (Map III). Pubs occupied all four corners of the central square in the cattle market opened at Copenhagen Fields in 1855, for at this time bargains were sealed over a drink. Pubs were the focus for the market-town's servant-hirings and fairs, and temperance reformers felt obliged to attack both. Some nineteenth-century employers—notably the Richardsons and Titus Salt, in their temperance utopias of Bessbrook and Saltaire respectively—tried to promote work discipline by banning pubs from the factory area.

The commuter's needs help to conceal a fundamental class-contrast in Victorian drinking habits; for, whereas at the beginning of the century different classes patronized the same pubs, by the 1860s the respectable classes were drinking at home, or not drinking at all. If free trade had been allowed to operate, if working men had laboured where they lived, and if recreational and business commuters had not existed, pubs would have been far less common in West than in East London. These complicating factors do not in fact completely conceal this underlying contrast. The 1887 map shows that the best London streets—Whitehall, Pall Mall, Piccadilly, and the Embankment—had very few pubs. Over a wide area to the north and west of the West End, pubs were again very sparse—in Bloomsbury (Map IV), Belgravia, and Kensington, all fashionable areas whose landlords (notably the Dukes of Bedford and Westminster) pursued a temperance policy. William Hoyle the temperance reformer

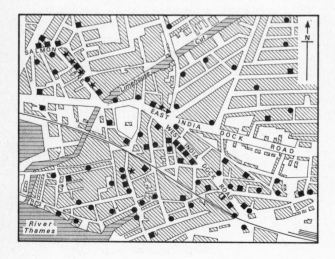

**III** Licensed premises in dockland, 1899. The many pubs on the West India Dock Road were a measure of the thirst of dockers working locally. There were many beer-shops, and the grocers' licences in Salmon Lane probably catered for the many Italians living nearby. Pubs clustered on the main thoroughfares, and in the area with the most poverty (41·4 per cent) to the south-west.

*Key and scale as for Map I*

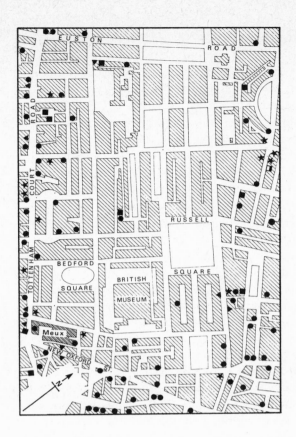

**IV** Licensed premises in Bloomsbury, 1899. The Dukes of Bedford
enhanced the value of their estates
by virtually excluding pubs, but
drinking facilities (especially Gladstone's grocers' licences) abounded
on the fringes because aristocratic
cellars had to be supplied.

*Key and scale as for Map I*

noted that in Lancashire's industrial towns, more socially homogeneous than London,
pubs were distributed far more evenly: 'this morning I have been for about an hour
riding about the West End', he told a select committee in 1877, 'where I did not see
a public-house at all'.[8]

If we turn from the quantity to the category of licences, the contrast becomes
very clear. By the mid-Victorian period the well-to-do were much more likely to
patronize some types of off-licence than to enter the pub. The off-licence was a Victorian invention, and a peculiarly urban phenomenon: the more scattered the
population, the less prevalent it became. The nineteenth century saw a marked shift
from on-consumption to off-purchase of drink. The change stems partly from changing class relationships and religious attitudes, and from the accompanying growth of
the suburb, but also from technological developments in the drink industry, which
expanded the trade in bottled beer. Evangelical families with a conscience, like the
Fremlins of Maidstone, felt fewer qualms at promoting the relatively respectable
'family trade'. By an Act of 1834, beer-house licences were divided into two categories: for on- and off-sales. In late-Victorian England and Wales there were over
twelve thousand of the latter, as against about thirty thousand of the former; by

1896 off-licences of all types accounted for a sixth of all drink-retailing licences in England and Wales.

There were relatively few beer-house off-licences in late-Victorian London, and these were not located in any particular area. But the relative prevalence in well-to-do areas of the off-licence in general stands out clearly from the L.C.C.'s licensing statistics for 1903–4. Among the eighteen London boroughs with fewer than average on-licences per head, there are eleven which have more than the average proportion of off-licences per head. There seems to be an almost inverse relation between the number of on- and off-licences per head in any London area. Furthermore, if one lists the eleven areas relatively well-endowed with off-licences, one finds oneself reading out a roll-call of what were then London's well-to-do suburbs: Westminster, Stoke Newington, Paddington, Lewisham, Kensington, Hampstead, Hammersmith, Hackney, Fulham, Chelsea, and Battersea.[9]

It is Gladstone's refreshment-house and grocers' licences for the sale of wine which explain the relative prevalence of the off-licence in wealthy areas. Gladstone claimed in 1860 that his licensing scheme would provide the poor with drinking facilities which were then being enjoyed only by the rich. But although his reforms did greatly open up the wine trade, and virtually created the firm of Gilbey, the 1899 map shows his wine-shops clustering only on the fringes of Clubland and the Bloomsbury estate. If we analyse thirty-three of Charles Booth's London districts comprising all levels of poverty, there is a negative association (significant at the 10 percent level) between the percentage of the population living in poverty in a London district and the proportion of its total drink licences accounted for by wine licences.[10] Booth's map shows only three refreshment-house licences east of Shoreditch, whereas in the Strand alone there are thirteen. Gladstone's grocers' licences, which in 1880–1900 accounted for nine-tenths of all his wine licences, had merely enabled the rich to replenish their cellars: his refreshment-house licences had merely enabled the businessmen to enliven their midday meals. If the temperance reformers are to be believed, wine licences also encouraged drinking among women—a view which gains support from Seebohm Rowntree's figures for York in 1899. He found that the customers of a local grocer's off-licence divided between 37 percent children, 35 percent women, and only 27 percent men. In the three pubs whose customers he surveyed on three days of the week, the percentage of men never fell below 47 percent and in one case rose as high as 81 percent.[11]

The distinction between on- and off-licences, and between work-time and recreational drinking, helps to explain why the association between pub density and the incidence of poverty is so weak. When one adds to these factors the campaign by late-Victorian magistrates and the L.C.C. to reduce the number of licences in slum areas, the fact that there is any association at all testifies to the immense importance of the pub in the residential areas of the late-Victorian working class. It also emphasizes the importance of considering the second major function of pubs in Victorian towns—the recreational function.

Late-Victorian London's breweries can almost all be found in working-class areas: in that inner ring of decayed suburbs which encircled the City (Map I). This forcibly impressed the young F. N. Charrington when, walking one evening to a local ragged-school from the family brewery in Mile End, he saw a working man come out of a pub and knock down into the gutter his wife, who was pleading for money; Charrington looked up to see his own name in huge gilt letters on the façade of the pub.[12] Particularly prominent in slum areas was the beer-house. In Booth's thirty-three London districts, there is a positive association (significant at almost the 10 percent level) between the percentage of the population in poverty and the number of beer-houses, expressed as a percentage of all local drinking-places. Created by the 1830 Beer Act, beer-houses were forbidden to sell spirits and were at first relatively free from magistrates' control. Beer-selling was popular with the prosperous working man who could employ his wife behind the bar. Pubs occupy strategic positions in the Victorian slum. Of the 160 pubs in the area bounded by Bethnal Green Road/Commercial Street/Whitechapel Road/Cambridge Road (Map I), 131 were situated on corners or opposite road junctions; two pubs stood guard over the entrance to many a side-street. Pubs with more than one entrance simultaneously attracted pedestrians from more than one thoroughfare. Statistics and maps cannot tell us what these pubs were doing: the historian must try to supplement the techniques of the social scientist with the insights of the novelist.

The Victorian slum pub must be seen in the context of street-life. All but the busiest streets at that time united rather than divided the community: in working-class areas 'the emphasis is not so much on the individual home, prized as this is, as on the informal collective life outside it in the extended family, the street, the pub and the open-air market'. Furthermore, economic, technological, and recreational factors ensured that, by modern standards, the pavements were alive with pedestrians many of whom felt obliged to subscribe to drinking customs on the way. Many people earned their living on the pavement—the beggars, stallholders, acrobats, organ-grinders, pedlars, whom Mayhew interviewed so brilliantly. In 1877 William Hoyle explained why pub density was so much greater in Manchester than in Bolton: 'there are a great many men in Manchester who are common porters, who loiter about the streets, and there is comparatively little of that in Bolton'. Nineteenth-century shops were more akin to stalls than they now are, less shut off from the street; glass seldom intruded between goods and purchaser. The pub was different, in that its goods and customers were shut off from public view by doors and frosted glass; but as its role was more recreational than that of the shop, this was a positive asset. Besides, the barrier between pub and street was easily crossed, for the two worlds were connected by great areas of glass, by first-floor balconies, by pavement seats and tables, by potmen carrying cans of ale in wooden frames to customers in nearby premises, and by a multitude of entrances; the 250 central London pubs investigated in 1897 had an average of three entrances apiece (Plates 28 and 30). Much to the temperance reformer's disgust, the street-corner was a social centre: the epitome of everything he disliked.[13]

The pub was marked off from nearby houses by large and colourful signboards; it became even more distinctive during the nineteenth century owing to at least two waves of expenditure on its façade and interior. It may not be coincidental that both these waves of expenditure occurred during decades when the temperance movement was booming. In the early 1830s the publican had every reason to follow the fashion for enriching shop façades which had gripped London in the 1820s, for the Beer Act of 1830 had created a new rival for his custom. A new phenomenon, the 'gin-palace'—with plate-glass windows, richly ornamented façade, gilded lettering and brilliant lamps—began to arouse comment. Its style soon became almost uniform in urban pubs, and still influences their design today. Its splendour accentuated the contrast between the pub and the squalor of its surroundings.

In towns very much darker at night than they now are, the huge and elaborate wrought-iron gas-lamps (Plate 30) which hung over the pub entrance extended the brilliance of the interior into the street, just as the pavement extended its floor. Temperance reformers were half-intoxicated by the brilliance of the scene: at 8.30 one Sunday evening in 1836, a temperance reformer observed the gin-palaces in the Ratcliffe Highway:

> at one place I saw a revolving light with many burners playing most beautifully over the door of the painted charnel-house: at another, about fifty or sixty jets, in one lantern, were throwing out their capricious and fitful, but brilliant gleams, as if from the branches of a shrub. And over the doors of a third house were no less than THREE enormous lamps, with corresponding lights, illuminating the whole street to a considerable distance. They were in full glare on this Sunday evening; and through the doors of these infernal dens of drunkenness and mischief, crowds of miserable wretches were pouring in, that they might drink and die.

Here, as elsewhere, publicans were profiting from the parsimony of the public authorities, and were introducing new upper-class comforts which working people could enjoy only communally.[14]

This external change accompanied an even more significant interior transformation. Simmel claims that 'cities are . . . seats of the highest economic division of labor': the urban predominance of the nineteenth-century gin-palace certainly illustrates his theory, for it was specially designed for the casual urban drinker. Whereas the pub had originally been nothing more than an enlarged home, city life demanded a large shop with specialized equipment and a bar. The cluttered interior which suited a small and relatively slow-moving community did not suit the London of the 1830s. What was needed was a long bar, enclosing several assistants; easy access to large quantities of alcoholic drinks, racked in attractively-painted casks on the back wall; a large area before the bar, where many customers could move freely under the manager's close supervision; and separate entrances for wholesale and family transactions.[15]

A second wave of expenditure took these developments further in the 1860s when, according to the slum missionary, the Rev. J. M. Weylland, 'there was a sudden enlargement of public-houses, and in the attractiveness of them'. By the early 1870s Ruskin was complaining that 'there is scarcely a public-house near the Crystal Palace but sells its gin and bitters under pseudo-Venetian capitals copied from the Church of the Madonna of Health or of Miracles'. The interior transformation also continued: 'many public-houses which had tap-rooms and parlors [*sic*] now have those rooms thrown into large bars', said Weylland in 1877; 'the people merely go in and drink their drams, stand there but for a short time and pass out again, hence it is that there are not so many people found seated and drinking themselves drunk as there used to be years ago.' Such expenditure must often have bewildered the seasoned drinker, especially when (as later in the century) elaborate carved mirrors and screens were introduced: like Tinker Taylor, he would have found such places 'too stylish . . . now for him to feel at home in'. But the sit-down drinker was never forgotten: there were always pubs whose many internal divisions promoted privacy, reduced opportunities for disorder, and preserved class distinctions.[16]

These changes are important, not so much for the luxury which so impressed contemporaries, as for the increase in the *size* of the pub. Looking back over the century, Rowntree and Sherwell in 1899 found that 'while Temperance workers have been steadily endeavouring to reduce the *number* of public-houses, the publicans and brewers have been busily intent upon increasing their *size*.' This probably helps to explain the fact that in the boroughs of 1896, holding size of household constant, there is a strong negative association (significant at the 1 percent level) between a town's population and its pub density; a doubling in the population is associated with a 20 percent rise in the ratio of persons per pub. The large size of urban pubs, together with licensing policy in the late-Victorian slum, may help to explain what is at first sight the surprising fact that, holding size of town constant, the more crowded the housing conditions (persons per house) in any town, the *lower* the pub density (significant at the 1 percent level). An increase of one in the average size of household is associated with an increase of thirty in the ratio of persons per pub. The fact that pub density rises the more scattered the population, and that the relatively small rural pubs were assessed to relatively low rates, reminds us that the steady reduction in pub density in England and Wales since the 1860s owes something to increased urbanization as well as to increased sobriety.[17]

The extravagant and crowded atmosphere of the pub helped Victorian publicans to pursue their important recreational role. Imagine the dram-shop's impact on a tired and bored working man, fleeing from his drab home, nagging wife or landlady, and crying children: 'there is light enough for the transformation scene of the pantomime, and noise enough for a fair', wrote 'Saunterer' of the *Bradford Observer*, who toured local dram-shops in 1871. 'We have some difficulty in obtaining a standing place beside the bright, pewter-topped counter, the crowd of drinkers being so great' (cf. Plate 29). The pub never became a mere shop, whose assistants were indifferent to its customers: it remained a social centre whose hold on working people was the greater because of their migratory lives. If Paris is any guide, in the rapidly-growing nineteenth-century towns which absorbed so many rural immigrants, there would probably be a temporarily low proportion of women to men, and a high proportion of adults to children: all the more need, then, for a 'masculine republic' in every street.[18] If working men were unemployed, in lodgings, 'flitting' from one house to another, or trapped in the bachelor trades, their dependence on the publican was complete. Pub density in some types of town increased, in 1896, with the likelihood of non-resident visitors. Holding size of town and size of household constant, pub density is greater in garrison towns than in market towns (significant at the 10 percent level); the same applies to resorts, though the association is not significant. In industrial towns and seaports, however, pub density is lower than in market towns, though not significantly so.

The close concentration of pubs outside the Knightsbridge Barracks on the 1887 map, and outside the Wellington Barracks on the 1899 map, reflects the heavy dependence of servicemen upon the pub. 'Have you ever thought of collecting some facts showing the demoralizing influence of the barracks in our large towns . . .', wrote that shrewd campaigner Richard Cobden to the pacifist Henry Richard in 1850; 'you might, through your own friends and members of the [Peace] Society, collect some startling information upon these points'. Publicans helped to recruit, to billet and to entertain the armed forces. Government policy, by discouraging servicemen from marrying, inevitably encouraged publicans in garrison towns and seaports to provide prostitutes, and to devour the savings which servicemen accumulated while overseas.

Pubs also lay at the heart of London's underworld. Although by the early-Victorian period the salacious public-house 'cock and hen' clubs may have been declining, the famous Cyder Cellars (Plate 32), Coal Hole, and Evans's Cave of Harmony still catered for the rabelaisian young men who kept late hours in the West End. Here one could find apprentices, clerks, guardsmen, undergraduates, clubmen, lawyers, and commercial men up from the country; 'it was no double meaning, but plain out', said the temperance missionary Jabez Balfour, of the songs he heard there. Renton Nicholson, a major figure in London's underworld, continued to preside at the Coal Hole's indecent Judge and Jury Society right into the 1860s; mock matrimonial cases were tried with the aid of 'female' witnesses (men dressed up in women's clothes), and in the view of one observer 'everything was done that could be to pander to the lowest propensities of depraved humanity.'[19] Robert Hartwell, standing as working-men's candidate at Stoke in 1868, felt obliged vigorously to rebut local accusations that he had been connected with the Cyder Cellars as a mock barrister: 'he had never been in the Cyder Cellars, and knew no more of that place than what he had heard by report.' Without such a denial, Hartwell had no hope of winning local dissenters and respectable working men to his side.

Here the two extremes of society met, for the pub's internal divisions could not prevent young bloods and aristocrats from sharing the pleasures of their humblest inferiors. 'When we dip down below the bourgeois and the regular working-classes', wrote J. A. Hobson, '. . . we find a lower leisure class whose valuations and ways of living form a most instructive parody of the upper leisure class.' *Household Words* in 1857 spoke of the Haymarket's 'sparring snobs, and flashing satins, and sporting gents, and painted cheeks, and brandy-sparkling eyes, and bad tobacco, and hoarse horse-laughs, and loud indecency'; a cruder sort of Haymarket could be seen every Saturday night in the East End's Ratcliffe Highway. Sir George Grey's Public-House Closing Act of 1864, which closed London's pubs between 1 a.m. and 4 a.m., was directed as much against prostitutes as against publicans. As seen from below in *My Secret Life*, it ensured that 'many nice, quiet accommodation houses were closed, and several nice gay women whom I frequented disappeared'; by the 1860s the puritans had made serious inroads on London's underworld.[20]

Sexual adventures were not the only pleasures which united the two social extremes: for generations, aristocrats and working men had centred their sporting activities on the pub. For whereas in the countryside one retreated there from the harshness of the elements, in the town one retreated into the pub from the harshness of urban and industrial life. Sport was a major consolation; the urban pub has always, even in its architectural styles, embodied the urban Englishman's desire to flee into the country. We have rightly been reminded that 'most of the new industrial towns did not so much displace the countryside as grow *over* it': the traditions, the ceremonial, the sociability, and even the sports of rural life were all preserved by urban publicans. Richard Nyren, innkeeper at Hambledon's Bat and Ball, is prominent in the history of cricket, and hanging over the entrance to Lord's first cricket-ground was an advertisement for wines and spirits, Lord's supplementary source of income. When Mayhew in the late 1840s attended the Graham Arms ratting session, all classes were present, and 'a young gentleman, whom the waiters called "Cap'an"' featured prominently in the proceedings. This was the world over which the Marquis of Hastings presided in the 1860s: 'his advent at a ratting match or a badger drawing was a signal to every loafer that the hour of his thirst was ended, and that henceforth "the Markis was in the chair".' When the R.S.P.C.A.'s early-Victorian inspectors interrupted pub cock-fights, they often found army officers presiding.[21]

The connections between drinking and racing were equally strong: the retired prize-fighters and sporting men who kept London sporting-pubs followed their customers to Epsom with tents and booths, and one day in the 1860s Taine was reminded of a recent racing event by the drunken men to be seen all along the road from Epsom to Hyde Park. 'Tom Spring's Parlour' (Plate 31), *alias* the Castle Tavern, Holborn, was conveniently placed midway between the East and the West End; it was a major centre of sporting gossip, attended by early-Victorians of all classes. Tom Spring, an impressive figure, had succeeded another prize-ring hero, Tom Belcher, as landlord in 1828, and died in 1851. On the night before a great (and illegal) prize-fight, his house was crowded by customers eager to learn the *venue*. Spring was deeply implicated, for instance, in the great Caunt–Bendigo contest of 1845. He was manager and chief supporter of Caunt, himself a London publican, and on the preceding night Caunt distributed coloured handkerchiefs as favours at a dinner held at the Castle. Frederick Gale claimed that Tom Spring, like other sporting men, had 'acquired that natural good-breeding which is engendered by associating with people much above them in society'.[22] Similar gatherings assembled at the Green Dragon, Fleet Street, in the 1860s, to meet Marwood the public executioner, who held court there at noon on execution days 'in the "select" section of the pub'. Here, then, are neglected haunts of popular Toryism in Victorian England: sources of that 'unsystematic, unintellectual support of familiar standards and habits of life' which has been attributed to the Tory party. Missionaries were not the only well-bred Victorians to bridge the social extremes by touring London slums. In the 1860s fashionable young aristocrats took a delight in exploring low taverns incognito at night. 'The aristocracy and the working class', Lord Randolph Churchill once declared, 'are united in the indissoluble bonds of a common immorality'.[23]

To a large extent the pub was a centre for male recreation, and the temperance movement liked to see itself as defending helpless women and children against male selfishness (Plates 33 and 34). But this was not the whole story. The 1899 map shows pubs strategically placed at the main entrances to the East End's Victoria Park. Suburban London publicans catered for Londoners taking a week-end walk, and at a pub like the Rosemary Branch, Islington, the entertainments provided (Plate 35) could be quite elaborate. During London's Easter recreations of 1825, balloons went up from the Eagle, and from the Star and Garter near Kew Bridge, while Greenwich Fair on the evening of Easter Monday ensured that 'every room in every public-house is fully occupied by drinkers, smokers, singers and dancers'.

The reputations of particular suburban pubs rose and fell according to their distance from the built-up area. Against this background, one can understand the passion aroused during the early 1850s in the debate on whether the Crystal Palace should sell drink and open on Sundays, for this was the first major opportunity for providing Londoners with a large drink-free suburban week-end pleasure-ground. If sabbatarians kept the place closed, or if temperance reformers kept it dry, the alternative was drunken sabbath-breaking at London's many suburban public-house tea-gardens—not pious and domestic respectability.[24]

Publicans catered for indoor recreational needs with the music-hall. The 1887 map, with its high pub density in the West End, clearly reveals the close link between pubs and recreation, for pub geography was governed by the evening recreational commuter as well as by the daytime business commuter. The early-Victorian music-hall evolved from three distinct institutions—the supper room, the variety saloon, and the tavern concert-room. The first of the music-halls proper evolved naturally out of the free-and-easies held at Charles Morton's Old Canterbury Arms at Lambeth, an important locality for popular recreation. In 1852 Morton opened his Canterbury Hall, which admitted ladies to every performance; despite puritanical criticism, its entertainment improved markedly on what had gone before. This was so successful that in 1854 Morton erected a larger building, and in 1856 added a picture-gallery. Preceded by Edward Weston in 1857, Morton crossed the river in 1861 and by 1866 London boasted twenty-three music-halls. Outside London there were at least three hundred in 1868—including nine in Birmingham, ten in Sheffield, and eight each in Leeds and Manchester. By 1908 there were as many as fifty-seven music-halls in London, attracting groups well below the theatre-goer in social grade: as a printer informed a parliamentary enquiry in 1892, 'it is to the music halls that the vast body of working people look for recreation and entertainment.'[25]

The links between the pub and the stage persisted for generations: in 1943 'Mass Observation' found that in Bolton 'the touring company is still on the side of the publican, constantly boosting beer, and often being sarcastic about teetotallers, temperance and parsons.' The temperance movement evolved an independent set of entertainers—notably the Shapcott and Edwards families, and the Poland Street handbell ringers—to provide music-hall recreations for teetotal audiences. But temperance reformers like F. N. Charrington and Cardinal Manning who tried to deprive the music-hall of its drink were merely accelerating an inevitable differentiation: for music-hall proprietors soon found that mass entertainment was profitable in its own right (Plate 36).[26] Music-halls had from the first been as Matthew Hanly described them in 1892: 'temperance halls at all times'.[27] Here, as elsewhere, publicans had the initiative to provide the community with a new service, then specialized in it, then lost control of it altogether.


The pub's third major social function—the provision of opportunities for public meetings of all kinds—flowed naturally from its prominence in the transport system and from the lack of alternative accommodation. *Laissez-faire* attitudes meant fewer public buildings; religious control over education meant that schools were seldom open to working men for political or trade purposes. 'Large rooms' rarely existed in the working man's home, whereas they could be taken free of charge from publicans confident of drink profits. Inevitably the pub became a centre for all kinds of working-class activity. Trade societies made pubs their 'houses of call', and customer and publican co-operated in building up the reputation of a house. A fashionable pub like the Cheshire Cheese stored up the autographs of its well-to-do customers, just as Charlie Brown's Railway Tavern in Limehouse stored up the valuable curios contributed by its sailor clientele. The Mile End Road's Bell and Mackerel displayed 20,000 specimens of animals in cases, originally collected by the East London Entomological Society.[28]

Many popular reforming movements originated in pubs. The London Corresponding Society was founded at a meeting in October 1791 between Thomas Hardy and three friends at the Bell, Exeter Street; the Hampden Club originated in 1812, at the Thatched House Tavern; the National Union of the Working Classes originated in some carpenters' meetings in the Argyle Arms, Argyle Street; and many of the factory movement's short-time committees in the North of England met in pubs. The government monitored such meetings through the licensing system, and London publicans in 1839 were threatened with the loss of their licence if they let their rooms to Chartists. There was an economic argument for instituting free trade in drink in the early nineteenth century, but it was the political argument which lent this radical campaign its fire. By the 1830s moral pressures against 'pothouse politicians' had become almost as powerful against radical meetings as threats to withdraw the licence of the publican who accommodated them. A committee of the National Union of the Working Classes in 1833 recommended that meetings be held outside pubs whenever possible because 'nothing will more effectually contribute to the success of our cause . . . than sobriety and good conduct'; but the committee admitted that 'this may, in the first instance, be attended with a little difficulty, and probably a diminution of numbers'. And when the Reform League's executive committee considered meeting outside pubs in 1865, the former Chartist J. B. Leno insisted that the League was 'compelled to use the public houses at present as other places were not open to us. It was a matter of necessity not choice.'[29]

Working men were not alone in holding meetings at pubs in the early-Victorian period. In 1856 Robert Lowery recalled that in Newcastle pubs during the 1830s

> all classes met . . . to compare notes and to hear individual remarks and criticisms on what occupied public attention . . . Every branch of knowledge had its public-house where its disciples met. Each party in politics had their house of meeting—there was a house where the singers and musicians met—a house where the speculative and free thinking met—a house where the literate met—a house where the artists and painters met—also one where those who were men of science met.

In mid-Victorian London, there were pubs for everybody's taste—for medical students, prostitutes, servicemen, sportsmen, actors, foreigners, and lawyers—in which it was often possible to reserve one's own seat. In the Strand at the Crown and Anchor, where the London Working Men's Association held its first public meeting in February 1837, John Bright made his London debut as an Anti-Corn Law League orator in February 1842. And according to Robert Owen, 'bigotry, superstition, and all false religions received their death blow' in the large room of the City of London Tavern, at his famous public meeting on 21 August 1817.[30]

London pubs feature prominently in the 1831–2 reform crisis. The Crown and Anchor, for instance, saw the origins of the National Political Union, accommodated the office of the Parliamentary Candidates' Society, and housed the finance committee of the Loyal and Patriotic Fund. Indeed, it was only in the mid-Victorian period that pubs ceased to be at the centre of party political organization. The Whig party could hardly have survived its long period of opposition before 1830 without the aid of publicans prepared to distribute its propaganda and accommodate the party's monthly dinners in London. A report of the London Tavern's dinner for General Sir Charles J. Napier (Plate 37) shows how lavish these entertainments could sometimes be. By 1866 the London Tavern was providing annual banquets for the officers of twenty-eight different regiments during May, for twenty-four of the City companies, and for many London charities.[31]

The pub's extensive social functions are perhaps best summarized with a brief glance at the pub geography of two provincial towns, Oxford (Map V) and York, in

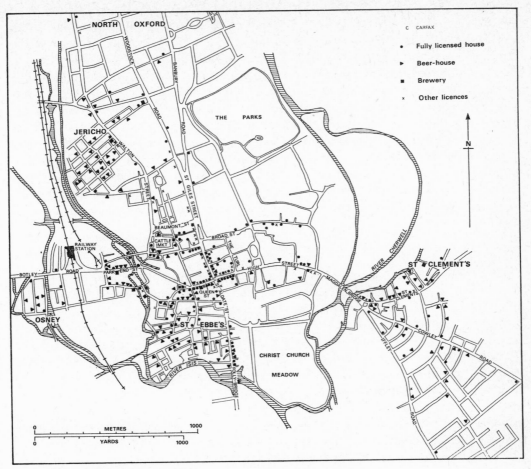

**V**   Drink map of Oxford, 1883

Source: Bodleian Library, Ref. No. C 17. 70 Oxford (7)

1883 and 1902, respectively. In both cities we can see the same concentration of breweries and pubs in the poorer central areas of the town—at Oxford in St Ebbe's and at York in the central areas coloured grey on Seebohm Rowntree's drink map; beer-houses cluster in the working-class areas of Oxford—in Jericho, St Clement's, and St Ebbe's. In both cities there is a concentration of pubs in the central trading areas to cater for the suburban visitor: in Oxford near Carfax and the cattle market, and in York's main Fossgate-Walmgate thoroughfare. But in both cities pubs are almost absent from the *best* central streets—from Oxford's Beaumont Street, and from York's Bootham, Monkgate, and Clifton. In Oxford, of course, the colleges had their own drink facilities, and there was no need for many pubs east of the Turl. In both towns, pub geography closely reflects major transport routes. Pubs cluster at the main entry-points to the city created by Oxford's peculiar water geography—

at Folly Bridge, Magdalen Bridge, and Park End Street. Rowntree reports that of the 236 on-licences at York in 1899, 111 had two entrances, 11 had three, and 1 had four.[32] Significantly, the one approach to Oxford notably lacking in pubs is the approach from the north, along St Giles and the Woodstock and Banbury Roads. Pubs are almost entirely absent from the fashionable suburb of North Oxford. The only type of drink required by the dons and professional people of North Oxford was wine to be consumed at home or in college, and wine-shops probably account for the licences marked 'other' on the west side of St Giles in the 1883 drink map. At York there are 136 licences of all kinds within a circle of a quarter-mile radius in the centre of the city; but doubling the radius adds only 121. With pubs as with churches, twentieth-century rationalization involved substituting suburban going concerns for central decayed institutions: with pubs, through compensation and licence transfer: with churches, through reunion of warring sects and concentration of resources.

These extensive transport, recreational, and political roles of the pub were for the first time powerfully challenged during the nineteenth century—partly by economic influences like the railway, and partly by religious and social groups who believed that social stability was best preserved through fostering sobriety and not drunkenness. In 1873 T. H. Green passionately rebuked W. V. Harcourt, Liberal M.P. for Oxford, over his libertarian attack on temperance legislation: 'I can scarcely think that, if you had seen much of the life of the working classes at close quarters, you c[oul]d have had the heart to speak as you did. Even here in Oxford . . . any one who goes below the respectable classes finds the degradation & hopeless waste wh[ich] this vice produces meet him at every turn.' Hear also the cries of Beatrice Potter from the East End in 1886: 'there are times when one loses all faith in *laisser-faire* and would suppress this poison at all hazards, for it eats the life of the nation.' It became common at temperance meetings to rebut the free traders and libertarians by quoting the working man's wife who said 'I can get my husband, sir, past two public-houses, but I cannot get him past twenty.'[33] When 'Saunterer' toured Bradford dram-shops in 1871, his response epitomized hostile reactions. 'Everywhere, the sights we see are saddening in the extreme', he wrote; 'poverty, misery, and wickedness go hand in hand.'

Still more serious, it was widely believed that pubs fostered revolutionary activity. Pubs assembled working people *in crowds*, and encouraged them to consume an article which might subvert their customary rational appreciation of the Government's power: wine-shops had indeed helped to transmit revolutionary ideas in France after 1789, and temperance reformers were eager to substitute a safe domesticity for the ominous public life of the working class. Many plots were hatched in pubs, whether it be for a poaching raid, for the Luddites' attack on Cartwright's Mill in 1812, or for the German Democratic Society's Continental conspiracies at the Red Lion, Soho, in the 1840s. Some pubs were notorious shrines for the worship of criminals like Jack Sheppard or Dick Turpin; several were well-known 'flash houses', where the police bargained regularly with the criminal underworld. In 1884, J. M. Weylland described the slums which were destroyed when New Oxford Street was built:[34]

> a criminal once reaching this 'city of refuge', considered himself safe from arrest. Within its precincts were many low beer-houses. The chief of these was known as 'Rat Castle'. Forty years ago, just before its removal, we penetrated to it, and found its low ceilinged, wretched rooms filled with desperadoes and youthful thieves. Bull-dogs, and others trained for ratcatching, mingled with the people, all of whom were more brutalized than the animals.

To the outsider, public-house debating clubs seemed merely to foment popular discontent. There were, of course, a few middle-class discussion groups in early-Victorian London pubs (Plate 38), but respectable debaters soon moved off to their clubs, temperance halls, literary and philosophical societies, and mechanics' institutes, leaving the publican to preside over the growth of working-class articulateness and self-confidence. During the 1839 Chartist convention Peter Bussey sent back reports to his Bradford beer-house, which was 'like a theatre; there was a rush for early places, and all paid for admission.' London's debating clubs were regularly reported by Ernest Jones in his *People's Paper* during autumn 1858, and in the Cogers' Hall at the Barley Mow off Fleet Street, many famous mid-Victorian radicals could be heard. In this 'long low room, like the saloon of a large steamer', dim with tobacco smoke, about a hundred debaters sat at the three long narrow tables which ran the length of the room; they were surveyed by departed distinguished members from the dingy portraits on the walls, and by the chairman from his elaborate seat on the dais. This was only the most famous of several such London debating clubs.[35]

At Birmingham's Hope and Anchor Inn, Navigation Street, a Sunday Evening Debating Society met continuously from the mid-1850s to 1886, and greatly fortified local radical opinion. The survival of its minute-books enables us to discuss its activities quite fully. At the meeting on 17 January 1886 George Bill, an old and regular speaker, described the Society as 'the best Sunday School for politics that had ever been established in our Town', and thanked Robert Edmonds, the landlord, who had 'thrown open his rooms for more than 30 years to enable us to educate each other'. From 8.30 to 11 every Sunday evening, almost without a break, twenty to forty members and (if the year 1864 was typical) over 150 spectators gathered to hear the topics introduced by regular speakers and then debated. The range and quality of the debates are remarkable: between 19 July 1863 and 6 November 1864, thirteen debates went on domestic politics, fourteen on foreign affairs, six on literary and cultural topics, five on religion, four each on labour questions, social problems and crime, two on science, and one on local affairs.[36]

The debaters' stamina is also remarkable. On 15 August 1858, so vigorous was the discussion on the motion 'Does the Mind of Man eminate [*sic*] from the Brain or from a higher Source', that an adjourned debate lasting two-and-a-half hours had to be arranged. From 7 August 1870 to 5 March 1871, thirty-two consecutive weekly debates were held on the Franco-Prussian War; about a hundred voted in the concluding debate, which condemned the French almost unanimously. In 1874 there were eight consecutive debates on miracles and seven nights were later devoted to Gladstone's pamphlet on Vaticanism. So excited was the Society in 1876 that it discussed the Eastern Question continuously once a week for over six months. The debates were permeated by a deep historical awareness, and could be ferocious in their moral judgments. When the Society debated the motion 'Was the Motive of Henry the 8th. at the Reformation of a Religious, Political, or Libidinous Character' on 9 June 1861, four votes were cast for the first, two for the second, and twelve for the third. In debating the motion 'What would be the best Mode of ensuring the Moral Character of the Priesthood?' on 3 August 1862, Mr Moreten, a regular speaker, won thirteen votes for castration—as against eleven for improving the education of women in morality, and only two for selecting priests more skilfully.

There was much to frighten the outside observer: the motion on 23 January 1859 for working-class enfranchisement was unopposed, and the monarchy lost by thirty-nine votes to sixteen in a debate on republicanism on 22 March 1863. On two occasions, 26 August 1866 and 21 April 1867, the Society was visited by prominent London Reform Leaguers: these included George Howell, who joined in the debates. The Society formally sent its condolences to the family of Ernest Jones on 1 February 1869: 'his Memory will long be cherished as one of the most able and honest advocates of the rights and liberties of the people that has ever lived to adorn our history with matchless eloquence.' And by twenty-three votes to fifteen, on 11 June 1871, the Society supported the Paris Communists. Nor was its radicalism exclusively political. On 21 August 1859, the strikers in the London building trade were supported by twenty-two votes to two: on 16 October 1864 the Midlands miners, on strike at the time, were supported by forty-five votes to eighteen: and on 12 March 1865, thirty-three voters branded the ironmasters' lock-out as 'unjust and tyranical [*sic*]', whereas only fifteen supported a milder motion hoping for arbitration. On 6 February 1859 the motion 'Has the Establishment and extension of Machinery tended to decrease the Wages of the employed' received unanimous support.

The cultural and political threat from pub culture lurked at the back of many a Victorian politician's mind: it was occasionally discussed in public when uncovered by the indiscretion of a Robert Lowe or by the wrath of a Carlyle. When the slums had been cleared from St Giles, the East End became identified with everything feared by the well-to-do, and the drinking habits of the poor were regarded with a mixture of fear and fascination. Several temperance reformers specialized in retailing to the rich the barbarities of the poor. In his prurient and unpleasantly moralizing *Night Side of London* (1857), the prohibitionist J. Ewing Ritchie exposed slum-life to upper-class eyes; and by the 1870s G. W. McCree, prominent missionary and temperance reformer, was profiting from lectures on topics like 'Lights and Shades of Life in London'.

180

In late-Victorian London, as in early nineteenth-century Paris, the worlds of crime and of labour were merging in the middle-class mind; in the melodramatic 'contrasts' often described in temperance works, Ratcliffe Highway's drunkenness symbolized the East End's threat to the West End's prosperity: 'there is not a sin which the imagination of man can conceive which is not rife in that north Bank of the river Thames', Archbishop Manning told a prohibitionist meeting in 1871.[37]

Yet it would be quite wrong to imply that a united working class, entrenched behind the pub, faced a united and exclusively middle-class temperance public. Such an interpretation would make nonsense of nineteenth-century temperance history. In reality the temperance movement was one of several Victorian reforming crusades which transcended the gulf between employer and employee, and emphasized instead the gulf between 'rough' and 'respectable' working men. During the nineteenth century, at least three ways of containing pub culture presented themselves: all three attracted considerable support from working men. Briefly, these three temperance strategies were restriction, prohibition, and insulation.

The first was embodied in the steadily extending Victorian restraints on drinking hours and on children in pubs. Although the Sunday-trading riots of 1855 held up restriction of opening hours for many years,[38] working-class opinion was divided both during 1855 and during the better-known licensing crisis of 1871–2. Some libertarian working men pointed to the aristocratic clubs, and branded licensing legislation as class legislation; but many others (Lovett and several ex-Chartists not least among them) were more apprehensive about a drunken and ignorant populace. Such men attacked the pub, not because they shared middle-class fears that it fomented radicalism, but because they believed that only a *sober* radicalism could ever be really effective. Working-class temperance enthusiasts are therefore sometimes found outside the formal temperance movement—operating either as individuals or as members of the secularist and self-improving working men's temperance groups which congregated on the fringe of official temperance organizations. But many respectable working men lent impetus to the second temperance strategy: to prohibitionism, as championed by the United Kingdom Alliance.

Founded at Manchester in 1853, the Alliance argued that ratepayers should enjoy the landlord's power to ban the drink trade from any locality. Several London landlords, including the Marquis of Northampton and the Dukes of Westminster and Bedford, excluded pubs from their property. Whereas there had been seventy-four pubs on the Bedford estate in 1854, by 1893 the owner's policy had reduced their number to thirty-four. On the 1887 map, the Duke of Bedford's Bloomsbury and Fig's Mead estates stand out from their surroundings by their lack of red spots. It was even argued that leasehold enfranchisement would deprive society of the great landlords' benevolent policies. But to prohibitionists, who were always democrats above all else, temperance by fiat was a very bad second-best. Besides, the objective of these landlords was not so much temperance as increased prosperity for their estates.

Prohibitionists were fired by zeal for local self-government and for the moral progress of the masses. Their cry was the Permissive Bill, or local option—that is, for prohibition enacted by a two-thirds ratepayer majority in a locality. The Alliance temptingly invited its supporters to mount simultaneous attacks on aristocratic privilege and pauper idleness. Prohibitionism attracted the middle levels of society, cemented the radical alliance between Nonconformists and respectable working men and, by making local option a major late-Victorian political issue, extended the Liberal Party's popular base. It was a policy so reliant upon the moral idealism of slum-dwellers that the Fabians later regarded it as utopian: 'legislation on the principle of asking the blind to lead the blind', they pronounced in 1898, 'is not up to the standard of modern political science': only a more broadly-based representative assembly could be expected to curb the drink trade.[39] Not till the end of the century did the Alliance begin to lose its democratic image and seem to be promoting a measure which would merely enable wealthy property-owners to exclude vulgarity from their midst; in the mid-Victorian period, Alliance leaders were in the vanguard of progressive thought.

'There are more than 600 Members sitting in this House', declared Samuel Smith in a local option debate of 1883, 'and I will venture to say that there are very few of them who have a public-house within sight of their residence.' The prohibitionists' parliamentary agent, J. H. Raper, regularly held up a sovereign at temperance meetings and offered it to anyone who could name a magistrate who had licensed a pub next door to his own house. With pubs, as with brothels, the rich were better placed than the poor to defend their respectability and property. Lady Henry Somerset, a prominent late-Victorian temperance reformer, produced maps before the Royal Commission on Liquor Licensing in 1897, and asked why a thoroughfare was held to justify pub licences in Whitechapel, but not in Belsize Park. Pubs, she concluded, 'exist absolutely regardless of the needs of the neighbourhood, and . . . the only places which are comparatively free are those places which are rich enough to maintain an effective opposition to their establishment'.[40]

Prohibitionist speakers often advertised the plight of the respectable working man, beleaguered by the pubs he never patronized. At a temperance meeting in 1871, Manning[41] claimed that the rich banned pubs from upper-class areas, yet if a pub were established

> in a part of the town where honest working men and their families live, where peace and quiet have hitherto reigned . . . between the dwellings of two honest labouring men . . . their wives and children . . . have to live all the day long and all the week round, with this moral pestilence on their threshold; and . . . the walls of the dwellings are so thin that the noise of revelry and the words, it may be, of impurity and blasphemy are heard in the chambers where they rest. But this atmosphere of pestilence will hang about the dwelling of the poor man, and he has not power to abolish it.
> He has no means whatever to purify the street where he lives, and to protect his family from infection.

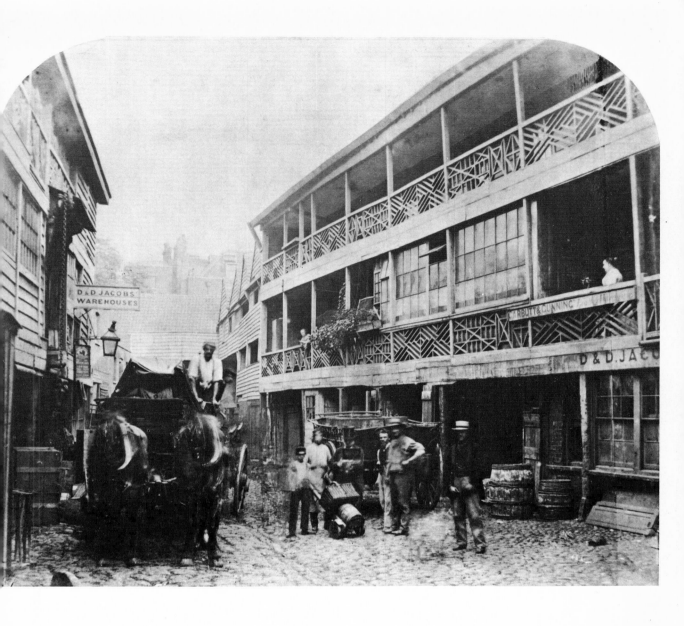

**25** A typical inn yard—the King's Head, Southwark, in 1900. The inn's major transport functions had long since been taken over by the railway, but such yards sometimes became loading bays for warehousemen. There are two such firms operating from this one, and the galleries themselves no longer serve the inn alone.
*Greater London Council*

**26** *above left*   The pub serving road transport in its heyday. The *Cambridge Telegraph* setting off from the White Horse in Fetter Lane. After the print by J. Pollard in the John Johnson Collection.
*Bodleian Library*

**27** *left*   A coaching inn nearing the end of its coaching days. The Bull and Mouth about 1830, shortly before becoming the Queen's Hotel, St Martin's-le-Grand. The placard in the bottom right-hand corner advertises coaches to all parts of the kingdom. After a steel engraving of a drawing by T. Allom.
*Guildhall Library*

**28** *above*   Idleness, extravagance, drunkenness, squalor: a London street-corner scene on a Sunday morning, from *Illustrated London News*, xxix (1856), 578.

**29** A London ginshop interior in 1852.
Crowded, smoky, noisy, this was the kind
of atmosphere which struck 'Saunterer' so
forcibly when he visited the Bradford gin-
shops in 1871. The combination of sporting
raffishness with humiliating squalor was
attacked at all points by the temperance
movement. This engraving by T. B. Smithies
comes from *Working Man's Friend*, i,
new series (1852), 56.

**30** The Old Oak, Mansfield Road, Hampstead. A typical street-corner brewers' pub of the late nineteenth century, complete with discreet frosted glass, prominent signboards, several entrances, the faded relics of the gin-palace's classical style, and a magnificent set of wrought-iron gas-lamps.
*R. B. Sawrey-Cookson*

**The Harmonic every Evening.**

**New and Splendid Rooms.**

## CYDER CELLARS,

MAIDEN LANE,

COVENT GARDEN,

### JOHN REGAN

Having at an immence expense completed his improvement trusts his exertions will merit from a discerning Public, a continuance of that support and general Patronage which this Old Established and Favourite Place of Resort has for so many Years experienced.

**Wines, Chops, Spirits Dinners, &c., of the best Quality, Moderate Charges.**

31 *above* Tom Spring's Parlour, *c.*1840. A centre of sporting gossip for all classes, run by a retired prize-fighter at the Castle in Holborn. *Guildhall Library*

**32** *below left* The Cyder Cellars, Maiden Lane, a centre of London's underworld, and one of the ancestors of the music-hall, from a handbill in the Norman Collection. *Guildhall Library*

**33** *above left* The bright window of the pub contrasts strongly with the drab surroundings, as wives wait for their husbands to leave off drinking on pay night. Temperance reformers sided firmly with wives and children in their claim on working men's wages. From S. C. Hall, *The Trial of Sir Jasper* (1872), p. 3

**34** *above right* Temperance reformers claimed, sometimes with excessive sentimentality, to be defending women and children against male selfishness. This picture records an alleged intervention at an Aylesbury temperance meeting by a railway employee. He said that on this occasion his five-year-old daughter, whom he carried every night to the beer-shop, begged him 'Father, don't go.' He turned back (and became a teetotaller) when he felt a tear fall from her as he was about to enter. Temperance tracts often emphasized the theme of the virtuous child reforming the drunken parent. From an engraving in *Band of Hope Review*, 1 March 1867, p. 297.

**35** *above*  Suburban entertainments at the
Rosemary Branch, Islington, one of several
suburban tea-gardens catering for weekend
recreation in the early nineteenth century. Their
prosperity was short-lived because the demand
for building land took away their gardens and
'views'. From the Crace Collection.
*British Museum*

**36** *below*  The Surrey Music-Hall, Lambeth,
where the audience was free to move about
during performances; in other music-halls the
audience remained seated while waiters took the
orders. From an undated picture in *Paul Pry*
no. 12, unpublished collection 'Pleasure Gardens
of South London', II, p. 96. By courtesy of the
Trustees of the London Museum.
*London Museum*

**37** Dinner at the London Tavern for Sir Charles
Napier in 1849. The leading pubs of London
could still cater lavishly for the best company.
For humbler gatherings in slum areas, the
publican's 'Large Room' was indispensable.
From a print in the Norman Collection.
*Guildhall Library*

**38** A middle-class discussion group in session at
the Belvedere, a London pub in Pentonville in
the 1850s, at ten o'clock in the evening. From G.
A. Sala, *Twice Round the Clock* [1859], p. 288.

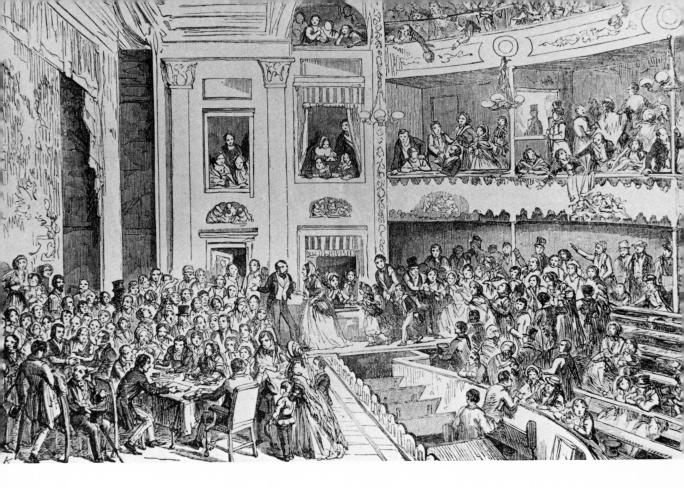

**39** Signing the pledge of total abstinence in
Sadler's Wells Theatre, 1854. Temperance
meetings were sometimes held in theatres during
the 1850s, partly because large numbers were
interested in the subject, but also because such
things could also be entertaining. This drawing
was made by George Cruikshank, a temperance
zealot himself, and comes from *Illustrated London
News*, xxiv (1854), 465.

**40** The Band of Hope, Littlemore, Oxon.
Towards the end of the nineteenth century, the
temperance movement, having failed to win over
the adults, sought to protect the children.
Children could hardly refuse to abjure temptations
they had scarcely experienced, especially when
asked to do so in the schoolroom, as in this
watercolour by Miss E. D. Herschel.
*Bodleian Library*

Prohibitionists were among the first free-trading Liberals to seek social progress through state intervention, for a respectable working man surrounded by drink-shops could hardly be expected to self-help his way to prosperity.

Prohibitionists spiced their diagnosis with hints of aristocratic conspiracy: they claimed that pubs were 'imposed' on respectable working people by an aristocracy anxious to keep them socially, educationally, and politically subordinate. 'I hold that no more efficient means for corrupting a people can be found', wrote William Lovett, 'than that of blending their amusements with the means of intoxication.' He was particularly bitter on this score because his National Hall school at Holborn was denied the music licence which the magistrates granted to the publican who succeeded him there in 1857: 'publicans can always have such licences', he wrote tartly, 'but not so those who would have music apart from the means of intoxication.' Pub geography in nineteenth-century London did of course protect the sobriety of the rich and obstruct the respectability of the poor; but to go further, and to ascribe this to deliberate aristocratic design, was to lose a sense of proportion. As Baron Bramwell pointed out, existing pub geography stemmed only from the fact 'that a public-house in a square in which the rich live would not pay.'[42]

The third temperance strategy was to insulate oneself from temptation. Insulation could be sought in two ways. The easy way was for the abstainer to husband his savings and move away from the slum: 'the home that had satisfied my wants as a drinker was not in harmony with my self-respect as a teetotaller', wrote Thomas Whittaker of his conduct after signing the pledge in the 1830s, 'and I soon put myself in possession of a house rented at twelve pounds a year.' In the 1820s, licensing restriction had been opposed by speculative builders eager to add value to their suburban estates by providing drink facilities. But by the 1880s, the climate had so changed that it was profitable to *exclude* pubs from one's estate. The Artisans, Labourers and General Dwellings Company specialized in building drink-free suburban utopias— at Queen's Park, Shaftesbury Park, and Noel Park. Like so many utopias, the nineteenth-century temperance estate suffered by the fact that it was embedded in a corrupt society: pubs clustered round its fringes. Yet Shaftesbury Park had charms for at least one of its residents: during the past year, he wrote in 1875, 'I have never heard the song of a drunkard, but during the summer evenings I have often listened to the songs, &c., of the people from the open windows.'[43]

This residential separation of teetotallers from drinkers in late-Victorian London probably accentuated the slumland weakness of a Liberal Party which sought to attract all classes. It was certainly more courageous to face the evil directly from inside the slum, for this involved braving ridicule and even violence from one's own class. Slum-dwellers disliked working men who 'gave themselves airs', and teetotallers were often insulted. Hence arose a second form of insulation. By taking the pledge, the sober slum-dweller could protect himself against temptation and insult by joining a group of the like-minded (Plates 39 and 40). If successful, such groups could purchase a temperance 'hall', or attach themselves to a Nonconformist chapel or mission.

But it was always a struggle, particularly in London, where dissenting chapels were weaker than in the North of England, and where temperance effort within the working class was fragmented by the gulf between Nonconformity and the relatively powerful secularist movement. In Booth's thirty-three districts, religious institutions exceed pubs in number only in the freak district of Holborn. The 1899 map shows that religious institutions, unlike pubs, were poorly sited for influencing the passer-by. Anglican churches (until the 1860s, likely to be anti-temperance) were sometimes well placed, because the community had often grown up around them. But Nonconformist chapels and missions usually huddled in backstreets and backyards; unlike pubs, they seldom clustered at the crossroads. In Booth's districts, an increased percentage in poverty is not accompanied by an increase in the ratio of religious institutions to drinking places: nor is there any significant relation, when population is held constant, between the number of religious institutions and the number of pubs. Yet the drinker lacked the temperance reformer's skill in making his political presence forcefully and continuously felt. From a host of obscure contests between drinkers and teetotallers in Victorian towns, the stuff of Victorian politics was made. Here religion impinged upon social class, recreation upon party politics.

These contests were at times very bitter: yet the bitterness conceals a fundamental similarity between the roles of pub and temperance society. Both provided individual working men with the chance of rising in society; both gave working men collective experience which could easily be applied to politics and wage-bargaining. Both recognized the social evils rife in Victorian towns: the publican palliated them, the temperance reformer tried (however ineffectually) to remove them. Teetotallers and heavy drinkers may even have tended to appear together in the same communities. We know from recent social surveys that teetotalism is now most common in areas of heavy drinking, and we have several individual nineteenth-century assertions that drunkenness was more prevalent in early-Victorian Glasgow and Lancashire, where the temperance movement was strong, than in London and the southern rural counties where the temperance movement was weak. But we lack statistical proof of these assertions.[44]

There are many other similarities between pub and temperance society. Both struggled to protect the newcomer from the loneliness and strangeness of town life. Urban sociologists tell us, somewhat pretentiously, that 'the city is characterized by secondary rather than primary contacts'—contacts which are relatively anonymous, segmentalized, utilitarian. Social anthropologists tell us that modern Africans moving from country to town often form new types of non-tribal voluntary association; these small private societies unite the like-minded, replace the community ties which lent structure to rural life, integrate the newcomer into urban society by initiating him into business habits, and assign prestige through elections to petty offices.[45] Organizations of this sort existed in nineteenth-century England, yet serious historians have so far ignored them. Instead, they tend to use the term 'urbanization' rather clinically, and conceal from us the shock of transition experienced by so many rural immigrants at the time. We need to know *how* the immigrant was socialized, what organizations catered for him, and how these were related to the contemporary social and political structure.

The temperance society, like the pub, could ensure that the newcomer to Victorian towns received recognition, education, employment, friends, advice, and support; it could encourage him to resist the temptations which the anonymity of urban life made so seductive; and it could provide a new framework for daily conduct. Like the urban chapels to which they were so often attached, temperance societies were 'havens of refuge in an utterly strange and alien landscape. Here, and here only, could the old links of identity with home be maintained, the familiar forms of worship be recovered.'[46] Their very names, not to mention their roles, closely resemble those of the voluntary association formed by newcomers to the modern African city.

Nor did pub and temperance society differ so markedly in their political tendency. Pub society was never so subversive as it seemed to the respectable outsider. The Conservative Party realized this when it promoted working men's drinking-clubs from the 1860s; indeed, in some ways the temperance society was far more radical. Pub society's traditionalism and chauvinism made drinkers unreceptive to Continental doctrines of revolution. 'Saunterer''s dram-shop criminals were less dangerous than he thought; they did not threaten the successful entrepreneur—they were his mirror-image. The Birmingham Sunday Evening Debating Society was really quite a conservative body. Mr Nuttall on 12 September 1864 raised twenty-two votes for his motion that the Chartists failed from propagating 'wild and impract[ic]able ideas and endeavouring to carry them out by physical force [,] thus setting all other classes against them'. The Society usually ensured that both sides of any question were presented, and like many other pub associations it encouraged respect for House of Commons procedure. By the 1880s and perhaps before, it was operating decidedly from inside the existing political party system. There was much presenting of testimonials, mutual congratulation, and Christmas punch-drinking at the landlord's expense: in short, much consciousness of respectability. The Society was, in fact, like the temperance society, a 'small-scale success system': it did not threaten the social structure.[47]

It is clear, then, that to a large extent pub and temperance society fought so fiercely because their roles were so similar. Indeed, as their rivalry grew more intense, temperance society and pub appropriated each other's attractions. Pubs acquired organs, hymn singing, and soft drinks; temperance societies acquired professional entertainers, sent their members into pubs to spread the new gospel, and even purchased pubs (though only for the purpose of turning them dry). In this context, then, as in the very different context described by Gladstone, 'there is often, in the courses of this wayward and bewildered life, exterior opposition, and sincere and even violent condemnation, between persons and bodies who are nevertheless profoundly associated by ties and relations that they know not of.'[48]

## Notes

1   See J. R. Kellett, *The Impact of Railways on Victorian Cities* (1969), and the essays by John Foster and E. P. Hennock, in H. J. Dyos, ed., *The Study of Urban History* (1968). I acknowledge gratefully here the most generous help I have received in interpreting the statistics in this article from my colleague Mr A. J. Glyn, Corpus Christi College, Oxford; Miss H. Karayannis helped me with the computations. Professor Peter Mathias, All Souls College, Oxford, was kind enough to provide valuable bibliographical help at an early stage.

2   The two maps are the National Temperance Publication Depot's *The Modern Plague of London* (c. 1887), and 'London 1899–1900', a map in the final volume of Charles Booth's *Life and Labour of the People in London* (1903 edn). Miss Joan Pollard of the London Museum kindly guided me to the former, which is kept in the London Museum, Kensington Palace; she also gave me much other painstaking help. For ideas on the study of local temperance societies, see my 'Temperance Societies', *Local Historian*, viii, nos 4 & 5 (1968–9). The social and other roles of drink and drinking-places in the 1820s and 1870s are fully discussed in my *Drink and the Victorians* (1971), chs 2, 14, 15. There is a mass of antiquarian literature on pubs, most of it worthless; but for an excellent discussion, see W. B. Johnson, 'The Inn as a Community Centre', *Amateur Historian*, ii, no. 5 (1955). The term 'pub' is used in this article to denote any type of public drinking-place, and not synonymously with the specialized term 'public-house'; there were several categories of 'pub' in nineteenth-century England, and these have been distinguished where necessary. The expression 'pub density', as used here, refers to density in relation to population, not in relation to area.

3   B. W. Matz, *The Inns and Taverns of 'Pickwick'* (1921), p. 9; I am most grateful to Professor Philip Collins of Leicester University for generous help on Dickens's attitude to pubs.

4   For early railways, see George Stephenson, in *Temperance Monthly Visitor* (Norwich), October 1860, 79; J. A. R. Pimlott, *The Englishman's Holiday* (1947), p. 88. For Gladstone, see National Temperance League, *Annual Report 1881–2*, 26.

5   *Collins Illustrated Guide to London & Neighbourhood 1871* (1871), p. 118; see also N. C. Selway, *The Regency Road: The coaching prints of James Pollard* (1957), pp. 21, 29; Charles Knight, *London*, IV (1843), pp. 310ff.; VI (1844), p. 313. For canals, see L. T. C. Rolt, *Narrow Boat* (1944), p. 59—a reference I owe to Christopher Harvie of the Open University.

6   J. Dunlop, *The Philosophy of Artificial and Compulsory Drinking Usage* (1839), p. 306; cf. *Parliamentary Papers* (*P.P.*), 1898, XXXVI, Royal Commission (R.C.) on the Liquor Licensing Laws, Third Report: Minutes of Evidence (C. 8694), Q. 26,312. For Leeds, see G. C. Dickinson, 'The Development of Suburban Road Passenger Transport in Leeds, 1840–1895', *Journal of Transport History*, iv (November 1960), 215; see also J. R. Kellett, op. cit., pp. 87ff., 139–40, 278, 281; and E. A. Pratt, *The Policy of Licensing Justices* (1909), ch. 8.

7   *P.P.*, 1898, XXXVII, R.C. on the Liquor Licensing Laws: Statistics (8696), p. 44 et seq.

8   *P.P.*, 1877, XI, Select Committee (S.C.) (H. of L.) on Intemperance, Third Report: Minutes of Evidence (418), Q. 8404.

9  Figures in G. B. Wilson, *Alcohol and the Nation* (1940), pp. 394–6; R.C. on Liquor
   Licensing Laws, Statistics, pp. 30–1; *London Statistics 1903–1904*, xiv (1904), 369; cf.
   H. J. Dyos, *Victorian Suburb* (Leicester, 1961), p. 154, and the interesting table in
   Charles Booth, *Life and Labour*, final volume (1903), p. 221.

10 The boundaries and poverty classifications of Booth's districts are in *Life and Labour*,
   1st series, II, Appendix, pp. 1–60; drinking facilities have been calculated from
   Booth's 1899 map. The following districts have been analysed: 44C, 2B, 48E, 48C,
   2D, 22E, 40A, 75B, 79B, 66A, 40B, 60A, 78A, 48D, 43A, 23A, 59B, 42A, 74C,
   43F, 43G, 41E, 2A, 63B, 80C, 23B, 41D, 48F, 92A, 43E, 86E, 41A, 88F. Two difficulties
   arise: the districts were classified ten years before the map was compiled, and during
   that decade the L.C.C. was pursuing a vigorous temperance policy. Second, Booth
   gives no details of the *size* of the drinking places.

11 B. Seebohm Rowntree, *Poverty: A study of town life* (Nelson edn, n.d.), pp. 371–83,
   390.

12 For brewery locations, see *Handbook to London As It Is* (John Murray, new edn,
   1879), p. 79; G. Thorne, *The Great Acceptance* (1913), pp. 20–1.

13 Quotations from M. Young & P. Willmott, *Family and Class in a London Suburb*
   (1960), p. 130; S.C. on Intemperance, Q. 8408. For street recreations, see
   A. R. Bennett, *London and Londoners in the Eighteen-Fifties and Sixties* (1924),
   pp. 47, 60. For drinking customs, see J. Dunlop, op. cit., p. 306; for pub entrances,
   see J. Rowntree and A. Sherwell, *Temperance Problem and Social Reform*
   (5th edn, 1899), p. 84.

14 Quotation from *Temperance Penny Magazine*, January 1836, 6. On gin-palaces,
   see *Sketches by Boz* (2nd edn, 1836), I, pp. 280, 282; S. and B. Webb, *The History of
   Liquor Licensing in England, principally from 1700 to 1830* (1903), pp. 120–1;
   John Hogg, *London As It Is* (1837), p. 287.

15 Simmel quoted in P. K. Hatt and A. J. Reiss, eds, *Cities and Society* (Chicago, 1957),
   p. 643; for an excellent account of the evolution of pub interiors, see M. Gorham and
   H. McG. Dunnett, *Inside the Pub* (1950), pp. 64–5, 94–113.

16 Weylland, S. C. on Intemperance, QQ. 9141, 9124. Ruskin is quoted in E. T. Cook,
   *Life of John Ruskin* (1911), I, p. 308; cf. Ruskin's preface to the 3rd edn of his
   *Stones of Venice*, in *Works*, ed. Cook and Wedderburn (1903), IX, p. 12.
   Tinker Taylor is in Thomas Hardy, *Jude the Obscure* (1957 paperback edn), p. 187;
   I owe this reference to Mr John Stothard, formerly of Corpus Christi College, Oxford.
   See also A. Shadwell, *Drink, Temperance and Legislation* (1902), pp. 204–5.

17 Quoted from J. Rowntree and A. Sherwell, op. cit., p. 83. For rating, see
   G. B. Wilson, op. cit., pp. 291–2; he prints figures for persons per pub on p. 236.

18 'Saunterer' in *Bradford Observer*, 19 January 1871: I owe this reference to
   Miss Peggy Rastrick, Killinghall Road, Bradford, who is studying the history of
   local temperance activity. The phrase 'masculine republic' was coined by
   H. W. J. Edwards, *The Good Patch* (1938), p. 158; I owe this reference to
   Dr W. R. Lambert, formerly of the Department of History, University College,
   Swansea. See also L. Chevalier, *Classes laborieuses et classes dangereuses à Paris
   pendant la première moitié du xixᵉ siècle* (Paris, 1958), pp. 225, 299.

19 Cobden quoted by J. A. Hobson, *Richard Cobden: The international man* (1918),
   p. 63; for Balfour, see *P.P.*, 1854, XIV, S. C. (H. of C.) on Public Houses:

Minutes of Evidence (367), Q. 1265; the observer was J. E. Ritchie, *The Night Side of London* (1857), p. 79. For Hartwell, see *Staffordshire Advertiser*, 14 November 1868, p. 6. I am most grateful to Paul Anderton, of the Historical Association's North Staffordshire branch, for this reference. For 'cock and hen' clubs, see *P.P.* 1849, XVII, S.C. (H. of C.) on Public Libraries: Minutes of Evidence (548), Q. 2783 [Lovett]. For London's underworld, see Guildhall Library, *Norman Collection*, G.R.1.1.5 (Inns and Taverns, II), 'Coal Hole' and 'Cyder Cellars'. For generous help in guiding me through this excellent collection, and for much other assistance, I must thank Mr Ralph Hyde, the Guildhall Library. For Judge and Jury clubs see James Greenwood, *The Wilds of London* (1874), pp. 99ff., and the illustration in T. McD. Rendle, *Swings and Roundabouts: A yokel in London* (1919), p. 196.

20  Quotations from J. A. Hobson, *Work and Wealth* (1914), pp. 155–6; William Acton, *Prostitution* (2nd edn, 1870), p. 21; *My Secret Life* (Amsterdam, n.d., British Museum copy), VI, p. 127. For Sir George Grey, see *P.P.*, 1871, XIX, R.C. on the Contagious Diseases Act: Minutes of Evidence (C. 408), Q. 18,152.

21  Quotations from E. P. Thompson, *The Making of the English Working Class* (2nd edn, 1968), p. 445; H. Mayhew, *London Labour and the London Poor* (1861), III, p. 6; Anon., *London in the Sixties (With a Few Digressions)* by One of the Old Brigade (1908), p. 35. For cockfights, see my 'Religion and Recreation in Nineteenth-Century England', *Past and Present*, no. 38 (1967), 118.

22  F. Gale, *Sports and Recreations in Town and Country* (1888), p. 4. See also Taine's *Notes on England*, ed. E. Hyams (1957), p. 36; Guildhall Library, *Norman Collection*, G.R.1.1.5 (Inns and Taverns, II), 'Thomas Spring's Parlour'; John Timbs, *Club Life of London* (1866), II, p. 235; K. Chesney, *The Victorian Underworld* (1970), pp. 268–9.

23  For Marwood, see *London in the Sixties*, p. 161; cf. p. 91ff. Other quotations from E. L. Woodward, *The Age of Reform* (1938), p. 120; Sir Oswald Mosley, *My Life* (1968), p. 18.

24  For 1825, see W. Hone, *Every-Day Book*, I, part 1 (1825), cc. 438, 442. For the Crystal Palace, see Percy Cruikshank, *Sunday Scenes in London and its Suburbs* (1854), p. 12; S. Couling, *History of the Temperance Movement* (1862), p. 221; P. T. Winskill, *The Temperance Movement and its Workers* (1892), III, p. 54.

25  Quotation from *P.P.*, 1892, XVIII, S.C. (H. of C.) on Theatres and Places of Entertainment: Minutes of Evidence (240), Q. 5177 [Matthew Hanly], Q. 864. Music-hall statistics from R. Mander and J. Mitchenson, *British Music Hall: A story in pictures* (1965), p. 19; *P.P.*, 1866, XVI, S.C. (H. of C.) on Theatrical Licences: Report (373), p. 307; *Collins Illustrated Guide to London & Neighbourhood* (1871), p. 124; *Era Almanack*, 1908, pp. 102–3. The *Almanack* does not confront the serious problems involved in defining the term 'music-hall'.

26  'Mass Observation', *The Pub and the People: A worktown study* (1943), p. 160. See also Mander and Mitchenson, op. cit., p. 21.

27  *P.P.*, 1892, XVIII, S.C. (H. of C.) on Theatres and Places of Entertainment: Minutes of Evidence (240), Q. 5171; cf. P. Snowden, *Socialism and the Drink Question* (1908), p. 82.

28  C. E. Lawrence, 'Public-House Museums', *Ludgate* (n.d., *Norman Collection* C. 23.1 T. 1895); *Graphic*, 8 December 1928, 410.

29   For the N.U.W.C. see *Poor Man's Guardian*, 6 July 1833, 217; I owe this reference
     to Dr Patricia Hollis, the University of East Anglia. Leno is in Bishopsgate Institute,
     *Reform League Executive Committee Minutes*, 25 August 1865; see also W. Lovett and
     J. Collins, *Chartism* (1840), p. 48.

30   Lowery, *Weekly Record of the Temperance Movement*, 21 June 1856, 107; Owen,
     quoted in J. F. C. Harrison, *Robert Owen and the Owenites in Britain and America*
     (1969), p. 92.

31   Guildhall Library, *Norman Collection*, Box C.23.1 (London Tavern); see also
     John Timbs, op. cit., II, p. 278.

32   B. S. Rowntree, op. cit., p. 363. The York map is in the 2nd edn, 1902.
     *The Drink Map of Oxford, 1883* is in Bodleian Library, ref. no. C.17.70 (Oxford), 7.

33   Quotations from Balliol College, Oxford: T. H. Green MSS., Black Box: T. H. Green
     to W. V. Harcourt, draft reply to Harcourt's letter of 7 January 1873; Beatrice Webb,
     *My Apprenticeship* (2nd edn, 1946), p. 238. For the working man's wife, see
     Rolleston, in *Alliance News* (Manchester), 19 October 1872, 739.

34   Quoted from J. M. Weylland, *These Fifty Years* (1884), p. 8. For plots, see F. Peel,
     *The Risings of the Luddites, Chartists and Plugdrawers* (1968 edn), p. 53ff.;
     A. R. Schoyen, *The Chartist Challenge: A portrait of George Julian Harvey* (1958),
     p. 135. For wine-shops in the French Revolution, see G. Rudé, *The Crowd in the
     French Revolution* (Oxford, 1959), p. 217.

35   For Bussey, see A. J. Peacock, *Bradford Chartism 1838–1840* (York, 1969), p. 20.
     Cogers's quotation from Guildhall Library, *Norman Collection*, G.R.1.1.5
     (Inns and Taverns, II).

36   See the Society's MS. Minutes (2 vols) in Birmingham Central Library, ref. nos
     103138–9. Mrs Corke of the Leamington Historical Association kindly referred me to
     this source.

37   *Alliance News*, 21 October 1871, 674; see also A. E. Dingle and B. H. Harrison,
     'Cardinal Manning as Temperance Reformer', *Historical Journal*, xii (1969), 504ff.

38   For a full account of this incident, see my 'Sunday Trading Riots of 1855',
     *Historical Journal*, viii (1965), especially 238–9. See also *Daily Telegraph*, 20 April 1871,
     5; 10 May 1871, 4; 19 June 1871, 5.

39   Fabian Society, *Municipal Drink Traffic*, Tract no. 86 (1898 edn), p. 5. For the
     Bedford Estate, see D. J. Olsen, *Town Planning in London: The eighteenth and
     nineteenth centuries* (New Haven, 1964), p. 165.

40   3 Hansard 278, c. 1324 (27 April 1883); R.C. on Liquor Licensing Laws, Q. 31, 377.

41   Manning, *Alliance News*, 5 October 1872, 706–7.

42   Quotations from W. Lovett, *Life and Struggles* (1876), p. 374; National Library of
     Scotland, Edinburgh, Combe MSS. 7365 f.89: Lovett to Combe, 25 November 1857;
     C. Fairfield, *Some Account of George William Wilshere, Baron Bramwell* (1898), p. 272.

43   Quotations from T. Whittaker, *Life's Battles in Temperance Armour* (1884), p. 66
     and *Alliance News*, 2 October 1875, 636. See also P. T. Winskill, *Temperance
     Movement and its Workers*, III, p. 113; J. N. Tarn, 'Some Pioneer Suburban Housing
     Estates', *Architectural Review*, cxliii (1968), 367; Rowntree and Sherwell, op. cit.,
     pp. 212–15. I am most grateful to Dr D. A. Reeder, Garnett College, London. for
     help on this topic.

44   For Glasgow and Lancashire, see W. Reid, *Temperance Memorials of the Late*

*Robert Kettle Esq.* (Glasgow, 1853), p. 13; British Museum Add. MSS. 44428
(Gladstone Papers), f.178: Bishop Fraser to Gladstone, 5 November 1870;
Joseph Livesey, *Preston Temperance Advocate* (Preston), July 1834, p. 53. For recent
surveys, see F. Zweig, *The Worker in an Affluent Society* (1961), pp. 130–1;
D. E. Allen, *British Tastes* (Panther edn, 1969), pp. 89, 143–4.

45 Wirth is quoted in Hatt and Reiss, op. cit., p. 54, but see also pp. 61, 631.
For social anthropologists, see W. B. Schwab, 'Oshogbo—an Urban Community',
in H. Kuper, ed., *Urbanization and Migration in West Africa* (University of
California Press, 1965), pp. 102–6; M. Banton, 'Social Alignment and Identity in
a West African City', ibid., pp. 143–4; P. Marris, *Family & Social Change in an
African City: A study of rehousing in Lagos* (1961), pp. 39, 42; G. Breese,
*Urbanization in Newly Developing Countries* (New Jersey, 1966), pp. 87–8, 98.
Dr Alan Macfarlane kindly directed me towards much of this literature.

46 I. G. Jones, in G. Williams, ed., *Merthyr Politics* (Cardiff, 1966), p. 52; cf. the revealing
quotation from B. G. Orchard, in R. B. Walker, 'Religious Changes in Liverpool
in the Nineteenth Century', *Journal of Ecclesiastical History*, xix (1968), 204.

47 J. Foster, in H. J. Dyos, ed., *The Study of Urban History*, p. 294.

48 W. E. Gladstone, 'The Evangelical Movement; its Parentage, Progress, and Issue',
*Gleanings of Past Years, 1843–79* (1879), VII, p. 224.

# 7    The Literature of the Streets

## Victor E. Neuburg

The massing of people in cities in the nineteenth century made a vast difference to the scale of many things. It meant not only higher densities on the ground but also new opportunities for communication on many different levels. These concentrations of people rapidly became the means and the ends of mass production, but they also provided the basis for new ways of life that depended at certain levels less on the household than on the street. The urban mass provided, too, a demand for various kinds of mass journalism, of which perhaps the most characteristically urban was that known as 'street literature'. It is a vague category and ought for our present purposes to be fairly narrowly defined. At its widest it can comprise cheap newspapers; sporting journals; song books; almanacks; broadsides; advertisement hoardings; political, religious, freethinking, or commercial leaflets or circulars; printed wrapping material; 'penny dreadfuls' like those issued by Lloyd, Purkess, and others; and even —though this is perhaps more arguable—the dumpy little books, both fiction and non-fiction, of which Milner and Sowerby's 'Cottage Library' was the most comprehensive series, although by no means the only one. More narrowly we can say that the most characteristic and typical kind of street literature was the broadside or street ballad.

The value of this narrower definition is based upon two factors: first, the Victorian broadside was produced almost entirely for the poor; second, it bore a superficial resemblance to a traditional form of popular literature. From the earliest days of printing, ephemeral sheets of this kind had circulated throughout Europe.[1] The broadside was the most substantial element in the literature of the poor, and there seems no reason to doubt that people living in the Victorian city accepted it as an unquestioned part of their background.

The broadside consisted of popular ballads or prose printed in 'broadside' form and hawked around the streets and in public houses. The sheets were essentially simple to produce. They were printed upon one side only of paper which was nearly always of the flimsiest; and sometimes they carried woodcut illustrations which were not seldom lively, and on occasion lurid. They varied in size, and the use of *ad hoc* typography, combined with the illustrations, gave many of them considerable visual appeal. The cries of the sellers—'Three yards a penny!' or 'Two under fifty for a fardy!'—were one kind of sales promotion; there were other sellers who sang the words of the ballads they had for sale; and there were the 'pinners up' who attached samples of their wares to a convenient wall or hoarding, or who exhibited their stock by affixing it to a pole.[2]

Henry Mayhew moved amongst this fraternity, and what little we know of them is due to his investigations.[3] 'Do I yarn a pound a week?' asked one street-seller of ballads rhetorically in response to Mayhew's query. 'Lor' bless you, no. Nor 15s., nor 12s. I don't yarn one week with another, not 10s. sometimes not 5s. . . . I am at my stall at nine in the morning, and sometimes I have walked five or six miles to buy my "pubs" before that. I stop till ten at night oft enough. The wet days is the ruin of us; and I think wet days increases.' This man sold his sheets at a half-penny a time, a penny if he could get it; and this seems to have been the usual price, although it must be said that the economics of the street trade are obscure. Depending upon the quality of the paper, songs were bought usually at twopence or even twopence-halfpenny a dozen. Manifestly weather was a crucial factor—on summer days trade was likely to be a great deal brisker than in winter, and it is clear that the seller of street literature depended upon the kindness of the weather for his livelihood quite as much as the mediaeval peasant had done centuries earlier.

From Mayhew's pages we are able to gather something at least of the life of the street-seller. It was precarious, and except upon the few occasions when a sensational murder took the public fancy, little money was to be made out of it. But in general the world of the itinerant vendor remains—Mayhew notwithstanding—obscure. There are one or two books which shed a flickering and uncertain light upon it. *The Life and Adventures of a Cheap Jack* is one, and 'Lord' George Sanger's *Seventy Years a Showman* is another: both show something of the shifting, insecure background of wandering sellers and showmen. From a somewhat earlier period there is David Love's autobiography, and William Cameron, a Scottish pedlar, wrote his autobiography.[4]

The most artless writing of this kind can often provide an imaginative key which sets more orthodox material into a sharper focus. Often this will be in the form of the memories of an old person who recalls the streets of his childhood more than seventy years ago. A description of Hoxton by Albert Jacobs, who was born in Nile Street in 1889, has this precise quality of simplicity and conveys a vivid sense of what it was like to be there:[5]

Life in the streets seemed quite interesting, first thing in the morning the lamplighter came round with his long pole turning out the street lamps and in the evening lighting them. There were many hawkers singing their wares, gypsies to sell you something or offer to tell your fortune, the cats meat man with his one wheel barrow followed by hungry cats hoping he would drop a piece while he cut slices for a customer, the milkman ladling out milk from a churn on a barrow into an oval metal container with a hinged lid or into your own jug. Sunday was the day of the Muffin Man, he came round balancing a large tray on his head packed with Muffins and Crumpets and ringing a bell while calling out 'Muffins'. He often had to go to the bakery for fresh supplies and there would be people there handing in tins containing their Sunday dinners to be cooked. In the afternoon there would be the winkle man calling out from his barrow with winkles, shrimps and cockles ... There was the Ballad Singer who sung a popular song and sold copies of it for a penny and again there was always the Hurdy-gurdy man, an Italian with a small organ on a short pole and a monkey trained to turn the organ handle ...

When, however, we come to ask what was the nature of the stock-in-trade of the street-sellers, then we are upon very much firmer ground, for much of it has survived; and this adds a significant historical dimension to the understanding of an important element in Victorian popular culture. In the British Museum there are the Baring-Gould and the Crampton collections, and, in a number of the larger provincial libraries, locally printed sheets are preserved. Not only, indeed, is there no shortage of original material, but also the rambling, untidy books—compilations, perhaps, is a better word—by Charles Hindley offer examples of street literature which but for him would have disappeared.[6] Nevertheless, this mention of the debt we owe to Charles Hindley does highlight the fact that there has been no real attempt to classify or quantify the output of broadsides. The two collections in the British Museum offer no classification either within periods or around episodes, presenting only selections of these sheets mounted in guard books; and it must be borne in mind that, because of the very nature of this literature, its survival poses an immediate problem. It may be that the most popular of its items were those most readily available for preservation; or is it in fact more likely that the less popular items, where copies remained unread and undiscarded, had the better chance of survival?

The material which we have is certainly sufficient to make possible some valid generalizations about its nature. There were four broad categories of street ballad: street drolleries; ballads about the Royal Family or politics; 'ballads on a subject'; and ballads concerning crime.[7]

The first of these covered general themes, in prose as well as in verse, some of which were 'cocks' or 'catchpennies', fictitious narratives offered to a gullible public as though they were true and topical. The keywords in the sales patter for such sheets were 'Horrible', 'Dreadful', 'Murder', 'Love', 'Seduction', 'Blood', and so on.

Mayhew has described the way in which these were sold: 'Few of the residents in London—but chiefly those in the quieter streets have not been aroused, and most frequently in the evening, by a hurly-burly on each side of the street. An attentive listening will not lead any one to an accurate knowledge of what the clamour is about. It is from a "mob" or "school" of running patterers, and consists of two, three, or four men.'[8] They shouted their wares, and the noisier they were the better they deemed their chance of good sales. Imaginary murders, usually with a lurid love interest, seem to have been the most popular, and could by a practised patterer be made to sound extremely plausible. Typical of these—and there were very many of this type—was one entitled 'Shocking rape and murder of two lovers'.[9] This was an account in prose and verse, embellished with a horrifying woodcut, of how one John Hodges, a farmer's son, raped Jane Williams and afterwards murdered her and her lover, William Edwards, in a field near Paxton. 'This', declares the anonymous author, 'is a most revolting murder. It appears Jane Williams was keeping company, and was shortly to be married to William Edwards, who was in the employment of Farmer Hodges.' John, his son, made approaches to the young lady 'who although of poor parents was strictly virtuous.' After the rape, Edwards came upon Hodges, who immediately turned upon him with a bill-hook, which he afterwards used to kill the girl. He was then apprehended and 'committed to take his trial at the next Assizes'. The last two of the 'Copy of Verses' which follows the prose accounts are typical:

> Now in one grave they both do lie,
> These lovers firm and true,
> Who by a cruel man were slain,
> Who'll soon receive his due.
>
> In prison now he is confined,
> To answer for the crime.
> Two lovers that he murdered,
> Cut off when in their prime.

In every way this 'cock' or 'catchpenny' is representative of its type of street literature. Less repetitive, and certainly more interesting, is the large sub-class of 'street drolleries' proper, though it is of course very much more difficult to select any title which typifies this category. Examples are 'The full particulars of "taking off" Prince Albert's inexpressibles'; 'The perpetual almanack'; 'How to cook a wife'; 'The Dunmow Flitch'; 'Secrets, for ladies during courtship'. Some of these are illustrated with woodcuts of which by no means all were relevant to the text—a characteristic of street literature, whose producers appeared to use woodblocks with inconsequential abandon. 'How to cook a wife', for example, has a dramatic woodcut showing a soldier with a knife, menacingly approaching two distressed females—one swooning—in a sylvan glade.

One of the most interesting titles is 'Railroad to hell, from dissipation to poverty, and from poverty to desperation. This line begins in the brewery, and runs through all public-houses, dram-shops, and jerry-shops, in a zigzag direction, until it lands in the Kingdom of hell.' Although undated, the imprint 'T. Such, Union street, Boro'' suggests that this broadside was issued, almost certainly not for the first time, in the 1870s.[10] Such was a commercial printer who carried a large stock of sheets, and the fact that he thought it worthwhile to exploit a temperance theme throws an interesting light upon the saleability of street ballads which took a strong line over the demon drink. Not many did, but the subject was not entirely unusual. More immediately striking, perhaps, is the railway imagery which is used in these leaden-footed verses:

> Such Taverns as these are Railroads to Hell,
> Their barrels are engines which make men rebel;
> Their jugs and their glasses which furnish their Trains,
> Will empty their pockets and muddle their brains.
> And thus drunkards ride to Hell in their pride,
> With nothing but steam from the barrels inside.

A companion piece from the same printer is 'The railway to heaven. This line runs from Calvary through this vain world and the Valley of the Shadow of Death, until it lands in the Kingdom of Heaven.' In this ballad the railway imagery is more pronounced:

> The Railway mania does extend,
> From John o' Groats to the Land's End;
> Where'er you ride, where'er you walk
> The Railway is the general talk.
>
> Allow me, as an old divine,
> To point to you another line,
> Which does from earth to heaven extend,
> Where real pleasures never end.
>
> Of truth Divine the rails are made,
> And on the Rock of Ages laid;
> The rails are fixed in chains of love,
> Firm as the throne of God above.

The final couplet, too, is worth quoting:

> 'My son', says God, 'give me thy heart,
> Make haste, or else the train will start.'

Examples of technology impinging upon popular literature are unusual. The railway symbolism had its origins in what Americans knew as 'The Great Awakening'— a shrill evangelical revival which found expression in the camp meetings held mostly in upper New York State during the 1830s. The evangelists later brought their message and their sons to England, where 'The railway to heaven' became popular at revival meetings in the North. In fact, Americans absorbed machinery into the imagery of their popular literature much more rapidly than did the English.

The tone is broadly evangelical, and mention is made—always with approval—of the Church of England, the Quakers, the Baptists, the Independents, and the Methodists 'both old and new'. Such an approach to religious matters is characteristic of street literature, which rarely if ever reflects the religious conflicts of the nineteenth century, and a simple explanation of this is the desire to achieve the widest possible sales. The fact that religion formed the subject-matter of broadsides at all appears interesting, for recent research has indicated that the working classes had little or no interest in formal religious practices. Why then should commercial printers have concerned themselves with the subject? The answer is probably that such sheets in most cases had a seasonal sale. A number of Christmas ballad sheets has survived, and it is possible that at this time of the year, and perhaps at Easter, ballads could be sold which appealed to a residual religious emotion which had nothing to do with church-going.

Many street ballads took as their subject the Royal Family, while others of course had political themes. The former often exhibited an adulatory, unsophisticated attitude to Royalty which remains a characteristic of much journalism today. Fairly typical of this group is 'A new song on the birth of the Prince of Wales', with its chorus:

> So let us be contented and sing with mirth and joy
> Some things must be got ready for the pretty little boy.

Where critical attitudes are to be found, they fall far short of anything approaching a full-blooded republicanism.

Political street ballads are in every way more interesting, and the striking feature of most of them is their moderation. There is seldom a strident note, and little rabble-rousing. 'The temper of the ballads on such questions as strikes and lock-outs', wrote a contemporary,[11] 'has struck us as singularly fair and moderate ... In the middle of the bitter struggle of the last three years in the building trades, we find nothing really violent or objectionable.' A verse, quoted in the *National Review* of October 1861, from 'The glorious strike of the builders' (i.e. the strike of 1859), catches the mood of many political broadsides:

> They locked us out without a cause—
> Our rights was our desires,—
> We'll work for Trollope, Peto, Lucas,
> For all the world, and Myers.
> If we can only have our rights,
> We will go to work much stronger:
> Nine hours a day, that's what we say,
> And not a moment longer.

Strikes apart, there were other issues which provided material for the political broadside. Reform was one, political personalities another. Then there were political litanies of various kinds, similar in form to those for which William Hone had been tried in 1817. Crimean ballads, too, fall into this category.

The political tone of street literature, then, was muted. 'The great battle for freedom and reform' is clearly reformist, but by no stretch of imagination extremist:

> With Gladstone, Russell, Beales and Bright
> We shall weather through the storm,
> To give the working man his rights,
> And gain the Bill—Reform.
>
> We want no Tory government
> The poor man to oppress,
> They never try to do you good,
> The truth you will confess.
>
> The Liberals are the poor man's friend,
> To forward all they try,
> They'll beat their foes you may depend,
> And never will say, die.

A sense of bitterness with their lot—and this is very different from revolutionary fervour—is to be found in those ballads which deal with wages and the cost of living. 'Fifteen shillings a week' provides a complete budget for a working man who was in receipt of this wage. Husband, wife and seven children! Rent cost one shilling and ninepence, tobacco eightpence, tea eightpence, fuel one shilling and tenpence halfpenny. Clothes were bought second-hand—a jacket for sixpence, threepence for socks. This particular ballad is of considerable interest, purporting as it does to outline working-class expenditure in the 1870s (a date which can be inferred from Such's imprint, though earlier versions may exist).

Similarly, 'How five and twenty shillings were expended in a week', gives in detail the weekly expenditure of a tradesman and his wife. This sheet is probably earlier than 1870, but there is no way of verifying this. In this case no children are mentioned. Rent costs three shillings and twopence, meat four shillings, tobacco sixpence, and so on. Most interesting, however, are the incidental comments:

> Last Monday night you got so drunk, amongst your dirty crew,
> It cost twopence next morning for a basin of hot stew.

Breakages, for example:

> There's a penny goes for this thing, and twopence that and t'other,
> Last week you broke a water jug, and I had to buy another.

Hygiene:

> A three farthing rushlight every night, to catch the bugs and fleas.

So far, then, as the cost of living is a political issue, these ballads were in essence political. More obviously so was 'Dizzy's Lament':

> O dear! Oh dear! What shall I do
> They call me Saucy Ben the Jew
> The leader of the Tory crew
>    Poor old Benjamin Dizzy.
> I'd a great big house in Buckinghamshire
> My wages was Five Thousand a Year;
> But now they have turned me out of place,
> With a ticket for soup, in great disgrace.
> I had a challenge last Monday night
> Billy Gladstone wanted me to fight;
> The challenge was brought by Jackey Bright
> To poor old Benjamin Dizzy.

Disraeli, Gladstone, Bright—clearly these were names which entered the consciousness of the humblest reader. It would of course be possible to offer further extracts from ballads of this kind. Almost always they were anti-Tory, but their keynote was reform rather than revolution. Ernest Jones's 'The Song of the Lower Classes' was circulated as a broadside round about 1848, and was later reprinted, once, together with an English translation of 'The Marseillaise', as a Socialist League broadside; there were titles like 'The Chartists are coming'; a number of Corn Law ballads were produced; but certainly in all the street ballads I have examined it remains true that anything more than a fairly mild reformism, and occasional support for Chartism, is entirely absent.

Those pieces which fall under the heading of 'ballads on a subject' show the kind of themes which could take the fancy of the public, and illustrate too the ingenuity of the unknown hack-writers who produced these effusions. Here we find them seizing upon every event which the contemporary scene provided; and, in earning commercial reward for the printers and street-sellers, they now provide for us aids towards re-creating that scene. As we might expect, the Tichbourne claimant, 'Bloomers', 'Wonderful Mr Spurgeon', the Volunteer forces, the opening of Holborn Viaduct, were all celebrated in street literature. So, too, were the death of the Duke of Wellington, the popularity of the polka when it reached this country about 1844, and the Great Exhibition of 1851, in ballads to which reference will be made later. The category of 'ballads on a subject' might be extended to include popular songs, some of the older ballads, and even music-hall songs, although the relationship between these and the street ballad is imprecise and as yet unexplored.[12]

The most popular subject of all, however, was crime. Sheets concerned with the execution of a criminal were the most numerous of all, and were bought with 'singular eagerness'. Almost all of them were illustrated—it was usual to see the criminal or criminals dangling from the gallows—and there was an account of the execution in

**41** *above* James Catnach's shop in Great St Andrew's Street, Seven Dials, from *Punch*, ii (1842), 183.

**42** *right* A ballad-seller, as drawn by Doré. From *London. A Pilgrimage* (1872), p. 84.

# MARRIAGE
# OF THE QUEEN.

TUNE.—" Billy O'Rooke."

Come grave or sad, and dull or mad,
    I'll not detain you long. sirs,
While I relate some odds and ends,
    I've worked into a song, sirs.
The other day the Park I cross'd,
    And in a crowd did mingle,
A snob sung out "God Save the Queen,"
    She no longer will live single.

CHORUS.
Prince Albert's come from Germany,
    To change his situation ;
So the house of Hanover now may last
    Another generation !

Spoken.—Why do you know Mrs. Tomkins,
as I came by Buckinham Palace the other day. I
was told the Queen had summon'd all her councillors into her Privy, to let them know she wanted a
husband. Oh ! stop there, Mrs. Knowall, that is
wrong ; you mean her Privy Councillors, but I'll
not interrupt you, so go on, well ; I heard there was
the Count of Strasbug, the Duke of Humbug, the
Prince of Wirtenbug, and Albert of Cobug, and a
whole host of other bugs ; but out of them she
fixed her eyes on Albert of Cobug, and to the as-
tonishment of all present, bawled out aloud, "that's
the man for me !"

In the Council hall the Queen did bawl,
    Prince Albert I will marry,
Don't fret your kidneys, gentlemen,
    For him I mean to tarry ;
The day I'm married I'll present,
    Aye, in my Royal Passage.
All single maids, from Albert's store,
    A polony or a sausage.

Spoken.—Oh, Crikey, Mrs. Skinflint, won't St.
Giles's be alive the day the Queen is married, for
the Prince will send a waggon load of herrings, a
ship load of murphys, and a quartern of the cra-
tur to every mother's son, that we may toast his
most Gracious Majesty's Royal Highness, that he
may live long, and be svrrounded by a host of little bugs, to the honour of the Queen, long life to

hers good luck to the pair of them say I, Mother
Flaherty — Dan O'Connell, Prince Albert, & Erin-
go-Braug

Through Ireland they will rejoi,
    The day our Queen is married,
And many a wench will cry aloud
    Sure, I too long have tarried ;
Victoria has a husband got,
    May nothing ere distress her,
And Albert gain the people's love,
    Then toast " the Queen, God bless her."

Spok —Oh ! Mrs. Jenkins, won't we have
a flare- the day the Queen is married,—there
is to be a bullock roasted in Clare Market another in Smithfield, lots of pigs and other poultry,
a large German sausage will be hung up to every
lamp post in St. James's Park, solely for the fe-
minine gender ; a man is not to have even a smell
of them, and should any man be found daring
enough to cut a slice off the forbidden meat, he will
be placed in the same state and along side of
Achiles in Hyde Park, for 48 hours. Oh ! dear
me, Mrs Bustle, O dear me, I would not look at
it for life, and perhaps without even a fig leaf to
hide —oh horrid, &c,

A bullock will be roasted whole,
    The day our Queen is married,
And German sausages on poles,
    Will though the streets be carried.
Such glorious sprees will be that day,
    Old Sal will treat her crony,
And Dublin Bet of Saffron Hill,
    Will sport a large polony.

Spoken.—Lord bless you, Mother Thingamy,
there will be such fun, nothing was ever like it,
nobody must be gloomy that day, under pain of
Royal displeasure. Now I should like to know
who this Albert is ? Why, that is his name, Oh,
nonsence ! I know that already ; but where does
he come from ? That I will tell you directly ; he
is the second son to the Grand Duke of Germany,
Master Manufacturer of German Sausages to the
Britfsh Empire, and worth 600 millions of screw-
bles, and he will give the Queen all he has got.

May Albert with her happy live,
    In gay and sweet content, sirs,
And their wedding day through England be,
    A day of merriment, sirs,
Oh ! may she have a happy reign,
    On her subjects never frown, sirs,
But quickly have a son and heir,
    To wear Old England's Crown, sirs.

BIRT, Printer, 39, Great St. Andrew Street; Seven Dials

---

**43** A characteristic broadside of 1840. The vignette came from stock. Birt, the printer, was
an important supplier to the street trade.
*Leslie Shepard*

# JOHN BULL & HIS PARTY

## Or, Do it Again.

Tune—Do it Again.

As the shamrock, the rose, and the thistle were
    meeting
Together one morning, so jovial and gay,
First in popped a Welchman and then came a
    Frenchman,
And loudly to old Farmer Bull thus did say ;
I think this great nation wants some alteration,
    All over the land and far over the main,
You once was victorious, done deeds bright and
    glorious,
But now do you think you can do it again.
Do it again, do it again, but now do you think you
    can do it again.

I met with young Albert, so buxom and all pert,
He was down in the nursery telling some tales,
In the royal palace to Addy and Alice,
    The young Duke of York, and the great Prince
    of Wales ;
Then he went in the passage and took up a sausage
    And strove for to banish all sorrow and pain,
He played up so charming, oh ! it was alarming,
    Buy a broom, ax my eye, and we'll do it again.

Then up stept Victoria, all England adores her,
    Russians, Prussians, and Frenchmen she loves
    to invite,
She likes you know what then, to travel to Scotland
    And gaze on the Highlands with joy and delight
Towns, counties, & cities, with sweet little kiddies
    By steam she'll supply, & send them by the train
If old Bull don't like it, why then he may pipe it,
    She has done it before and she'll do it again.

Then up stept old Nosey so blythe and so cosey,
    With his cocked hat and feather, believe it's true
His cannons rattled as if 'twas in battle,
    When he faced poor Boney at famed Waterloo,
Like a soldier afloat with his sword, sash, & coat,
    He had travelled through Houndsditch and Pet-
    ticoat Lane,
Singing, buy old clotnes, hey day, elts, powder,
    and pipe clay,
I am getting too old for to do it again.

Then rateatching Bobby jumped up in the lobby,
    And to old Neddy h— these words he did say,

You know as I will state they have broke down
    the toll gates,
    While you was a hopping in Kent t'other day ;
Jemmy G— with letters of hymen and fetters,
    Came creeping and weeping in sorrow and pain,
When his nose it went right slap into Bobby's rat
    trap,
    And old Bull holloa'd out will you do it again.

Up came Gladstone a blinking with old Mr. Lin-
    coln,
    And as in the Enclosure together they stood,
Said Gouldbourn to Lincoln by jingo I'm thinking
    They will hang us all up in the forests & woods ;
Then old Harry Hardinge with a bag of half-far-
    things,
    Got a good situation right over the main.
So says he off I'm jogging, I was once fond of flogg-
    ing,
    And I shan't come to England to do it again.

Like winking did up run Mr. Tommy Duncombe,
    And in Finsbury Square he began for to dance,
He was followed so quickly by Alderman Wakley,
    Who out of his pocket did pull a great lance,
Saying Duncombe so clever we'll struggle together
    And throw our enemies into great pain,
We will strive for to righten, we must not be
    frightened,
    I have bled them before and I'll do it again.

Up came Mr. Daniel saying now don't I stand well,
    Against all oppression and shocking bad law,
Repeal now and glory and no whig and tory,
    The Lakes of Killarney and Erin go bragh ;
I will not be frighted till Erin is righted,
    For the repeal of the union my nerves I will strain
You know well Hibernia, repeal does concern her,
    I have beat them before and I'll do it again.
Do it again, do it again, I have beat them before
    and I'll do it again.

BIRT, Printer, 39, Great St. Andrew Street,
Seven Dials.

44   An unillustrated sheet on sale about 1850, also supplied by Birt.
*Leslie Shepard*

# What do you think of Mister Billy Roupell.

It is now all over Lambeth, there's a grand flare-up we see
Abnot a well-known gentleman, who once was their
   M.P.;
A worthless, cunning fellow, everybody knew him well,
And many a jolly row has been about Billy Roupell.

Funny things we see, he's a man you know full well,
In every street in Lambeth they knew Billy Roupell,
And Billy was resolved to have the whole lot or none.

Though Billy was a natural son, he a gentleman would be,
It was Bill Roupell, Esquire, and afterwards M.P.,
When Bill Roupell possession of the property had got,
He didn't care who went without so he had got the lot.

He got Roupell Park, at Brixton and every other place,
By roguery and forgery now he is in disgrace ;
And when his poor old father died, was not he a naughty
   chap,
He even prigged his father's breeches, and his poor old
   mother's cap.

Was'nt he a mem'er of Parliament, a wicked naughty
   man,
Was'nt he, good folks of Lambeth, a disgrace unto the

Twas once, Roupell for ever, sounding through every
   street,
And now I say, 'tis Bill Roupell, how is your poor feet ?

Bill carried on a stunning game, he wanted the whole
   lot,
He even sold the frying-pan, the scrubbing brush and
   mop;
Bill was a wicked brother, and a good-for-nothing son
Not satisfied without he had the whole lot or none,

Billy was a gentleman who'd have thought it, I declare ?
Billy was an officer in the Rifle Volunteers;
He was a member of Parliament, a rogue to the back-bone
Determined he was for to have the whole lot or none.

Billy made the money fly, how he would sport and play,
And when the game was finished then Billy ran away.
They had him down at Guildford, for the naughty deeds
   he'd done,
When he told them to their face he'd have the whole lot
   or none.

It is no joke, you Lambeth folk, for one avoricious
   brother,
To guilty be of forgery, just for to rob another ;
But I'll tell you what the end will be for the wicked deed
   he's done,
In a little time he'll have to go the whole hog or none.

Well, now you Roupell, M.P. in sorrow may bewail,
For forgery and perjury he lies within a gaol ;
Reflecting on the wicked deeds which he for lucre done.
So Bill Roupell will have to go the whole hog or none.

This gentleman round Lambeth is
   By every one known well.
He was, you see, the great M.P.,
   The wonderful Roupell.

TAYLOR,
Printer, 92, Brick Lane, Spitalfields.

**45** A topical broadside of 1862, telling a story of belated justice. William Roupell forged a will in 1856 but was not brought to book for six years, when he was given penal servitude for life.
*Leslie Shepard*

# THE STRIKE
# Of the London Cabmen!

Ryle and Co., Printers, Monmouth Court,
Seven Dials.

OH! here's a great and glorious row,
  All over London. sirs, I vow,
A few words of which I'll tell you now,
  The strike of the London Cabmen.
Some days ago they pass'd an act,
About the cabs—it is a fact—
Which made old swells and codgers smile,
That they should ride at a tanner a mile ;
And if not pleased, then all around,
The cabman had to measure the ground,
  And that's the reason I'll be bound,
  Has caused the strike of the cabmen.

Cut him! slash him! here's a go,
All over town come up, gee wo,
The law was hard you all do know,
  So strike did the London Cabmen

On Tuesday last, oh! what a sight,
The thing was done and all was right,
Just at the hour of twelve at night,
  All strike did the London Cabmen.
There was not a cab upon the ground,
And never a Cabman to be found,
Swells and cripples on did steer,
Singing out, oh! law, oh! dear ;
They did not know there was a strike,
They bawl'd and squall'd with all their might,
They hunted up and down all night,
  But could not find a Cabman.

Soon after twelve the sky look'd dark,
A City Barber, and his clerk
On London Bridge made this remark,
  ' There's a strike among the Cabmen.'

Now I did this expect awhile,
When whip along, a tanner a mile,
We through London streets could go,
In wet and dry, come up! gee wo.
Well I must really now confess,
Indeed I did think nothing less,
This tanner job did so oppress,
  That strike would the London Cabmen.

As I was going down the Strand,
I met a poor old feeble man,
Upon his legs he scarce could stand,
  And he roar'd aloud for a Cabman
But never a one was to be had,
He bawl'd and holloa'd cab, cab, cab,
I am tired out and nearly mad,
Now is not my condition sad ?
He was unable on to roam,
When down he squatted on the stones,
Saying, I shall never more get home,
  All through the London Cabmen.

While coming home from Drury Lane,
I tumbled over Bet and Jane,
Who said the Act was much to blame,
  To cause the strike of the Cabmen.
Indeed! indeed! said lovely Kate,
I know they gave in all their plates,
And told their masters they should go,
To dwell in South Australia, O.
Behold how dismal is the streets,
No cab or carriage can we meet,
And we must travel on our feet,
  All through the London Cabmen.

Now if comes a thunder shower
If it rains, or if it pours,
You may be about the streets for hours,
  And never find a Cabman.
And won't it too make many fret,
To see the ladies muslin wet,
And see them thro' the streets 'o scud,
With their backs behind all cover'd in mud
And won't it cause them to bewail,
To wash their petticoats and tails,
Cause thro' the dirt they have to trail,
  All through the London Cabmen.

**46**   Catnach retired in 1838 and left his business to his sister, Annie Ryle, who continued it till
1841 as Ryle and Co. This ready commentary on a passing event appeared during this period.
*Leslie Shepard*

# SHOCKING MURDER
# OF A WIFE
# And Six Children.

Attend you feeling parents dear,
While I relate a sad affair ;
Which has filled all around with grief
    and pain,
It did occur in Hosier Lane.

On Monday, June the 28th,
These crimes were done as I now state,
How horrible it is to tell,
Eight human persons by poison fell.

In London city it does appear,
Walter James Duggin lived we hear,
And seemed to live most happily,
With his dear wife and family.

They happy lived, until of late,
He appear'd in a sad desponding state,
At something he seem'd much annoy'd,
At his master's, where he was employ'd

He was discharged, and that we find,
It prayed upon his anxious mind,
Lest they should want——that fatal day
His wife and children he did slay.

Last Sunday evening as we hear,
To the Wheatsheaf he did repair,
Then homewards went as we may read,
For to commit this horrid deed,

To the police he did a letter send,
That he was about this life to end,

And that he had poisoned, he did declare
His wife, and his six children dear.

To Hosier Lane in haste they flew,
And found it was alas, too true,
They found him stretched upon the bed
His troubles o'er—was cold and dead.

They searched the premises around,
And they the deadly poison found ;
And the shocking sight, as you may hear
Caused in many an eye a tear.

They found upon another bed,
The ill-fated mother, she was dead,
While two pretty children we are told,
In her outstretched arms she did enfold

It is supposed this wretched pair,
First poisoned their six children dear,
Then took the fatal draught themselves,
Their state of mind no tongue can tell.

Of such an heartrending affair,
I trust we never more may hear,
Such deeds they make the blood run cold
May God forgive their sinful souls

This wholesale poisoning has caused
    much pain,
It did take place in Hosier Lane.

Disley, Printer, 57, High Street, St, Giles

47  This tissue of fact and fiction belonging to the 1860s comes from a man who once worked for Catnach and specialized in crime sheets.
*Leslie Shepard*

prose, followed by a 'copy of verses' often alleged to have been written by the condemned felon in his cell on the eve of execution.

Occasionally such a broadsheet was memorable. The 'Confession of the Murderess', which was published on a sheet entitled 'The Esher tragedy. Six children murdered by their mother', has a quality of horror which is both credible and moving:

> 'On Friday last I was bad all day; I wanted to see Mr Izod, and waited all day. I wanted him to give me some medicine. In the evening I walked about, and afterwards put the children to bed, and wanted to go to sleep in a chair. —About nine o'clock, Georgy (meaning Georgianna) kept calling me to bed. I came up to bed, and they kept calling me to bring them some barley water, and they kept calling me till nearly 12 o'clock. I had one candle lit on the chair—I went and got another, but could not see, there was something like a cloud, and I thought I would go down and get a knife and cut my throat, but could not see. I groped about in master's room for a razor. I went up to Georgy, and cut her first; I did not look at her. I then came to Carry, and cut her. Then to Harry—he said "don't mother". I said, "I must" and did cut him. Then I went to Bill. He was fast asleep. I turned him over. He never woke, and I served him the same. I nearly tumbled into this room. The two children here, Harriet and George were awake. They made no resistance at all. I then lay down myself.' This statement was signed by the miserable woman.

Few other broadsides rival this in style; the mounting tension and understatement give one the sense of being present at a nightmare. For the most part these murder sheets possess for us all the dullness of sensational news that has passed into obscurity. The prose and verse are largely stereotyped, while the illustrations are scarcely credible. This, however, is what the nineteenth-century public wanted—the continuing popularity of broadsides dealing with crime bears this out. As a street-seller said to Henry Mayhew, 'There's nothing beats a stunning good murder after all.'

The producers of street literature were printers in London and in the larger provincial towns and cities.[13] The Worrall family in Liverpool, Bebbington in Manchester, Harkness in Preston, were amongst the leading provincial printers in this field, and the list could be considerably extended. A great deal of plagiarism went on —successful items were shamelessly copied—and local themes were of course exploited by local printers. Production of street ballads could be readily and easily undertaken by any printer when there was material about to catch the public fancy, and it was easy to combine this kind of work with the usual jobbing tasks—labels, notices, letterheads, catalogues, and so on—which formed the greater part of his work.[14]

The most noted specialist in producing street literature was James Catnach,[15] who supplied many hawkers in London and elsewhere with the wares which they cried in the street, sold at fairs and races, or offered for sale by 'pinning up'. His business was founded in London in the second decade of the nineteenth century, and was flourishing in the hands of his successors for well over fifty years. Catnach himself died in 1841 and was buried in Highgate Cemetery, having made a great deal of money out of street literature (and incidentally out of publishing cheap books for children). It is said that his sheets were sold to their sellers for coppers, his employees were paid in pennies and halfpennies, and he would hire a hackney coach each week to convey the coins to the Bank of England. Even so, he was the recipient of many bad pence, and legend has it that these were embedded in plaster of Paris in the kitchen behind his printing office. Catnach was the doyen of street printers and a specialist in this kind of publication, besides being sufficiently astute a businessman to pick up job lots of printers' old stock, including blocks a century and more old which he used to excellent effect.

It is almost entirely due to the industry of Charles Hindley, Catnach's biographer, that we know something of the life and work of this printer. Catnach's neighbour and rival printer, John Pitts, has been the subject of a recent book; and in it, rescued from the limbo of the nineteenth-century periodical press, there is a vivid account of Pitts's manager, Bat Corcoran, selling ballad sheets to hawkers and others:[16]

> But let us see Bat amidst his customers—see him riding the whirlwind— let us take him in the shock, the crisis of the night when he is despatching the claims of a series of applicants. 'I say, Blind Maggie, you're down for a dozen "Jolly Waterman", thirteen to the dozen.—Pay up your score, Tom with the wooden leg. I see you are booked for a lot of "Arethusas".— Master Flowers, do you think that "Cans of Grog" can be got for nothing, that you leave a stiff account behind you.—Sally Sallop, you must either give back "The Gentlemen of England" or tip for them at once.—Friday my man, there are ever so many "Black-eyed Susans" against you.—Jimmy, get rid of the "Tars of Old England" if you can; I think "Crazy Janes" are more in vogue. What say you to an exchange for "Hosier's Ghost"?'

Although this account dates from 1825, the method of selling ballads wholesale cannot have changed significantly throughout the century. It is, moreover, the only description of this aspect of the trade which appears to have been written, or at any rate to have survived.

Little was said anywhere about the writers of street literature. Who were they? Unknown hacks in the truest sense. Henry Mayhew tracked one of them down; so too did Charles Hindley in 1870.[17] This was John Morgan, who had worked for Catnach, and recalled rather bitterly how difficult it had been to secure adequate payment from him. The printer, of course, was in a difficult position, for if a ballad sheet was successful it was immediately pirated, and much of the profit was dissipated. How then could he afford to pay more than one shilling, or more rarely half-a-crown, for a work which would cease to be his as soon as it was published? A persistent legend has it that Catnach himself was the author of many of his own broadsheets, and this may have been true. What is more certain is that of the approximate sum of £12,000 which Henry Mayhew estimated was spent upon broadside ballads and the like in the late 1840s and early 1850s,[18] only a very tiny part could have found its way into the pockets of the unknown authors of so much of it.

All these factors must be borne in mind in assessing street literature and its place in working-class life. Attitudes and tendencies within a society do not, of course, change their emphasis or direction at points which can be committed to even a verbal chart; they develop gradually, and these ballad sheets reflect such a development. The authors received a trifling recompense for a product which was short-lived in the extreme, and there was the pressing commercial need for its sellers to reach as wide a public as possible in order to earn a meagre living. The printers were the only ones who did reasonably well out of it, and even then Catnach's success was unusual, and due partly to the fact that he exploited other markets with skill. There is no evidence to suggest that any of those concerned in the street trade ever set himself the task of forming attitudes. Events were followed, seized upon, and exploited.

The method of exploitation was simple and direct, and a striking example of this is provided by the death of the Duke of Wellington. As victor of Waterloo he had been a popular hero: as a Conservative Prime Minister this was clearly not the case. His death on 14 September 1852 was followed by a lying-in-state at Chelsea Hospital from 10 to 17 November, and he was buried at St Paul's on 18 November. The demise of a man so widely known, and the splendour of his funeral, presented street printers with an opportunity for unusually large sales, and it was seized in a characteristic way. Wellington is presented simply as a popular hero, with no mention of his political activities:

DEATH OF WELLINGTON

On the 14th of September, near to the town of Deal,
As you may well remember who have a heart to feel,
Died Wellington, a general bold, of glorious renown,
Who beat the great Napoleon near unto Brussels town.

Chorus
So don't forget brave Wellington, who won at Waterloo,
He beat the great Napoleon and all his generals too.

He led the British army on through Portugal and Spain,
And every battle there he won the Frenchmen to restrain,
He ever was victorious in every battle field,
He gained a fame most glorious because he'd never yield.

He drove Napoleon from home, in exile for to dwell,
Far o'er the sea, and from his home, and all he loved so well.
He stripped him quite of all his power, and banished him away,
To St Helena's rocks and towers the rest of his life to stay.

Then on the throne of France he placed Louis the king by right,
In after years he was displaced all by the people's might,
But should the young Napoleon threaten our land and laws,
We'll find another Wellington should ever we have cause.

He's dead, our hero's gone to rest, and o'er his corpse we'll mourn,
With sadness and with grief oppress'd, for he will not return,
But we his deeds will not forget, and should we ere again,
Follow the example that he set, his glory we'll not stain.

So don't forget brave Wellington, who won at Waterloo,
He beat the great Napoleon and all his generals too.

The language is simple, and the emphasis is upon Wellington's martial glory. It requires no great leap of the imagination to picture this sheet selling in its thousands to the crowds who watched the funeral procession or who filed past the catafalque. Not all its purchasers would have been working-class readers, but in both style and form it is a typical product of street literature. One of the surviving copies of this ballad, together with a similar one entitled 'Lamentation on the death of the Duke of Wellington', was printed by John Harkness of Preston, Lancashire, and this illustrates the way in which topical themes, usually originating in the metropolis, were pirated immediately by provincial printers. The converse is less true, and examples of ballads on anything like national themes originating in provincial towns and being subsequently printed in London are virtually non-existent.

A topical theme of a rather different kind is represented in a ballad called 'Jullien's Grand Polka'. Louis Antoine Jullien, born in France in 1812, was one of the many foreign musicians who performed in England during the nineteenth century. He was the first to take advantage of the popularity which the polka was achieving since its introduction into this country. The street ballad on the subject is satirical about the craze, and illustrates the way in which a theme which took the public fancy could be exploited right across the social spectrum: at the fashionable end the dance itself at routes and parties, the vogue for 'polka' jackets and bonnets; at the other a street ballad comment tilting against the pretensions of the upper and middle classes. Much earlier in the century, when Pierce Egan's *Life in London* had achieved an immense success both in book form and on the legitimate stage, Catnach had brought out a twopenny edition which, together with the versions which were staged at the penny theatres of Lambeth and elsewhere, provides an almost exact parallel—the adventures of Corinthian Tom and Jerry Hawthorne being enjoyed simultaneously at opposite ends of the social scale.

JULLIEN'S GRAND POLKA
Oh! sure the world is all run mad,
The lean, the fat, the gay, the sad,—
All swear such pleasure they never had,
Till they did learn the Polka.

Chorus

First cock up your right leg so,
Balance on your left great toe,
Stamp your heels and off you go,
To the original Polka. Oh!

There's Mrs Tibbs the tailor's wife,
With Mother Briggs is sore at strife,
As if the first and last of life,
Was but to learn the Polka.

Quadrilles and Waltzes all give way,
For Jullien's Polkas bear the sway,
The chimney sweeps, on the first of May,
Do in London dance the Polka.

If a pretty girl you chance to meet,
With sparkling eyes and rosy cheek,
She'll say, young man we'll have a treat,
If you can dance the Polka.

A lady who lives in this town,
Went and bought a Polka gown,
And for the same she gave five pound
All for to dance the Polka.

But going to the ball one night,
On the way she got a dreadful fright,
She tumbled down, and ruined quite,
The gown to dance the Polka.

A Frenchman he has arrived from France
To teach the English how to dance,
And fill his pocket,—'what a chance'—
By gammoning the Polka.

Professors swarm in every street,
'Tis ground on barrel organs sweet,
And every friend you chance to meet,
Asks if you dance the Polka.

Then over Fanny Ellsler came,
Brilliant with trans-Atlantic fame,
Says she I'm German by my name,
So best I know the Polka.

And the row de dow she danced,
And in short clothes and red heels pranced,
And, as she skipped, her red heels glanced
In the Bohemian Polka.

But now my song is near its close,
A secret, now, I will disclose,
Don't tell, for it's beneath the rose,
A humbug is the Polka.

Then heigh for humbug France or Spain,
Who brings back our old steps again,
Which John Bull will applaud amain
Just as he does the Polka.

As will be seen, 'Jullien's Grand Polka' did convey a hint of class antagonism—
but it could justify no stronger description than that. At the same time two of the
lines in the ballad drew upon a rich vein of folklore:

The chimney sweeps on the first of May
Do in London dance the Polka.

The survival of this custom in Victorian cities demonstrates not only its persistence,
but also a range of shared, or perhaps remembered, experience which was rarely
referred to in nineteenth-century popular literature. The Victorian street ballad
throws very little light upon urban folklore, and the extent to which the popular
customs of a rural past survived in an urban setting remains obscure.

Another ballad for which there would have been a ready public deals with the
Great Exhibition of 1851, and is called 'Crystal Palace':[19]

Britannia's sons an attentive ear
One moment lend to me,
Whether tillers of our fruitful soil,
Or lords of high degree.
Mechanic too, and artizan,
Old England's pride and boast,
Whose wondrous skill has spread around,
Far, far from Britain's coast.

Chorus
For the World's great Exhibition,
Let's shout with loud huzza,
All nations never can forget,
The glorious first of May.

From every quarter of the Globe,
They come across the sea,
And to the Chrystal Palace
The wonders for to see;
Raised by the handiwork of men
Born on British ground,
A challenge to the Universe
It's equal to be found.

Each friendly nation in the world,
Have their assistance lent,
And to this Exhibition
Have their productions sent.
And with honest zeal and ardour,
With pleasure do repair,
With hands outstretch'd, and gait erect,
To the World's Great National Fair.

The Sons of England and France
And America likewise,
With other nations to contend,
To bear away the prize.
With pride depicted in their eyes,
View the offspring of their hand,
O, surely England's greatest wealth,
Is an honest working man.

It is a glorious sight to see
So many thousands meet,
Not heeding creed or country,
Each other friendly greet.
Like children of one mighty sire,
May that sacred tie ne'er cease,
May the blood stain'd sword of War give way
To the Olive branch of Peace.

But hark! the trumpets flourish,
Victoria does approach,
That she may long be spared to us
Shall be our reigning toast.
I trust each heart, it will respond,
To what I now propose—
Good will and plenty to her friends,
And confusion to her foes.

Great praise is due to Albert,
For the good that he has done,
May others follow in his steps
The work he has begun;
Then let us all, with one accord,
His name give with three cheers,
Shout huzza for the Chrystal Palace,
And the World's great National Fair!!

The tone here is unmistakably one of triumph and self-congratulation. Chauvinism and fervour for the Royal Family are the keynotes. This fact in itself is hardly remarkable, and the lines—

> O surely England's greatest wealth
> Is an honest working man

are entirely consistent with the tone of the ballad. There is, however, some evidence to suggest that working men did not see the matter in this light. In 1851 G. J. Holyoake produced a pamphlet entitled 'The Workmen and the International Exhibition', and although priced at a halfpenny it was in fact designed to be given away to visitors to the exhibition. Its aim was to show the conditions in which many working men lived, and the misery which existed in workshops and houses where so many of the striking exhibits had been prepared. The cost in human terms was thus stressed by Holyoake.

Now Holyoake's pamphlet was not in any sense street literature, and the comparison does seem to show that the tendency of the latter was to romanticize reality—to offer a kind of cultural jingoism—in order to achieve as wide a sale as possible where vast concourses of people were gathered together on specific occasions.

The three street ballads quoted are typical products of their time. Quite apart from the verse, which is often slipshod, they exhibit, like most street literature, a superficiality which provides heroes whose less attractive qualities are conveniently ignored. If themes are exploited with any directness and clarity there is little evidence in the sheets of anything more than a vaguely sketched class-consciousness—class and economic antagonisms, indeed, are played down despite the general mildly reformist nature of the political ballads. Of evocative phrases there are few.

Street literature is, however, worth a closer scrutiny than it has yet received. A contemporary, writing in the *National Review* for October 1861 (to which reference was made earlier), said of these ballads that 'they are almost all written by persons of the class to whom they are addressed', and urged that they were worthy of study because they provided 'one of those windows through which we may get a glimpse at that very large body of our fellow-citizens of whom we know so little'. This was the literature of the urban working class, and with all its defects it provides one of the few insights we have into their popular culture. Occasionally there are ballads which look back to a rural past, but these are few. In its format, even in its size, the Victorian street ballad perhaps bears a resemblance to the tabloid newspaper which in many ways—concern with sex, crime, Royalty—it anticipated in a somewhat crude way. Only sport is missing.

This sense of looking forward to the tabloid newspaper of the twentieth century is further strengthened when the Victorian street ballad is contrasted with the eighteenth-century chapbook. The ballad sheet attempted, often with some success, to deal with topical themes and to exploit news and events of the day. The chapbook, on the other hand, preserved the fragments of an older tradition petrified in print, with 'Guy of Warwick', 'The Seven Wise Masters', 'Old Mother Shipton', and others together with a good deal of folklore, and many of the jests and rhymes which had earlier formed an important element in the oral lore of the English peasantry.[20]

Clearly these differences in the popular literature of the eighteenth and nineteenth centuries[21] are evidences of a fundamental change in mass reading habits, and in attitudes to life. But there is another reason for looking more searchingly at this kind of publication. Although we cannot be absolutely certain who bought and read such sheets, contemporaries suggested strongly that they circulated almost entirely amongst the poor,[22] and such circulation figures as we have are impressive. 'The execution of F. G. Manning and Maria, his wife'—based on a celebrated case in 1849—sold two and a half million copies, and 'The trial and sentence of Constance Kent' one hundred and fifty thousand. These are considerable figures, and not by any means unique for the street trade. They seem even more striking when we compare them with the sales figures for Henry Milner's cheap editions of Burns and Byron, which sold 183,333 and 126,514 copies respectively over a much longer period.[23]

Figures of this kind for the sale of broadsides, taken in conjunction with the enormous stocks carried by Catnach, are a strong indication that such ephemeral literature was an important element in the development of the mass reading-public. Like the chapbook in the eighteenth century, the street ballad provided the means by which those who could read—an ability which was not always gained too easily by the nineteenth-century poor—could exercise their skill. Ballad sheets were readily available, and they were short. This last point is an important one, for as a London vicar pointed out, 'it needs more than an average love for reading to be able to turn with interest or profit to books, when mind and body are wearied with a long day's toil'.[24]

Through street literature we are able to penetrate, however vicariously, the world of feeling of the poor in Victorian cities. The ephemeral nature of the street ballad symbolizes the precarious quality of their lives. It was, of course, the cheap newspaper towards the close of the nineteenth century which killed the street ballad, and the singer in Hoxton whom we noticed earlier, who sang a popular song and sold copies of it at a penny a time about seventy years ago, must have been one of the last of his kind.

What was the quality of life in the Victorian city? How did it seem to those who lived in the slums and rookeries of Victorian London, Manchester, Liverpool? These are large questions. The street ballad offers us one view, from below as it were, of elements in the culture of the urban poor.

## Notes

1   In Germany, they were called 'fliegende Blätter'; in Russia, the 'lubok'; in England, 'broadsides'. See, for example: R. Lemon, *Catalogue of a Collection of Printed Broadsides in the Possession of the Society of Antiquaries of London* (1866); William A. Coupe, *The German Illustrated Broadsheet in the Seventeenth Century:*

*Historical and iconographical studies* (2 vols, Baden-Baden, 1966, 1967); Y. Ovsyannikov and A. Shkarovsky-Raffé, *The Lubok* (Moscow, 1969), in which substantial English abstracts are given throughout.

2 See Henry Mayhew, *London Labour and the London Poor* [4 vols, 1861–2], I, p. 222, for a daguerreotype of a vendor of street literature. (Facsimile reprints of the four volumes published in 1967 by Cass and by Dover, New York.) There is a picture of two female ballad singers in 'P. Parley' [George Mogridge], *Tales about Christmas* (1838), p. 65. William B. Jerrold, *The Life of George Cruikshank* (1883 edn), p. 90, shows Cruikshank's delineation of a mendicant ballad seller.

3 Mayhew, op. cit., I, pp. 213–51, 272–85.

4 Charles Hindley, ed., *The Life and Adventures of a Cheap Jack* (1881 edn); 'Lord' George Sanger, *Seventy Years a Showman* (1910); *The Life, Adventures and Experiences of David Love, written by Himself* (3rd edn, Nottingham, 1823); William Cameron, *Hawkie: The autobiography of a Gargrel*, ed. John Strathesk (Glasgow, 1888).

5 'A. Jaye' [Albert Jacobs], 'Looking Back', *Profile* (Hackney Library Services), II, no. 11 (August 1969), 2; no. 12 (September 1969), 2.

6 C. Hindley, *The Catnach Press* (1869); (ed.) *Curiosities of Street Literature* (1871); *The Life and Times of James Catnach, late of Seven Dials, Ballad Monger* (1878); *The History of the Catnach Press* (1886). See also John Ashton, *Modern Street Ballads* (1888). Several of these titles have been reprinted in facsimile editions.

7 I have followed Hindley's arrangement of street ballads. His *Curiosities of Street Literature* (1871) is divided into four sections, and this seems the most suitable broad classification of such material.

8 Quoted by Hindley, *The Catnach Press* [p. 15].

9 Unless otherwise stated, the ballads and prose quoted are from Hindley's *Curiosities of Street Literature* and Ashton's *Modern Street Ballads*. Not only are their contents representative of the genre as a whole, but they are also the range of material which is most readily available for study. Patrick Scott, *Index to Charles Hindley's Curiosities of Street Literature* (Victorian Studies Handlist 2, University of Leicester Victorian Studies Centre, 1970) greatly facilitated the use of this anthology.

10 In 1871, when ballad printing had passed its heyday, there were still four printers in London who specialized in this kind of work:
W. S. Fortey (Catnach's successor), Monmouth Court, Seven Dials.
Henry Disley, 57 High Street, St Giles.
Taylor, 92 & 93 Brick Lane, Spitalfields.
H. Such, 177 Union Street, Borough. (Such's business had been established in 1846, and in 1950 some of his woodcuts were said to survive in the premises of S. Burgess in Of Alley, off Villiers Street, in London. The present writer attempted to see them, but had no success.) There is a copy of Such's *Catalogue of Songs Constantly kept in Stock* (undated), listing over 800 titles, in the Mitchell Library, Glasgow.

11 Anon., 'Street Ballads', *National Review*, xiii (1861), 412.

12 Even the extent to which favourite music-hall songs were published as street ballads is a matter for conjecture.

13 No satisfactory account of London street ballad printers exists. Catnach and his successors, Ryle, then Fortey, dominated the trade in the metropolis, but a large

number of other printers were at one time or another involved in it. V. E. Neuburg, *Chapbooks: A Bibliography of References to English and American Chapbook Literature of the Eighteenth and Nineteenth Centuries* (1964), pp. 16–27, lists, with dates, a number of provincial printers.

14  For a valuable account of such a local printer see [C. R. Cheney *et al.*], *John Cheney and his Descendants, printers in Banbury since 1767* (Banbury, for private circulation, 1936).

15  Little or no recent research has been done upon Catnach. Various magazine articles have appeared, and in 1955 the Book Club of California published in a limited edition *Catnachery* by P. H. Muir, which is delightfully produced but nothing more than a newly arranged account of what is already known, with no attempt at critical judgments of any kind.

16  Leslie Shepard, *John Pitts: Ballad printer of Seven Dials, London, 1765–1844* (Private Libraries Association, 1969), p. 71.

17  Mayhew, op. cit., I, pp. 301–2; *History of the Catnach Press*, pp. xiv–xxx.

18  Quoted by Shepard, op. cit., p. 81.

19  This is the version given in Ashton, *Modern Street Ballads*, pp. 284 ff.

20  For chapbooks see John Ashton, *Chap-books of the Eighteenth Century* (1882). (Facsimile reprints published in 1970 by the Seven Dials Press, Hatfield, and also in 1967 by Benjamin Blom, New York.)

21  See Neuburg, op. cit., for a guide to sources in chapbook and street literature.

22  C. J. Montague, *Sixty Years in Waifdom; or The ragged school movement in English history* (1904), pp. 17–20, provides an example of this. (Reprint published in 1969 by Woburn Press.)

23  Figures for the sale of broadsides are those quoted by Hindley, *Curiosities of Street Literature*, p. 159. Those for Milner's books are from Milner and Co. stock book, quoted by H. E. Wroot, 'A pioneer in cheap literature, William Milner of Halifax', *Bookman*, xi (1897), 174.

24  Robert Gregory, *Sermons on the Poorer Classes of London* (1869), p. 109.

# 8     The Metropolis on Stage

## Michael R. Booth

The theater was quick to recognize in the growing numbers and multifarious activities of urban life in the nineteenth century a really dramatic opportunity. It was not only that these human concentrations provided more promising openings for theatrical managers or emotional reactions of a peculiar kind and intensity among the crowds themselves. The real achievement of the theater in this age of cities was to make theaters of the cities themselves. A deliberate artistic and thematic use of the city as a moral symbol and an image of existence, as well as a strikingly visual and human presentation of the realities of its daily living, originates in the theater with the Victorian stage rather than with any earlier period in the development of English drama. It is true that scenes are laid in London and that characters are drawn from the London milieu in the drama of the seventeenth and eighteenth centuries, but in such drama the urban setting is a background for plots and intrigues rather than a foreground that frequently dominates both characters and narrative. The conflict between courtier and citizen is an interesting aspect of seventeenth-century comedy, but attention here focuses on intrigues and tensions between the two parties and not on the locale of their conflict. The wits and gallants of Restoration comedy inhabit a world of chocolate- and coffee-houses, the Mall, the Park, and all the resorts of fashion; in comical inferiority, aldermen and rich cits leave their counting-houses and lock up their wives and daughters, usually in vain. Once again the scenery provides illusional backing to the action on the forestage, and, given English staging techniques in the late seventeenth century, it could hardly do anything else. In the eighteenth century the counting-house and the merchant became more respectable, the class structure of both the drama and its audiences broader, and yet there was no attempt (again there were technical difficulties) to put the real life of the city on stage. In the nineteenth century, however, the attempt virtually to make the city a character in the drama was made and became common practice. The urbanized drama was born.

For the Victorians the city of drama was London. Despite the growing network of provincial circuits and the expansion of theater in the new manufacturing towns, the English drama and theater remained very much London-centered. First the London star and then the London touring company went out to the provinces; conversely, the desire of all provincial actors was to secure a hearing and a reputation in the West End. A dramatist like H. J. Byron (1834–84) might write melodramas specially for provincial audiences and a star like Barry Sullivan (1821–91) might be more popular in the provinces than in London, but nevertheless London was the heart of the theatrical world. Importing young actors and dramatists, London exported stars and the drama to all parts of the British Isles. As communications improved and provincial audiences grew, London companies found touring appearances profitable, and their tours slowly strangled the old provincial stock companies. These new audiences wanted to see London successes, not local plays, and by the end of the nineteenth century the metropolis, like a great leech, was sucking the native theatrical life of the provinces dry. Indeed, London and the life of London became one of the dominant themes in the drama of the day. *The Heart of London* (1830), *The Scamps of London, or The Crossroads of Life* (1843), *London by Night* (1845), *London Vice and London Virtue* (1861), *The Work Girls of London* (1864), *The Streets of London* (1864), *The Poor of London* (1864), *Lost in London* (1867), *The Great City* (1867), *The Great Metropolis* (1874), *The Lights o' London* (1881), *The Great World of London* (1898)—almost all these, and many more with similar titles, are Victorian in origin and character.

Although in the first half of the nineteenth century the relative growth in the population of the larger manufacturing towns was even greater than that of London, the number of theaters catering to the new urban proletariat was much higher in London than anywhere else. Moreover, the drama produced for this proletariat (preserved, when it was preserved at all, in cheap acting editions), though it was diffused all over the country and adapted to local situations where necessary, remained recognizably a London export. During the first third of the century the drama and theater ceased to be the mainly middle-class territory they had been in the eighteenth century. Then, if the lower classes went to the theater at all, they inhabited the upper galleries of the patent theaters—Drury Lane, Covent Garden, and the Haymarket—and watched a drama largely aimed at the tastes and concerns of their betters. Now, however, for the first time in the history of the English theater, playhouses were built and a drama was written exclusively for the working and lower-middle class. By 1837 most of these playhouses were already open: the Surrey, the Victoria, the Bower, and Astley's on the South Bank of the Thames; the City of London, the Pavilion, and the Standard in the East End. The Britannia in Hoxton was to follow in 1841, the Effingham in Whitechapel and the Grecian in Hoxton in 1843. At these theaters the physical and moral simplicities of melodrama, farce, and pantomime were paramount; their audiences were mostly illiterate and cared nothing for the tragedy and refined comedy of an earlier age. What they wanted was the colour, action, excitement, illusion, poetic justice, and moral satisfaction that constituted an escape from the dreary monotony and daily discomfort of lives spent mostly in the business of survival. Such an escape the dramatists and managers of the popular theater set out to provide for them, and they succeeded so well that the types of drama that they produced froze quickly into a set of readily identifiable conventions which entertained millions of spectators for the rest of the century. Dickens concisely summed up this new popular taste when he described the ordinary patron of the Victoria Theatre in 1850:[1]

> Joe Whelks, of the New Cut, Lambeth, is not much of a reader, has no great store of books, no very commodious room to read in, no very decided inclination to read, and no power at all of presenting vividly before his mind's eye what he reads about. But put Joe in the gallery of the Victoria Theatre; show him doors and windows in the scene that will open and shut, and that people can get in and out of; tell him a story with these aids, and by the help of live men and women dressed up, confiding to him their inmost secrets, in voices audible a mile off; and Joe will unravel a story through all its entanglements and sit there as long after midnight as you have anything left to show him. Accordingly, the Theatres to which Mr Whelks resorts are always full; and whatever changes of fashion the drama knows elsewhere, it is always fashionable in the New Cut.

Quite possibly Dickens's Mr Whelks had grown up in a small village and come to London either by himself or with his parents. In any event, emigration had its effect on urban theater as well as on urban economics, and two of the particular characteristics of Victorian melodrama were its idealization of the village home and its denigration of London. The former was symbolically equated with the state of man before the Fall and represented virtue, innocence, beauty, peace, and a known place in God's world, while the latter stood for vice, the loss of innocence, squalor, degradation, bitter suffering, and helpless anonymity. The song 'Home, Sweet Home,' written for an operatic melodrama of 1823, *Clari, or the Maid of Milan*, by John Howard Payne, referred to a village home. The heroine of Edward Lancaster's *Ruth* (1841), after asking 'Who would dwell in cities, where our days are passed in obscurity?' sings 'My Own Village Home.' Such songs were common in village melodrama. The most convenient device for carrying this weight of moral dogma was the heroine, at first happy and tranquil in her village home, then miserable and imperiled in London. Once in the second state she invariably recalled the first. T. P. Taylor's temperance melodrama, *The Bottle* (1847), set in London, has the agonized Ruth, wife to the drunken Thornley, beg the bailiff to allow her to keep one precious possession:

I must beg you not to take that; it is the picture of the village church where I worshipped as a girl, that saw me wedded in my womanhood; there are a thousand dear recollections connected with it, humble though they be. There was a meadow close by, over whose green turf I have often wandered, and spent many happy hours, when a laughing merry child; and dearer far it is to me, for beneath a rude mound in that sad resting-place poor mother and father lie.

In a later scene Ruth, ill, starving, and separated from her drunken husband, is looking for work; she is assisted by her friend Esther, who is trying to keep alive by

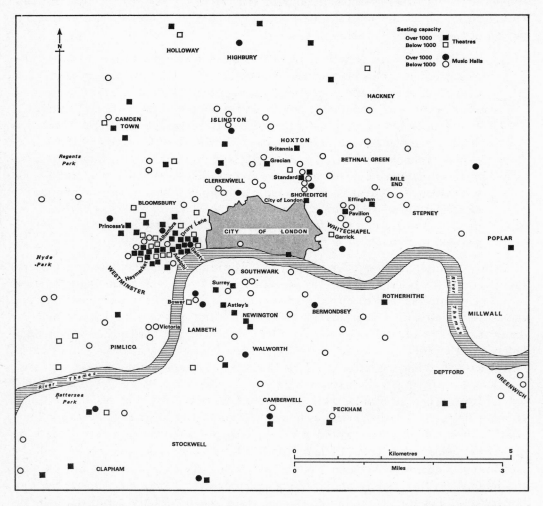

**VI**  London theaters and music-halls known to have been open in the period 1875–1901. Places mentioned in the text are named. Source: Diana Howard, *London Theatres and Music Halls 1850–1950* (1970), which contains an extensive gazetteer and bibliography, and some illustrations.

# SADLER's WELLS.

Licensed by the **Lord HighChamberlain**, *pursuant to the* **Act 6 & 7 Vic. Cap. 68**
Under the Management of **THOMAS LONGDEN GREENWOOD**,
Melbourne Cottage, White Hart Lane, Tottenham.

☞ **First Night of a New National Local Drama.**
Last Six Nights OF THE ENGAGEMENT OF **Mr. R. W. PELHAM.**

**MONDAY, Nov. 13th, 1843, and DURING THE WEEK.**
The Performances will commence with (FIRST TIME) an entirely new National Local Characteristic, Metropolitan, Melodramatic Drama of the day, in 3 Acts, correctly exhibiting Life and Manners in innumerable novel and interesting Phases, called The

# CROSS ROADS
## *OF LIFE!*
### OR THE
# SCAMPS OF LONDON.

The Groundwork of the Drama founded on the celebrated Play, "LES BOHEMIENS," now attracting the attention of all France, and applied to the circumstances and realities of the present moment, by the Author of **TOM & JERRY**, &c

The New Scenery, (from Actual Authorities) by **Mr. F. FENTON** and Assistants. The New Flash Medley Overture, and Slang Dramatic Music, by Mr. W. MONTGOMERY. The Action of the Piece arranged by Mr. C. J. SMITH. The Dresses by Mr. HAMPTON & Miss BAILEY. The whole produced under the direction of Mr. H. MARSTON.

Deverex, alias Fox Skinner, alias ██████ (a Swell Cove out of Luck, King of all the Scamps & Greeks in London) Mr H. MARSTON
Mr Dorrington (a wealthy Liverpool Merchant, on a visit to London) MR. ROMER.
Frank Danvers .... (a British Naval Officer, just arrived from the Indies) .... Mr BIRD.
Herbert Danvers ........ (His Younger Brother, a ruined Roué, pigeoned by the Greeks) ....... Mr MELVIN,
Mr Hawkworth Shabner { Principal Proprietor of a Silver Hell at the West End, Director of a Company, Capital One Million, Bill Discounter & Anythingarian where there's anything to be got } Mr P. WILLIAMS
Bob Yorkney .... (the Duffer, tired of the Lay) .... Mr W. H. WILLIAMS
Tom Fogg, alias Old Deady, alias The Animal, { a Gin-drinking Vagabond suffering under delirium tremens } ....... Mr C. J. SMITH,
alias The Savage, alias ██████
Ned Brindle .... (the Magsman—a Half-and-Half Cove) .... Mr CORENO.
Joe Onion (the Crocodile—an Out-and-Out Cove, Cadger and Creature of Deverex's) Mr C. FENTON
Dickey Smith (the Wakeful Bird) a young Gentleman in no ways particklar to a shade, picking up a living how he can) Mast. G. MASKELL
Ikey Bates { Landlord of Rats' Castle, otherwise the Dyot Street Hotel, Proprietor of twenty two-penny dabs and a most respectable bagatelle Board, having cut bumblepuppy as too low } Mr LAMB
Waiter at the Cat and Bagpipes Tavern, Mr SMITHSON, Inspector of the XYZ Division. Mr FRANKS.
Miss CAROLINE RANKLEY
Louisa, .. (the Victim of an ill-requited attachment)
Miss Charlotte Willers, { a young Lady with her Cat, &c., from the Country, betrothed to Mr Yorkney amusing her leisure hours in shoe-binding, waistco and gaiter making } Mrs R. BARNETT,

♥ After which, the Interesting Drama of

# GWYNNETH VAUGHAN

Evan Pritchard, Mr C. J. SMITH, Owen Williams, Mr BIRD, Morgan Morgan, Mr W. H. WILLIAMS,
Hugh Morgan, Mr ROMER, David, Mr LAMB, Thomas Johns, Mr SMITH, Pryce Mr GRAMMAR,
Gwynneth Vaughan, Miss C. RANKLEY. Lyddy Pryce Mrs R. BARNETT,
Betsy Thomas, Miss STEPHENS, Taffline, Miss MORELLI, Phœbe, Mrs ANDREWS.

**Mr. R. W. PELHAM** will, for the First Time at this Theatre, give his

## NIGGER LECTURE ON LOCOMOTIVE.
And Description of his Courtship wid de Black Girls down in Louisiana.
To conclude his Black Art of de Evenin, he will, for de benefit of all dose who hab de Blues, dance his new Solo Reel
**HOP, SKIP, AND A JUMP**, and dat will sure to cure dem.

To conclude with a Melo-Drama, in Two Acts, by T. E. WILKS, Esq, entitled The

# ROLL OF THE DRUM.

Ernest Viscount d'Obernav. Mr BIRD, Captain Charles Aubri,, Mr LAMB, Lucius Junius Brutus, Mr ROMER.
Oscar, Mr HENRY MARSTON, Valentine, Mr CORENO, Peter Peaflower, Mr W. H. WILLIAMS,
ailie, Countess de Renville, Miss CAROLINE RANKLEY, Martha, Miss COOKE, Rosalie, Mrs R. BARNETT

**48** An early metropolitan drama of low life, better known by its sub-title, *The Scamps of London*. It was adapted in 1843 by W. T. Moncrieff from a novel by Eugène Sue. The full supporting programme set forth on this poster was a well-established practice.
*Victoria & Albert Museum: Enthoven Collection*

# PRINCESS's THEATRE.

LICENSED BY THE LORD CHAMBERLAIN TO

# MR. VINING

(ACTUAL & RESPONSIBLE MANAGER), UPPER MONTAGUE STREET, RUSSELL SQUARE.

## Doors Open at Half-past Six o'clock, To commence at Seven.

## Saturday Next, August 8th,

The Performances will commence at SEVEN with the Popular FARCE, by J. M. MORTON, Esq., of

# POOR PILLICODDY.

| | | |
|---|---|---|
| Mr. Pillicoddy, | — | Mr. DOMINICK MURRAY. |
| Captain O'Scuttle, | | Mr. W. D. GRESHAM. |
| Mrs. Pillicoddy, | | Miss EMMA BARNETT. |
| Mrs. O'Scuttle, | | Mrs. ADDIE, |
| Sarah Blunt, | | Miss POLLY MARSHALL. |

After which, **AT EIGHT O'CLOCK,**

### A NEW DRAMA, IN FOUR ACTS, entitled

# AFTER DARK

## A TALE OF LONDON LIFE.

BY

# DION BOUCICAULT.

The subject of this Work is derived from a Melodrama by Messrs. D'ENNERY & GRANGÉ, with their permission.

| | | |
|---|---|---|
| Gordon Chumley, | (Light Dragoons) | Mr. J. G. SHORE. |
| Sir George Medhurst, (under the assumed name of Hayward) | | Mr. H. J. MONTAGUE. |
| Chandos Bellingham. | | Mr. WALTER LACY. |
| Old Tom, | (a Boardman) | Mr. VINING. |
| Dicey Morris, | (a Keeper of a low Gaming House, near Leicester Square, and Proprietor of the Elysium Music Hall, Broadway, Westminster) | Mr. D. LEESON. |
| Pointer, | (A Division) | Mr. W. D. GRESHAM. |
| The Bargee, | | Mr. R. CATHCART. |
| Crumpets, | | Mr. MACLEAN. |
| Area Jack, | (a Night Bird) | Mr. HOLSTON. |
| Sam and Josey, | { Kerbstone Vocalists by day, and Elysium Artists by night } | Messrs. H. & J. MARSHALL. |
| The Coleen, Mr. TAPPING. | | Nick, Mr. CHAPMAN. |
| Marker, | Mr. TRESSIDDER. | |
| Eliza, (once a Barmaid at the Elysium, Sir George's Wife) | | Miss ROSE LECLERCQ. |
| Rose Egerton, (an Heiress, Sir George's Cousin) | | Miss TRISSY MARSTON. |

## THE PERIOD,    THE SUMMER OF 1868.

## ENTIRELY NEW SCENERY by Mr. F. LLOYDS,

MR. W. HANN, and numerous Assistants.

Music Composed and Arranged by Mons. E. AUDIBERT.

Scene 1.

# VICTORIA STATION

## AND GROSVENOR HOTEL.

Returning from the Derby—The Sensation Column in the Times—Fifty Pounds Reward—Dicey Morris finds a Lost Heir—The Hansom Cabman No. 8941—Old Tom the Boardman—How the Medhurst Estate was Left to the Lost Heir.

### Scene 2. No. 5½, LITTLE COMPTON MEWS.

Eliza, the Cabman's Wife, refuses to be accommodating—The Compact.

Scene 3.

# SILVER HELL.

Chicken Hazard—Dicey gives wrong change for a five pound note—Sir George arrives, and he renews his acquaintance with Champagne—The Proposition—The Barmaid and the Baronet.

### Scene 4. No. — RUPERT STREET, HAYMARKET.

The Gambler's Wife—How Eliza proposes to Liberate her Husband.

### Scene 5. THE STRAND, NEAR TEMPLE BAR.

Old Tom's History—Fanny Dalton and Richard Knatchbull—Father and Daughter.

SCENE 6.

# Blackfriars Bridge

## ON CRUTCHES,

AND

# THE THAMES BY NIGHT.

The Nest of the Night Birds—Bankside Hotel (Limited)—Airy Rooms—Water always laid on—The Kerbstone Drama—The Suicide.

ACT II.

### Scene 1. DRY ARCHES Under Victoria Street,

Old Tom sends for his Friend, and takes his Farewell to Liquor—After Dark, Light will come—How Eliza got a Situation.

Scene 2.

# THE LILACS.

How the Confederates worked—Rose and Sir George—The Confession—How Eliza finds an unexpected Friend in her New Mistress.

### Scene 3. GARDEN GATE.

How Bellingham meets with his match, and Old Tom finds a clue.

### Scene 4. GREEN CHAMBER.

How Rose showed Eliza the Bracelet—The Bridegroom makes a Confession and a Happy Mistake.

ACT III.

### Scene 1. ELYSIUM MUSIC HALL,

## IN BROADWAY, WESTMINSTER.

The Provident Mudlarks' Benefit—How Bellingham dealt with Chumley—Old Tom objects, and how he is suppressed—A visit of the Police—All serene.

### Scene 2. WINE CELLARS.

Old Tom's Adventures in Subterranean London—A Murder in the Dark.

SCENE 3.

# UNDERGROUND RAILWAY.

Something on the Track—Old Tom destroys wilfully the Property of the Company—The Night Express.

ACT IV.

# THE LILACS.

Bellingham's Triumph—Eliza in search of a Father—Dicey Morris throws over an old friend.

To conclude with the FARCE of

# NO. 1

# ROUND THE CORNER.

| Flipper, | - | - | - | Mr. J. G. SHORE, |
| Bobbler, | - | - | - | Mr. R. CATHCART. |

| Stage Manager, | - | - | - | Mr. J. G. SHORE. |
| | Musical Director, | - | Mons. E. AUDIBERT. |
| Secretary, | Mr. T. ROBERTS. | | Treasurer, | Mr. T. E. SMALE. |

N.B.—Box-office Open Daily from Ten o'clock until Five, under the Direction of Mr. WADE.

Any person wishing to secure places, can do so by paying One Shilling for every party not exceeding Six, which places will be retained the whole Evening.

Dress Circle, 5s.　Boxes, 4s.　Pit, 2s.　Gallery, 1s.

Orchestra Stalls, 6s.

Private Boxes, £2 12s. 6d., £2 2s., and £1 11s. 6d.

"Messrs Some Road," W. S. JOHNSON, 60, St. Martin's Lane, W.C.

49  *After Dark* was a 'sensation' drama by Dion Boucicault, derived from a melodrama by D'Ennery & Grangé but set in the entirely contemporary London scene of 1868. The cheapest seats were a shilling.
*Victoria & Albert Museum: Enthoven Collection*

# THEATRE ROYAL,
## DRURY  LANE.

Sole Lessee and Manager' ... ... Mr F. B. CHATTERTON.

## ATTRACTION FOR THE HOLIDAYS.

EASTER-MONDAY, April 22nd, & EVERY EVENING DURING THE WEEK

At SEVEN o'clock, HER MAJESTY'S SERVANTS will perform a New Comedy-Drama, in Four Acts, entitled—THE  *1867*

# GREAT CITY

(*Written by* ANDREW HALLIDAY.)

THE NEW AND MAGNIFICENT SCENERY BY

## MR. WILLIAM BEVERLEY.

The Music and Original Overture composed and arranged by Mr. J. H. TULLY.
The Character Dances arranged by Mr. J. CORMACK.

The Dresses by Mrs. LAWLER and Mr SWAN.     Machinery by Mr. J. TUCKER.     Properties by Mr. NEEDHAM.
The whole produced under the direction of .. .. .. .. Mr. EDWARD STIRLING.

| | | | |
|---|---|---|---|
| Lord Churchmouse' ... | | ... | Mr C. WARNER |
| The Hon. Mr Dawlish ... | ... | ... | Mr F. MORTON |
| Major O'Gab ... | ... | (Half-Pay) ... | Mr FITZJAMES |
| Arthur Carrington ... | ... | (a Young Gentlemen) ... | Mr C. HARCOURT |
| Mendez ... | ... | (a Jew) ... | Mr F. VILLIERS (His First Appearance at this Theatre.) |
| Jacob Blount, M.P. ... | ... | ... | Mr J. C. COWPER (His First Appearance at this Theatre.) |
| Mogg ... | ... | (a Convict) ... | Mr W. McINTYRE |
| Jenkinson ... | ... | (a Footman and a Man of Business) ... | Mr J. ROUSE (His First Appearance at this Theatre.) |
| Ragged Jack ... | ... | (a Street Arab) ... | Mr J IRVING (His First Appearance at this Theatre.) |
| The Bos ... | ... | (Steward of the Beggars' Club) ... | Mr J. B. JOHNSTONE |
| Doctor ... | ... | ... | Mr NAYLOR |
| Railway Porter ... | ... | ... | Mr CULLEN (His First Appearance at this Theatre.) |
| First Policeman ... | ... | ... | Mr J. MORRIS |
| Inspector Brown ... | ... | ... | Mr WEAVER |
| Edith ... | ... | ... | Miss MADGE ROBERTSON [later Mrs Kendal] (Her First Appearance at this Theatre.) |
| Mrs Mauvray ... | ... | (a Young widow) ... | Miss R. G. LE THIERE |
| Aunt Judith ... | ... | ... | Mrs WARLOW |
| Fanny ... | ... | ... | Miss C. THOMPSON (her First Appearance at this Theatre) |

Street Passengers, Beggars, Police, Paupers, Swells-Extremes of St. James's and Giles's.

SCENERY AND INCIDENTS:

# CHARING CROSS HOTEL.

Alone in the Great City—The Faithless Lover—A Friend in Need—Home Again.

# A STREET NEAR ST. PAUL'S.

The Plot—The Meeting—The Recognition—The Compact.

**50**  A programme of a performance of Andrew Halliday's *The Great City* in April 1867.
This was another 'sensation' drama of considerable topographical ingenuity, culminating

# WATERLOO BRIDGE.

A Discovery—Despair—The Rescue.

## BELGRAVIA !

# DRAWING ROOM IN EDITH'S HOUSE.

Fortune—Grand Society—Pride—A Proposal and a Rejection—A Mysterious Visitor—Pride Humbled—The Awakening of Love and Gratitude—A Midnight Mission.

# GATES OF THE WORKHOUSE.

The Theory and Practice of the Poor Law—A Jew's Commentary—Meeting of the Lovers—Suspicion.

# THE JOLLY BEGGARS' CLUB.

The Beggars at Home—The Supper—JOLLY BEGGARS' DANCE—A Strange Story—Tracked—The Escape.

# THE BOARD-ROOM.

The Renewal of Love—Jenkinson's Grand Scheme—HOW TO GET UP A COMPANY (LIMITED)—Startling Information—A Jew's Friendship—A Jew's Vengeance.

## ROOM IN EDITH'S HOUSE.

A Daughter's Devotion—The Lover's Trial.—A GARRET—The Hole in the Wall—The Escape and Pursuit.

# LONDON by NIGHT

## THE HOUSETOPS.—Desperation—The Last Chance.

CHAMBER IN EDITH'S HOUSE.    The Accusation—Counter Accusation—The Last Wish—Happiness.

## STREET NEAR ST. PAUL'S.

# THE RAILWAY STATION.

## REALISATION OF FRITH'S CELEBRATED PICTURE.

THE ARREST.        THE END.

---

To conclude with the Farce, in One Act, by T. L. GREENWOOD, Esq., entitled

# THAT RASCAL JACK !

| | | |
|---|---|---|
| Mr Maddleton | ... | Mr J. NEVILLE |
| Mr George Granby | ... | Mr C. WARNER |
| Rascal Jack | ... | Mr JOHN ROUSE |
| Waiter | ... | Mr BEDFORD |
| Amelia | ... | Miss BESSIE ALLEYN |
| Lucy | ... | Miss C. THOMPSON |

---

| | |
|---|---|
| Stage Manager | Mr EDWARD STIRLING. |
| Musical Director | Mr J. H. TULLY. |
| Treasurer | Mr JAMES GUIVER. |

Private Boxes, One, Two, Three, Four, and Five Guineas.   Stalls, 7s.   Dress Circle, 5s.   First Circle, 4s.   Balcony Seats, 3s.
Pit, 2s.   Lower Gallery, 1s.   Upper Gallery, 6d.   NO HALF PRICE.

Box Office open from Ten till Five daily.      Doors open at Half-past Six, the Performances to commence at Seven o'clock.

E. W. MORRIS & COMPY.'S STEAM PRINTING WORKS, WILDERNESS LANE, WHITEFRIARS.

in a reconstruction of W. P. Frith's painting of Paddington station. See nos 63 and 342.
*Victoria & Albert Museum: Enthoven Collection*

**SOLE PROPRIETOR AND MANAGER, MR. BENJAMIN WEBSTER.**

Licensed by the Lord Chamberlain to Mr. BENJAMIN WEBSTER, Actual and Responsible
Manager. Kennington Park.

# LOST IN LONDON.

Mr. BENJAMIN WEBSTER, finding recovery from his present serious
Illness to be impossible without perfect rest and relief from professional anxieties,
has yielded to the advice of his Medical Adviser, EDWIN CANTON, Esq.,
and his Friends, and prevailed upon Mr. HENRY NEVILLE to undertake
the Character originally written for Mr. WEBSTER.

## FIRST NIGHT
### OF A
## New and Original Drama, in Three Acts,
By **WATTS PHILLIPS, Esq.,**
Author of "THE DEAD HEART," &c., entitled

# LOST IN LONDON,
### WITH
## ENTIRELY NEW SCENERY AND ADELPHI EFFECTS,

**Mr. HENRY NEVILLE,** (His First Appearance at this Theatre.)
**Mr. J. L. TOOLE,**
**Mr. PAUL BEDFORD,** **Mr. ASHLEY,**
**Miss NEILSON,** (who has been expressly engaged for this Drama.)
**Mrs. ALFRED MELLON,** (Late Miss Woolgar.)

# The MOUNTAIN DHU!
## EVERY NIGHT.

**SATURDAY, MARCH 16th, MONDAY, MARCH 18th, 1867,**
**AND DURING THE WEEK.**
To commence at SEVEN with (FIRST TIME) a New and Original DRAMA, in Three Acts,
by WATTS PHILLIPS, Esq., Author of the "Dead Heart," &c., entitled

# LOST IN LONDON.

## THE NEW SCENERY BY MESSRS. DANSON.
The Machinery by Mr. CHARKER. The Appointments by Mr. T. IRELAND.
The Music Arranged by Mr. EDWIN ELLIS.
The whole Produced under the Direction of Mr. R. PHILLIPS.

| | | |
|---|---|---|
| Gilbert Featherstone, | (Owner of the Bleakmore Mine) | Mr. ASHLEY, |
| Sir Richard Loader, | (his Friend) | Mr. BRANSCOMBE, |
| Job Armroyd, | | Mr. H. NEVILLE, (His First Appearance here). |
| Jack Longbones, | (Miners) | Mr. PAUL BEDFORD, |
| Dick Raine, | | Mr. ALDRIDGE, |
| Noah Morehead, | | Mr. TOMLIN, |
| Benjamin Blinker, | (a London Tiger) | Mr. J. L. TOOLE, |
| Thomas, | (a Footman) | Mr. W. H. EBURNE, |

| | | |
|---|---|---|
| Tops, | (a Post Boy) | Mr. C. J. SMITH, |
| | Guests, Miners, &c. ; | |
| Nelly, | | Miss NEILSON, |
| | | (Who has been expressly engaged for this Drama.) |
| Tiddy Dragglethorpe, | | Mrs. ALFRED MELLON, (late Miss Woolgar.) |
| Florence, | | Miss A. SEAMAN. |

## LANCASHIRE.
### ACT I.
SCENE 1 **JOB ARMROYD'S COTTAGE.**

Scene 2.—**BLEAKMOOR.**

SCENE 3. **BLEAKMOOR MINE!**

## LONDON.
### ACT II.

Scene 1.—**INTERIOR OF THE FERNS' VILLA.**

Scene 2.—**ANTE ROOM AT THE FERNS' VILLA.**

SCENE 3. **Exterior of the Ferns' Villa in Regent's Park**
**(BY NIGHT.)**

Scene 4.—**ANTE ROOM AT THE FERNS' VILLA.**

Scene 5—**BALL ROOM.**

### ACT III.
**INTERIOR OF A COTTAGE IN THE NEIGHBOURHOOD OF LONDON.**

### PROGRAMME OF MUSIC.

| | | | | |
|---|---|---|---|---|
| Overture, | ... | "IL BARBIERE DI SIVIGLIA," | ... | Rossini. |
| Valse, | ... | "DEBATEN," | ... | J. Gung'l. |
| Quadrille, | ... | "LINDA," | ... | D'Albert. |
| Galop, | ... | "WEDDING," | ... | C. Coote, Junr. |
| Valse, | ... | "SHADOWS OF DESTINY," | ... | Captain Colomb, R.A. |
| Overture, | ... | "MOUNTAIN DHU," | ... | Edwin Ellis. |

Musical Director, Mr. EDWIN ELLIS.    Solo Cornet, Mr. W. H. HAWKES.

To conclude with the New and Original GRAND EXTRAVAGANZA, by the Author
of the Celebrated Burlesque of "KENILWORTH," entitled The

# MOUNTAIN DHU!
## OR, THE KNIGHT, THE LADY AND THE LAKE.

Fitzjames (an errant knight [wi' Burns] who, pursuing his little *game* among the mountains, discovers a little *dear*, and being engaged with the *dear's talking*, finds himself on the horns of a dilemma, by which he is naturally *stag*-gered) Mrs. A. MELLON

Malcolm Græme (the original "bonnie laddie, highland laddie," who will give himself all sorts of Scotch airs [with v-air-iations] it is hoped to the satisfaction of the public) Miss HUGHES

Roderick (the genuine Mountain Dhu, a fiery spirit considerbly O. P. [which being interpreted means over proof], the wool-gatherings of Toole-ittle John—also a Mountain Do, whose crest, being a Caledonian Pine [*Fur Scotticus*] sufficiently indicates his character) Mr. J. L. TOOLE

The Douglas (the definite article of his clan, a Scotch heavy *f[e]ather*, very much *down* on his luck) Mr. PAUL BEDFORD

Malise (a young [*electric*] spark of the period, who flashes about the Highlands and kindles the flame of freebooting patriotism) Miss EMILY PITT

Red Murdoch (Rough and *Red*-dy, Roderick's *M*actotum, descended [*very low*] from an ancient line of [*Highway*] Robbers) Mr. ASHLEY

Norman (a Scotch Norseman, or *Sandy Knavian*) Mr. R. ROMER

Ellen (the Blue Belle Ellen of Scotland, lately taken from the Greek by Paris, now taken from Paris by the Scotch, also very much taken with Fitzjames, and no doubt the public will be very much taken with her) Miss FURTADO

Allan Bane (a transparent medium, a spirit wrapper and a spirit tapper, gifted with second sight, or the art, when in liquor, of seeing double) Mr. C. J. SMITH

Box-Office Open Daily from 10 till 5, where Private and Family Boxes and
Places can be taken without Fee a Fortnight in advance.
N B.—No gratuities to Box-keepers, or for Bills of Performance allowed.

Acting Manager, Mr. J. KINLOCH.   Treasurer, Mr. J. W. ANSON.   Stage Manager, Mr. R. PHILLIPS
Nassau Steam Press—W. S. JOHNSON, 60, St. Martin's Lane, W.C.

**51** The first night of *Lost in London*, 16 March 1867. This was a drama by Watts Phillips and dealt with the seduction of a coalminer's wife by an aristocratic mine owner who takes her to live at a villa in Regent's Park. See no. 64.
*Victoria & Albert Museum: Enthoven Collection*

**52** *right*  The Surrey Theatre in Blackfriars Road, Lambeth. It was opened in 1782 as the Royal Circus but was converted into a theater in 1810. It later became a variety theater and eventually a cinema. It was demolished in 1934. From an engraving in R. Wilkinson, *Londina Illustrata* (1819–25), II, facing p. 190.

**53** *right*  The Adelphi Theatre Royal in the Strand, one of the most famous of the minor theaters. Opened as the Sans Pareil in 1806, it took its new name in 1819. Moncrieff's *Tom and Jerry; or, Life in London* had a long run here in the 1820s. From a watercolor.
*Photo: R. B. Fleming & Co. Ltd Guildhall Library*

**54** *far right*  The Adelphi in 1840, suitably enriched so as to give 'the spectator a correct idea of the entrance to a theatre.' The frontage was enlarged still more in the rebuilding of 1858, when the seating capacity reached 1,500. From *Mirror*, xxxvi (1840), 271.

**55** *right* The London Pavilion, Tichborne Street, *c.*1870. This theater grew out of a hall erected on the yard of the Black Horse inn on the left, first used as a waxworks exhibition. It became a sing-song saloon in 1859 and a music-hall with a capacity of 2,000 two years later. It was rebuilt on a new site in 1885 following street improvements.
*Guildhall Library*

**56** *below* The Alhambra Theatre of Varieties, Leicester Square. This building replaced the original structure of 1854, built as an exhibition hall known as the Panopticon but soon converted into a theater and destroyed by fire in 1882. The second building had a maximum capacity of over 3,000.
*Photo: G. W. Wilson*
*Aberdeen University Library*

**57** *left*  The second Theatre Royal, Haymarket, on its opening night in 1821. From an engraving in R. Wilkinson, *Londina Illustrata* (1819–25), II, facing p. 160.

**58** *below*  The Garrick Theatre in Whitechapel, a low working-class theater, presenting *Starving Poor of Whitechapel*, while a policeman gets the worst of it in the pit. The original theater was opened in 1831 and burnt down in 1846. The auditorium shown here was raised in tone in 1873. It was closed finally about 1880. From Gustave Doré and Blanchard Jerrold, *London. A Pilgrimage* (1872), p. 164.

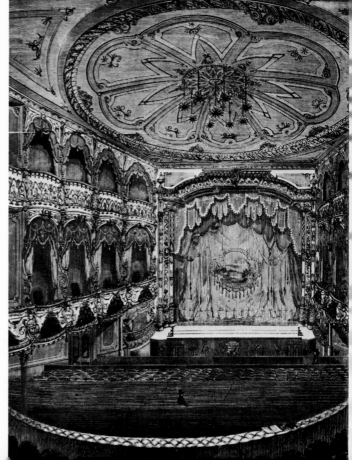

**59** *above left*  The Gaiety Theatre, Strand, opened by John Hollingshead in 1868. An earlier building on this site was known as the Strand Musick Hall. George Edwardes's famous productions began here in 1886. The building was demolished in 1902. From *Illustrated London News*, liv (1869), 20.

**60** *left*  The Grecian Theatre, Shoreditch, built on ground once occupied by pleasure gardens, and managed by the Conquests from 1851 to 1879. It had by then become the largest theater in the East End, eventually holding 3,400. It was sold to the Salvation Army in in 1881 and staged no more productions. From *Builder*, xxxv (1877), 1105.

**61** *above*  The Britannia Theatre, Hoxton, the most famous of East End theaters, opened in 1841 at the back of a tavern and remained under the management of the Lane family till 1899. This auditorium dates from 1858. From *Builder*, xvi (1858), 763.

**62** *above* *The Streets of
London*, Princess's Theatre,
August 1864. This was another
Boucicault play. One reviewer
wrote of the 'union of an exact
picture with all the movement
and mechanical aids which are
appropriate to the scene . . . of
Charing-cross at midnight, with
its lighted lamps, its Nelson
column, its gleaming windows of
Northumberland House, its
groups of rich and poor wending
their way to club or garret . . .
perhaps the most real scene
ever witnessed on the stage in
London.' From *Illustrated
Times*, v (1864), 129, 131.

**63** *above right* *The Great City*,
Drury Lane Theatre, May 1867.
The scenes were set 'amidst
the maze of the metropolis' and
contained some improbable
developments, including a house-
tops chase of a convict who
escaped by hanging from telegraph wires. From *Illustrated
Times*, x (1867), 276.

**64** *right* *Lost in London*,
Adelphi Theatre, April 1867.
The final scene. From *Illustrated
London News*, l (1867), 341.

**65** *The Long Strike*, Lyceum Theatre, September 1866. A play by Boucicault adapted from *Mary Barton*, which 'endeavours, after the example of the late Mrs Gaskell in her novels, to place before the audience the actual life of the world —a narrow world, too—the world of Manchester, with its discontented workmen and its manufacturing despots.' A metropolitan viewpoint, from *Illustrated London News*, xlix (1866), 290, 309.

sewing. Fearful of the landlady's demands for rent, which she cannot pay, Esther says, 'Work, work, work, and yet of no avail; it will not clear away the poverty by which I am surrounded. The dreadful threat of the few things I have got together being taken from me, the fear of being thrust forth homeless, checks every zealous intention, defies all industrious efforts. Well, well, I must try—still struggle on.' On Esther's wall is the same picture of the village church, which she has rescued from a sale; Ruth sees it and cries, 'Why does it hang there, as if to remind me of the past— to tell me what I might have been?'

London was indeed the City of Dreadful Night for melodramatists, and since all melodrama dealt in moral and material extremes, the village innocent often became, in the course of the same play, the urban sufferer caught in a vicious circle of poverty and sin. J. T. Haines's *The Life of a Woman, or The Curate's Daughter* (1840) is based upon 'The Harlot's Progress' and 'realizes' Hogarth's pictures on the stage. Fanny, the daughter in question, is seduced in London; her aged uncle suffers greatly; her honest village lover seeks her; and Fanny herself is consumed with guilt and agony of mind. Similarly, Susan, the village heroine of John Stafford's *Love's Frailties, or Passion and Repentance* (1835), is lured to London by her seducer. Maddened by guilt and horror, she throws herself into the Serpentine, but is rescued by her brother, who has come to London to look for her. (Carefully included in this scene is '*the view of the new Bridge across the Serpentine*'.) The virtuous Agnes of W. T. Moncrieff's *The Lear of Private Life* (1820) is betrayed by her city lover into leaving beloved father and village home and eloping with him to London. Living there as a kept woman she realizes that he means never to marry her, and she flees to her father and her childhood home. In Douglas Jerrold's *Martha Willis, the Servant Maid* (1831), the heroine, 'a good girl, the darling of our village,' goes into domestic service in London, is falsely accused of theft, and suffers under sentence of death in Newgate until the real criminal is discovered. The preface points directly to the moral-urban theme: 'It is the object of the present drama to display, in the most forcible and striking point of view, the temptations which in this metropolis assail the young and in-experienced on their first outset in life.' The blissful innocence of Martha's village life, in contrast to the corruption that later overwhelms her, is evident from her speech when she arrives in London and unpacks her box, which contains

> my best stuff gown, my four cotton ones, and my white aprons for Sundays, and here are the ballads, 'Crazy Jane,' 'The Dusty Miller,' 'Sheep Sheering,' and 'Blue-eyed Mary,' and there's the Charm for the Tooth Ache, and there's 'The Babes in the Wood,' and 'Lady Godiva,' and my grandmother's wedding-ring, and the needle case Ralph Thomas would give me, and there's the dream book, and Doctor Watts, and my sampler when I was a little girl. Oh, those were happy days! And here's the picture of our church and village, that Mr. Carmine painted for me, and told me always to keep by me, and—but where are the ribbons?

Nelly, the heroine of Watts Phillips's *Lost in London* (1867), carried off from her

Lancashire mining village to a life of kept luxury in London, awakens after repentance and severe illness and looks out of the window:

> London! (*She gazes for some moments steadfastly at the distant city, the red light of the setting sun falling full upon her face.*) The shining city of my dreams—my dreams! Its spires are bathed in light. (*As she gazes the light fades from her face and her voice changes from one of exultation to one of deep sadness.*) But the darkness is creeping down, and a shadow rises between me and the fading light.

At the end of the play Nelly dies and her husband Job tears aside the curtains, revealing '*the distant city, now brought out in strong light by the rising moon.*' Job declares that 'though lost in London (*he indicates by a gesture the city now bright with moonbeams*) I shall foind her theer,' pointing to Heaven. The polarity of London and Heaven is an obvious one, and to make the identity of London as a symbolic character in the drama even plainer, Phillips adds a note requiring a great width of window at the back of the scene, because 'I wish the great city to appear *most distinctly*, as a background to the last act of the drama.' This symbolic view of London is by no means at variance with the life-like treatment of the London streets and the people to be found on them; symbol and verisimilitude go hand in hand in nineteenth-century melodrama.

The men of Victorian drama go as badly astray in London as the women, although their suffering is caused mainly by gambling and drinking. Drink is a separate problem whose place in urban drama will be briefly examined below, but the village innocent in the capital of vice takes just as quickly to gambling. Young Wildflower, up from a Yorkshire village to buy an estate for his father with £5,000, loses it to gamblers in A. V. Campbell's *The Gambler's Life in London* (1829). Stephen Lockwood, a good farmer in W. B. Bernard's *The Farmer's Story* (1836), draws a lottery ticket worth £20,000 and sets up fashionably in London, where, ruined by drink and gambling, he sinks into poverty. The first two acts are entitled 'The Village—Labour and its Lesson' and 'The Metropolis—Wealth and its Temptations.' The honest Lancashire hero of Tom Taylor's *The Ticket-of-Leave Man* (1863), befuddled by the unaccustomed pleasures of London and duped by a gang of counterfeiters, complains, 'I used to sleep like a top down at Glossop. But in this great big place, since I've been enjoying myself, seeing life—I don't know (*passing his hand across his eyes*)—I don't know how it is—I get no rest—and when I do, it's worse than none—there's great black crawling things about me.' Job Armroyd, the betrayed miner husband of *Lost in London*, sums it up simply: 'It be a dreadful and a dreary place, this Lunnon, for them as are weak an' wi' no hand to guide 'em.'

Praise of country life at the expense of the city has been a theme common in Western literature since the days of Rome, but its expression in nineteenth-century drama is rather different and peculiarly of the age of great industrial cities—peculiarly Victorian. There is nothing like it in previous English drama and it can hardly be found before the 1820s. What is praised is specifically the village, not rural life in general, a village that is no longer a real place but a dream, a lost Eden in the sharpest contrast to the dirty streets and the wretched dwellings which the rural poor now inhabited. That life in the village was so hard did not, apparently, take long to forget, and the village of Victorian melodrama is like no other village that ever existed or could exist; it was a village of shimmering sweetness, sentiment, nostalgia, and beauty. It appears again and again in plays seen and enjoyed by metropolitan audiences in their tens of thousands, and the great London in which these audiences lived, in these same plays, vanished before the Ideal Village from which thousands of them came (or thought they came), many of them long ago. This is what countless Londoners saw as the stage version of their own past—illusion, it is true, but with all the complex significance of illusion. After 1860 drama of this sort was not so prevalent. Perhaps it was because the villager had stopped seeking his economic salvation in London or other cities, and because urban audiences had ceased comforting or amusing themselves with illusions of a simpler and purer rural life.

The living conditions of rural migrants to the city had become a theme of the Victorian popular theater. The only form of Victorian drama that dealt with social issues, clumsily and emotionally oversimplified in presentation though they were, was melodrama, which was also the form in closest touch with the needs and dreams of the urban masses. It is therefore to the melodrama that we must turn to see some reflection of their lives. By the 1840s melodrama had already become a crude theater of social protest and had taken up such matters as slavery, industrialization, class conflicts, game-laws, and other problems of contemporary society. As for London, melodrama was full of its homeless poor, and of their crime, drunkenness, and nostalgia for the lost life of the village. To give only one example of its social range, melodrama was a powerful weapon in the armory of temperance reform. *Fifteen Years of a Drunkard's Life* (1828), *The Drunkard's Doom* (1832), *The Drunkard's Glass* (1845), *The Drunkard's Fate* (1847), *The Drunkard's Progress* (1847), *Drink, Poverty, and Crime* (1859), *Drink* (1879), *Destroyed by Drink* (1879), *Intemperance* (1879), *Gin* (1880)—these are titles of some of the English temperance melodramas. Most of them end in the redemption of the drunkard and his family by the influence and direct intervention of the temperance spokesman, but in a few drink pursues its course unchecked, causing poverty, crime, madness, and death.

Two such plays can be examined as metropolitan examples of their school: T. P. Taylor's *The Bottle* (1847) and the same author's *The Drunkard's Children* (1848), both based on Cruikshank's temperance engravings, each one being 'realized' in a stage picture. The opening scene of *The Bottle*, entitled 'The Happy Home,' shows Richard Thornley, a mechanic, with his wife and two children, celebrating a tenth wedding anniversary in a '*neatly-furnished room*' in Finsbury. The bottle is brought out for the first time despite the wife's admonitions and fears. Soon there is no stopping Thornley on his slippery downward path. Ignoring the pleas of his loving wife and his best friend (who refuses to touch a drop), he continues to drink, both at home and in the 'High-Mettled Racer,' and is fired from his job for continued absences from work; at the end of Act I the Thornley furniture is removed for non-payment of debts, all having been spent on drink. In Act II, three years later, Thornley's son is taken into a gang of thieves to save him from starvation; his daughter becomes a prostitute for the same reason; his baby dies; he murders his wife in a fit of drunken rage ('Ha, Ha! The bottle has done its work!') and dies raving in Bethlehem madhouse, which he describes in a sane moment as 'warmer here, and better than the cold and muddy streets.' *The Drunkard's Children* is a sequel to *The Bottle* and traces the fortunes of Thornley's two surviving children. The son, now a dissipated thief, frequents beer-shop and gin-palace alike, gambles, is convicted of robbery, transported, and dies in the hulks. The daughter falls into a life of drink and prostitution, and, homeless and starving, ends her life in the dark, cold waters beneath Waterloo Bridge. The sins of the father have been visited on the children, and the Demon Gin (that favorite figure of temperance literature) has done his work.

The saloon or public-house figures prominently in *The Bottle* and *The Drunkard's Children* and most temperance dramas. It was almost always depicted as a place of evil and corruption, although in J. P. Hart's *Jane, the Licensed Victualler's Daughter* (1840), one character speaks in favor of the public house: 'Next to my own house I consider this my resting place from the toils of business, and I contend that a respectably-conducted tavern is one of the greatest blessings a nation can enjoy—it is in the social parlour that rational pleasure sweetens the care of trade.' Because of the high moral tone of Victorian melodrama, sentiments like this were rarely heard on the stage, although one hardly needs to draw attention to the ubiquity and popularity of the public house. Not only do the heroes of temperance melodrama fall further into physical and moral degradation in the public house, but it is also the scene of unseemly brawls and sometimes murders. In some plays the hero progresses downward from his pleasant rural home, through the horrors of a vile saloon, to poverty and despair on the streets. In an American temperance play with a happy ending, W. H. Smith's *The Drunkard, or The Fallen Saved* (1844), the reformed drunkard and his wife are happily reunited, not in New York, where in his un-regenerate state the husband had been fighting in saloons and sleeping in the street, but in the same country cottage in which they lived happily in the first act, with '*vines entwined, roses &c. The extreme of rural tranquil beauty.*' To this cottage, away from the foul metropolis, they return at the end of the play, '*everything denoting domestic peace and tranquil happiness. The sun is setting over the hills.*' To the melody of a flute the welcoming villagers quietly sing 'Home, Sweet Home.'

In order for the dramatization of urban social problems such as poverty, o melessness, and drink, to hold the attention of London working- and lower-middle-class audiences—who knew these things well from first-hand experience of them—at least a surface realism had to be created. By the early years of Victoria's reign the theater was able, through a series of technical advances such as the development of the box set, the controlled use of gas lighting, and the perfection of stage mechanisms, to present a more realistic and detailed picture of contemporary life than was possible before. At the same time the tendency of the arts, including the theater, was to move toward a greater fidelity to the surface of life, a tendency that faithfully reflected the ever-increasing materiality and emphasis on the business of daily living. A stage art that concerned itself primarily with reproducing the surface details of life began reconstructing the immediate physical environment of the lives of London audiences, as well as exterior views of the main sights of the city. In this way the drama was, in a sense, true to life, and in this way its presentation of character and situation could carry sufficient conviction for the occasion. The fact that the basic content of such drama was in many respects notably unreal, the dream world of the popular melodrama or the middle-class 'drama,' was an added reason for enjoyment rather than the reverse; a taste for the real and an indulgence in the illusory could be satisfied simultaneously. Such a duality lies at the heart of Victorian drama.

The stage realism of the 1840s was greatly stimulated by *Les Bohémiens de Paris* (1843), a dramatic version of Eugène Sue's novel *Les Mystères de Paris* (1842–3), which contains many scenes of Parisian low life. In London there were several adaptations of *Les Bohémiens de Paris*, and they all concentrated on the realistic depiction of London scenes. In Moncrieff's *The Scamps of London* (1843), the opening stage direction sets the scene with some care:

> *London Terminus of the Birmingham Railway. Curtain rises to bustling music.*
> DICK SMITH (*with Congreves*), *Cabmen, Baked Taters, Fried Fish, Lucifer*
> *Matches, and other Vendors and Hawkers, with Miscellaneous Vagabonds,*
> *discovered.* TOM FOGG *seen lying on the ground, leaning against a kerb stone,*
> *on one side, in a half-stupefied state, taking no notice of any one. Various cries of*
> 'Baked Taters, all hot,' 'Fried Fish, a penny a slice,' 'Lucifer Matches,'
> *&.c. heard confusedly mingling together.*

Later in the scene '*eight o'clock strikes, and bell rings, whistle of engine is heard, and train arrives*'; the train being, at this juncture in theater technology, offstage. Another scene displays Waterloo Bridge by moonlight, with the homeless settling down for the night under the dry arches; in a few moments the heroine throws herself off the bridge (a popular activity in Victorian melodrama) and is saved by a boat putting off below. Other scenes include the pleasure gardens of the suburban Cat and Bagpipes Tavern and Terpsichorean Saloon, and the '*Interior of miserable room in Rat's Castle, the Rookery, Dyot Street, St. Giles's. At the back of bagatelle board,* NED BRINDLE, JOE ONION, DICK SMITH, CADGERS, *and* VAGABONDS *of every description divided into groups, sitting, smoking, drinking, &.c.*' Charles Selby's *London by Night* (1845) adds the brickfields of Battersea and a low public house; in Dion Boucicault's *After Dark* (1868), the climactic scene occurs in the Underground, with semaphore signals working, signal lights changing, tunnels converging in perspective, and a train (onstage this time) bearing down on the drugged body of the hero. *The Drunkard's Children* contains scenes of a beer-shop, a gin-palace, and the sleeping-room of a cheap lodging-house. Henry Leslie's *Time and Tide, A Tale of the Thames* (1867) depicts among other things the Embankment Works, Waterloo Bridge, the Houses of Parliament, and the departure of an emigrant ship from the London docks. In

219

Andrew Halliday's *The Great City* (1867) audiences were much excited by a real hansom cab driving through the Waterloo Bridge toll-gate.

Scenes of high life could be presented as thoroughly as scenes of low life or the common sights of London. In *Lost in London* the third scene of Act II is an exterior view of a villa in Regent's Park with '*a picturesque view of other villas in varied perspective:*'

> *This set should partake of those characteristics which form what is called a realistic and sensational scene. A great snow effect. Scene brightens gradually, as the various windows and distant gas lamps are lighted up. As scene progresses, broughams, &.c. can be driven on if necessary, and all the minor out-door details which accompany the giving of a grand evening party.* FEATHERSTONE'S *villa has handsome portico, with large practical doors . . .*
> *Snow falling in scattered flakes at first, afterwards more thickly.*

Two scenes later the interior of the house is revealed, and the effect is equally elaborate and equally detailed:

> *Handsome suite of rooms in* FEATHERSTONE'S *house. Decorations blue and white, profusely relieved by gilt work. Furniture rich, and elegant mirrors adorn the walls, so as to multiply the reflection of the vases and statuettes placed about; chandelier hangs from ceiling of inner room. The two rooms open into each other by a broad arch, surmounted by a handsome cornice, from which fall velvet curtains, drawn up at sides so as to show table spread with refreshments, wines, fruits, &.c. &.c., the whole giving idea of elegant but prodigal luxury.*
> *Music and laughter as* GUESTS (*all in full toilet*) *come crowding from inner room.*

*Time and Tide* was performed at the Surrey, one of the working-class theaters on the South Bank in the same year (1867) as *Lost in London* was put on at the Adelphi, a West End playhouse catering predominantly for the middle class. Whatever their class, London audiences wanted to see the city scene recreated faithfully before their eyes, and demands for this kind of realism not only affected the development of Victorian dramas, but also enabled playwrights, managers, stage carpenters, and gasmen to present a composite stage-picture of London that was indeed metropolitan in its scope and variety.

This realism was not, however, merely a realism of display, of bridges, buildings, squares, and railway stations. Such a realism was only half of it; the other half had to do with people. Londoners, especially the poorer classes, daily rubbed shoulders with countless other people; their pleasures were communal, their apartments were overflowing, their streets were crowded. The stage could not reproduce the street-thronging thousands, but it could offer both serious and comic characters pursuing a variety of occupations, characters entirely recognizable to audiences who encountered them every day in the course of ordinary business. The preface to *Martha Willis* points out that 'this great metropolis teems with persons and events, which, considered with reference to their dramatic experience, beggar invention. . . It is these scenes of everyday experience—it is these characters which are met with in our hourly paths that will be found in the present drama.' *Martha Willis* contains only a coach-office porter, a pawnbroker, a shopman, a bawd, a gang of thieves, and prison officers, but no one could see (or even read) melodramas like *The Bottle* or *The Drunkard's Children*, both essentially plays of the streets, without being conscious of the drama's wide selection from contemporary London character-types and occupations. The *dramatis personae* of *The Bottle* include, besides the hero (a mechanic) and his family, a recruiting sergeant, a police constable, a bailiff, a thief, a needle-woman, a master engineer (the hero's employer), and a lodging-house keeper. The comic woman is a shoe-binder, the comic man, Coddles, a potboy and then a pieman. Scenes are laid in apartments, streets, garrets, and public houses in the areas of Finsbury, the Bank, Chick Lane, and Moorfields. The geography and the characters would have been perfectly well known to the audience, for *The Bottle* was first given at the City of London Theatre in Norton Folgate. Many aspects of the play's life and sentiments would have been known to them, too—drink, crime, the rent, poverty, hunger, the police, and the old village home. A character like Coddles, trying to sell an unwanted stock of meat pies, with his livelihood depending on their sale, but keeping a sense of humor about his failure, would have been dear to their hearts. *The Drunkard's Children* is even more crammed with life: safecracker, thimble-rigger, costermongers, dancers, publicans, casino manager, prison chaplain and jailor, barmaid, threepenny lodging-house keeper, dog fancier and stealer, prizefighter, dustman, lascar, and others.

Over thirty years later the staging of London scenes had become elaborately realistic and the trouble taken to establish local atmosphere more painstaking. A rather shocked Clement Scott described the last-act setting of George Sims's *The Lights o' London* (1881), the Borough market on a Saturday night:[2]

> It is a marvellous example of stage realism, complete in every possible detail ... If anything, it is all too real, too painful, too smeared with the dirt and degradation of London life, where drunkenness, debauchery, and depravity are shown in all their naked hideousness. Amidst buying and selling, the hoarse roar of costermongers, the jingle of the piano-organ, the screams of the dissolute, fathers teach their children to cheat and lie, drabs swarm in and out of the public house, and the hunted Harold, with his devoted wife, await the inevitable capture in an upper garret of a house which is surrounded by police.

These examples of the realistic portayal of London street life and the surface of London character have been drawn mainly from the lower-class popular melodrama, but enough evidence from the whole range of Victorian drama could be produced to show that the eye of playwright and stage manager for the details of urban character extended to all classes of drama. From whatever social class they came, London audiences liked their stage London to look like real London and their stage Londoners to act like people they knew; in this wish they were satisfied.

Because Victorian melodrama and the 'drama' possess a certain sweep of external events and often chose to depict a cross-section of metropolitan life, they were better suited to a broad portrayal of the London environment and the handling of urban themes than was the more circumscribed comedy or the domesticated farce. The farce was often citified in settings and characters, but since it was commonly a one- or two-act afterpiece with a necessarily inexpensive interior set, it lacked any sort of urban scope and contented itself largely with the comical and extravagant treatment of domestic trivia and misunderstanding. Comedy, the more serious parts of which were almost indistinguishable from melodrama, had a wider range, and from comedy, as well as from melodrama and 'drama,' we can select a Victorian theme that had not properly appeared in drama before and was intimately connected with the City of London: the theme of commercial life, high finance, and speculation. Such a theme had previously only touched drama, and that incidentally, as in Steele's *The Conscious Lovers* (1722), Lillo's *The London Merchant* (1731), and Cumberland's *The West Indian* (1771). Hovering in the background of these plays and others like them are beneficent merchants and noble men of commerce; since Addison's Sir Andrew Freeport, the merchant (and later the substantial tradesman), ceased to be the automatic figure of fun and scorn that he had been in seventeenth-century comedy. However, on the Victorian stage the world of business does not merely supply the plot and intrigue mechanism of an earlier drama of settlements, contracts, wills, and property dealings; it now becomes the thematic center of plays that occupy themselves with this world. Here, of course, we have moved out of a working-class and into a middle-class theater; to be 'something in the City' was taken to be the sole ambition of generations of middle-class youths and their parents.

The general theme of business and its accompanying ambitions appears in many plays of the period, some of them comedies, but most of them serious. A dramatist who turned more than once to it was Tom Taylor, in his vigorous career at one time or another tutor, barrister, journalist, Professor of English, and editor of *Punch*. His comedy *Still Waters Run Deep* (1855) treats of the final and rightful assertion of authority in the home by an apparently down-trodden husband, Mildmay. One of the means by which Mildmay commends himself to the audience is his refusal to be taken in by the speculating villain, Hawksley, and the shares the latter is selling in his fraudulent Galvanic Navigation Company. Hawksley declares proudly that a man may 'chance his hundred thousand on the up or down of the Three percents, every month of the twelve, and he may cultivate domestic felicity at his box at Brompton in the respectable character of a man of business.' He then lectures Mildmay on the stock market and how huge financial advantages are to be gained from investing in Inexplosible Galvanic Boats; the lecture is a long one and must have been calculated to hold the audience's interest as well as Mildmay's. Mildmay replies with a long speech tracing Hawksley's connection with a forged bill presented at a share-discounting house in the City. The plot of the play hangs on the exposure of Hawksley as a roué and a swindler, but the business theme is more than a plot device: Mildmay, in a sense, proves himself a man by a cool and competent demonstration of business knowledge and ability, for he too was 'something in the City.' The second act of another play by Taylor, *Payable on Demand* (1859), is almost entirely taken up with the frenzied speculations of Reuben Goldsched on the eve of Napoleon's abdication, and his attempts to pour money into a falling market so that he can be sure of an immense profit when he sells on the rising market which the news of the abdication (brought to him in advance by fast carrier-pigeon from Paris) will be sure to create. The tension of the act is purely financial, mounting steadily as messengers arrive with reports of the market and Goldsched issues orders to buy and sell. The substance of *Settling Day* (1865), whose second act is laid in a carefully described City broker's office, is financial speculation and financial crisis as the hero struggles to save his bank from ruin. Again, the dialogue is full of stock-market phraseology. *The Ticket-of-Leave Man* is concerned with the attempt of ex-convict Brierly to rehabilitate himself socially. He is taken into Mr Gibson's City office, turned away when his past is revealed, and finally places Mr Gibson in his debt by preventing a robbery. (As in *Settling Day*, the act laid in the broker's office is commercially solid and authentic in setting.) The certain implications of the happy ending are that Brierly can resume his rise to City prominence and City wealth, thereby taking the respected place among the seats of Commerce to which he so deeply aspires. A revealing passage of dialogue in Act III points directly to Brierly's prospects beyond the happy ending:

> MR. GIBSON. Go on as you've begun—keep a bright eye and an inquiring tongue in your head—learn how business is done—watch the market—and from what I've seen of you the six months you've been here, I shouldn't wonder if I found a better berth than messenger for you one of these days.
> BRIERLY. Mr. Gibson—sir—I can't thank you—but a lookout like that— it takes a man's breath away.
> MR. GIBSON. In the City there's no gap between the first round of the ladder and the top of the tree.

Other dramatists also developed the motifs of success in the City, speculation, and financial disaster. George Henry Lewes's *The Game of Speculation* (1851), adapted from Balzac's *Mercadet*, presents the manipulative wizardry of Affable Hawk, who twists his creditors round his little finger as he bluffs his way towards a Stock Exchange hoax of vast proportions that will save his tottering fortunes. While there is nothing of the London scene in the play, its dialogue is heavy with investments, bonds, mortgages, loans, and stock, and the character of Affable Hawk is that of the over-ambitious speculator whose swindles on the London Stock Exchange were exposed from time to time in a blaze of publicity. 'All our morals,' he says, 'lie in dividends. . . In these days credit is everything—credit is the wealth of commerce, the foundation of the state.' Holding up half-a-crown, Hawk declares 'Here lies modern honour. Chivalry has shrivelled into that'—and he acts accordingly. Hawk is properly redeemed by a stroke of coincidental good fortune just as he begins to carry out his swindle. A more ruthless speculator is Bloodgood, the villain of Boucicault's *The Poor of New York* (1857), which was successfully adapted as *The Streets of London* in 1864. Two financial crises, in the 1830s and 1850s, drive the hero's family into poverty (in *The Streets of London* they beg in a snow-covered Trafalgar Square), since Bloodgood has absconded with their fortune, which was deposited in his bank. All comes right in the end, but in the meantime much dramatic interest is attached to the business transactions carried on in Bloodgood's bank in Act I, and to his reputation as a speculator on the stock market.

The London of commercial speculation, financial panic, and the promise of riches and status was, as we have noted, not a working- or lower-middle-class London at all. The most significant fact of English theatrical history in the second half of the nineteenth century is the slow but sure upper-middle-class takeover of both the theater and the drama, and the steady rise of theater into that middle-class respectability it is even now trying so hard to shake off. Consequently, the lower-class dramatic vision of London retreated to the dwindling number of neighborhood theaters still open, which by the end of the century meant the Britannia, Standard, Pavilion, Surrey, Elephant and Castle, and the West London. The West End playhouses were given over entirely to the middle class, except the galleries in theaters like Drury Lane, the Adelphi, and the Princess's, which were mainly filled by a lower class of patron. In the East End, urban themes were dramatized in much the same way as in the 1840s, and low-life scenes and characters abounded; in the West End the increasing taste for visual realism brought forth more and more ponderous reconstructions of the London landscape. The annual autumn drama at Drury Lane, an institution that lasted from the 1880s until after the First World War, offered the most elaborate effects of all, especially in portraying the pleasures, occupations, and public resorts of the upper classes: Derby Day, Ascot, Goodwood, the Grand National, Rotten Row, Hurlingham, the Stock Exchange, the House of Commons, Westminster Abbey, the promenade at the Empire, the Military Tournament at Earls Court—all staged with the full scenic and mechanical resources of Drury Lane, which were considerable.

As a spectacle of life, therefore, or as a commercial jungle, a moral lesson, a monster of poverty and darkness, or a reminder of a lost heritage, London fascinated Victorian audiences, even those outside London, and was staged for them in different types of drama, different kinds of theaters, and before different classes of people, again and again. In the theater it was London above all, and neither before nor since has the metropolis exercised such a hold on the imaginations and dreams of English theater audiences.

### Notes

1 'The Amusements of the People,' *Household Words*, i (1850), 13–15.
2 *Theatre*, October 1881, 239–40.

# Index

Figures in italic type indicate illustrations; those in bold type indicate principal entries. Superior figures refer to notes.

## A

Aberdeen, 139
  overcrowding, 23
Acorn, G., 152, 160[239]
Acton, W., 188[20]
Adams, W. E., 151, 160[238]
Addison, J., 222
Adelphi Arches, sleeping rough in, 128–9
Adelphi Theatre, *53, 54, 64*; 220, 224
Adickes, F., 56[66]
Africa, South, rate of urban concentration, 41 (table)
Africa, urban population growth, 34
  urbanization, 33
Alhambra Theatre of Varieties, *56*
Allen, D. E., 190[44]
Alpert, H., 120[23,33]
Amato, P. W., 55[59]
America, Latin, agglomeration of population, 9
  child-woman ratio, 37
  demographic characteristics of immigrants, 37
  fertility, 37
  migration of foreigners, 15

  mortality rates, 34
  population concentration, 8, 41
  urban population growth, 34
  urbanization, 32, 33 (table)
America, North, concentration of population, 8
  density of population, 26
  effect of births on natural resource consumption, 43
  urbanization, 32, 33 (table), 34
  *see also* United States
Anderson, A. M., 157[118]
Anderson, M., 122[71]
Anerley, 126
Anti-Corn Law League, 161, 176
Argentina, annual rate of urban concentration, 5 (table)
  child-woman ratio, 37
  concentration of population, 10, 34
  rate of urban concentration, 41 (table)
  vital statistics, 35 (table)
Armstrong, W. A., 97, 104[64]
Artisans, Labourers and General Dwellings Company, 183
Ashton, J., 208[6,9,19,20], 209

Ashton, T. S., 101[12], 102[15]
Ashton-under-Lyne, 127, 128
Ashworth, H., 103[34]
Ashworth, W., 54[51], 119[10]
Asia, agglomerations of populations, 9
  demographic characteristics of migrants, 37
  urban population growth, 34
  urbanization, 32, 33 (table)
Astley's Theatre, 212
Athens, as primate city, 39
*Aurora Leigh*, 90
Australasia, annual rate of urban concentration, 5 (table)
  concentration of population, 8, 10
  population growth, 34
  urbanization, 32, 33 (table)
Australia, urban transformation, 42
  population, 8
  rate of urban concentration, 41 (table)
  vital statistics, 35 (table)
Austria, annual rate of urban concentration, 5 (table)
  marriage rates of urban

Austria—*continued*
  population, 18
Aves, E., 135
Azad, Q., 56[67]

# B

Bagshawe, J. R., 147, 159[204], 160[213]
Baker, A. B. M., 104[65]
Balfour, J., 172
Baltimore, population, 9
  slum conditions, 25
Balzac, H. de, 223
Banbury, 127
Banks, J. A., **105–22**, 121[57,58,59], 122[64,65]
Banks, Olive, 121[58], 122[64,65]
Banton, M., 190[45]
Barker, T. C., 103[34]
Barnes, G. N., 156[72]
Barnes, H. F., 120[32]
Barracks, Wellington and Knightsbridge, pubs near, 166, 172
Barraclough, G., 48[1]
Barrow-in-Furness, 125
Bass, Ratcliff and Gretton, records of, 145
Battersea, gypsies, 130
  off-licensed premises, 168
Baumeister, R., 54[51], 56[66]
Bavaria, annual rate of urban concentration, 5 (table)
  infant mortality, 25
Bedford, Bishop of, 95
Bedford, Duke of, temperance policy, 165, 166, 167, 181
Bedfordshire, marriage-rates, 17
Beer Act (1830), 169, 170
Belcher, T., 173
Belfast, migration to, 13
  overcrowding, 23
Belgium, annual rate of urban concentration, 5 (table)
  mortality, 27, 35 (table)
  vital statistics, 35 (table)
Belgravia, scarcity of pubs, 166
Bell, G. D., 57[71]
Bell, Lady, 125, 154[18]
Bennett, A. R., 187[13]
Bentham, J., 87
Berger, B. M., 56[66]
Berkshire, migrants from, 133
Berlin, age structure of migrants to, 17
  as agglomeration of suburbs, 29
  birth-rate, 19
  crude mortality, 21 (table)
  infant mortality, 24
  mortality, 20

population, 9
  as primate city, 39
Bermondsey, 139
Bernard, W. B., 216
Berry, B. J. L., 55[62]
Berthoff, R. T., 153[5]
Besant, W., 160[236]
Bessbrook, pubs banned, 166
Bethnal Green, density of population, 26
  employment, 134, 137
  labour-yard of Employment Association, *10*
  licensed premises, 164 (map)
  migrants, 152
  overcrowding, 23
Bevan, G. P., 52[32]
Beverley, 6
Birmingham, crude mortality, 21 (table)
  migration through, 117
  mortality, 20
  music halls, 174
  Night Refuges, 142
  population, 9
  pub debates, 179–80, 185
  Society, 86
Birth control, 114–15
  as an urban development, 114
  in working-class families, 115
Birth-rate, *see* Fertility
Bishopsgate, transport-inns, 162
Blackburn, fair, 131
Blake, N. M., 52[32]
Blaug, M., 101[9]
*Bleak House*, 103[31]
Bleicher, H., 51[28]
Bloch, M., 92
Bloomsbury, licensed premises, 167 (map)
  scarcity of pubs, 166
Blunt, R., 155[63]
Boeckh, R., 13, 50[14]
Bolton, link between pub and stage, 175
  pub density, 169
Bombay, 9, 36
Booth, C., 14, 50[16,19], 51[23], 92, 93, 94, 96–7, 103[48,50], 112, 120[38], 121[52], 126, 130, 136, 140, 154[12ff], 155[50ff], 156[69ff], 157[111ff], 158[152], 159[206,209,210], 160[216ff], 164, 165, 168, 169, 184, 186[2], 187[9]
Booth, J. B., 160[231]
Booth, M. R., **211–24**
Booth, General W., 155[52]
Bose, A., 56[66]
Boston, as agglomeration of suburbs, 29
  birth- and death-rates, 14

foreign-born population, 50[15]
  infant mortality, 25
  migration to, 14
  population, 9, 14
Boucicault, D., *49, 62, 65*; 219, 223
Boulding, K. E., 57[74]
Bournemouth, overcrowding, 22
Bow Common, 151
Bower Theatre, 212
Boyd-Orr, Lord, 57[69]
Bradford, 99
  dram-shops, 178
  mortality, 20
*Bradford Observer*, 171
Bradlaugh-Besant trial, 115
Bramwell, Baron, 183
Brazil, housing deficits, 37
  rate of urban concentration, 41 (table)
  rate of urban growth, 37
  urban natural increase, 37
Breese, G., 190[45]
Breslau, overcrowded housing, 24
Breslaw, J., 57[73]
Briggs, A., 6, **83–104**, 103[44], 104[59,71], 119[11], 122[67]
Bright, J., 176, 198
Brighton, 125, 139
  lodging-houses, 127
  return of migrants, 144
Britannia Theatre, *61*; 212, 224
British Association, statistical section, 90
*British Towns: A statistical study of their social and economic differences*, 98
Brix, J., 53[38]
Broadsides, *see* Street literature
Brodbeck, M., 104[62]
Bromyard, 138
Brougham, Lord, 90
Brown, G. H., 57[70]
Browning, Elizabeth Barrett, 90
Bruckner, N., 51[23,26]
Brussels, as agglomeration of suburbs, 29
  crude mortality, 21 (table)
  population, 9
  as primate city, 39
Bryson, R. A., 57[72]
Bücher, K., 122[69]
Buckingham, migrants from, 133
Buckle, H. T., 101[4]
Budapest, population, 9
  as primate city, 39
Buenos Aires, effect of population concentration, 38
  population, 9
  primacy, 38
  rate of population growth, 37

Bulgaria, rate of urban concentration, 41 (table)
Bull and Mouth (Queen's Hotel), 27; 162
Burchard, J., 56[66], 57[73]
Burgess, E. W., 102[22]
Burton-on-Trent, migrants to, 143, 144–5
Suffolk maltsters, *20*
Bussey, Peter, 179
Byron, H. J., 212

# C

Cairncross, A. K., 50[12], 120[18]
Cairo, population, 9
Calcutta, infant mortality, 36
population, 9
Cambridge Circus (London), pubs, 166
Camden Pratt, T., 160[228]
Cameron, W., 192, 208[4]
Campbell, A. V., 216
Canada, annual rate of urban concentration, 5 (table)
child-woman ratio, 36
migrants to, 15
rate of urban concentration, 41 (table)
vital statistics, 35 (table)
Canning Town, 143
Caracas, effect of population concentration on, 38
Cardiff, Tiger Bay, 123
Carlisle, Lord, 102[31]
Carlyle, Thomas, 89, 180
Carmarthenshire, winter migrants in, 143–4
Carnegie, A., 31
Casual wards, *9*; 128, 135, 142
payment for, 142
Catnach, J., *41, 46*; 199–200, 201, 202
Census, when instituted, 94
Census of England and Wales (1851), 4
(1881), 7
(1891), 17
(1911), 114
(1931), 6
Ceylon, infant mortality, 36
Chadwick, Edwin, 87, 88, 89, 96, 101[8]
Chartist attacks, 102[27]
Chaloner, W. H., 121[51]
Channing, W. E., 87, 88, 102[21]
Charing Cross, tramps, 129
Charlton, 129
Charrington, F. N., 169, 175
Chartist movement, 161, 179, 185, 198

public meeting rooms denied to, 175
Chase, Ellen, 139, 143, 158[141], 159[179]
Cheapside (London), *12*
Checkland, S. G., 119[12, 14]
Chelsea, off-licensed premises, 168
*see also* Embankment
Chemnitz, infant mortality, 24
overcrowded housing, 24
urban illegitimacy, 19
Cheshire, migration through, 117
Chesney, K., 188[22]
Chevalier, L., 92, 97, 104[63], 187[18]
Chicago, as agglomeration of suburbs, 29
migration to, 14
mortality, 27
population, 9
slum conditions, 25
Children, activities, 61, 62, 68, 69, 73, 74, 78
attitudes to, 63, 64, 66, 67
in factories, 86
games, 60, 61, 72
mortality, 16, 23–7
Chile, annual rate of urban concentration, 5 (table)
child-woman ratio, 36, 37
rate of urban concentration, 41 (table)
rate of urban growth, 37
urban natural increase, 37
vital statistics, 35 (table)
Christaller, W., 56[65]
Churchill, Lord Randolph, 174
Cities, definition, xxvii–xxviii
dependence on migration, 112
development, 31–2
dominance of large over small, 39
growth, 4–15
need for 'qualitative' and 'quantitative' evidence for study of, 83
new ideas originating from, 111
nodality, 40
numbers, 99
quantitative growth of wealth and population, 31
study of society based on, 93
Victorian attitude to growth, 84
*see also* England; Urbanization; individual cities and countries
*City Development. A Study of*

*Parks, Gardens, and Culture Institutes*, 31
Clapham, J. H., 113, 120[39], 121[46]
Clapham, M. H., 113, 120[39], 121[46]
Class, social, in relation to fertility, 12, 28–9
Classes, middle, attitude towards children, 63, 64, 66, 67
attitude towards destitute, 65, 68
attitude towards working classes, 63, 65, 66, 67
children's activities, 63, 64, 65, 66, 67
employment of servants, 63, 65, 66, 67
leisure activities, 63–4, 67
moral attitudes, 64, 67
occupations, 64, 65, 66, 67
*see also* Suburbs
Classes, upper, meeting with lower classes in pubs, 172–4
portrayed in late Victorian drama, 224
poverty among, 70
pubs banned near residences, 182
servants, 70–1
Classes, working, apprenticeship of, 77
attitude of upper classes to, 67, 68, 74–5
attitude to children, 61, 62, 69–71, 73, 74, 77
attitude towards neighbours, 72, 75, 78
attitude to police, 75, 78, 80
attitude to religion, *see* Religion
attitude to wealth, 62
begging, 80
children's activities, 61, 62, 68, 69, 73, 74, 78
and criminal class, 75–6, 77
family occupations, 61, 67, 71, 72, 73, 76
fighting as pastime, 62, 77
gulf between city and country, 69
illiteracy, 61, 73, 77
interviews, **60–80**
living conditions, 72, 206
manners, 62, 73, 74, 76, 77
meeting with upper classes in pubs, 173–4
and prohibitionism, 181
and temperance movement, 183
thieving, 78, 79, 80

Classes—*continued*
  *see also* Housing; Occupations;
    Poverty
Clerkenwell, Italians in, 135
Cleveland, migration to, 14
  population, 9
  size of families, 19
Cleveland, H. W. S., 54[52]
Coaching inns, 162
  modernization, 163
Coal Hole, 172
Coale, A. J., 51[23]
Cobbett, W., 134, 157[102]
Cobden, R., 172
Coffee-shops, 127, 128
Coger's Hall, 179
Cole, G. D. H., 121[44]
Coleman, T., 155[54]
Collett, E. B., 52[36]
Collins, J., 189[29]
Colombia, foreign migration to,
    37
  rate of urban concentration,
    41 (table)
  urban growth, 37
  urbanization and per capita
    income, 37
Colombo, child-woman ratio, 36
Communications, *see* Transport
Computers, use in quantitative
    analysis, 98
Comte, A., 110
*Condition of England, The*, 96
Constantinople, population, 9
Contagious Diseases Acts (1864,
    1866, 1886), 116
Cook, E. T., 187[16]
Cook, T., 113
Cooke Taylor, W., 5, 10
Cooley, C. H., 29
Co-operative societies, 113
Copenhagen, 18
Copenhagen Fields, pubs, 166
Conservative Party, *see* Tory
    party
Corcoran, B., 200
Cornwall, economic decline, 109
Couling, S., 188[24]
Coulsdon, overcrowding in, 99
Coulthart, Dr J. R., 128, 155[38, 40]
Coupe, W. A., 207[1]
Covent Garden, market, 100
  pubs, 166
  sleeping rough, 128
  theatre, 212
Coventry, migrants, from, 133
Crabb, J., 156[88]
Crawford, J. H., 15
Cresy, E., 155[37]
Crime, growth, 107

as subject of street literature,
    198–9
Cripplegate, Night Refuge, 142
Croydon, migrants from, 133,
    138
  tramps, 129
Cruikshank, G., 39
Cruikshank, P., 188[24]
Crum, F. S., 50[15], 51[25, 28]
Crystal Palace, 21
Cubitt, T., employment of
    migrants, 146
Cumberland, R., 222
Cyder Cellars, 32; 172

**D**

Dagenham, 99
Davis, K., 33n
De Tocqueville, A., 6, 49[5]
Deane, Phyllis, 49[10], 50[13], 52[37],
    55[61]
Dearle, N. B., 159[194]
Death-rate, *see* Mortality
Demography, *see* Population
Denmark, marriage-rates of
    urban population, 18
  rate of urban concentration,
    41 (table)
  urban birth-rate in, 19
Denvir, J., 138, 154[14, 17],
    157[126, 129]
Deptford, 143
  Mill Lane, 126
Derby, lodging-houses, 127
Derbyshire, migrants, 144
Derry, overcrowded housing, 23
*Descriptive and Statistical Ac-
    count of the British Empire*,
    84
Destitute Sailors' Asylum, 142,
    146
Detroit, 9, 14
Dewnsnup, E. R., 22, 23, 52[33]
Dickens, Charles, 84, 85, 86, 91,
    102[31]
Dickinson, G. C., 186[6]
Dingle, A. E., 189[37]
Disraeli, Benjamin, 87, 121[51],
    198
*Division of Labour in Society*, 110
Djakarta, population of, 9
Domestic service, employment
    of country girls in, 115
Dominican Republic, child-
    woman ratio, 37
Doré, G., 3, 42, 57
Dou Chang, Sen, 49[9]
Downing, A. J., 29, 54[48]
Drama, commercial, 222, 223
  high moral tone, 218

life in London as theme, 48–51,
    62–4; 212, 215–17, 222, 223
  symbol and verisimilitude in,
    216
  temperance, 217–18
  themes, 213–18, 222–4
  upper-class life as theme, 224
  *see also* Theatres
Dresden, urban illegitimacy, 19
Drink, argument for free trade,
    175
  off-purchase, 167
  prohibition, 181–3
  restriction of hours, 181
  and sporting activities, 173–5
  as theme of Victorian melo-
    drama, 217
  and women, 78, 168
  *see also* Drama; Gin-palaces;
    Pubs; Temperance move-
    ment
Drury Lane, soup-kitchens, 123
  theatre, 63; 212
Dublin, overcrowded housing, 23
Dubos, R. J., 43, 48, 57[71]
Dudley, 138
Dumfries, fair, 131
Duncan, R., 120[19]
Dundee, overcrowding, 23
  whalers, 24
Dunfermline, 31
Dunlop, J., 163, 186[6], 187[13]
Dunnett, H. McG., 187[15]
Durham, overcrowding, 23
Durkheim, É., 109–10, 111–12,
    117, 120[20, 29, 34], 122[68]
Dyos, H. J., 54[49], 98, 104[64, 65, 67],
    186[1], 187[9], 190[47]

**E**

Ecology, human:
  abuse of human ecosystem,
    42–8
  application of cost-benefit
    analyses to ecosystem, 47
  future plans for environment,
    48
  welfare-accounting technique
    applied to environmental
    policies, 47
  *see also* Pollution
Ecuador, vital statistics, 35
    (table)
Edgeworth, F. Y., 94
Edinburgh, effect of migration,
    13
  Night Refuge, 142
  overcrowding, 23
*Edinburgh Review*, 89, 101[13]
Edmonds, E. L. and O. P., 101[5]

Education, provision of, 86
  *see also* School
Edwards, H. W. J., 187[17]
Edwards, R. D., 120[17]
Effingham, 213
Egan, P., 202
Egypt, rate of urban concentration, 41 (table)
  urbanization and per capita income, 37
Ehrlich, P., 48
Elephant and Castle, pubs, 166
  theatre, 224
Elson, G., 156[85]
Embankment, Thames, scarcity of pubs, 166
  tramps on, 129
  winter employment, 146
Embankment, Victoria, 165
Employment, industrial, competition with agriculture, 133
  Christmas increase in, 149
  growth of regular, 153
  lack of in late winter, 150
  for migrants, 148
  slackness of, 137
  *see also* Occupations
*Encyclopaedia Britannica*, xxvii, 92
Engels, F., 3, 121[51]
England, annual rate of urban concentration, 5 (table)
  home ownership, 25
  increase in town and country population, 14, 15
  industrialization of labour force and product, 11 (table)
  internal migration, 15
  marriage-rates for urban population, 18
  migration to towns, 13
  mortality, 20, 24
  overcrowding, 23
  population concentration, 11 (table), 12
  population, 6, 8
  sex and age structure of population, 16–17
  size of households, 25
  size of rural population, 12, 15
England and Wales, growth of cities, 39
  nineteenth-century growth of population, 105
  *see also* Census; Great Britain
Entertainment, travelling circuses, 131
  *see also* Fairs; Music halls; Pubs; Theatres
Epsom Downs, Derby Day at, *5, 159;* 124

Essex, migrants to, 135
Europe, concentration of population, 8
  increase in urban and rural populations, 14
  urban birth- and death-rates, 14
  urbanization, 32, 33 (table)
Euston, pubs, 163
Evans, G. E., *20;* 132, 144, 156[86], 159[182,187,191]
Evans's Cave of Harmony, 172
Everton, gypsies at, 129
Ewing Ritchie, J., 157[126], 180, 188[19]
*Eyes of the Thames*, 137

**F**

Fairfield, C., 189[42]
Fairs, autumn, 140
  spring migration of showmen to, 131
  summer migration to, 136
Family, changes in relationships, 60, 114
  growing economic independence of children, 114
  migration, as escape from, 113–14, 121[51]
  size, 61
  standards of behaviour, 62
Farr, W., 95, 103[55]
Faucher, J., 52[38]
Fawcett, H., 91
Fayers, T., 157[108]
Fertility, child-woman ratio as measure of, 36
  class differences, 53[44]
  highest in mining and agricultural families, 114
  in London, 49[11]
  negative correlation with socio-economic status, 27, 40
  parity between mortality and, 34
  relation between size of agglomeration and, 19
  rural compared with urban, 51[29]
  in urban populations, 18, 114
Fielding, K. J., 102[31]
Finchley, Common, 150
Finland, child-woman ratio, 36
  rate of urban concentration, 41 (table)
Finsbury, gypsies in, 130
  overcrowding, 22, 23
Fisher, R. A., 94
Flanagan, J., 126, 154[21]

Fleetwood, shipping trade in, 146
Fletcher, J., 101[1]
Flinn, M. W., 101[8]
Fogel, R. W., 103[56]
Ford, B., 102[24]
Ford, G., 101[4]
*Fortnightly Review*, 96
Foster, J., 186[1], 190[47]
Foundling hospitals, 80
France, age and sex structure of population, 51n.
  annual rate of urban concentration, 5 (table)
  concentration of population, 4
  death-rate in cities, 13
  decreasing internal migration, 15
  effects of migration on cities, 13
  mortality, 20, 35 (table)
  rate of urban concentration, 41 (table)
  research on urbanization, 97
  vital statistics, 35 (table)
  *see also* Paris
Frankenberg, R., 120[24]
Frankfurt-am-Main, age structure of migrants to, 17
*Fraser's Magazine*, 88
Fredur, T., 157[103]
Freeman, A., 156[7]
Freeman, T. W., 54[53], 119[7]
Friedmann, J., 55[59]
Frith, W. P., *50*
Fulham, off-licences, 168

**G**

Gaiety Theatre (London), *59*
Gale, F., 173–4, 188[22]
Galton, F., 27, 121[54]
Garden cities, advantages, 31
  *see also* Howard, E.
Garrick Theatre (London), *58*
Gaskell, Mrs, 86, 88
Gateshead, overcrowding, 22, 90
Geddes, P., 31, 48, 54[52]
Genzmer, F., 53[38]
Germany, effect of migration on growth of cities, 13
  marriage-rates of urban population, 18
  sex and age structure of urban population, 16–17
  vital statistics, 35 (table)
Gibbon, S., 158[157]
Giffen, Sir R., 93
Gin-palaces and gin-shops, *29, 33;* 170

Gladstone, W. E., 163, 180, 185, 190[48], 198
  grocers' licences, 167, 168
  refreshment house licences, 165, 168
Glasgow, concentrations of population, 38
  drunkenness, 184
  mortality, 20
  overcrowding, 22, 23
  population, 9
  tramps, 129
Glass, D. V., 52[31, 37], 121[53]
Gloucester, lodging-houses, 127
Gloucestershire, economic decline, 109
Godstone, migrants to, 133
Golden, H. H., 33n.
Gorham, M., 1871[15]
Graham, J. Q., 103[56]
Gravesend, migration from, 138
  migration to, 140
Gray, B. Kirkman, 102[17]
Great Britain, birth-rate, 10, 11, 35 (table)
  concentration of population, 41
  death-rate, 10, 35 (table)
  effects of urban transformation, 10
  Gross National Product, 11
  growth of cities, 8
  income per capita, 11
  internal migration, 15
  level of urbanization, 35 (table)
  mortality, 27, 35 (table)
  population, 6, 10
  prices, 10
  *see also* England and Wales
Great Exhibition (1851), 198, 204
Grecian Theatre (London), *60*
Greece, rate of urban concentration, 41 (table)
Green, T. H., 178
Greenwich, migration to, 140
Greenwood, J., 124, 153[6], 154[24], 159[176], 160[235], 188[19]
Greg, W. R., 86, 101[13]
Gregory, R., 209[24]
Grey, Sir G., 173
Groome, F., 154[9]
Guillou, J., 50[18]
Gypsies, and the law, 130
  hop-picking, 138
  in and near London, *4, 5, 13, 16*
  on outskirts of towns, 142–3
  outward movement from London, 132
  sites of encampments, 129–30

*see also* Migrants; Migration; Tramps

## H

Hackney, off-licensed premises, 168
  skating on marshes, 151
Hackney Wick, gypsies, 130
Hadley, A. T., 28, 29, 54n.
Hagen, E. E., 35n.
Haines, J. T., 215
Haiti, child-woman ratio, 37
Halliday, A., *50*
Hamburg, birth-rate, 19
  population, 9
Hammersmith, off-licensed premises, 168
Hammond, J. L. and Barbara, 119[12]
Hampden Club, 175
Hampshire, migration via, 117
Hampstead, Heath, 150
  off-licensed premises, 168
Handlin, O., 56[66], 57[73]
Hanly, M., 175
Hansen, G., 27
Harcourt, W. V., 178
*Hard Times*, 84, 85, 86
Hardy, T., 175, 187[16]
Harris, B., 38, 55[60]
Harris, C. D., 56[67]
Harrison, A., 121[40]
Harrison, B. H., **161–90**, 189[37]
Harrison, J. F. C., 189[30]
Hart, J. P., 218
Hartwell, Robert, 172
Hastings, Marquis of, 173
Hatt, P. K., 187[15], 190[45]
Hauser, P. M., 33n., 52[29], 55[56, 58, 59], 56[64], 104[61]
Hawley, A. H., 54[53]
Haymarket (London), 173
  theatre, *57*; 212
Health, advances in bacteriology 95
  demand for national policy, 96
  effects of improvements in medicine, 10, 30
  *see also* Disease; Sanitation; Water systems
Health, medical officers of, reports, 94
Health of Towns Association, 95
Heberle, R., 120[32]
Henderson, W. O., 121[51]
Hennock, E. P., 104[67], 186[1]
Herefordshire, level of nuptiality, 17
  migrants, 137, 138
Hertford, employment of migrants, 144

Hertfordshire, 22
Herzfeld, H., 54[49]
Higgs, Mary, 42
Hill, A. H., 160[231]
Hill, Octavia, 26, 139
Himes, N. E., 56[66], 121[58]
Hindley, C., 154[10], 156[75, 78], 158[151], 160[224], 193, 208[4, 6, 7, 8, 9]
Hirsch, W., 122[65]
*History of England*, 100
Hitchin, tramps, 126
Hobsbawm, E. J., 108, 119[13], 120[15], 121[62]
Hobson, J. A., 28, 53[46], 172, 187[19], 188[20]
Hogben, L., 121[53]
Hogg, J., 187[14]
Holbeach, migrants to, 133
Holden Pike, G., 159[202]
Hollingshead, J., *59*; 141, 158[164]
Holmes, G. K., 53[41]
Holyoake, G. J., 121[44], 206
Homestead Act (U.S.A., 1862), 108
Hone, W., 188[24], 197
Hongkong, population, 9
Hooper, W., 92
Hop-picking, *22*
  *see also* Migrants
Horsfall, T. C., 52[38]
Horsley, J. W., 126, 154[28]
Hotels, growth of, 163
House, H., 102[31]
*Household Words*, 173
Housing, inadequacy, 106
  as an increasing urban problem, 22
  in United States, 25–7
  *see also* Lodging-houses; Suburbs; and individual cities
Housing, overcrowding in, 22
  causes, 25–7
Houseless Poor Asylum, 143
Hove, 144
Howard, Diana, 214n.
Howard, E., 30–1
Howarth, E. G., 158[159]
Howell, G., 180
Hoxton, 192–3, 213
  Theatre, *61*
Hoyle, W., 166–7, 169
Hoyt, H., 56[66]
Huddersfield, lodging-houses, 127
Hugill, S., 155[57]
Hull, waterfront industries, 147
Hungary, annual rate of urban concentration, 5 (table)
  migration from, 15

Hutchins, Barbara L., 121[40]
Hutchinson, T. W., 103[47]
Huyton-with-Ruby, population, 99
Hyams, E., 188[22]
Hyndman, H. M., 92

# I

India, effect of births on natural resource consumption, 43
  housing deficits, 37
  migration to cities, 41
  mortality-rates, 34
  urbanization and per capita G.D.P. in, 38
  vital statistics, 35 (table)
Indonesia, migration to cities, 41
Industrial Revolution, effects of, 4
  on population, 11
  on the working classes, 108
Industrial-urban transformation, *see* Urban transformation
Industrialism, features of, 10, 11
Inglis, K. S., 122[74]
Innes, J. W., 121[55]
*International Encyclopaedia of the Social Sciences*, 94
Interviews, *see* Oral history
Ipswich, English-born population, 118
Iraq, rate of urban concentration, 41 (table)
  urbanization and per capita income, 37
Ireland, annual rate of urban concentration, 5 (table)
  migrants from, 108
  overcrowded housing, 23
  *see also* Belfast; Dublin; Irish
Irish, concentrations of, 165
  as hay-makers, 134
  as hop-pickers, 125
  in market gardens, 135
  as migrants, 124, 125, 133, 134, 138, 149
  seasonal movements, 140
  women migrants, 137
Islington, tramps, 126
  'World's Fair', 141
Italians, 166
  as migrants, 135, 149
Italy, decreasing internal migration, 15
  effects of migration on growth of cities, 13
  mortality, 27, 35 (table)
  vital statistics, 35 (table)

# J

Jackson, J. A., 122[75]
Jacob, H., 56[63]

Jacobs, A., 192
Jaffe, A. J., 51[29]
James, H., 93, 100, 104[72]
Japan, migration to cities, 14
  mortality in cities, 36
  population restriction, 36
  rate of urban concentration, 41 (table)
  urban demographic transition, 35
  urbanization, 34, 35 (table)
  vital statistics, 35 (table)
Jarrow, 6
Jeffery, J. R., 119[5]
Jerrold, D., 215
Jerrold, W. B., *3*; 208[2]
Jevons, W. A., 157[104]
Jews, exclusion by street-gangs, 76
John, A. H., 159[184]
Johnson, S. C., 120[16,17]
Jones, Ernest, 179, 180, 198
Jones, I. G., 190[46]
Juillard, E., 56[65]
Jullien, L. A., 202

# K

Kaplan, A., 104[62]
Kay-Shuttleworth, Sir J. P., 90
Kellett, J. R., 98, 104[66], 155[54], 186[1,6]
Kendall, M. G., 103[54]
Kenilworth, migrants to, 133
Kenney, R., 155[57]
Kennington, turnpike gate, 120
Kensington, off-licensed premises, 168
  Park Gardens, 112
  scarcity of pubs, 166
Kensington, West, gypsies, 130
Kent, migrants to, 132, 135, 138
Kettle, A., 88, 102[24]
Kettle, J., 54[52]
Kilmarnock, overcrowding, 23
King's Cross, Fair, 133
  pubs, 163
King's Lynn, fair, 132
Kingsley, C., 29, 84, 90, 101[2]
Kirwan, D. J., 128, 155[45]
Kitson Clark, G., 106, 119[9]
Knight, C., 186[5]
Köllman, W., 50[19]
Königshütte, overcrowded housing, 24
Korea, rate of urban concentration, 41 (table)
  urbanization and per capita income, 37
Kuczynski, R., 51[22]
Kuper, H., 190[45]
Kuznets, S., 56[68]

# L

Labour force, growth of, 49n.
Lackington, T., 55[59]
Lambert, Royston, 103[53], 104[58]
Lambert, W. R., 187[18]
Lambeth, half-gypsy colony, 141
  music hall, *36*; 174
Lampard, E. E., *3–57*, 49[3], 52[29], 55[60,65,66], 56[64], 104[61]
Lancashire, drunkenness, 184
  high marriage-rates for employed women, 18
  infant mortality-rates, 24
  migrants from, 137
  nuptiality for urban and rural adults, 17
  pub distribution, 167
  *see also* Liverpool; Manchester
Lancaster, E., 213
Landlords, attitude to tenants, 78
  *see also* Bedford, Duke of
Lasker, B., 134, 157[105]
Lavoie, E., 56[63]
Law Courts (London), 146
Lawrence, C. E., 188[28]
Lawton, R., 119[4,6]
Le Play, F., 110
Leeds, effect of migration, 13
  mortality, 20
  population, 9
Legoyt, M. A., 51[21]
Leicester, crude mortality, 21 (table)
  Domestic Mission Society, 113
  English-born population, 118
  mortality, 20–1
  overcrowding, 22
Leicester Square, employment of boardmen, 150
  soup kitchen, 123
Leipzig, birth-rate, 19
  illegitimacy, 19
Lemon, R., 207[1]
Leningrad, migration, 14
  population, 9
Leno, J. B., 176
Leslie, H., 219
Lettsom, J. C., 85, 101[7]
Levasseur, Émile, 13, 50[14], 51[27]
Levi, Leone, 159
Lewes, G. H., 223
Lewis, R. A., 102[19]
Lewis-Faning, E., 56[66]
Lewisham, off-licensed premises, 168
  swimming baths, 322
Liberation Society, 161
Libraries, provision of, 113, 146
Licensed premises (maps)

Licensed premises—*continued*
  Bethnal Green and Spital-fields, 164
  Bloomsbury, 167
  dockland, 166
  Strand, 165
  *see also* Pubs
*Life and Adventures of a Cheap Jack, The*, 149, 192
*Life in London*, 202
Lillo, G., 222
Limehouse, Charlie Brown's Railway Tavern, 175
  Strangers' Home, *2*
Limerick, overcrowding, 23
Lincolnshire, migrants to, 133, 134, 143
Liverpool, 106
  building trade, 146
  English-born population, 118
  Irish, 118
  lodging-houses, 127
  mortality, 20, 21 (table)
  population, 9, 13
  shipping trade, 146
  tramp shelters, 129
  waterfront industries, 148
Llewellyn Smith, Sir H., 50[19], 94, 103[50], 112, 120[38]
Lloyd, A. L., 156[72]
Lloyd, J., 156[76]
Lodging-houses, conditions, 127–128
  desertion at hopping time, 138
  tramps' use, 126, 127
London, as agglomeration of suburbs, 29
  birth-rates, 49n.
  as centre of drama and theatre, *48–65*; 212, 224
  City, *see below*
  city-size distribution, 39
  coffee shops, 127
  concentration of population, 38–9
  Corresponding Society, 175
  County Council, inception, 94
  crude mortality, 21 (table), 49n.
  density of population, 26, 106
  East End, *see below*
  effects of migration, 13
  inns, *25, 26, 27*
  lodging-houses, 127
  migration from, 133, 139
  migration to, 49n., 139, 141
  music halls, 174, 175
  Night Refuges, 142
  population, 4, 9
  sleeping rough, 128
  Statistical Society, 86–7

van-dwellers at Agricultural Hall, *16*
  Working Man's Association, 176
  *see also* Drama; Housing; Pubs; Street life; Suburbs; Theatre; and individual institutions and place-names.
London, City of, xxvii
  population, 4, 7–8
  portrayed in drama, 222, 223
  pub density, 163
  Theatre, 212, 221
  transport inns, *26–7*; 162
London, East End of, attitude of wealthy to, 180,
  migrants from, 135
  Sailors' Home in, *1*
*London: A pilgrimage, 3; see also* Doré, G.
London Bridge, pubs, 163
  sleeping rough near, 123, 128
Longstaff, G. B., 50[16,18]
Los Angeles, migration to, 14
  population, 9
Love, D., 192, 208[4]
Lovett, W., 183, 189[29,42]
Low, S. J., 54[49]
Lowe, R., 180
Lowery, R., 176
Lowestoft, 140
  migrants to, 143
Loyal and Patriotic Fund, 176
Lubbock, B., *24*
Lubove, R., 53[41]
Luddites, 178
Lumley, W. G., 122[73]
Lyceum Theatre (London), *65*
Lynch, K., 104[70]

**M**

Macarthy, D., 151
Macaulay, T. B., 100, 101
McCulloch, J. R., 84, 85
MacDonagh, O., 108, 120[17]
McGee, G. W., 180
Mackenzie, J. S., 6, 49[5]
McKenzie, R. D., 102[22]
Madras, population, 9
Madrid, population, 9
Mairet, P., 54[52], 57[76]
Malthus, Rev. T. R., 86, 101[11]
Manby Smith, C., 140, 158[150]
Manchester, agglomeration of suburbs, 29
  building trade, 146
  crude mortality, 21 (table)
  fair, 131
  housing, 22
  infant mortality-rates, 24

mortality, 20
  music halls, 175
  Night Refuges, 142
  population, 9, 13
  pub density, 169
  Statistical Society, 86, 88
  tramps, 128, 141
  *see also* Gaskell
*Manchester Examiner and Times*, 91
*Manchester Guardian*, 91, 146
Mander, R., 188[25,26]
Mann, P. H., 121[56]
Manning, Cardinal, 175, 181, 182
Margate, 125
Marriage, advocation of post-ponement, 28
  chances of, in towns, 113
  demographic consequences of early, 114
  fluctuations in marriage-rates and population growth, 91
  rates, 17–19
Marris, P., 190[45]
Marshall, A., 27, 28, 30, 54[50], 93, 103[47]
Marshall, W., 158[140]
Martley, 138
Marwood (public executioner), 174, 188[23]
Marx, K., 3, 110
*Mary Barton*, 65; 88, 101[13]
Marylebone, workhouse, 9
Massachusetts, birth-rates, 19
  foreign-born population, 50[15]
  high marriage-rate, 18
  infant mortality, 25, 26
  mortality, 20
Masterman, C. F. G., 96, 104[60]
Matthiessen, F. O., 103[49]
Matz, B. W., 162, 186[3]
Mayhew, A., 150
Mayhew, Henry, 88, 89, 101, 102[23,28], 124, 125, 132, 143, 154[11,25], 156[74ff], 157[109,124], 158[144ff], 159[173,180], 160[224], 225,234, 169, 173, 188[21], 192, 199, 200, 201, 208[2,3], 209[17]
Mechanics' Institutes, 113
Meek, G., 139, 158[142]
Mehta, S. K., 55[61]
Melbourne, population, 9
*Memoirs of a Social Atom*, 151
Merthyr Tydfil, 'China' in, 126
Merton, infant mortality, 99
Meuriot, P., 51[22]
Mexico, rate of urban concentra-tion, 41 (table)
  rate of urban growth, 37
  urban natural increase, 37
  vital statistics, 35 (table)

Mexico City, population, 9
Middle classes, *see* Classes, middle
Middle East, urban population in relation to gross domestic product, 37–8
Middlesbrough, age of population, 99, 100
  as boom town, 125
  'moral density', 117
  sex of population, 116
Middlesex, migrants to, 137
  wages, 133
Migrants, long-term: adaptation to town life, 118
  age, 112
  contact with villages of origin, 117–18
  cultural shock felt by, 184–5
  economic opportunities, 108–9
  French, 138
  Irish, 108
  living conditions, 217
  marriage opportunities, 113
  sex-distribution of, 112
  Welsh, 138
Migrants, seasonal: as agricultural itinerants, 132, 133, 134, 136, 137
  attracted by pubs, 172
  in breweries, 44
  Christmas increase in employment, 149
  cultural shock felt by, 184–5
  decline, 153
  different classes, 124, 134
  hay-making, 134
  hop-picking, 125, 133, 134, 135, 136, 137, 138, 139
  industrial employment, 148
  influence of weather, 131, 150–1, 152
  lack of employment, *7*; 150
  legislation against, 153
  in market gardens, 135
  occupations, 124, 134, 135, 136, 145
  relation to urban social economy, 15
  respectability of, 152
  sailors, 146–8, 151
  sleeping places, 127–8
  street-trading, 149
  wages, 133
  work for women, 133
  *see also* Irish; Italians; Occupations; Tramps
Migration, age of population at time of, 16–17
  as component of urban increase, 12–17
  effect on urban theatre, 213
  effects on American cities, 14

effects on European cities, 13
international, 14–15
rural-urban, 105, 108–9, 112–118, 139, 143
seasonal nature, 139
undertaken in stages, 117, 142, 
urban-rural, 136–7
Milford Haven, shipping trade, 147
Mill, J. S., 48, 87, 88, 91
Miller, D. P., 156[78]
Miller, T., 128, 155[46]
Milner and Sowerby's 'Cottage Library', 191
Milwaukee, mortality, 27
Mining towns, infant mortality, 24
Minneapolis, migration to, 14
Mint, the, pubs near, 166
  tramps near, 166
Mishan, E. J., 57[73]
Mitchell, B. R., 49[10], 50[13], 52[37], 55[61], 118[3], 119[4]
Mitchenson, J., 188[25, 26]
Mols, R., 50[11]
Moncrieff, W. T., *48, 53*; 215, 219
Monmouthshire, winter migrants 143
Monod, S., 101[4]
Montague, C. J., 209[22]
Morden, 99
Morgan, D., 160[240]
Morgan, J., 200
*Morning Chronicle*, 88
Morocco, rate of urban concentration, 41 (table)
Morris, R. N., 102[22]
Morse, R., 39, 56[64]
Mortality, and environment, 19–23
  and fertility, 34–6
  declining rate, 27, 95–6
  effects of decline in urban, 27–8
  infant, 16, 23–7, 53[43], 95
  in London, 49[11]
  of men, 16
  *see also* Population
Morton, C., 174
Morwood, V., 155[67]
Moscow, migration to, 14
  population, 9
Moser, C. A., 98–9, 100, 104[69]
Mosley, Sir Oswald, 188[23]
Mouat, F. J., 103[36]
Mudd, J., *84*
Muir, P. H., 209[15]
Mumford, L., 31, 54[51]
Munich, overcrowded housing, 25
Murdock, K. B., 103[49]

Murphey, R., 55[61]
Murray, J. F., 54[49], 155[44]
Music halls, *36*
  evolution, 174
*My Secret Life*, 173

**N**

Nagle's, employment by, 150
Napier, Sir C., *37*; 176
Naples, population, 9
National Association for the Promotion of Social Science, 90, 91
National Political Union, 176
*National Review*, 196, 206
National Union of the Working Classes, 175, 176
Navy, methods of recruitment, 79
Netherlands, Dutch, infant mortality, 25, 35 (table)
  mortality, 20, 35 (table)
  population, 4
  vital statistics, 35 (table)
Neuburg, V. E., *191–209*, 209[13, 21]
New England, reasons for growth, 14
New Orleans, mortality, 27
New South Wales, sex ratio of population, 16
New York, Booth's attitude to, 94
  city-size distribution, 39
  crude mortality, 21 (table)
  infant mortality, 25, 26
  'metropolitan district', 52[30]
  mortality, 20, 24, 26, 27
  population, 9
  size of families, 19
  slum conditions, 25–6
New Zealand, different pattern of urban transformation, 42
  rate of urban concentration, 41 (table)
  urbanization and per capita gross domestic product, 38
  vital statistics, 35 (table)
Newark, employment of migrants, 144
Newcastle-upon-Tyne, crude mortality, 21 (table)
  'hopping', 131
  pubs, 176
  slums, 22
  tramps, 129
Newmarch, W., 91
Newsholme, A., 22, 52[33], 102[18]
Newton, Mary P., 119[5]
Nicholson, R., 172
*Night Side of London*, 180
Nisbet, R. A., 120[25]

Nixon, President R., 57[70]
Noel Park, pubs excluded from, 183
Norfolk, migrants from, 143
Northampton, migration through, 117
Northampton, Marquis of, temperance policy, 181
*Northern Star*, 88
Norway, annual rate of urban concentration, 5 (table)
Norwich, English-born population, 118
Notting Dale, gypsies, *4*; 130
  migrants' return, 140
  tramps, 126
Nottingham, English-born population, 118
  overcrowding, 22
  tramps, 125
Nuisance Removal Acts (1855–8), 22
Nyren, R., 173

**O**

O'Connor, T. P., 118
Occupations, change from indoor to outdoor, 132
  depicted in theatre, 221
  of migrants, 124
  number of new, 109
  of street-sellers, 193
  winter-time, 139–40, 143–4, 145–51
Oddy, D. J., 103[34]
Odessa, migration to, 14
Ogle, W., 51[24], 91, 121[49]
Ohlin, G., 57[69]
Okun, B., 51[29]
Olsen, D. J., 189[39]
Omnibus, introduction of, 6
Oral history, possibilities of, 60–80
Orchard, B. G., 190[46]
Organ-grinders, 136
Osaka, infant mortality, 36
  population, 9
Osborne, F. J., 54[51]
Oslo, as primate city, 39
Ovsjannikov, Y., 208[1]
Owen, R., 176
Owenites, 87
Oxford, pubs, 176–8
Oxfordshire, wages in, 133

**P**

Paddington, off-licensed premises, 168
  station, *50*
Paddock Wood, 139

Page, J. K., 57[72]
Pakistan, effects of births on natural resource consumption, 43
  migration to cities, 41
  vital statistics, 35 (table)
Pall Mall, scarcity of pubs, 166
Paris, 94, 181
  age and sex structure, 51[29]
  crude mortality, 21 (table)
  density of population, 26
  mortality and fertility, 20
  population, 9, 171–2
  as primate city, 39
Park, R. E., 102[22]
Parliamentary Candidates' Society, 176
Parsons, T., 120[23]
Pask, A. T., 137, 157[123]
*Past and Present*, 89
Patterson, A. T., 121[42]
Pavilion Theatre (London), *55*; 212, 224
Payne, J. H., 213
Peabody Trust, 26
Peacock, A. J., 189[35]
Pearson, K., 94
Peel, Mrs C. S., 121[47]
Peel, F., 189[34]
Peking, population, 9
Penge, tramps, 126
*People's Paper*, 179
Perkin, H. J., 101[6]
Perloff, H. S., 56[65]
Perth, 31
Peru, housing deficits, 37
  rate of urban concentration, 41 (table)
  urbanization and per capita income, 37
  vital statistics, 35 (table)
Philadelphia, as agglomeration of suburbs, 29
  population, 9
  slum conditions, 25
Phillips, W., *51*; 215–16
Piccadilly (London), scarcity of pubs, 166
  transport inns, 162
*Pickwick Papers*, 162
Pimlott, J. A. R., 121[41], 186[4]
Pinchbeck, Ivy, 121[50]
Pitts, J., 200
Pittsburgh, population, 9
Plumstead, gypsies, 130
Plymouth, migration through, 117
Police, attitude to tramps, 129
Political Economy Club, 87
Pollard, A., 102[13]
Pollard, J., *26*

Poll-books, use of, in assessing political motivation, 98
Pollution, of air, in United States, 43
  laws against, 47–8
  reduction, in air, 30
Poor Law, workhouses, *10*
  *see also* Poverty
Poplar, 139
Popplewell, F., 156[83]
Population, age structure of urban, 16–17, 99
  agglomeration, 7, 8
  concentration, 7, 8, 13
  density, 109
  effects of increase in urban, 28, 30, 107
  fecundity, 13, 17, 36
  growth, 7, 105
  growth of world and world urban, 33 (table)
  increase in 'surplus' women, 116
  and pub density, 171
  sex structure of urban, 16–17
Porter, G. R., 84, 93
Portlock, J. E., 101[10]
Portsmouth, 125
  migrants from, 139
Portugal, annual rate of urban concentration, 5 (table)
Potter, Beatrice, *see* Webb
Poverty among migrants, 143
  causes, 59
  homeless, *6, 9, 14*
  national policy needed, 96
  in relation to pub density, 168
  unofficial enquiries into, 94
  in upper classes, 70
  of working-class families, 61–2
  *see also* Classes, working; Crime; Mayhew; Prostitution; Poor Law
*Poverty*, 96
Prague, density of population, 26
Pratt, E. A., 186[6]
Prest, A. R., 104[66]
Priestley, J. B., 6, 7, 21, 49[6]
Prince Miller, D., 156[78]
Princess's Theatre (London), 224
*Progress of the Nation*, 84
Prohibitionism, *see* Drink
Prostitutes
  in pubs, 173
  travelling, 142
Prostitution, 116
Prussia, annual rate of urban concentration, 5 (table)
  internal migration, 15
  mortality, 20
  population, 4, 10
  rural fertility, 18

Public House Closing Act (1864), 173

Pubs, **161–90**
appearance, *28, 30, 34*; 170, 171
as centre for public meetings, 175
and commuter travel, 163, 165
debates held in, 179–80
density, 162, 163–7, 172
dependence of migrants on, 171, 172
discussion groups, *38*; 179–80
entertainment, *31, 35, 37*; 174
exclusion from building estates, 183
increasing size, 171
lack of class distinction, 172
licences, 167
in London underworld, 192
number in relation to churches, 184
political tendencies, 185
and railway travel, 162, 163
as recreational centres, 168, 169, 171
revolutionary activities accredited to, 178
in rural society, 161
similarity of role to temperance movement, 184–5
siting, 164n., 165–9
and sporting activities, 173–4
as transport centres, *26*; 162
variety of, 176
working-class, 166, 167
*see also* Drink; Licensed premises; Temperance movement; and individual cities
Pudney, J., 121[45]
*Punch* (London Charivari), *6*; 22, 85, 222
satirical treatment of statistics, 89

**Q**

Queen's Park, pubs excluded from, 183

**R**

Railway, Metropolitan, 146
provision of employment, 153[4]
Railways
arches used as shelters, 129
effect on other transport, 162
as imagery in street ballads, 195–6
mobility increased by, 107, 117

and pubs, 162
stations, and migrants, 125
in Europe, 125
*see also* individual stations
statistics of urban, 98
and suburban commuters, 163
Rammell, T. W., 154[33]
Ranger, W. C. E., 154[35]
Ranyard, Ellen, 158[156]
Raper, J. H., 182
Ratcliffe Highway (London), 123, 142, 173
drunkenness, 181
gin-palaces, 170
Rauchberg, H., 50[19], 51[26]
Ravenstein, E. G., 50[17], 100, 116, 117, 122[66,70,72]
Rawson, Sir Rawson W., 101[1], 103[41]
Reading
fair, 132
migrants from, 139
photographic printing works, 229
Redford, A., 122[70]
Reeder, D. A., 54[49]
Refuges, Night, 128, 150
closing down, 131, 132
for the destitute, 143
financing, 142
opening, 142
Regent Street (London), 100
Registrar-General, the, 19–20, 24
Reid, W., 189[44]
Rein, S. R., 49[9]
Reiss, A. J., 187[15], 190[45]
Religion, middle-class attitude to, 63, 64, 66, 67, 68
Religion, working-class attitude to, 61, 69, 71, 72, 73, 77, 80
Rendle, T. McD., 188[19]
Reynolds, G. M. W., 87
Ricardo, D., 85
Rice, J., 160[236]
Richard, H., 172
Rilke, R. M., 6
Rio de Janeiro, population, 9
Ripley, W. Z., 28, 53[47]
Roberts, D., 119[11]
Rochdale, infant mortality rates, 99
Rodgers, B., 103[35]
Rolt, L. T. C., 186[5]
Rome, crude mortality, 21 (table)
Rotherhithe, 123, 129
Rowe, R., 153[3]
Rowney, D. K., 103[56], 104
Rowntree, B. Seebohm, 93, 96, 97, 103[44], 134, 154[16], 157[105],

168, 187[11], 189[32]
drink map of Oxford, 177
Rowntree, J., 171, 187[13,17], 189[43]
R.C. on Elementary Education (1847), 126
R.C. on Labour (1892–4), 132, 134
R.C. on Liquor Licensing (1897), 182
Royal Statistical Society, 91, 92
*see also* London, Statistical Society
Royston Pike, E., 199[9]
Rubin, M., 51[26]
Rudd, R., 55[55]
Rudé, G., 189[34]
Ruhrgebiet, population of, 9
Rural life, as theme of nineteenth-century drama, 216–217
considered superior to urban life, 108–11
difference between urban and rural population, 69–70, 100
Ruskin, John, *219*; 29, 89, 103[33], 171
Russia, mortality, 27
sex ratio of population, 16
*see also* U.S.S.R.
Russian Empire (Europe), annual rate of urban concentration, 5 (table)
growth of cities, 8
Rutland, level of nuptiality, 17
Ryle, Annie, *46*

**S**

Safdie, M., 54[52]
St George's Circus (London), 166
St Giles's, migrants' return, 140
tramps, 126
workhouse, 138
St James's Park, frost fair, *11*
tramps, *14*
St Louis, population, 9
St Pancras, pubs, 163
St Petersburg, crude mortality, 21 (table)
population, 9
Saltaire, pubs banned, 66
Salvation Army, 80, 142
Samuel, R., **123–60**, 160[240]
Samuelson, P. A., 57[74]
San Francisco Bay, migration to, 14
population, 9
Sanger, 'Lord' G., 132, 141, 151, 156[80,89], 158[165], 160[237], 192, 208[4]

Sanitation, effects on growth of London, 14
  lack of provision, 106–7
  pride in improvements, 85
  statistical knowledge, 95
  in United States, 25
Santiago, effect of population concentration, 38
São Paulo, population of, 9
Saville, J., 118[2]
Saxony, annual rate of urban concentration, 5 (table)
  infant mortality, 24
  internal migration, 15
  legitimate birth-rates, 19
  migration of foreigners to, 15
Scandinavia, effect of migration on growth of cities, 13
Schnore, L. F., 52[29], 54[49], 55[60], 56[64], 98, 104[61,68], 120[23]
School, attendance, 80
  middle-class attitudes, 63
  punishment, 65, 76
  violence, 62
School Board visitors, 153
Schoyen, A. R., 189[34]
Schumpeter, J. A., 101[9]
Schwab, W. B., 190[45]
Scobie, J. R., 54[53]
Scotland, annual rate of urban concentration, 5 (table)
  migration of foreigners, 15
  overcrowding, 23
  population, 8
  sex ratio of population, 16
Scott, C., 221
Scott, P., 208[9]
Scott, W., 98–9, 100, 104[69]
Selby, C., 219
Selway, N. C., 186[5]
Senior, Nassau, 86
Seoul, population, 9
Serbia, sex ratio of population in, 16
Seven Dials, James Catnach's shop, 41
*Seventy Years a Showman*, 192
Sewers *see* Sanitation; Water systems
Sexby, J. J., 156[69]
Shadwell, 139
  pubs, 166
Shadwell, A., 23, 52[32,35], 53[43], 187[16]
Shanghai, population, 9
Shannon, H. A., 50[12]
Shaw, S., 126, 154[31]
Sheffield, employment, 134
  mortality, 20
  music halls, 174
  population, 13
Shephard, L., 209[16,18]

Sheppard, J., 179
Sherwell, A., 171, 187[13,17], 189[43]
Shields, 125
Shkarovsky-Raffé, A., 208[1]
Shoreditch, Grecian Theatre, 60
  overcrowding, 23
Simey, Margaret B., 103[43,46,51]
Simey, T. S., 103[43,46,51]
Simmel, G., 122[69], 170
Simon, Sir J., 94
Simpson, G., 120[29]
Sims, G. R., 16; 155[51,67], 160[231], 221
Singer, S. F., 57[72]
Skalweit, A., 53[38]
Smith, Adam, 28, 53[45], 89
Smith, G., 143, 155[58], 156[90], 159[178]
Smith, Sir Henry, 158[155]
Smith, Samuel, 182
Smith, T. L., 55[58]
Smith, W. H., 218
Smithies, T. B., 29
Snowden, P., 188[27]
Social science, statistics in relation to, 91, 92
  urban problems encouraging growth of, 91
  *see also* Statistics
Socialist League, 198
Soho, sleeping rough, 123
Solly, H., 54[50]
Somerset, Lady Henry, 182
Somerville, A., 158[145]
Southwark, Borough High Street, 162
  King's Head, 25
  tramps, 126
Spain, rate of urban concentration, 41 (table)
Spencer, H., 27
Spitalfields, licensed premises, 164 (map)
  tramps, 129
  weavers, 129
Spring, T., 31, 173
Staffordshire, infant mortality rates, 24
  migrants from, 137
Standard Theatre (London), 212, 224
Statistics:
  appointment of statistical Officer by L.C.C., 94
  contrasts in nineteenth- and twentieth-century information, 99
  difficulties in categorization, 98
  health improvements stemming from, 95–6
  main categories, 99

  methods of using, 92–3, 97
  official collections, 94
  qualitative evidence, 95
  quantitative evidence, 95, 97
  relation of qualitative to quantitative evidence, 97, 100
  in relation to economics, 93, 94
  of urban railways, 98
  value of quantitative analysis, 101
  Victorian attitude towards, 84–6, 97
Steel, Robert W., 119[6]
Steele, Sir R., 222
Stephenson, G., 186[4]
Stepney, fair, 133
  Union workhouse, 136
Stevenson, T. H. C., 53[44]
Stockholm, as primate city, 39
Stoke Newington, off-licensed premises, 168
Stolnitz, G. J., 55[55]
Stone, L. O., 54[53]
Stourbridge, 138
Strand (London), licensed premises, 165
  pub density, 163, 165
  refreshment-house licences, 168
  theatre, 59
Strauss, A. L., 104[70]
Street-folk, ballad-sellers, 41, 42
  crossing sweepers, 150
  sandwich-board men, 17; 136, 150
  traders, 149, 192, 193, 194, 239
  *see also* Street life
Street life, 141
  mobile circus, 19
  musicians, 7, 18
  scenes, 12, 28
Street literature, **191–207**
  anticipation of tabloid newspaper by, 206, 207
  character of broadsides, 43–7; 191–2
  circulation figures, 207
  cost of living revealed in, 197
  crime as subject-matter, 45, 47; 198–9
  irrelevant nature of illustrations, 194
  as literature of urban working class, 191, 197, 201, 206
  political themes, 196–8
  polka as subject, 198, 202–4
  production, 199–200
  religious subject-matter, 196
  Royal Family as subject, 196, 206

subjects, 193
superficiality, 206
temperance encouraged in 195
writers, 200
Sturt, G., 158[139,149]
Suburbs, effect of improved transport, 23, 29–30
entertainment, 35
growth, 13, 15
as remedy for problems of city density, 29
Sue, E., 48, 219
Suffolk, migrants from, *20*; 143
Suicide, in cities, 117
Sullivan, B., 212
Surrey, migrants to, 133, 139
migration through, 117
Surrey Theatre, *52*; 212, 220, 224
Sussex, hopping in, 138, 139
migrants, 133, 138, 144
Sweden, marriage rates of urban population, 18
rate of urban concentration, 41 (table)
rates of increase in population, 14
rural fertility, 18
vital statistics, 35 (table)
Swinstead, J. Howard, 158[163]
Switzerland, annual rate of urban concentration, 5 (table)
infant mortality, 25
Sydney, as agglomeration of suburbs, 29
primacy, 38
sex ratio of population, 16

**T**

Taeuber, Irene, 9n., 14, 50[14]
Taine, H., 173, 188[22]
Tarn, J. N., 189[43]
Taylor, G. R., 57[72]
Taylor, Tom, 216, 222, 223
Taylor, T. P., 213, 217
Taylor, W. C., 49[4]
Temperance movement, *34, 39, 40*; 161
activities, 181–5
entertainments started by, 175
in relation to party politics, 162
role compared with pubs, 184–5
as subject of melodrama, 213, 217–18
as subject of street ballads, 195
support of women, 174
among the working class, 183
Ten Hours (Amendment) Act (1860), 113

Theatres, distribution in London, 214 (map)
division between East End and West End of London, 224
growth, 211
increasing respectability, 224
stage realism, 218–22
technical advances, 218
for urban proletariat, 212–13, 224
*see also* Drama
Theatre Royal (London), 57
Thompson, E. P., 88[21], 102[26]
Thompson, P., **59–80**
Thompson, W., 53[39]
Thompson, W. S., 51[29]
Thorne, G., 187[12]
Thorne, W., 156[83], 160[223]
Tientsin, population, 9
Tillett, Ben, 156[77]
Tillotson, Kathleen, 102[24]
Tillyard, F., 121[40]
Timbs, J., 188[22], 189[31]
Tokyo-Yokohama, child-woman ratio, 36
infant mortality, 36
population, 9
Tönnies, F., 110–11, 120[26,31]
Tory Party, 185
traditions, 174
working men's drink club promoted by, 185
Tothill Fields, 126
Town councils, social composition, 98
Town-planning, reasons for development, 107
Tramcars, effect on housing, 23, 30
routes, 163
Tramps, *15*
and police, *14*; 129
sleeping places, *9, 392*; 125–6, 127, 128–9
*see also* Migrants
Transport, as remedy for problems of city density, 29–30
pubs as centre for, 162
river, 165
role of coaching inn, 162
*see also* Railways; Tramcars
Tremenheere, H. S., 85, 101[5]
Trevelyan, C. E., 159[174]
Tsuru, S., 57[73]
Turpin, Dick, 179
Turvey, R., 104[66]

**U**

*Unemployment*, 134
United Kingdom Alliance, 181, 182

United States, agglomeration of population, 9
annual rate of urban concentration, 5 (table)
concentration of population, 4, 10, 11 (table)
evangelical revival, 195
fertility, 43
growth of cities, 8
industrialization of labour force and product, 11 (table)
interest in urban problems of low-income countries, 41
internal migration, 15
international migration, 14
level of urbanization, 35 (table)
marriage-rates of urban population, 17
mobility of female population, 15
pollution, 43–4
sex ratio of urban population, 16
size of family units, 19
size of households, 25
urban population, 7
urbanization and per capita gross domestic product, 38
vital statistics, 35 (table)
*Unto this Last*, 89
Urban transformation, demographic processes in, 11–12
effects of, 28
meaning of urban-industrial transformation, 45
metropolitan phase, 12
manifestations of industrial, 40
nineteenth-century, 4–10
sex and age structure of population in later phases of, 17
*see also* Cities; Mortality; Population
Urbanization, causes, 34
correlation with city-size distribution, 39
correlation with non-agricultural labour force, 38
definition of, 49[8]
gross domestic product in relation to, 37–8
impact, 107–8
level and rate of world, **33** (table)
as social progress, 97, 105
of society, 4
selective character, 42
*see also* Cities; Mortality; Population
Urbanize, meaning of, 5
Uruguay, rate of urban concentration in, 41 (table)

U.S.S.R., rate of urban concentration, 41 (table)
urbanization and per capita gross domestic product, 38
urbanization, 32, 33 (table)
vital statistics, 35 (table)

# V

Vaughan Williams, R., 156 [72]
Venezuela, migration of foreigners to, 37
rate of urban concentration, 41 (table)
Victoria Theatre (London), 212, 213
*Victorian Cities*, 85, 98, 100, 101n.
Vienna, crude mortality, 21 (table)
infant mortality, 24
migration of foreigners, 15
population, 9
Vietnam, urbanization and per capita income, 37
Vincent, J. R., 98, 104 [67]
Von Jurashchek, F., 52 [38]
Von Ungarn-Sternberg, R. 56 [66]

# W

Wales, annual rate of urban concentration, 5 (table)
concentration of population, 11 (table)
increases in town and country population, 14, 15
industrialization of labour force and product, 11 (table)
internal migration, 15
marriage-rates of urban population, 16–17
migration to towns, 13
mortality, 20, 24
overcrowding, 23
population, 6, 8
sex and age structure of population, 16–17
size of households, 25
see also England and Wales; Great Britain
Walford, C., 51 [21]
Walker, R. B., 190 [46]
Wandsworth, 130
Wanstead Flats, fair, 133
Wappäus, J. E., 18, 19, 51 [27]
Ward, D., 52 [35]
Ware, employment of migrants, 144

Warsaw, population, 9
Warwick, migration through, 117
Washington, D.C., mortality rates, 27
Water systems, effects of improvements, 10
importance, 21–2
lack of provision, 106–7
pride of improvements, 85
provision of public baths, 146
Wateringbury, 139
Waterloo Road (London), pubs, 163
Webb, Beatrice (née Potter), 93, 103 [45], 155 [42], 178, 189 [33]
Webb, S., 155 [42], 156 [83], 159 [208], 160 [217,226], 187 [14]
Weber, A. F., 5, 7, 8, 9n, 13, 14, 19, 20, 26, 27, 30, 41, 48 [2], 50 [12,14,16,17,19], 51 [20,24,26,29], 53 [39,41,44], 54 [48], 55 [61], 112, 120 [36], 121 [48], 122 [70]
Wedderburn, A., 187 [16]
Weldon, W., 94
Wellington, Duke of, as subject of street ballad, 198, 201–2
Welton, T. A., 52 [37], 119 [8], 120 [22,37]
West Bromwich, English-born population, 118
West Ham, as boom town, 125
West India Dock Road, pubs, 166
West London Theatre, 224
Westergaard, H., 51 [26]
Westminster, Duke of, temperance policy of, 166, 181
Westminster, off-licensed premises, 168
tramps, 126
Weston, E., 174
Weylland, Rev. J. M., 171, 179, 189 [34]
Weylland, S. C., 187 [16]
Whipple, G. C., 55 [56]
Whitby, 23; 147
Whitechapel, Bull's Eye, 3
pubs, 182
soup kitchens, 123
theatre, 213
Whitechapel Road, pubs, 164, 165
Whitehall, scarcity of pubs, 166
Whittaker, T., 183
Whittle, P. A., 156 [75]
Wilkinson, E., 156 [92]

Wilkinson, R., 52, 57
Wilkinson, T. O., 56 [67]
Wilkinson, T. W., 130, 155 [51,66], 158 [163]
Willcox, W. F., 50 [17], 51 [20]
Willesden, sleeping rough in, 128
Williams, F. S., 153 [4]
Williams, G., 190 [46]
Williams, R., 159 [211]
Williams, T. Desmond, 120 [17]
Willmott, P., 56 [66], 187 [13]
Wilson, G. B., 187 [9,17]
Wilson, Mona, 158 [159]
Wingo, L., 56 [65]
Winskill, P. T., 188 [24], 189 [43]
Wirth, L., 102 [22]
Women, growth of opportunities, 115–16
as migrants, 74, 113–14, 137
predominance over men in numbers, 116
in telephone service, 148
see also Population
Woodcock, H., 155 [67]
Woodward, E. L., 121 [43], 188 [23]
Woolwich, migration to, 140
Worcestershire, migrants to, 138
Wordsworth, W., 85
Working classes, see Classes, working
Worthing, 99
Workhouse, *10*
Wright, C. D., 53 [41]
Wright, E., 102 [13]
Wright, T., 135, 157 [110]
Wrigley, E. A., 49 [11], 51 [26], 104 [64]
Wrong, D. H., 53 [44], 56 [66]
Wroot, H. E., 209 [23]

# Y

Yarmouth, 140
migrants to, 143
herring sales, *8*
Yaziki, T., 56 [67]
York, poverty, 96
pubs, 176–8
women drinkers, 168
Yorkshire, migrants to, 133
Young, G. M., 120 [39]
Young, M., 56 [66], 187 [13]
Yudkin, J., 103 [34]
Yule, G. U., 94

# Z

Zollschau, G. K., 122 [65]
Zweig, F., 190 [44]

Index by Marie Forsyth